Kennie

301-9170 Mary St
Chilliwack BC
V2P 4H9

In The Morning

Biographical Sketches of the Veterans
of
Victoria County, Cape Breton
that served in both World Wars

They shall grow not old, as we that are left grow old:
Age shall not weary them, nor the years condemn.
At the going down of the sun and ***IN THE MORNING***
We will remember them.

Poems For the Fallen
Laurence Binyon

The UCCB Press acknowledges the support received for its publishing program from the Canada Council's Block Grants program.

Cover design by Goose Lane Editions, NB
Book design by Gail Jones, Sydney, NS
Printed and Bound in Canada by Kromar Ltd., Winnipeg, Manitoba CANADA

Canadian Cataloguing in Publication Data

Main entry under title:

In the morning

ISBN 0-920336-79-5

1. World War, 1914-1918 -- Veterans -- Nova Scotia -- Victoria (County) -- Biography. 2. World War, 1939-1945 -- Veterans -- Nova Scotia -- Victoria (County) -- Biography. 3. Victoria (N.S.: County) -- Biography. I. Thornhill, Bonnie, 1948- II. MacDonald, W. James.

FC2345.V52Z48 1999 940.53'71693'0922 C99-950099-6
F1039.V515 1999

University College of Cape Breton Press
Box 5300
Sydney, Nova Scotia
CANADA B1P 6L2

The war is dreadful.

It is the business of the artist to follow it home to the hearth of the individual fighters - not to talk in armies, nations and numbers - but to track it home.

D.H. Lawrence in 1914
(1885-1930)

In the Morning
Biographical Sketches
of
W.W. I and W.W. II Veterans
Victoria County, Nova Scotia

Editors:
Bonnie Thornhill
James MacDonald

Associate Editors:
*Leslie Buffett
James Cook
Thelma Grant
Katherine Kerr
Mabel MacEachern
Theresa MacDonald
John Graham MacInnes
Katherine MacLean
Vincent MacLean
*Robert S. MacLeod
*Allison MacMillan
*Rod C. MacNeil
Wallace MacRae
Walter Matheson
Donald N. Morrison
Barbara Nicholson
Edmund Nicholson
Ervin Robinson
Katherine Robinson
Clarence Roberts
Mary Roberts
Nancy Smith

***Veterans**

Dedicated to

The Victoria County veterans, of both World Wars,

who

sacrificed their lives

in

our country's wars

and

in everlasting gratitude

to

those who, daring to die,

survived.

Preface

Following Remembrance Day, 1993 a core group of volunteers met and considered the possibility of compiling a memorial book to commemorate the lives of the men and women who served in the two great wars from Victoria County, Nova Scotia. The inspiration arose from the war memorials situated in various communities - some displayed names - others did not. It begged the following questions: Could we complete a comprehensive list of names and identify those individuals whom we collectively credit with our freedom? Would it be possible to note a short but significant biography for each one? If this could be accomplished, it would preserve under one cover a lasting tribute to these veterans.

Our research focussed on those persons indigenous to Victoria County. The guidelines for those who make up the roll in this book includes the veterans who enlisted or were conscripted, whose place of birth was Victoria County or who came as a child and were raised and nurtured here during their formative years. There were a few individuals whose properties crossed or abutted county lines. They were included since they had attended Victoria County schools and while growing up were an integral part of the social fabric of Victoria County communities. This occurred in Middle River and in Boularderie. Unfortunately, the scope of the project did not include the Peace Keepers nor the war veterans who following the wars chose to call this county "home" and who contributed greatly to their respective communities. Example of such individuals include the late Rev. A.W.R. MacKenzie, founder of the Gaelic College, St. Ann's; R. Fisher Hudson, Lawyer and former M.L.A.; and Leonard Jones, Merchant and past Director of the Gaelic College, David Smith and the late Alton Langille plus so many others. Perhaps a sequel will be considered and the original data base be expanded to include all such individuals.

Most of the material used to compile the information contained herein was gathered by dedicated volunteers from veterans, family members and senior citizens throughout Victoria County and beyond. Oral histories provided much of the data base. Attics were searched and long stored away photographs and faded military papers were dusted off and kindly shared with committee members. Sometimes our research evoked sorrowful memories. We recognize that with the passing of so many years, memories begin to dim and some inaccuracies are apt to occur. Most birth dates for the First World War Veterans were extracted from the 1901 census. We are aware of discrepancies between some of these dates and those noted in family records. Therefore, despite our utmost effort to verify all data, some inadvertent errors may exist. Regretfully we recognize that some deserving individuals may have been missed due to the very nature of the project. Since no complete official lists were readily available we attempted to gather what information we could on an ad hoc basis. The blank page at the conclusion of the book is purposefully left there in case someone remembers a veteran or veterans whom we have not included. Hopefully this space will be used to detail what is applicable to that person or persons. At best, this book is an imperfect record but, hopefully, this first attempt will elicit additional information and corrections. Sadly, in some cases, there are those veterans who remain unidentified except for their surname and initials. If further clarification can be made, please contact any research member and an updated registry will be compiled and maintained for future reference. In the event of a second printing these revisions could be included at that time. With regard to veterans who served in both wars their biography is found under the First World War section. For identification purposes we have in many cases included known nicknames or titles by which the person was familiarly known. With so many who have the same or similar name, this feature became a necessary component of this biography. Without including such, some might well remain unrecognizable. We have taken the liberty to list all the Mc's and Mac's under Mac as the task to determine the spelling generally used by some became an impossible one.

We in no way meant this book to be either an in-depth record of anyone's military career or a log of an individual's personal life. Although a battalion may be noted in an individual's history this person may well have served in other units. Recruits from non-combat units were commonly transferred to fighting battalions. Therefore, the synopsis while it is as accurate as we could ascertain, it by no means reveals any veteran's entire story. Hopefully, it will inspire and enable others to pursue further research. This book is solely a means to remember and to honour Victoria County's sons and daughters who enlisted to protect Crown and Country. Their sacrifice all to often of life and limb, resulted in their precious legacy to us of freedom and democracy.

To them, may this book be a reminder of their selfless lives and be an expression of our thankfulness.

Acknowledgements

In preparing this book we were fortunate to have so many dedicated research volunteers. They unselfishly donated their time and expense to collect the database for this project.

There were an inestimable number of individuals who shared memories and contributed documents and photographs. Because of their sheer number, donors shall have to remain anonymous. Due to the vast number of photographs, we are unable to accredit each one individually. Most of the undated clippings were from local newspapers (not identified). In addition to the photographs and clippings, the contributors readily extended warm hospitality to the members of the research team who collected the information.

Without such assistance and co-operation from both groups, this book could not have become a reality. Their effort can never be repaid. We thank all who in any way 'remembered' our county veterans.

Thank you to Betty Hanam, Big Baddeck for perserving the military memorabilia of the Anderson family from South Side Baddeck River. Thank you for donating their photograph which graces the cover of this book. Thank you to Harve Grant, Boularderie, Angus MacLeod, Goose Cove, and John Urquhart, Baddeck, for sharing their illustrations and ideas regarding a cover design. Thank you to Conrad Lawrence, Cape North, for processing photographs. Thank you to John Clarke, Cape Breton Highlanders Museum, Sydney, for his interest and support. Thank you to veteran E. Douglas MacLean, Sydney, for sharing his research material which he and the late veteran Donald MacDonald, Sydney, meticulously recorded and preserved.

Our gratitude goes to Daniel Chaisson, Baddeck, for giving of his legal services in establishing the Victoria Heritage and Culture Society and to Lydia MacKinnon, Halifax, formerly of Little Narrows, for her monumental undertaking in editing the manuscript.

The role played by the Gaelic College, St. Ann's, is immeasurable. Two people deserve special recognition, Sam MacPhee, Executive Director of the Gaelic College for his generosity for allowing us access to the staff and equipment and Jennifer Daisley for her patience and willing dedication to type and process every word of the text onto computer disks. Jennifer has won a special place in our hearts. To Sam MacPhee and Jennifer Daisley we are eternally grateful.

For all the times during this project when 'our lives were placed on hold' I want to especially thank my husband, Roland Thornhill, for his capable assistance and encouragement.

Thank you to Penny Marshall for her invaluable support, direction and guidance on an ongoing basis. Thank you to University College of Cape Breton for accepting this project and agreeing to publish it.

For each and every one who played a part, because of your volunteer effort *In the Morning* is a lasting remembrance of Victoria County veterans.

December 3, 1998
Bonnie Thornhill

The Veterans Research Committee of the Victoria Culture and Heritage Society expresses its appreciation of the generous financial support of the following:

Royal Canadian Legion, Baddeck
John Chisholm, Nova Construction
Municipality of Victoria County
Village Commission of Baddeck
St. Marks # 35 Masonic Lodge
Middle River Historical Society
Royal Canadian Legion, Grandona
Royal Canadian Legion, Neil's Harbour
Royal Canadian Legion, Ingonish
West Novas Memory Club
Peter and Sandra Smith
Inverary Resort
Murdena Morrison Eldridge
Jean MacLeod Buck
Wallace MacRae
Scotland St. Ann's Waipu Connection
Baddeck Public Library
Everett MacAskill
Edna Dowling
George MacLean
Barbara Nicholson
Thelma MacLellan
Middle River Garden Club
Victoria Farmers' Co-Op, Baddeck
Baddeck Volunteer Fire Department
North Shore Historical Society
Mary MacInnis
Baddeck Branch, Royal Bank
Midway Motors Ltd., Middle River
D.W. Matheson & Sons
Ernie Mingo - Silver Dart Lodge
Lakeside Computers, Baddeck
Baddeck Lions Club
St. Margaret's Village Central Co-Op Society
Mary R. MacDonald
Gordon and Ruth MacAulay
Scotiabank, Ingonish
Alfred MacLeod Service Station, Dingwall

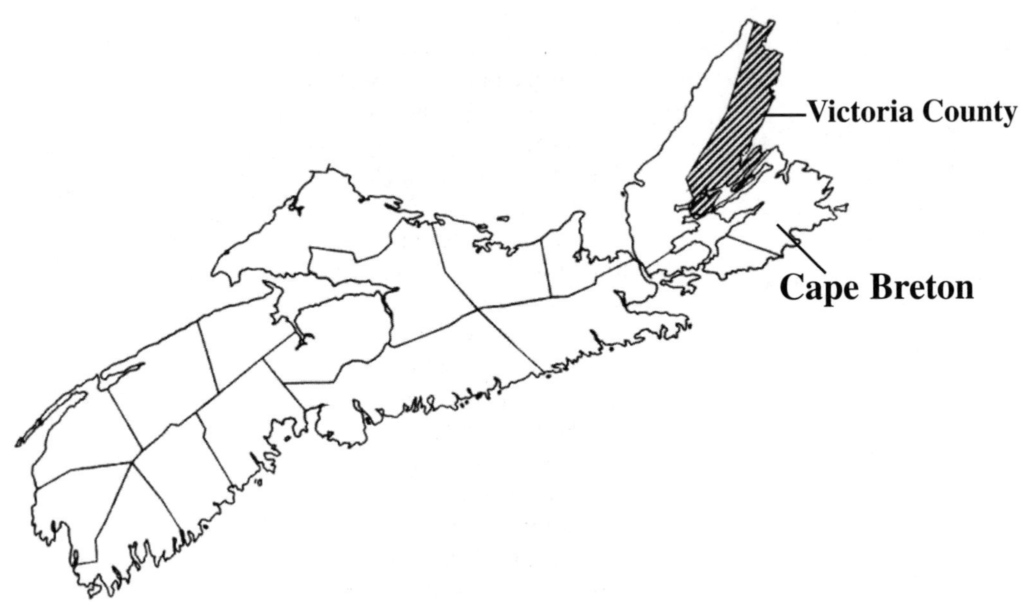

Nova Scotia, Canada

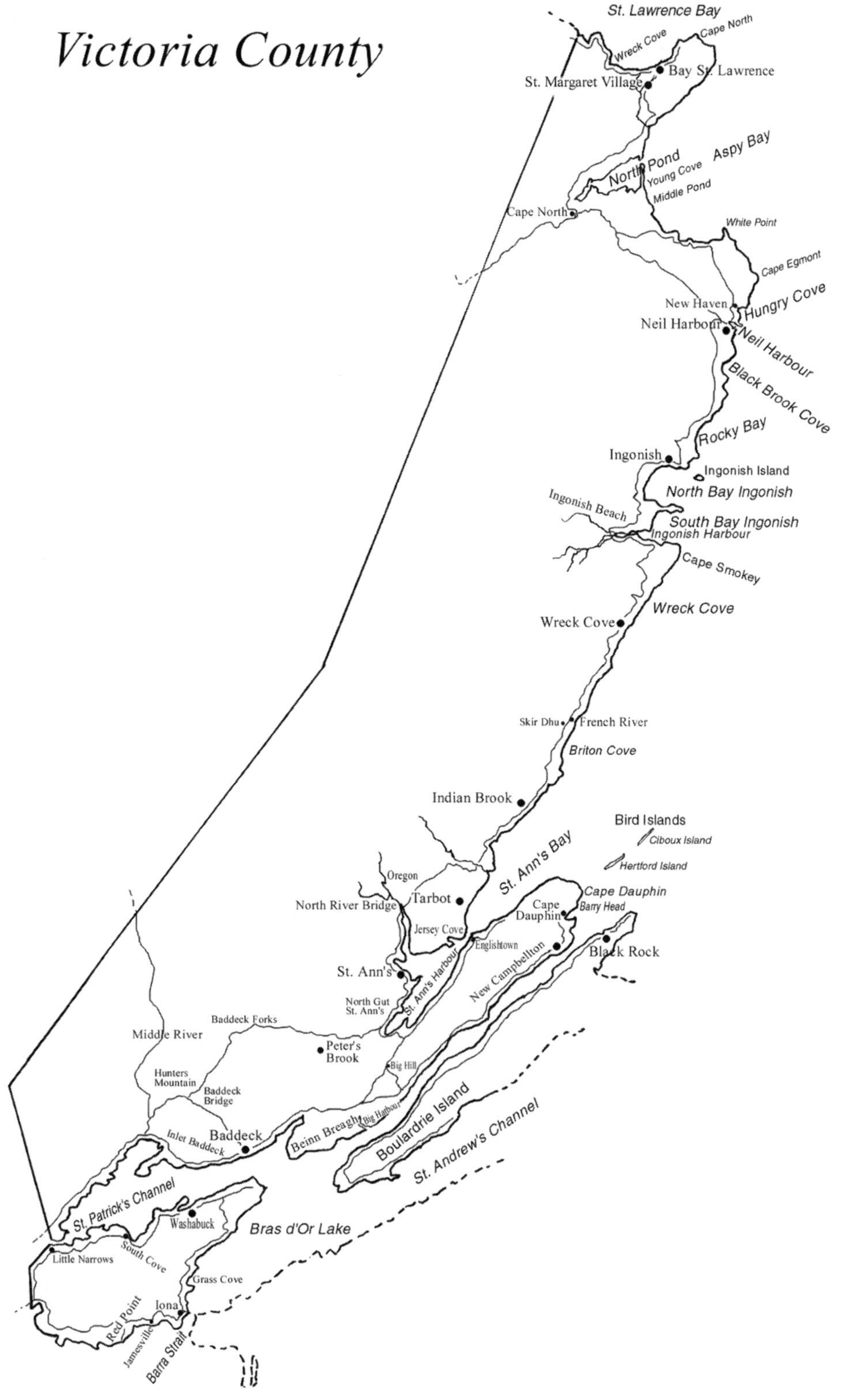
Victoria County
St. Lawrence Bay
Wreck Cove
Cape North
Bay St. Lawrence
St. Margaret Village
North Pond
Young Cove
Aspy Bay
Middle Pond
Cape North
White Point
Cape Egmont
New Haven
Hungry Cove
Neil Harbour
Neil Harbour
Black Brook Cove
Rocky Bay
Ingonish
Ingonish Island
North Bay Ingonish
Ingonish Beach
South Bay Ingonish
Ingonish Harbour
Cape Smokey
Wreck Cove
Wreck Cove
Skir Dhu
French River
Briton Cove
Indian Brook
Bird Islands
Ciboux Island
Hertford Island
St. Ann's Bay
Cape Dauphin
Oregon
Tarbot
North River Bridge
Cape Dauphin
Barry Head
Jersey Cove
Englishtown
New Campbellton
Black Rock
St. Ann's
St. Ann's Harbour
North Gut St. Ann's
Baddeck Forks
Middle River
Peter's Brook
Big Hill
Hunters Mountain
Baddeck Bridge
Boulardrie Island
St. Andrew's Channel
Inlet Baddeck
Baddeck
Beinn Breagh
Big Harbour
St. Patrick's Channel
Washabuck
Bras d'Or Lake
Little Narrows
South Cove
Grass Cove
Iona
Red Point
Jamesville
Barra Strait

World War I

Adie, Harry

Harry Adie hailed from Plaister Mines. He was raised by William and Christy (MacMillan) MacLeod.

He served during World War I. After the war, he married and settled in Halifax.

Anderson, Daniel William 223167

Dan Anderson of Big Baddeck was born on March 29, 1888, and served overseas with the 85th Battalion # 14 Platoon. His mother, Minnie Anderson, worked in the United States, so following the war he moved there as well. He married, but had no issue. He died while living in Massachusetts and is buried there.

Anderson, James Archibald, M.C.

Three Anderson siblings served in World War I. Archie was born on January 29, 1894, to Alexander and Susan (Archibald) Anderson, Poplar Grove Farm, S.S. Baddeck River, Big Baddeck.

After enlisting in the 85th Nova Scotia Highlanders in October of 1916, he quickly moved through the ranks to become a Captain and Major. In September 1918, he was wounded on a Cambrai battlefield. He was awarded the **MILITARY CROSS** for his bravery in action

"... for conspicuous gallantry and devotion to duty during

(Formal photograph of Anderson family. Seated - M. Blanche Anderson, James A. Anderson [centre] and [right] Percival W. Anderson)

the Bowston Wood operations in front of Cambrai. On September 29, 1918, when his company was ordered to rapidly form an outpost line covering an important village, he himself reconnoitered the position, and, one by one, rushed his posts out to advantageous positions over ground which was kept under a constant sweep of enemy machine-gun fire. Though wounded while doing so, he carried on until his line was established."

He was a graduate of the Nova Scotia Agricultural College in Truro and a recipient of the Governor General's medal. He married, but had no issue. He died on April 30, 1964 and is buried in the family plot in St. John's Old Cemetery in MacCharles Cross, Big Baddeck.

Anderson, Minerva Blanche R.N.

M. Blanche Anderson, Field Hospital

Blanche Anderson was born on February 10, 1889, the daughter of Alexander and Susan (Archibald) Anderson, S.S. Baddeck River, Big Baddeck. She served as a Nursing Sister during the great War of 1914-1918. She was a graduate of the Royal Victoria Hospital School of Nursing and McGill University in Montreal. For many years she was Director of Nurses at the Sydney City Hospital in Sydney. At the time of her death, May 22, 1981, she was the last surviving member of her immediate family. She is buried in St. John's Old Cemetery, Big Baddeck.

Anderson, Percival William, M.C. P1163

'Percy' was the eldest Anderson sibling to serve in World War I. He was born on July 7, 1885, the son of Alexander and Susan (Archibald) Anderson, S.S. Baddeck River, Big Baddeck.

He enlisted a few months following his 30th birthday in October, 1915.

"He was remembered as a superb officer and a leader of men - a splendid example of a Cape Breton Highlander, displaying outstanding conduct throughout his military career. During one exploit he single-handedly performed a deed of heroism which won him the **MILITARY CROSS**. Rather than asking any of his men, he crossed the battlefield while it was raked with rifle, and machine gun fire and carried on his back one of his wounded men to safety." He was awarded the **MILITARY CROSS** on August 16, 1916, for " ... conspicuous gallantry and devotion to duty."

Major Anderson is featured in Pierre Burton's book entitled *Vimy*.

While commanding "D" Company of the 85th Nova Scotia Highlanders at Passchendaele, he was killed in action. As he stood in a crater, a heavy enemy shell landed nearby and blew him against the side of the crater. As he lifted his hands to his face, drops of blood fell from his nose and comrades believed he was only wounded.

(The Memorial to the men of the 85th Battalion [N.S. Highlanders] who sacrificed their lives on October 27, 28 and 29, 1917 at Passchendaele, was erected by the men of the battalion in February, 1919, with 156 names of the fallen men. Major P. Anderson is the first name on the monument).

M. F. B. 440.

In reply please quote No6D.43-A-33

MILITIA AND DEFENCE.
HEADQUARTERS, MILITARY DISTRICT No.6,
HALIFAX, NOVA SCOTIA

22nd.March 1918.

MILITARY DISTRICT No. 6
HALIFAX. N. S.
MAR 22 1918
M. D. No. 6 ....

REGISTER

To
Mr.A.Anderson,
Poplar Grove Farm,
S.S.Baddeck River,
Nova Scotia

Dear Sir,

I am to acknowledge the receipt of Mrs. Anderson's letter of the 15th.instant.

I am forwarding you herewith by registered mail the Military Cross awarded to your son, the late Captain and Acting Major Percy William Anderson, 85th. Battalion, Canadian Infantry, C.E.F., and am to express to you the personal sympathy of the Honourable the Minister, and the General Officer Commanding Military District No.6 and his Staff, in the great loss you have sustained of a son who proved himself to be such a gallant soldier.

Kindly send me a receipt for the Military Cross at your earliest convenience

Yours truly,

Beverley Armstrong

Lt.Colonel,
for A.A.G., Military District No.6

The wound proved fatal and Major Anderson died on October 28, 1917. Major Anderson is buried at Ypres (Menin Gate) Memorial Cemetery, Belgium.
Like so many other parents, Mr. and Mrs. Alexander Anderson, received the following message from King George V.

BUCKINGHAM PALACE.

I join with my grateful people
in sending you this memorial
of a brave life given for others
in the Great War.

George R.I.

Archibald, Charles

'Chas' was born on February 23, 1888, the son of James W. and Mrs. Archibald, Baddeck.

He served during World War I. His father operated an early tannery in Baddeck.

Arsenault, John Samuel 224498

'John S' was born on March 10, 1888, the son of Joseph A. and Catherine (MacLean) Arsenault, Baddeck.

Sergeant Arsenault served with the 85th Battalion Canadian Expeditionary Force in Canada, England, France and Belgium.

He married Frances Hartlen, Halifax, and they resided in Baddeck. He was Ferry Captain on the Ross Ferry at Big Harbour for many years.

Bain, William 68275

William was born in 1895, the son of Charles and Euphemia (MacVicar) Bain, New Harris. Lance Corporal Bain served with the 94th Regiment and was taken on strength with the 85th Battalion in Halifax on March 25, 1915. He died of wounds on August 24, 1916, and is buried in Reninghelst New Military Cemetery, Belgium.

The following is an excerpt from the *25th Battalion, Canadian Expeditionary Force* by F.B. MacDonald and John J. Gardiner.

" ... For a battalion (85th) that suffered 4,496 wounded casualties including 783 dead, it left a lasting mark. In a province that responded so generously in that war, perhaps many a district still remembers that it gave beyond the normal measures; - along the northern shore of the Bras d'Or Channel every farm between the little village of New Campbellton and Scalpie Mountain (approximately New Harris) sent at least one young man to war, and of them all only one returned."

On left, William Bain .

Bates, Harry

Harry hailed from Baddeck. He served during World War I.

Beaton, John L. 878254

John served in the 185th Canadian Infantry Battalion. His birthplace was given as Big Bras d'Or.

Bethune, John Hamilton Gordon

Gordon was born on August 26, 1892, the son of Dr. John L. (M.D.) and Mary C. (Jones) Bethune, Baddeck. He served overseas during the war.

He married Mabel Hickey, North Sydney. After the war, he was left a young widower and lived in Toronto for a time.

Bethune, Norman Leslie

Norman was born on August 6, 1899, the son of Dr. John L. (M.D.) and Mary C. (Jones) Bethune, Baddeck. He enlisted in 1916 and served with the 94th Regiment Argyle Highlanders. He served in Canada.

He was predeceased by his first wife, Dolly MacIntosh, North Sydney. He later married Mary Stanbury, Halifax. They resided in Baddeck. For years he was the proprietor of Bethune's Garage. A leading citizen of his community, he contributed greatly to the betterment of others. He was a worthy patron of the Gaelic College, St. Ann's. He died in June, 1986, and is buried in Greenwood Cemetery.

Bethune, Dr. Roderick Owen, M.D., C.M.

Roderick was born on September 16, 1887, the son of Dr. John L. (M.D.) and Mary C. (Jones) Bethune, Baddeck. Dr. Bethune was a 1913 graduate of Dalhousie Medical School. Colonel Bethune served overseas as a medical officer in both World Wars.

He married Margaret C. Hiltz. They resided in Berwick. He practiced medicine in Tusket and Berwick. He died in September, 1947, and is buried in Berwick.

Bird, John 468243

John hailed from Neil's Harbour. Private Bird enlisted in Halifax and served overseas in the 16th Battalion. He was killed in action on October 9, 1916, and his name is inscribed on the Vimy Memorial, France.

Blanchard, Benjamin H.C.

Ben was born in February, 1890, the son of N. Percy and Julia (Calkin) Blanchard, Baddeck. He enlisted in 1914 and served in France with The Bombers.

His father was a barrister and played a large role in putting through the legislation that secured "Village Incorporation" for the district of "Baddeck Centre." He was credited, to a large extent, for street and sidewalk construction and upgrading.

Blanchard, Rev. Henry H.

Henry was born on April 4, 1893, the son of N. Percy and Julia (Calkin) Blanchard, Baddeck. He served overseas with the 85th Battalion during World War I. In civilian life he was an ordained clergyman.

Bragg, Walter 3180937/F31984

'Braggy' was born on October 30, 1896, the son of Captain and Mrs. Grove, New Haven. He enlisted in the Canadian Army and served in France during the First Great War. Walter Bragg, F 31984, enlisted in July, 1942, and served in the Second World War.

He married Polly Smith, New Haven. He tended the lighthouse at Neil's Harbour. He died in 1986 and is buried in St. Andrew's Cemetery, Neil's Harbour.

Brewer, Henry 877130

'Harry' was born on January 6, 1896, a twin son of Samuel and Mary (Curtis) Brewer, (Backlands), Ingonish. He was a steelworker prior to the war. Private Brewer served overseas and was severely wounded.

He married Mary Clements. He died on June 15, 1925, as a result of wounds that he sustained during combat.

Brewer, Thompson 85904

Thomas was born on June 15, 1896, the son of (harbour master) Frank Colin and Susan (Cann) Brewer, Creek Road Beach, Ingonish. Driver Brewer served with the 3rd Brigade, Canadian Field Artillery In Canada, Britain and France. Twenty-four year old Brewer died in Halifax from the effects of influenza on April 20, 1916, and was buried in Holy Cross Cemetery, Sydney, Nova Scotia.

Buchanan, Alexander

'Sandy' was born on March 8, 1896, the son of Charles and Catherine (MacDonald) Buchanan, Sugar Loaf. Sergeant Buchanan served with the 85th Battalion. He was wounded in France on March 22, 1918. He was discharged on June 11, 1919. He died tragically in Boston. He went there to visit his sister who was in nurses' training. En route to meet her, he met with foul play on April 4, 1925. He is buried in Aspy Bay Cemetery.

(Dan Buchanan and his war bride, Annie Hancock)

Buchanan, Daniel

Dan was born in 1884, the son of John and Effie (MacLeod) Buchanan, River Bennett. He served overseas. He married Annie Hancock, Rossshire, Scotland. Dan and his war bride returned to Canada on July 21, 1919 on the troop ship *Cedric*. Following military discharge he went to British Columbia and died in New Westminister, after a brief illness, on December 24, 1919. He is buried there. His young widow and infant daughter, Donna, remained in River Bennett.

Buchanan, Donald William, M.D., M.M.

'Weetie' was born on March 22, 1900, the son of Angus A. (merchant) and Mary Isabel (MacLeod) Buchanan, Neil's Harbour. He served in Siberia during World War I. According to the family history he was awarded the **MILITARY MEDAL** for gallant conduct in the field in Siberia. During his service in Siberia, he developed chronic heart disease. Eventually, he succumbed to this condition.

Dr. Buchanan was a graduate of Mount Allison University and received his medical degree from Queen's University. He married Susan Carpenter, who was believed to be from Detroit. He died on November 12, 1949, in Bath, New Brunswick. He is buried in the Presbyterian Cemetery, Neil's Harbour.

Buchanan, John MacLeod 222044

'Mac' was born on January 31, 1897, the son of merchant Angus A. and Mary (MacLeod) Buchanan, Neil's Harbour.

He attended Mount Allison University in Sackville, New Brunswick. Later, while attending university in Halifax, he enlisted on September 29, 1915 and served with the 85th Battalion. He also served with the Cape Breton Highlanders in World War II. He married Ethel Peel, Oxford, Nova Scotia. They settled in Sydney. He was employed at the Steel Plant. He died on October 19, 1953, and is buried in the Presbyterian Cemetery, Neil's Harbour.

Buchanan, John William

Jack was born on November 28, 1894, the son of Charles and Catherine (MacDonald) Buchanan, Sugar Loaf. Corporal Buchanan served overseas in the 85th Battalion. He returned from France on May 2, 1919.

He married Bessie MacLeod MacRae. As he was mowing a hay field on his property by the waters of Aspy Bay, the land gave way and he went down with his tractor and was tragically killed on August 18, 1956. He is buried in Aspy Bay Cemetery.

Burke, Pius O.

Pius was born on October 2, 1886, the son of Patrick and Mary A. (Burke) Burke, Ingonish Harbour. He served during the war. He was wharfinger at South Bay, Ingonish. He was a choir member at St. Peter's Church. He and his wife, Regis, resided in Ingonish Beach.

Burton, James Isaac 1033234

James was the son of James Isaac and Hannah (MacIntosh) Burton, Bay St. Lawrence. He served in both World Wars. Private Burton served with the 97th Battalion during World War I. He served again during World War II. He married Susan Young. He died on November 16, 1959, and is buried in St. Margaret Village Cemetery.

Burton, John P.

John P. Burton hailed from Bay St. Lawrence. He served in the United States Navy. He is buried in St. Margaret's Village Cemetery.

Burton, John W.

John W. hailed from Cape North. He served during the war.

Burton, Joseph 4050338

Joe was born on October 7, 1896, the son of George and Effie Ann (Morrison) Burton, Cape North. Private Burton served overseas with the 85th Battalion. He was wounded and lost a leg in active duty.

He resided in Ontario. He is buried in MacPherson Cemetery, Cape North.

Burton, William 818013

William was born in January, 1896, the son of John and Mary (MacDonald) Burton, Glen Nevis.

Private Burton served overseas with the 25th Battalion. While serving with the 140th Battalion, he was killed at Vimy Ridge on April 9, 1917. He is buried in Thelus Military Cemetery.

Buzzan, William

William was the son of Mary (Campbell) Buzzan. He was raised by his uncle and aunt, Alex and Christy (MacNeil) Campbell, Red Point.

Bugler William Buzzan served with the Canadian Garrison Regiment.

Cameron, Michael

Michael was born on May 17, 1889, the son of Archibald A. and Bridget Cameron, Sugar Loaf. Private Cameron served with the 1st Depot Battalion.

Campbell, Albert Hart

(W.W. I)

(W.W. II)

'Bert' was born on April 7, 1893, the son of Charles and Elizabeth (Ross) Campbell, Baddeck. He served in both World Wars. He married Olive Anthony, Liverpool. They resided in Baddeck.

During World War II Lance Corporal Albert Hart Campbell (F97316) served with the Royal Canadian Army as a member of the Veterans Guard. While serving as a prison guard in Ontario, he was killed on December 28, 1942. He is buried in Greenwood Cemetery, Baddeck.

Campbell, Alexander A.

'A.A.' was born on February 10, 1882, the son of Archibald and Flora (MacDougall) Campbell, Red Point. Sergeant Campbell served in the 1st Depot Battalion.

Campbell, Angus

Angus was the son of Allan and Catherine (MacNeil) Campbell, Gillis Point. Private Campbell served in the 1st Depot Battalion.

Campbell, Angus Rory 2125035

'Angus R.' was born on June 1, 1883, the son of Rory and Maggie (MacNeil) Campbell, Jamesville West.

Sergeant Campbell served in the Canadian Railway Troops, No. 1 Section in Canada, United Kingdom, and Northwest Europe.

He married Jessie Scott. In civilian life he worked as a stationmaster for the Canadian National Railway.

Campbell, Daniel J.

Dan was born on July 18, 1891, the son of John and Ann (Patterson) Campbell, West Middle River. Private Campbell served as a sniper in the United States Army. He married Hazel John and they lived in Missouri.

(Left - Daniel Campbell)

Campbell, Daniel Joseph 878345

'D.J.' was born on April 10, 1898, the son of Donald and Margaret (MacDonald) Campbell, Baddeck.

He served overseas with the 185th and 85th Battalions. Miss Mary Campbell, Baddeck, received the following message:

France, September 18, 1918

Dear Miss Campbell - You will have already heard of the death of your nephew, 878345 Pte. D.J. Campbell. He was killed on September 2nd in the great battle fought by the Canadians east of Arras.

On the 5th of September I buried him in the British military cemetery in Vis-en-Artoi.

All the Catholics of the 85th battalion were at holy communion a few days before the battle in preparation for it, you can have the consolation of knowing that your nephew was well prepared and also that he died nobly in the greatest fight for right that the world has ever known.

I offer you my sincerest sympathy in your bereavement. Yours very truly, A. MACDONELL, Chaplain, 72nd Seaforth Highlanders.

Campbell, Dan Roderick

'Dan Rory' was born on June 30, 1897, the son of James and Katie (MacNeil) Campbell, Jamesville. Sergeant Campbell served in the 64th Battalion Canadian Infantry. He was wounded in action. He married and resided in Western Canada.

Campbell, Gerald 415736

Gerald was the son of merchant John E. and Mary Ann Campbell, Baddeck.

Private Campbell enlisted on August 7, 1915, in Sydney and served with the 40th Battalion.

Campbell, Hugh A.

Hugh was born on October 2, 1883, the son of Archibald and Flora (MacDougall) Campbell, Red Point.

Private Campbell served in the 94th Regiment.

Campbell, J.D. 878405

Private Campbell, Baddeck, served overseas with the 185th Battalion, No. 3 Platoon.

Campbell, Jerry 16289

Jerry was born on May 18, 1886, the son of Hugh and Sarah (MacNeil) Campbell, Jamesville East.

Private Jerry Campbell served overseas in the infantry with the British Columbia Regiment. While serving with the 7th Battalion, he was killed in action on June 3, 1916, in the Battle of Mount Sorrel. He was thirty years of age. His name is inscribed on the Menin Gate Memorial, Belgium.

Campbell, John James 878344

'John J.' was born on July 9, 1891, the son of Hector (Ban) and Mary (MacKenzie) Campbell, Baddeck.

He enlisted on April 20, 1917, and served overseas with the 85th Battalion, Canadian Infantry. Private Campbell was wounded on September 2, 1918.

He married a Miss Corkery, Sydney. He was injured in an explosion in Princess Colliery, Sydney Mines, on December 6, 1936. Two days later, he died in Harbourview Hospital in Sydney Mines. He is buried in St. Mary's Cemetery, Sydney.

Campbell, Kenneth Charles 222499

Kenneth was born on January 8, 1895, the son of Charles J. and Elizabeth (Ross) Campbell, Baddeck. He joined the 85th Battalion No. 14 Platoon on October 1, 1915. He was promoted to L. Sergeant on June 13, 1917, and was wounded at Lens on June 28, 1917. He resided in the USA and died there.

Campbell, Malcolm Hugh

Malcolm Hugh was born in 1892, the son of Ronald and Henrietta (Morrison) Campbell, Estmere. Private Campbell served in the war.

His parents died when he was three years old. He was raised by Charles and Flora MacDonald, Estmere. He married Margaret Calahan. They resided in Estmere. He was a master carpenter and built many of the local homes. He died in 1970 and he was the last person buried in the Grant Cemetery, Estmere.

Campbell, Malcolm R.

'Malcolm R.' was born on February 20, 1880, the son of Hugh and Sarah (MacNeil) Campbell, Barra Glen. Sergeant Campbell served in the 94th Regiment in Canada.

He married a school teacher, Eliza MacKenzie, Birch Point, and they resided in St. Columba. He died on February 26, 1969, and is buried in St. Columba Cemetery.

(Malcolm Campbell and his wife, Eliza)

Campbell, Michael L. 878150

Michael was born on May 4, 1884, and hailed from Cape North. He served with the 185th Canadian Infantry Battalion. He was a miner at the time of his enlistment.

Campbell, Murdoch J.

'Murdoch Arthur' was born in June, 1897, the son of Sea Captain Arthur and Mary (MacLeod) Campbell, South Gut. He served in the American Army. He married Margaret Morrison, Englishtown. They resided in Massachusetts. He died in 1995 in Brockton. Interment was in Riverside Cemetery, North River.

Campbell, Norman K.

Norman was born on June 3, 1890, the son of John and Ann (Patterson) Campbell, West Middle River. Private Campbell served overseas as a sapper in the Canadian Army. He married Margaret Campbell, Scotland. He and his war bride resided in the United States.

Campbell, Peter J. 3180734

'Peter J.' was born on May 11, 1893, the son of Dan H. and Annie (MacLean) Campbell, Baddeck. He joined the 1st Depot Battalion. Private Campbell served with the 25th Battalion Canadian Expeditionary Force. He died on December 24, 1924, and is buried in St. Michael's Cemetery, Baddeck.

Capstick, Maurice

Maurice was the son of William and Mollie Capstick, Capstick. Private Capstick served with the 1st Depot Battalion. He is buried in the United States.

Carmichael, David Kenneth 68278

David was raised in the home of Alexander Tailor MacRae, Middle River. He was a brother to Belle, Mrs. Dan MacQuarrie, Middle River. Corporal Carmichael served overseas with the 25th Battalion. He died of wounds on August 15, 1918, and is buried in Crony British Cemetery, France.

Carmichael, John Archie 878334

John Archie was born on October 3, 1894, the son of Norman and Mary (MacLeod) Carmichael, Tarbot. This family moved from Tarbot to Plaister Mines and eventually some members returned to Tarbot.

He served overseas with the 185th and 85th Canadian Infantry Battalion. He was wounded on October 30, 1917, in Passchendaele and died on November 4, 1917. He is buried in Etaples Military Cemetery, France.

Carmichael, John Hector

John Hector was born on October 3, 1894, the son of Archibald and Effie (Urquhart) Carmichael, Munroe's Point. He served in the war. He married Sadie Morrison, Loch Lomond. They moved to the United States.

Carmichael, John J.

'John J.' was born on November 15, 1872, the son of John and Jessie (Bain) Carmichael, Tarbotvale. He served overseas. He worked in the United States and later returned to Tarbot. Unmarried, he died in Tarbot on September 28, 1963. He is buried in Pine Hill Cemetery, River Bennett.

Carmichael, John William

John William Carmichael was born on October 3, 1894, the son of Daniel and Mary Belle (MacLeod) Carmichael, New Harris. At the outbreak of the war, he was working in the United States. He served in the army and was stationed in the Southern United States. He is buried in Mount Repose Cemetery, New York.

Carmichael, Neil John 877684

Neil was born on November 16, 1893, the son of Norman and Catherine (Matheson) Carmichael, Baddeck. He served with the 185th Canadian Infantry Battalion. It is believed that his family moved to Whitney Pier.

Christie, Joseph Bernard 877257

Joseph Bernard Christie hailed from Sugar Loaf. He served with the 185th Canadian Infantry Battalion.

Clarke, Daniel Alexander

Dan Alex was born on June 4, 1895, the son of Charles and Jessie Mary (MacPhee) Clarke, Cape Dauphin. Private Clarke served in the Infantry in Canada during the war. He married Cassie MacRae, Middle River. He and his wife resided in Cape Dauphin. He died on August 7, 1973, and is buried in New Campbellton Cemetery.

Clements, Frederick 877968

Fred was born in May, 1879 and hailed from Ingonish. He was a painter at the time of his enlistment and his address was given as Sydney Mines. He served with the 246th Battalion.

Clinch, George

George was born on March 11, 1886, the son of George and Elizabeth (Wadman) Clinch, New Haven. He served in the Merchant Marine. He was a fisherman and he resided in New Haven.

Crowdis, Angus

Angus was born on March 10, 1896, the son of Matilda MacPhee, Big Baddeck. He served in France. He is featured in the book entitled *Away* by Gary Burrill.

He married Sarah Morrison, Big Glen, and they settled in the United States. By trade he was a carpenter. He displayed great musical talent and was an accomplished violinist. He died on February 8, 1982, in Massachusetts.

Crowdis, Edward Chandler 715913

Edward was born on March 26, 1894, the son of Henry and Annie (Clarke) Crowdis, Inlet Baddeck. He enlisted on January 25, 1916, in Sydney. He joined the 106th Overseas Battalion and served in Canada, Britain and France. Private Crowdis was discharged on April 12, 1919. He married Christine MacPherson, Cape

North. They resided in Sydney. He died in 1978 and was buried in MacGregor Memorial Cemetery, Sydney River.

Curtis, Lawrence A. 877725

Lawrence was born on September 22, 1887, and he hailed from Ingonish. He worked as a miner. His name is entered in the recruiting ledger of the 185th Battalion.

Curtis, Thomas D.

Tom was born on April 14, 1895, the son of Thomas D. and Annie Curtis, South Ingonish. Private Curtis served with the 85th Battalion, Canadian Infantry.

Donovan, Alonzo Charles 488735

Alonzo hailed from Ingonish. J. Donovan was listed as his next of kin. Private Donovan enlisted in Halifax on November 9, 1915, and served with the 63rd Regiment First Reinforcing Draft.

Donovan, George 488232

George was born on December 16, 1895, the son of Thomas and Ada M. Donovan, South Ingonish. Private Donovan served overseas with the 27th Battalion. Twenty-one year old Private Donovan was killed in action on September 15, 1916. His name is inscribed on the Vimy Memorial, France.

Donovan, George 878326

George was born on May 24, 1895, and hailed from Ingonish. He was a farmer. His name is entered in the recruiting ledger of the 185th Battalion.

Donovan, Herbert A.

Herbert was born on September 9, 1894, the son of Timothy John and Mary Emma (MacDonald) Donovan, South Ingonish. Private Donovan served overseas with the 17th and 25th Battalions Canadian Infantry. 'Following a particular patrol assignment only two men answered the roll - Donovan and Doyle. Herbert Donovan and Mick Doyle, both from Ingonish, were the two soldiers who survived the assignment.' (Per Leo Donovan, Ingonish)

He was involved with the construction of the Cape Breton Highlands National golf course. Affectionately known as 'Old Herb,' he was unmarried and resided in Ingonish. He is buried in St. Peter's Parish Cemetery.

Doucette, John D.

'John D.' Doucette hailed from the parish of South Ingonish. Private Doucette served overseas with the 25th Battalion and was wounded during combat.

Doucette, John James 3181346

Jack was born on August 31, 1889, the son of James and Mary (Robinson) Doucette, South Bay, Ingonish. Private Doucette served with the 85th Battalion, Canadian Infantry. He was wounded and gassed in action. He was hospitalized in a military hospital in Epsom. For the remainder of his life, he suffered ill health.

He married a school teacher, Mary Helen Lord, Port Hood. He was edu-

cated at St. Francis Xavier College and his name is inscribed on their roll of honour. He worked for the gypsum company in Ingonish and for the Canada Cement Company in Halifax. He also worked at the Cape Breton Highlands National Park, Ingonish. He died in October, 1956, and is buried in St. Peter's Parish Cemetery, Ingonish.

(Right: Thomas Hines, Left: Jack Doucette)

Doucette, Thomas Leo

Thomas Leo was born on July 15, 1897, the son of John and Jane (Brewer) Doucette, Clyburn Valley, Ingonish. He enlisted in September, 1914 with the Royal Highlanders of Canada in the 13th Battalion of the Black Watch Regiment. He served at Vimy and Ypres. He was discharged in March, 1919. He married Agnes Lucy Devenish, London, England. He and his war bride took up residence in Ingonish. He died on October 18, 1963.

(Thomas Doucette and his wife, Agnes Lucy)

Dowling, Ambrose Gordon 488225

Gordon was born on October 31, 1886, the son of Ambrose and Celestine Dowling, Neil's Harbour. He joined the Canadian Expeditionary Force on November 20, 1915, and served overseas in the Composite Branch of Reinforcement. After the war, he moved to the United States.

Doyle, George A.

George hailed from South Ingonish. Private Doyle served with the 25th Battalion, Canadian Infantry. He was wounded in action.

Doyle, Michael D.

'Red Mick' was born on August 17, 1896, the son of Joseph and Christy Annie (Young) Doyle, Ingonish.

Private Doyle served overseas with the 25th Battalion Canadian Infantry.

For a short while, he was married to Widow MacNeil. He resided in Ingonish. He was an industrious man and was very involved with the actual construction of the Cape Breton Highlands National Park, Ingonish. He is buried in St. Peter's Parish Cemetery, Ingonish.

Duggan, James Benjamin

'Jimmie' was born on October 21, 1896, the son of Angus and Mary Julie (Daisley) Duggan, Dingwall. Private Duggan served with the 1st Depot Battalion. He was also a veteran of the World War II. His wife hailed from Inverness. She died in childbirth and he was left a young widower. He is buried in St. Joseph's Cemetery, Dingwall.

Dunlap, Frank

Frank hailed from New Campbellton. Private Dunlap served in Canada.

Farquharson, John 488228

John Farquharson hailed from Ingonish Centre. He was the son of Rev. Alexander and Barbara (MacLeod) Farquharson.

He served during the war.

He married Marjorie Crowdis. He was game warden in the Cape Breton Highlands National Park. He is buried in Sydney.

Ferguson, Angus Campbell 877362

Angus was born on June 15, 1897, the son of Archie and Catherine (Kate) (Campbell) Ferguson, New Campbellton.

He served overseas with the 185th Canadian Infantry Battalion.

He married Jennie MacDonald and they resided in Florence. He worked in the insurance business and later with the school board.

Fisher, William Henry 877954

'Willie' was born on October 5, 1898, the son of Abraham and Jessie Fisher, Birmingham, England. He was raised at the home of John Dougal and Christy (Murray) MacFadgen, Bucklaw.

Private Fisher enlisted in 1914 and served overseas. He was severely wounded in action.

In 1919, he went West to the harvest fields in Saskatchewan. He married Judith Nansen and moved to Oregon, USA. He died there in April, 1982.

Fitzgerald, Emery T. VR2748

Emery was born on May 11, 1899, the son of Caleb and Sarah (Duggan) Fitzgerald, White Point.

He served overseas in the Royal Canadian Naval Volunteer Reserve from November 16, 1916, to March 25, 1919. He served in the Veterans Guard of Canada during the Second World War. He was predeceased by his first wife Christina Dixon and his second wife Mary MacIntosh. His third wife was Mary Barron, Ingonish. He tended various lighthouses. He retired to Dingwall and he died on October 10, 1978, and is buried in Dingwall Cemetery.

Fraser, George

George was born on February 9, 1896, the son of Alexander G. and Mary Jane (Fraser) Fraser, South Side Boularderie. He enlisted in British Columbia with the Black Watch. He served overseas for three years.

He and his brother worked in the mines in Ontario. Unmarried, he died on January 23, 1972. He is buried in MacDonald Cemetery, Boularderie.

Fraser, James 715478

James was the son of Hugh and Margaret (MacDougall) Fraser, Upper Washabuck. Private Fraser served overseas in the 106th Battalion, Canadian Infantry. His father died when he was a young child and he was raised by his maternal grandparents Michael and Bessie (MacDonald) MacDougall, Washabuck. His wife hailed from Christmas Island. They lived and died in the United States.

Fraser, John Roderick

'John R.' was born on October 12, 1895, the son of David and Isabel (MacLeod) Fraser, Ross Ferry.

He served in both World Wars. He enlisted in the army and served in Siberia during the First Great War. He served in the navy during World War II and was aboard a vessel which was torpedoed by the enemy. One of the men who helped rescue him was fellow veteran Donald Ryan, Baddeck.

He served on the Victoria County municipal council and served as Warden of Victoria County for nine years. Unmarried, he died on February 25, 1992 and is buried in Man O' War Cemetery, Ross Ferry. "Fois Air Anam" is the Gaelic inscription on this grave marker. Literally translated, it means "Peace on His Soul."

Frost, Harold

Harold was born in England. He was raised at the home of Malcolm William and Mary Ann MacLeod, Jubilee. Private Frost served in the infantry. Upon his return from war he deboarded the train at Orangedale and walked to his old home at Jubilee.Mrs. MacLeod, his foster mother, died in childbirth leaving her husband with their young family. Malcolm W. MacLeod's sister, Johena MacLeod, returned home from Boston to help raise the children, including Harold. Private Frost, while in England, located his birth mother and sent her picture to his family at Jubilee. Harold Frost married and lived in New York.

Gillis, Daniel Joseph

Dan Joe was born on July 12, 1895, the son of James and Lucy (MacInnis) Gillis, McKinnons Harbour. Sergeant Gillis served in the 1st Depot Battalion. He married Mary Campbell, Prince Edward Island.

Grant, Alexander David

Alexander was born on January 7, 1896, the son of Duncan and Elizabeth (Corbett) Grant, South Side Boularderie. He enlisted on January 3, 1917, in Regina, Saskatchewan, with the 28th Battalion Reinforcement Draft (Trans 5th Battalion). He served in Canada, England and France. He was discharged in Halifax on January 8, 1919. He married Isabel MacDonald, Boularderie Centre. Alexander died on March 14, 1971, and is buried in MacDonald Cemetery, Boularderie.

Griffiths, George Edward 715448

'Ted' was born in England in 1896 and raised in Birch Plain by Rory MacLeod. Private Griffiths served with the 106th Overseas Battalion Canadian Expeditionary Force. He married Jennie Burns and they resided in New Waterford. He died in April, 1969.

Gunn, Wilfred

Wilfred was born on February 20, 1896, the son of Alexander and Harriet A. (Hood) Gunn, New Harris.

During the first war, Sergeant Gunn served in France with the 85th Battalion in # 15 Platoon. He also served during World War II. He married Catherine MacAulay, Sydney. They lived in Sydney Mines. He was an agent with London Life Insurance.

Gwynn, Hugh J.

Hugh J. Gwynn hailed from the Cape North area. He served during the war. His picture was obtained from the collection of war veterans photographs at the Cape North Museum.

Gwynn, Hugh Thomas 167047

'Hughie Josie' was born on March 29, 1898, the son of Joseph and Effie (Morrison) Gwynn, Cape North. He enlisted in Sydney Mines on November 18, 1915 with the 2nd Pioneer Battalion. Private Gwynn served overseas in the infantry for three years. His wife hailed from Prince Edward Island. They resided in Boston and retired to Prince Edward Island.

Gwynn, James William

(Right - Jim Gwynn)

James was born on April 1, 1894, the son of Joseph and Effie (Morrison) Gwynn, Cape North. He served two and one-half years with the Royal Canadian Engineers during the war. He lived in Boston where he was an electrician. He is buried in Aspy Bay Cemetery.

Gwynn, Wilson James 6428442

Wilson was born on October 7, 1899, the son of Alexander MacLeod and Effie Ann Gwynn, Sugar Loaf.
Private Gwynn enlisted on May 9, 1919 and served until August 11, 1921, with Troop G 5th U.S. Cavalry, Columbus, Ohio. Sergeant Gwynn , F476273, served in the infantry from 1943 to 1945. He married Sarah Hughena Wilkie. He tended the lighthouses at Money Point and St. Paul's Island. He died on January 21, 1986 and is buried in Aspy Bay Cemetery.

Hanam, John 469627

Jack the son of Morgan and Hannah (Hayward) Hanam, Rose Blanch, Newfoundland, was born on March 17, 1876. At eight years of age, he came with his family to St. Paul's Island and then to Baddeck. He had been a member of the Coast Guard and later enlisted with the 64th Battalion on August 13, 1915. Private Hanam served in Canada, England and France. He was wounded at Vimy. He served until May, 1918. He married twice. His first wife was Elizabeth Williams and his second wife was Alexandrina Anderson. He settled in South Side Baddeck and carried on farming. He died on July 2, 1949 and is buried in Greenwood Cemetery, Baddeck.

Hanam, Walter 478516

Walter was a son of Morgan and Hannah (Hayward) Hanam. He was born on January 10, 1880, in Newfoundland and came to Baddeck at four years of age.

Private Hanam served overseas with the Royal Canadian Regiment. He was killed in action on June 5, 1916, and is buried in Lijssenthoek Military Cemetery, Belgium.

Hart, Harold Alexander 3181998

Harold was born on November 21, 1891, the son of merchant Albert and Frances (Wilson) Hart, Baddeck.

Private Hart enlisted on April 26, 1918, and was released from active service on February 21, 1919. He served with the No. 1 Depot Battalion, Nova Scotia Regiment in Canada. According to the family history, deafness had disqualified Private Hart from earlier wartime service.

He was a fruit farmer in the Annapolis Valley. He married Ethel Alley from Hantsport, Nova Scotia, and they resided there. He died on May 28, 1951, and is buried in Hantsport.

Hart, Joseph

Joseph was born on October 31, 1892, the son of Phillip and Mary (MacLeod) Hart, Inlet Baddeck. He served in World War I. He married Tina MacDonald, North River. He left the area and did not return.

Hart, Joseph Ernest 1262742

Ernest was born on January 9, 1884, the son of merchant Albert and Frances (Wilson) Hart, Baddeck. Gunner Hart served with the 5th Brigade, Canadian Field Artillery. He died of wounds on July 14, 1917, and is buried in Bethune Town Cemetery, France.

He kept a descriptive diary about his war experiences. It was in his sister's possession for many years and after her death the diary was mailed to a relative but, unfortunately, it did not reach the person to whom it was mailed.

Hatcher, John Thomas 3180505

Johnny was born on October 2, 1895, the grandson of Phillip and Catherine Hatcher, New Haven.

Private Hatcher served in the Depot Battalion, Nova Scotia Regiment. He died of pneumonia on April 2, 1918, and is buried in St. Andrew's Cemetery, Neil's Harbour.

Hawkins, George Francis 488223

George Hawkins was born on October 29, 1897, the stepson of William Ward and son of Susannah (Hawkins) Ward, Neil's Harbour.

He enlisted with the Royal Canadian Regiment and served overseas. He died of wounds on November 16, 1917, and his name is inscribed on the Menin Gate Memorial, Belgium.

Hawley, Matthew Wilson 877152

Matthew Wilson was born on October 25, 1894, the son of light keeper Matthew and Annie Hawley, Ingonish Harbour.

He enlisted with the 185th Canadian Infantry Battalion and served until April 18, 1916. He married and lived in Ingonish where he was a fisherman.

Hines, Angus A.

Angus was born on November 14, 1895, the son of Alexander and Willena (Smith) Hines, Ingonish Ferry. Private Hines served overseas with the 5th Brigade. Unmarried, he resided in Ingonish. He was a cook aboard the SS *Aspy*. He is buried in St. Peter's Parish Cemetery.

Hines, Augustine

'Gus' was the son of Johnny and Mary (Hawley) Hines, Ingonish Ferry. Private Hines served with the 5th Brigade.

Later in life, he married a widow, Annie Colin Hawley. They resided in Ingonish where he was a fisherman. He is buried in St. Peter's Parish Cemetery, Ingonish.

Hines, George H.

'George H.' was born on August 17, 1891, the son of George A. and his first wife, Mary Hines, South Ingonish.

Private Hines served with the 3rd Battalion, Canadian Infantry. After the war, he moved to New Waterford and worked in the coal mines.

Hines, Otis 877665

Otis was born on April 30, 1895, and hailed from Ingonish.

He worked as a boiler maker and his name is entered in the recruiting ledger of the 185th Battalion.

Hines, Thomas J.

Tom was the son of John and Mary (Hawley) Hines, Ingonish Ferry. Private Hines served with the 25th Battalion Canadian Infantry.

He married a school teacher, Tena, from New Waterford. They resided in Ingonish where he was a fisherman.

(Right: Thomas Hines, Left: Jack Doucette)

Hooper, Charles Arthur 68281

Charles was born on May 24, 1893, in Birmingham, England. He was raised at the home of Alfred and Mary (MacRae) MacLeod, Middle River.

He had been a member of the 94th Regiment for seven years prior to enlisting on March 25, 1915, in Halifax. He served with the 25th Battalion Canadian Expeditionary Force in Canada, England and France. He was wounded in 1915 and again during the Battle of the Somme in 1916. Corporal Hooper was discharged in Halifax on February 11, 1919.

In civilian life he was a steam engineer.

Horton, John William 222561

Jack was born on February 7, 1896, the son of Alexander and Annie (MacDonald) Horton, New Campbellton. Private Horton served with the 85th Battalion, # 15 Platoon.

He married Marion Christie, Englishtown. For eleven years, they were light keepers on Birds Island. He died on March 15, 1944, and is buried in New Campbellton.

Hunter, Daniel 222385

Dan was born in Hunter's Mountain son of Catherine Hunter.

He served overseas with the 85th Battalion as a armourer sergeant. Dan Hunter died in Halifax circa 1939 and is buried in Middle River Cemetery.

Hutchison, Daniel Colin 2330327

Dan was born on October 3, 1889, the son of David and Margaret (MacIver) Hutchison, Inlet Baddeck.

Private Hutchison served in the two World Wars. He enlisted on April 27, 1917, and went overseas with the 85th Battalion. He served in France and sustained a leg wound in battle. He was discharged on March 31, 1919.

He married Margaret MacLean, Big Baddeck. Their son David was an internationally recognized artist. His painting entitled 'Keep the Lantern Lit' became the focal point for the Victoria County Memorial Hospital Charitable Foundation.

Private Hutchison F32783 joined the Veterans Guard of Canada on January 5, 1943. He served as border guard at St. Stephen, New Brunswick and then transferred to the German Prison Guard at Montrith, Ontario. When the war ended, he accompanied a boat load of prisoners to their homeland. He was discharged on July 18, 1946.

He died in April, 1969, and is buried in Greenwood Cemetery, Baddeck.

Hutchison, Joseph J.

Joe was born on July 6, 1894, the son of David and Margaret (MacLean) Hutchison, Inlet Baddeck.

He served overseas during the war. Joe and his brother, Dan, mailed postcards home to their mother on the same day from the same place in France. Neither one was aware that the other was in the same town.

Joe died in 1945 in the United States. His remains were brought home and he is buried in Knox Auld Kirk Cemetery, Bay Road, Baddeck.

Jackson, Daniel

Dan was born on October 20, 1892, the son of Henry and Elizabeth Jackson, Ingonish Centre. He served during the war.

He married and lived in the United States.

Jackson, John Bunyan 715848

'John B.' was born on June 7, 1891, the son of Jesse Lewis and Sarah Ellen (Brewer) Jackson, West Ingonish.

Private Jackson served with the 106th Overseas Battalion. He enlisted on February 25, 1916, in Truro. He served in Canada, Britain and France and was discharged on April 11, 1919, in Halifax.

He married Elizabeth Noseworthy, Newfoundland. In 1925, he and his brother, James Ward Jackson, formed a partnership and established Jackson Brothers, a fruit and confectionery store, Commercial Street, North Sydney. In 1928, fire destroyed their business establishment. John B. died in 1935.

Jackson, Thomas Carl 488227

Carl was born on July 26, 1896, the son of Henry and Elizabeth (Hardy) Jackson, Ingonish.

He served overseas during the war.

He married Caroline Roper, Ingonish. He was light keeper on Ingonish Island from 1924 to 1961.

James, Alexander

Alexander was born on June 30, 1885, on St. Paul's Island. He was the son of Joseph James, Newfoundland. His father is believed to have operated the first lobster factory on the North Shore.

He served overseas. Private James died as a result of wounds on April 2, 1919 in Halifax. He is buried in Oceanview Cemetery, Birch Plain.

James, George 222759

It is believed that George James was an English child who was raised with a family in Boularderie. His next of kin is listed as William J. James.

He enlisted in Sydney on October 5, 1915. Private James served overseas with the 85th Battalion, #15 Platoon.

James, Harry 222564

Private James enlisted with the 85th Battalion in Sydney on October 5, 1915. His next of kin was M.D. MacKenzie, New Harris.

James, William

Willie, brother to Alexander James, was born on February 9, 1884. He lived with his uncle, Rory MacLeod, Wreck Cove.

He served during the war. He resided in Pennsylvania.

Janes, Benjamin

Ben was born on April 17, 1896, the son of Richard and Charlotte (Hardy) Janes, West Ingonish.

He served during the war.

Jobe, Seward James 715479

Seward was born on January 22, 1888, the son of Phillip and Johanna Jobe, Ingonish.

Private Jobe served with the 106th Battalion. He was wounded while serving with the 26th Battalion and died of wounds on April 27, 1917. He is buried in La Targette British Cemetery, France.

Julian, John

John Julian hailed from Wagmatcook. Private Julian served during the war.

Kavanaugh, Daniel

Private Kavanaugh hailed from St. Margaret's Village. He served during the war. He resided in St. Margaret's Village and was buried in St. Margaret's Cemetery.

Kavanaugh, John

Johnnie hailed from Bay St. Lawrence. He served as a flight pilot in the United States Air Force. He is buried in New York.

Kerr, John Donald 3182490

Jack was born on March 4, 1894 the son of Rod and Mary (MacDonald) Kerr, Englishtown.

Private Kerr served as a sapper on the front lines in France during World War I. For fifty-one years he was a member of the Brotherhood of Locomotive Engineers and an employee of the Sydney and Louisbourg Railway.

He married Mary MacPherson, R.N., Glace Bay. They resided in Glace Bay. His brother, Dr. A.E. Kerr (WW I veteran, born Louisbourg), served as president of Dalhousie University. John D. Kerr died on December 30, 1979, and is buried in Greenwood Cemetery, Glace Bay.

Latham, John Gesner 878340

John was born on March 20, 1895, the son of William and Catherine (Morrison) Latham, Oregon, North River.

Private Latham served with the 185th Canadian Infantry Battalion. He was killed in action on August 9, 1918, and his name is inscribed on the Vimy Memorial in France.

Livingstone, Alexander

Alexander was born on June 9, 1884, the son of William and Sarah (MacLean) Livingstone, Big Bras d'Or.

Captain Alexander served with the American Merchant Marine in transport shipping out of New York.

He married Ruby Gurney. He was a captain with the United Fruit Company, New York. He maintained the original homestead in Big Bras d'Or. He died on July 19, 1968 in New York and is buried in St. James Cemetery, Big Bras d'Or.

Livingstone, Daniel Archibald, M.M. 469120

Dan was born on October 5, 1895, the son of William and Sarah (MacLean) Livingstone, Big Bras d'Or.

He had been sailing out of New York at the outbreak of war. He left and returned to New Brunswick to join the 64th Battalion.

He was an officer in charge of scouts of the 25th Battalion Unit. Although struck twice while reconnoitring front lines, he managed to crawl back a considerable distance. Shot through the thigh,

(Brothers Daniel Livingstone - left, and Capt. William Livingstone - right)

he unbuckled his Sam Browne belt and applied it as a tourniquet. He sustained the other shot through his neck. He was reported missing on April 7, 1918, but he likely lived for several days on the battlefield. The body of Lieutenant Livingstone was found on May 3, 1918. He is buried in Wailly Orchard Cemetery, France.

He was awarded the **MILITARY MEDAL.**

"... This man was attached to the Brigade Staff as a Battalion Runner. He was the first runner to visit me in the front line after the capture of Courcelette and from that time to the time of our relief on the morning of the 18th he was backwards and forwards with messages and parties continually. He never once failed in his duties and his devotion to duty was magnificent.

He was the last runner to come up to the Brigade to guide out myself and a few others who remained until the relief was complete." (Medals and Honors form)

Livingstone, David Stanley

Stanley was born on October 16, 1888, the son of William and Sarah (MacLean) Livingstone, Big Bras d'Or. He was named for his grand uncle, the famous Dr. David Livingstone, African explorer and missionary.

At the outbreak of the war, he was working as a street car conductor in Philadelphia. He gave up his work and served in the U.S. Marines. He was a French translator and author. He married in France. Stanley moved to Staten Island, New York. He wrote a book about the sea entitled *Full and Bye.* He married again and at the time of his death, he was living in Florida.

Livingstone, Harrison Lincoln 716207

Harrison was born on August 13, 1897, the youngest son of William and Sarah (MacLean) Livingstone, Big Bras d'Or. He enlisted following a recruitment meeting at the Big Bras d'Or schoolhouse. He served overseas in France with the 106th Battalion. Twice he was wounded in battle. Because his brother was an officer, they were not permitted to speak when they met in the trenches. At three o'clock one morning he was commanded to "Report to cemetery." Instinctively he knew that his older brother Daniel had been killed. Risking his life as he went on foot overland until he finally reached the cemetery to find his brother's burlap-wrapped body. After the chaplain and officers arrived, "they buried him and that was it."

A lengthy interview with Mr. Livingstone and other veterans is featured in the *Cape Breton Magazine* Issue # 33. Here he revealed this poignant quote, "My biggest regret was leaving my widowed mother on the farm." He is also featured in the book *Twenty-fifth Battalion - C.E.F.* by MacDonald and Gardiner.

He married Elizabeth Matheson, Boularderie. They resided in Montreal where he was employed in an airplane factory. In 1945, they moved to Halifax where he served in the Civil Service. His ashes were spread on his farm overlooking the beautiful Bras d'Or Lakes at Marble Mountain.

Livingstone, Lauchlan 222759

'Lochie' was born on September 3, 1893, the son of Archie and Mary Livingstone, Big Bras d'Or.

L/Sergeant Livingstone served overseas with the 85th Battalion and was killed in action on June 13, 1917. He was survived by his young widow, Christena (Tena) MacAskill Livingstone. She was a sister to Campbell MacAskill who was killed in action during World War II. L/Sergeant Livingstone is buried in Cabaret Rouge British Cemetery, Souchez, France.

Livingstone, William Angus, M.C. and Bar

William Angus was born on October 5, 1892, the son of William and Sarah (MacLean) Livingstone, Big Bras d'Or.

Commanding Officer Livingstone served overseas from July 20, 1915, to November 19, 1919, with the D Company, 25th Canadian Infantry Battalion. Five times wounded, he was promoted on the field and earned the nickname of 'Wild Bill' because of his fearlessness. He was an expert shot with a pistol and held the highest score at the Canadian Corps training camp in France. Lt. A/Captain Livingstone was awarded the **MILITARY CROSS** and **BAR**

" ... for conspicuous gallantry in action. He led his section of the raiding party with marked gallantry in action. He led his section of the raiding party with marked gallantry, inflicting many casualties and capturing several prisoners. He set a fine example to his men" - "for conspicuous gallantry and devotion to duty. He led his company in an attack until held up by machine-gun fire. He then went forward with a small party under heavy fire and killed the gun crews, thereby permitting his men to advance. Later, accompanied by one non-commissioned officer, he attacked and drove in a bombing post, killing three of the enemy. His magnificent courage and determination contributed materially to the success of the operation."

Source - *London Gazette*. He was recommended for the **VICTORIA CROSS** by the Colonel of the 22nd Battalion for retaking a trench at Hill 70. However, his own battalion commander wouldn't approve the recommendation.

En route home he met Nursing Sister Edith E. Clarke, R.N., Annapolis Royal, who had served overseas with the Canadian Medical Corp. They married and their son, Grant Livingstone (World War II), was born in 1922 and was the first child to be born in the Grace Maternity Hospital, Halifax. Their daughter, Caroline, R.N., served overseas as a Nursing Sister during World War II. It is believed that Edith and Caroline Livingstone may have been the only Canadian Nursing Sisters where a mother and daughter both served overseas - one in the First World War and the other in the Second World War. William Angus was a graduate of Dalhousie University and became a barrister-at-law. When he was appointed to the bench, he was the youngest judge in Nova Scotia. He died on May 14, 1950, and is buried in Mountain View Cemetery (Military Section), Vancouver.

MacAskill, Angus

Angus was born on January 23, 1897, the son of Norman and Mary (Campbell) MacAskill, Mill Cove, St. Ann's. He served overseas in Germany. He was a prisoner of war for two years. His first wife was Wilena Florence Fader, Englishtown. They resided in the United States. He was a skilled draftsman and designer of buildings. He was a merchant mariner and travelled to Africa many times.

MacAskill, Angus

Angus was born in 1868, the son of Duncan and Catherine (Matheson) MacAskill, Englishtown. He served during the war. He married twice. In later years he and his second wife, Rena MacDonald MacAskill, ran a boarding house in Sydney. He died in 1946.

MacAskill, Annabel R.N.

Annabel was born on May 27, 1891, the daughter of Charles and Jessie (MacKay) MacAskill, Big Baddeck/ Baddeck.

A Registered Nurse, she was a graduate of the Newport Hospital School of Nursing. She served as a Nursing Sister in the United States Army in 1918, stationed at Camp Merritt, New Jersey. She returned to Baddeck in 1930 and joined the staff of the Victoria County Memorial Hospital in 1948. She was a Deputy Registrar of Deaths, Births and Marriages for fifty years. She died on November 2, 1990, and is buried in St. Andrew's Cemetery, Baddeck Forks.

MacAskill, Campbell 477556

Campbell was born on August 5, 1895, the son of Norman and Mary (Campbell) MacAskill, Mill Cove, St. Ann's. Private MacAskill served overseas with the Royal Canadian Regiment. He was killed in action on April 9, 1917, and is buried in La Chaudiere Military Cemetery, Vimy.

MacAskill, Charles Bannington 1258130

Charles Bannington was born on April 26, 1899, the son of Murdoch D. (The Bishop) and Margaret (MacPhee) MacAskill, Baddeck. At seventeen years of age, while attending Dalhousie University, he enlisted in World War I. He served in the 10th Siege Battalion and entered Germany with the occupation army.

At the conclusion of the war, he returned to Baddeck and again enrolled in university to complete his studies. He graduated from Dalhousie with his Bachelor of Law degree. He served as the Stipendiary Magistrate, Registrar of Deeds and Judge of Probate in his home town of Baddeck. He married Neta Little. They resided in Baddeck. He died in May, 1947, at forty-eight years of age.

MacAskill, Reverend John J.

'John J.' was born on May 26, 1871, the son of Hugh and Kate MacAskill, Hazeldale. Captain MacAskill served as a chaplain during the war. He was ordained in 1901 and inducted that same year as minister in Fort Kent, Maine, USA. Later he moved to Maisonneuve, Montreal, and then returned to reside in Fort Kent, Maine.

MacAskill, Norman Angus 471082

Norman was born on June 28, 1881, the son of Alexander and Annie (MacLean) MacAskill, Englishtown. He enlisted on February 12, 1916, in Halifax. Private MacAskill served overseas with the Canadian Army Expeditionary Force and was discharged on July 17, 1919. Unmarried, he died tragically as the result of a sawmill accident in Englishtown. He is buried in Englishtown.

MacAskill, Norman James 2605883

'Norman J.' was born on November 9, 1892, the son of John and Annie (MacLeod) MacAskill, Birch Plain. Gunner MacAskill served in the Canadian Field Artillery, Canadian Expeditionary Force in Canada, England, France and Belgium. He was discharged on April 5, 1919. On December 6, 1917, while serving in Halifax, he witnessed the Halifax Explosion. He was a skilled orator and on the anniversary of this event, he often attended local schools and related his experiences to the students.

Norman J. MacAskill, # F40864, also served in World War II. From April 5, 1941 to August 10, 1945, he served with the 18th Company Veterans Guard of Canada. Norman married a local school teacher, Wilena Brewer. He felt great commitment to support and promote the Gaelic culture. He was closely associated with the Gaelic College and was an active member in his church and community. He died on May 17, 1969, and is buried in Oceanview Cemetery, Birch Plain.

MacAskill, William Ross 716260

'W.R.' was born on December 5, 1890, the son of Ewen G. and Minnie (MacKay) MacAskill, Baddeck. He was a pilot with the Royal Flying Corps - 20 Squadron. Lieutenant MacAskill was a prisoner of war. He died of wounds on June 19, 1917. He is buried in Hajebrouck Cemetery, France. A cross fashioned from the propeller of his aircraft was erected at his grave site by his comrades.

MacAulay, Alexander

Alex was born on December 25, 1897, the son of Norman and Norrie (Morrison) MacAulay, North Gut, St. Ann's. He served overseas with the Royal Canadian Regiment. He married Isobel Crosby, Yarmouth. He was a member of the Nova Scotia Police Force and later the Royal Canadian Mounted Police. We worked in the electrical department of HMC Dockyard during the Second World War. He was secretary of Nova Scotia Tartan Ltd., Halifax. He died on October 1, 1977 and is buried in Harbourview Cemetery, South Haven.

MacAulay, Alexander Malcolm M.D.

Alexander was born on November 1, 1876, the son of Donald William and Margaret (Fraser) MacAulay, Baddeck Bay. He taught school prior to entering medical school at Manitoba University. He was a 1907 medical graduate and later, he took further study at Mayo Clinic, Rochester, Minnesota. He practiced as a physician and surgeon in Great Falls, Montana.

'Dr. Alex' enlisted during the war and served overseas in the United States Army Medical Corps. He was commissioned as a First Lieutenant and was subsequently promoted to Captain. After the war, he returned to his medical practice in Montana. He was a member of the Veterans of Foreign Wars. He married Anne Eitelgeorge, Illinois. He died on July 23, 1940. His ashes are interred in his mother's plot in Highland Cemetery, Baddeck Bay.

MacAulay, Allan, M.C., D.C.M. 432935

Allan was born on February 29, 1892, the son of Norman and Norrie (Morrison) MacAulay, North Gut, St. Ann's.

He enlisted in Edmonton, Alberta, on January 25, 1915, with the 49th Battalion, Canadian Infantry, Alberta Regiment. His engagements were Ploegstrict, Missiner Front, Ypres, Somme, Courcolette, Vimy Ridge, Canal Du Nord, Cambrai and Valenciennes.

He received the **DISTINGUISHED CONDUCT MEDAL** on January 1, 1918, and the **MILITARY CROSS** on August 26, 1918. The supplement to the *London Gazette*, February 1, 1919 reads:

" ... The **MILITARY CROSS** was awarded for conspicuous gallantry and devotion to duty during the operations east of Aaras from August 26 to August 29, 1918. When the officer in charge of the bombing attack was killed and the advance held up, he (Allan MacAulay) immediately went forward, re-organized the attack and personally led it, bombing down the trench and inflicting heavy casualties on the enemy. Throughout the whole time he displayed great courage and determination and his fine example did much to bring about the complete success of the operation." Major MacAulay was demobilized in Winnipeg, Manitoba on April 4, 1919.

He served as chieftain of the Clan MacAulay. The keynote address at the opening of the Gaelic Mod, St. Ann's, on July 30, 1941, by Stuart McCawley was dedicated to Major MacAulay. Unmarried, he was tragically drowned at Ross Ferry on March 8, 1950. He is buried in Harbourview Cemetery, South Haven.

MacAulay, Angus Bannington 877278

'AB' was born on June 18, 1891, the son of Alexander and Catherine (MacAskill) MacAulay, Big Baddeck. He served in the militia and then enlisted with the 185th Canadian Infantry Battalion. He married a school teacher, Florence Matheson. He farmed in Big Baddeck. He died on August 3, 1971, and is buried in St. Andrew's Cemetery, Baddeck Forks.

MacAulay, Angus D. 67498

'Angus D.' was born on May 29, 1886, the son of John and Margaret (Ferguson) MacAulay, Hazeldale. He enlisted on November 20, 1914 and served in the 25th Battalion Canadian Expeditionary Force. Private MacAulay served in Canada, Britain and France. He was a member and medallist of a tug-of-war team which was a recreational component of the military. He married Katie Belle MacRitchie, Hazeldale. He died in 1944 and is buried in Little Narrows Cemetery.

MacAulay, Daniel A., M.D.

Dan was born on November 9, 1879, the son of Donald and Katherine (MacDonald) MacAulay, Englishtown. He graduated from Dalhousie University Medical School in 1911. Dr. Dan enlisted on July 21, 1915, with the medical detachment which aided the Empirical Army which was then holding the long line until the Empire could muster its forces. He was detailed for duty with the 27th British division serving with them at Ypres. He transferred to the Canadian Army in 1919 and served as Senior Medical Officer in charge of a hospital ship which sailed from England to Halifax. Unmarried, Dr. Dan died on June 16, 1928, while practising in Baddeck, Nova Scotia. He is buried in Bayview Cemetery, Englishtown.

MacAulay, Donald

Donald was born on February 28, 1891, the son of John and Carrie (MacInnis) MacAulay, Baddeck. He served during the war. He moved to the United States.

MacAulay, Ian A.

Ian MacAulay was born on May 27, 1894, the son of John and Carrie (MacInnis) MacAulay, Baddeck. He served during the war. He moved to the United States.

MacAulay, John

John MacAulay, Baddeck, served during the war.

MacAulay, William Murdock

William was born on January 17, 1865, the son of Alexander and Catherine (MacAulay) MacAulay, Beinn Bhreagh/Baddeck Bay Road. He served during the war. He died, unmarried, in Langley, British Columbia.

MacAulay, William Ross 2770018

(right - W. Ross MacAulay)

Ross was born on February 14, 1899, the son of Donald and Katherine (MacDonald) MacAulay, Englishtown. He enlisted on September 18, 1918, in Sussex, New Brunswick. He served overseas with the 260th Battalion Canadian Rifles. He was discharged on June 13, 1919. He served as municipal councillor for the Englishtown district. He was active in both community and provincial politics. He married Annabelle Morrison, Englishtown. He died on April 15, 1963 and is buried in Bayview Cemetery, Englishtown.

MacCharles, Farquhar John

'Fred' was born on September 22, 1890, the son of Angus D. and Mary (MacRae) MacCharles, MacCharles Cross, Big Baddeck. Prior to World War I he served in the militia. Lieutenant MacCharles enlisted on August 4, 1914, with the 94th Highlanders and in August, 1916, transferred to the 185th where he served until demobilization in June, 1919. He was a graduate of the Nova Scotia Agricultural College. He became a staff officer with the Canada Department of Agriculture, Truro. He was a life member of the Canadian Hereford Breeders Association. He married Margaret MacKay, Baddeck. They resided in Baddeck. He died on June 22, 1969, and is buried in Greenwood Cemetery, Baddeck.

MacCharles, Hector D. 2204789

Hector 'Plant' was born on June 20, 1882, the son of John (Plant) and Jessie (Campbell) MacCharles, Upper Middle River.

He enlisted on April 20, 1918, and served in the army with the 54th Railroad Construction Corps. He served in Canada and France. Private MacCharles was discharged on demobilization on March 24, 1919. He married Jessie Campbell, Scotland. He and his war bride returned to Middle River. He died on April 9, 1969, and is buried in Middle River Cemetery.

MacCharles, Herbert Kitchner

'Herb' was born on December 26, 1899, the son of Angus D. and Mary (MacRae) MacCharles, MacCharles Cross, Big Baddeck. He served in both World Wars. He graduated from Nova Scotia Agricultural College and Ontario Agricultural College in 1923. In 1939, he enlisted with the North Nova Scotia Highlanders and was discharged in 1945 with the rank of Major. He shared quarters with Dr. Sidney Gilchrist of Africa fame. They remained friends throughout the succeeding years.

Herb was a well recognized agriculturalist and served as district supervisor of the Canada Department of Agriculture. He married Elizabeth Johnson and they resided in Moncton. He died on October 6, 1963, and is buried in Moncton, New Brunswick.

MacCharles, Malcolm Donald 111350

Malcolm was born on March 17, 1889, the son of Angus D. and Mary (MacRae) MacCharles, MacCharles Cross, Big Baddeck. Trooper MacCharles enlisted on April 19, 1915, in Amherst with the 6th Regiment Canadian Mounted Rifle. He served overseas with the Canadian Mounted Rifles, 6th Regiment. He was a prisoner of war for two and one-half years.

He married Mabel MacAulay, Baddeck. He was an agricultural representative of the Nova Scotia Department of Agriculture in the Pictou area until he retired in 1954. He died on February 8, 1974, in Pictou and is buried in the Haliburton Cemetery, Pictou, Nova Scotia.

MacCorrison, Leslie G.

Leslie was raised in Nyanza, a grandson of a Mrs. Johnson who lived on the Donald MacPhail property. Lieutenant MacCorrison served overseas with the Cape Breton Highlanders, an officer with "C" Company. He served for the duration of the war. He sold his grandparents' property to Donald MacPhail who moved to Nyanza from Whycocomagh Mountain. After the war, he bought a property from merchant M.N. MacRae in Nyanza. He had siblings, but it is unknown if he was the only one who came to Cape Breton. The MacCorrison family lived in Maine. He moved to Glace Bay where he worked as a letter carrier for the Postal Department. He married, worked and died in Glace Bay.

MacDermid, Alexander

'Sandy' was born on January 25, 1884, the son of Kenneth and Annie (Morrison) MacDermid, Wreck Cove. He served overseas and suffered shrapnel wounds. When the shrapnel was removed, he saved a piece and made it into a pendant for his daughter, Annie Mae MacDermid.

He married Christy Ann MacLeod, Birch Plain. A very capable master carpenter, he designed and built churches, schools and homes. He authored a booklet about religious revivals on the North Shore entitled *The Awakening on the North Shore* and a booklet of poems entitled *Simple Lines for Simple Folks*. He resided in Wreck Cove and died on October 21, 1967.

MacDermid, Rachael Florence R.N.

Rachael was born on April 19, 1889, the daughter of Murdoch A. and Annie (Gillis) MacDermid, Crowdis Mountain/Baddeck. She was a Registered Nurse and a graduate of the New England Hospital for Women and Children School of Nursing in Boston. Nursing Sister MacDermid served in France during the War. She became Superintendent of Nurses at the Suburban General Hospital, Belleview, Pittsburgh, Pennsylvania. She died on July 26, 1942 in Pittsburgh, Pennsylvania, and is buried in Knox Auld Kirk Cemetery, Bay Road, Baddeck.

MacDonald, Alexander

'Sandy John X' was born on February 2, 1894, the son of John X. and Mary (Urquhart) MacDonald, North Shore. He served overseas. He married Irma Phelps. They resided in Massachusetts where he died on August 11, 1941.

MacDonald, Alexander John 150145

Alexander was born on May 6, 1885, the son of John S. and Jennie (MacAulay) MacDonald, Cain's Mountain.

He moved to Western Canada circa 1908 and worked in Winnipeg as a streetcar conductor. He enlisted in Winnipeg on July 24, 1915, and served overseas with the 16th Battalion (Winnipeg Regiment). He was killed in action on September 6, 1917, at the Battle of the Somme. Private MacDonald's name is inscribed on the Vimy Memorial, France.

MacDonald, Alexander Joseph

Alexander was born on December 4, 1884, the son of Allan and Sarah (MacNeil) MacDonald, St. Columba. Lieutenant MacDonald served in the 94th Battalion Canadian Infantry, Canadian Garrison Regiment.

He was predeceased by his first wife, Mary Ann MacKinnon. His second wife was Edna MacNeil. He was a merchant in North Sydney.

MacDonald, Alexander N.

Alexander was born on October 22, 1890, the son of Stephen A. and Mary Ann (MacNeil) MacDonald, St. Columba. Private MacDonald served in the 94th Battalion. He served in Canada. Unmarried, he died on February 1, 1972, and is buried in St. Columba Parish Cemetery, Iona.

MacDonald, Alfred Smith

Alfred Smith was an English child from the Middlemore Home, Birmingham. This tow-headed boy came to live with Angus and Mary (MacLeod) MacDonald, West Tarbot. His widowed birth mother kept in contact with Freddie and sent him a photograph of herself, her second husband and his half -siblings. It was his most treasured possession. 'Freddie' enlisted in the army and returned home on leave in 1917, before he disembarked for overseas. After the war he married and remained in England.

MacDonald, Angus Hugh 3187045

Angus was born on October 29, 1898, the son of John L. and Christy (MacKenzie) MacDonald, Oregon, North River. He enlisted in the 1st Depot Battalion, Nova Scotia Regiment, Canadian Expeditionary Force, on May 30, 1918, in Sydney. Rifleman MacDonald served with the 260th Battalion in Canada and sailed to Siberia on the *S.S. Empress* of Russia on May 19, 1919. He was discharged on July 7, 1919, in Halifax. He lived in Alberta and then in British Columbia. Unmarried he died in British Columbia.

MacDonald, Angus

Angus was born on December 9, 1882, the son of Michael and Sarah (MacNeil) MacDonald, Jamesville West. Lieutenant MacDonald served in the 257th Battalion Canadian Infantry.

MacDonald, Angus

Angus was born in 1875, the son of Peter and Ellen (Donahue) MacDonald, St. Margaret's Village. Captain MacDonald served in the United States Navy. He died on December 27, 1968, and is buried in St. Margaret's Village Cemetery.

MacDonald, Angus A.

'Angus Archie' was born on September 26, 1894, the son of Archie and Effie (MacLeod) MacDonald, Big Intervale.

He served overseas during the war. After the war, he went to the state of Washington, but returned home during the Great Depression years of the 1930's. He farmed in Big Intervale and the farm's large red barn situated beside the Cabot Trail is a local landmark (extant). He is buried in Cape North Cemetery.

MacDonald, Charles 715491

Charles was born on April 23, 1890, the son of Angus and Elsie (Williams) MacDonald, South Ingonish Beach. Private MacDonald enlisted on December 17, 1915, in Sydney and served overseas with the 106th Battalion, Canadian Infantry. He was killed in action on September 25, 1918, while fighting with the 26th Battalion. He is buried in Sun Quarry Cemetery, Cherisy, France.

MacDonald, Charles Jones

Charlie was born on April 22, 1897, the son of Neil and Mary (Gillis) MacDonald, Middle River. He served as a Sergeant with the 94th Battalion in the militia. He served overseas in the Great War. He moved to Edmonton circa 1922. Unmarried, he died there on July 27, 1964.

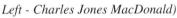

Left - Charles Jones MacDonald)

MacDonald, Dan K.

Dan was born on March 13, 1886, the son of Donald (Peddler) and Rebecca (MacKenzie) MacDonald, Middle River. Dan MacDonald moved to the Yukon Territory where he enlisted. He served in the war. Following cessation of hostilities, he came to Middle River and then returned to the North. Dan visited Middle River in 1967. Unmarried, he died and is buried in the Yukon.

MacDonald, Dan Murdock

Dan was born on May 12, 1887, the son of Murdoch and Mary (MacLeod) MacDonald, Baddeck. He served during the war.

'Captain Dan' was the captain on the mail and passenger boats running between Baddeck and Iona. He was predeceased by his first wife, Bessie MacLeod, Big Baddeck. Captain Dan and his second wife, Christy MacLeod, Cape North, resided in Baddeck. Captain Dan MacDonald died on March 6, 1956, and is buried in Greenwood Cemetery, Baddeck.

(Capt. Dan MacDonald and his daughter, Marian)

MacDonald, Dan Neil

'Danny Neil' was born on March 11, 1891, the son of Neil and Mary (Gillis) MacDonald, Middle River.

He was a Sergeant in the 94th Regiment Argyle Highlanders from 1907 to 1914. He served on guard duty from 1914 to 1915. He served as a Lieutenant in the 185th Battalion Canadian Expeditionary Force from 1916 to 1917 and as a Lieutenant in the Royal Canadian Regiment in France December from 1917 to 1919. Captain MacDonald served with the Cape Breton Highlanders from 1921 to 1933. His decorations included the **LONG SERVICE MEDAL** in the Colonial Auxiliary Forces. He married Hattie Campbell, Middle River. He died in February, 1979 and is buried in Middle River Cemetery.

MacDonald, Daniel 463651

Daniel 'Deanie' was born on March 14, 1867, the son of John and Mary MacDonald, Boularderie East. He served overseas and was wounded in battle. He married Sadie Maloney, North Sydney. He died in 1937 and is buried in Man O' War Cemetery, Boularderie.

MacDonald, Daniel

Dan was born in 1880, the son of John and Annie (Morrison) MacDonald, Ingonish Ferry. This family was originally from Wreck Cove and later moved to Ingonish Ferry. Private MacDonald enlisted on March 29, 1915, in Montreal. Sergeant MacDonald served with the Canadian Overseas Railway Construction Corps. He worked with Dominion Bridge Company in Montreal. He and his wife, Aldena, later resided in Winnipeg where he died in 1975.

(Daniel MacDonald and Montgomery children)

MacDonald, Daniel D. 67627

Dan was born on September 23, 1892, the son of Dougal and Margaret (MacCharles) MacDonald, Red Head, Beinn Bhreagh. He enlisted in Halifax on November 26, 1914, and served with the Canadian Expeditionary Force, 25th Battalion. He served in Canada, Britain and France. Private MacDonald was killed in action on October 12, 1915, while serving with the 25th Battalion. His name is inscribed on the Menin Gate Memorial, Belgium.

MacDonald, Daniel E. 878111

'Daniel E.' hailed from Victoria County. In civilian life he was a miner. He served in the 185th Canadian Infantry Battalion.

MacDonald, Daniel John 222576

'Danny Johnny Ban' was born on June 29, 1885, the son of John James (Ban) and Bella (Morrison) MacDonald, Baddeck. He served with the 94th Argyle Highlanders and the 85th Battalion, No. 14 Platoon. He was a machine gunner and was wounded in action. Lance Corporal MacDonald was recuperating in hospital in France when the Armistice was signed. He married and he and his wife resided in North Sydney where he served with the Royal Canadian Mounted Police. They moved to the United States where he died on July 2, 1977.

MacDonald, Donald 116438

Dan was born on November 16, 1888, the son of Donald and Ann (MacLean) MacDonald, South Ridge.

Private MacDonald served in the Highland Regiment, 25th Battalion. He was killed in action on August 21, 1917, and his name is inscribed on the Vimy Memorial, France.

MacDonald, Donald

Donald was born on May 10, 1889, the son of John and Sarah (MacLean) MacDonald, Bay Road Valley. Private MacDonald served with the 85th Infantry Battalion. He was wounded in France on August 8, 1918. He returned from France on February 15, 1919. He married Elizabeth MacDougall, Aspy Bay. He and his wife resided in the United States where he was a carpenter. He is buried in Boston.

MacDonald, Hector Joseph 167067

'Hector J.' was born in 1893, the son of Ronald and Lizzie Ann MacDonald, Ottawa Brook. He was raised by a family in Gillis Point. He served with the 9th Battalion, Canadian Railway Troops. Sapper MacDonald served in Canada, England and Europe.

He married Mary Dixon, Scotland. He died on June 19, 1965 and is buried in St. Columba Cemetery, Iona.

MacDonald, Helen Catherine

Helen Catherine was born circa 1887, the daughter of Captain John and Jessie C. MacDonald, Little Narrows. Nursing Sister MacDonald served in France during the war.

MacDonald, Hugh 415212

'Hughie Johnny Ban' was born on September 20, 1893, the son of John James (Ban) and Bella (Morrison) MacDonald, Baddeck. Private MacDonald enlisted on August 7, 1915, and served overseas with the 40th Battalion. He married Helen Goodfellow, Scotland. He and his war bride resided on the Big Farm Road. He died on May 24, 1954, and is buried in Greenwood Cemetery, Baddeck.

MacDonald, Hugh Bert 150159

Hugh was a twin born on February 8, 1888, the son of John and Katie (Morrison) MacDonald, New Campbellton. Private MacDonald served overseas with the 8th Battalion. He was reported missing in action on September 26, 1916. His name is inscribed on the Vimy Memorial, France.

MacDonald, Ian T.

Ian was born on March 15, 1890, the son of John and Margaret MacDonald, Baddeck. He served during the war.

MacDonald, J. Fraser

'Fraser Lion' was born in 1874 in Boularderie East. He served overseas with the 239th Battalion Canadian Expeditionary Force. After the war, he lived at Ross Ferry. He was a master craftsman and furniture builder. Some of his work is extant and continues to grace local homes. He was an expert at moving buildings using a roller and wedge method. Like his brother, he was a blacksmith. Fraser died in 1965 and is buried in St. Joachim Cemetery, South Side Boularderie.

MacDonald, James Peter

James Peter was born on August 18, 1893, the son of Peter and Catherine (MacNeil) MacDonald, Ottawa Brook. Private MacDonald served in the 94th Battalion Canadian Infantry. He married Margaret MacNeil, Red Point.

MacDonald, John

'Johnny Strawberry' was born on April 19, 1881, the son of Flora (MacRitchie) MacDonald. He was raised in the home of Mrs. Maggie MacKenzie, West Middle River. Private MacDonald served during the war. He married a widow, Mrs. Staples, and they resided in Glace Bay. He is buried in Glace Bay.

MacDonald, John 2330335

John MacDonald hailed from McKinnons Harbour. Mrs. Bridget MacDonald was listed as his next of kin. Private MacDonald enlisted in Truro on April 28, 1917, and served with the 2nd Forestry Battalion.

MacDonald, John Allan

'John A.' was born on June 5, 1875, the son of Allan and Sarah (MacNeil) MacDonald, St. Columba. Lieutenant MacDonald served in the 94th Regiment and the 6th Battalion Canadian Garrison Regiment in Canada. He married Mary Agnes MacKinnon, Shenacadie. He was a merchant in Iona. His business was located on the site of the former co-operative store. He represented the district of Iona on the municipal council. He was appointed to the Legislative Council of the Province of Nova Scotia on June 2, 1925. He and his wife moved to Halifax in 1934. He died on June 22, 1955, and is buried in Gate of Heaven Cemetery, Lower Sackville.

MacDonald, John Angus 878327

'Johnny William' was born on July 18, 1894, the son of William and Catherine (Roberts) MacDonald, Nyanza. Sergeant Major MacDonald served overseas with the 185th Battalion. He was killed in action on March 15, 1918, and is buried in Thelus Military Cemetery. A memorial stone was placed in the Middle River Cemetery by his mother.

MacDonald, John Archibald

'John A.' was born on April 7, 1894, the son of Stephen A. and Mary Ann (MacNeil) MacDonald, St. Columba. Private MacDonald served in the 94th Regiment. Unmarried, he died on November 12, 1974, and is buried in St. Columba Cemetery, Iona. His military photographs and documents have been placed in the Beaton Institute, Sydney.

MacDonald, John Clyde 469664

'John C.' was born on November 15, 1897, the son of Duncan and Flora (MacPherson) MacDonald, Englishtown/Plaster. His father was a merchant in Englishtown who also served as a Member of the Legislative Assembly for Victoria County.

Private MacDonald served overseas with the 4th Battalion Canadian Expeditionary Force. He was wounded at the Somme on October 14, 1916, and died of gunshot wounds on October 21, 1916, at No. 1 N.Z. Hospital. He is buried in St. Pierre Cemetery, Amiens, France (one of eleven Canadians buried there). His name is inscribed on the Vimy Canadian War Memorial and there is a memorial stone in the family plot in Plaster Cemetery, North Shore.

MacDonald, John Daniel

'John D.' was born on May 9, 1888, the son of Michael and Sarah (MacNeil) MacDonald, Jamesville West. Private MacDonald served in the 1st Depot Battalion. He married Dolena Gillis, MacKinnon's Harbour. He died in 1951 and is buried in St. Columba Cemetery, Iona.

MacDonald, Kenneth A.

'Kennie Archie' was born on November 12, 1897, the son of Archie and Effie (MacLeod) MacDonald, Big Intervale. He served overseas during the war. He received his military training in England. Tragically, he died on September 11, 1924, and is buried in Cape North Cemetery.

MacDonald, Kenneth John

Kenneth was born on April 9, 1891, the son of John James (Ban) and Bella (Morrison) MacDonald, Baddeck. He served during the war. He married Lillian MacKenzie, Plaister Mines. They moved to Detroit where he was employed with the Ford Motor Company.

MacDonald, Laughlin Edwin

'Laughie A.Y.' was born on January 23, 1893, the son of A.Y. and Alice (Crowdis) MacDonald, Baddeck. He served with the 94th Regiment and transferred to F Company, 6th Battalion, Canadian Garrison Artillery. His service spanned from August 6, 1914 to December 18, 1918.

He served as High Sheriff in Victoria County for forty years. He was predeceased by his first wife, Sara Brown. His second wife is Philena MacDonald. He died at age ninety-seven and is buried in Greenwood Cemetery, Baddeck.

MacDonald, M.W.

'M.W.' has his name inscribed on the war monument in Little Narrows. Private MacDonald served during the war.

MacDonald, Malcolm 877277

Malcolm was born on April 30, 1881, the son of Stephen J. and Catherine (Campbell) MacDonald, Upper Washabuck.

At the time of his enlistment he was working as a miner. Sergeant MacDonald served in the 185th Battalion Canadian Infantry. He was wounded in action. He is buried in Holy Rosary Cemetery, Washabuck.

MacDonald, Mary Simpson R.N.

Mary was born on September 20, 1892, the daughter of Alexander Y. and Alice (Crowdis) MacDonald, Baddeck. She was a Registered Nurse and served overseas as a Nursing Sister during the war. She married George Jarvis Farnsworth. They were the parents of triplets. They resided in Detroit and she died there in 1962.

MacDonald, Michael A.J.

'M.A.J.' was born on March 4, 1863, the son of Allan and Sarah (MacNeil) MacDonald, St. Columba. Major MacDonald served in the 94th Battalion and 6th Battalion, Canadian Garrison Regiment, Canadian Expeditionary Force. He married Mary MacDonald, Soldier's Cove. He was a Canadian National Railway agent and station master in Iona. He died on May 16, 1925, and is buried in St. Columba Cemetery.

MacDonald, Michael John 715536

Michael was born on August 31, 1896, the son of Stephen A. and Mary Ann (MacNeil) MacDonald, St. Columba.

Private MacDonald served in the 106th Battalion Canadian Infantry. Nineteen year old MacDonald died in Truro (en route overseas) with pneumonia on March 2, 1916. He is buried in St. Columba Cemetery, Iona.

MacDonald, Murdoch 877125

Murdoch was born on July 7, 1885, the son of Angus and Margaret (MacInnis) MacDonald, Tarbot. Private MacDonald served with the 85th and 185th Battalions. He enlisted in Sydney on March 6, 1916. Thirty-three year old Private MacDonald was killed in action on August 9, 1918, and is buried in Fouquescourt British Cemetery. He had been a carpenter in civilian life. He was alleged to have the ability of "second sight" and prior to his departure overseas he revealed to his sister, Mrs. Norman (Margaret) Munroe, that he knew he would not return from the war. Incidentally, his six Munroe nephews from Jersey Cove served their country in World War II.

MacDonald, Murdoch 877125

Murdoch was born on June 29, 1883, a twin son of Donald and Ann (Campbell) MacDonald, Rocky Side, St. Ann's.

He enlisted on July 6, 1917 with the Royal Canadian Naval Volunteer Reserve as a submarine engineer. He served in Canada and on the high seas. He was discharged in Halifax on June 30, 1919. During World War II, he served as an engineer in the Merchant Marine.

Prior to the war, he skippered various boats for Dr. Alexander Graham Bell. He married Maggie Bell MacNeil, Iona. They resided in North Sydney. He died on February 21, 1957, and is buried in North Sydney.

MacDonald, Neil, M.M. 715661

Neil was born on December 13, 1895, the son of Angus and Margaret MacDonald, South Ingonish Beach. Private MacDonald served with the 106th Battalion, Canadian Infantry. He enlisted in Sydney on December 17, 1915, and served in Canada, Britain and France. He was awarded the **MILITARY MEDAL**. This is documented on his record of service. He was discharged in Halifax on September 20, 1919.

He married a school teacher, Helen Jane MacQuarrie, St. Rose, and settled in New Waterford where he worked in the coal mines. He died on October 25, 1966, and is buried in Mount Carmel Cemetery, New Waterford.

MacDonald, Neil Alexander 877786

Neil was born on April 25, 1896, the son of Donald (Dan) and Kate (Morrison) MacDonald, French River. He had been a miner in civilian life. Private MacDonald served overseas with the 185th Canadian Infantry Battalion. He was killed in action on March 23, 1917, and his name is inscribed on the Vimy Memorial, France.

MacDonald, Neil Angus 1060211

'Neily Murdoch' was born on December 18, 1897, the son of Murdoch D. and Effie (MacDonald) MacDonald, "The Point," South Gut. He enlisted on November 24, 1916, with the 246th Battalion Canadian Expeditionary Force, Nova Scotia Highlanders - "C" Company. Private MacDonald served overseas. As a result of terrible conditions in the trenches, he suffered from rheumatic fever and was discharged on July 8, 1918. Unmarried, he died on December 30, 1938, and is buried in Goose Cove Cemetery, St. Ann's.

MacDonald, Neil John 715507

Neil was born on July 30, 1883, the son of Murdoch and Mary (MacLeod) MacDonald, Baddeck. Private MacDonald was a veteran of the Boer War and World War I. Private MacDonald enlisted on December 28, 1915, in Sydney and served with the 106th Battalion. 'Neil Tailor' operated a tailoring business in Baddeck. He married Dolly MacLean, Glace Bay. After her death, he and their three daughters moved to Vancouver. He married again and the family remained in British Columbia.

MacDonald, Norman

Norman was born on October 26, 1878, the son of William and Effie (MacDonald) MacDonald, Breton Cove. Private MacDonald was a member of the 94th Regiment (later known as the Nova Scotia Garrison Regiment). He was stricken by a hemorrhage while on duty at Marconi Tower and died in hospital in Glace Bay on September 1, 1918. His remains were transported to his old home in Breton Cove.

MacDonald, Roderick A. 2700441

Rod was born on December 15, 1874, the son of Alexander and Bella MacDonald, Boularderie. He served in the Boer War and also enlisted on September 15, 1914, with the 94th Battalion, 106th Canadian Garrison Regiment. Private MacDonald was discharged on November 30, 1918.

He married Jessie MacKay, Rear Baddeck Bay. They settled in Rear Baddeck Bay where Rod carried on trapping and farming. He died on August 21, 1951, and is buried in Highland Cemetery, Baddeck Bay.

MacDonald, Roderick Alexander

'Rory Alexander' was born on September 30, 1893, the son of Michael and Sarah (MacNeil) MacDonald, Jamesville West. Private MacDonald served in the 1st Depot Battalion.

MacDonald, Roderick John 2100080

Roddie was born on October 10, 1895, the son of Angus and Bella (MacPherson) MacDonald, Middle River.

He enlisted on August 14, 1914. He served with the 94th Regiment and transferred in March 1917 to the 8th Battery Canadian Garrison Artillery. He served as a gunner. He was discharged on demobilization in May, 1919.

He married Alice MacLeod, Middle River. He died on March 30, 1966 and is buried in Middle River Cemetery.

MacDonald, Ronald 3190505

Ronald was the son of Angus R. and Annie (MacIntosh) MacDonald, Bay St. Lawrence. He served with the Nova Scotia Regiment. He is buried in MacIntosh Cemetery, Bay St. Lawrence.

MacDonald, W.T.

'W.T.' has his name inscribed on the war monument in Little Narrows. Private MacDonald served during the war.

MacDonald, William A. 877478

'William A.' was born on January 1, 1896, the son of William Henry and Christy Effie (MacLeod) MacDonald, Cape North. Private MacDonald served overseas with the 185th and 85th Battalions from March 23, 1916, to March 27, 1919. He married and resided in the United States.

MacDonald, William Gordon

William Gordon was born on April 11, 1895, the son of Captain John and Jessie MacDonald, Little Narrows. Sergeant Major MacDonald served during the war.

MacDougall, Allan Douglas

Douglas was born on March 20, 1893, the son of Michael and Mary (MacLellan) MacDougall, Aspy Bay. Private MacDougall served during the war. He married Catherine Stevens. They resided in the United States and eventually returned to the old home in Aspy Bay. He died on August 19, 1965, and is buried in St. Margaret's Village Cemetery.

MacDougall, Hector 878031

Hector was born on May 10, 1882, the son of Michael and Bessie (MacDonald) MacDougall, Upper Washabuck. He was a miner at the time of his enlistment. He served with the Cape Breton Highlanders for six years. He served with the 185th and 85th Battalions, Canadian Infantry in Canada, the United Kingdom and Northwest Europe. He was wounded in action. His first wife, Lucy Warren, Glace Bay, died while he was overseas. His second wife was Mary MacKinnon, Lower Washabuck. He and his wife resided in Paschendaele, Glace Bay. He died in 1958 and is buried in St. Anthony's Cemetery, Paschendaele, Glace Bay.

MacDougall, John Dan

John Dan was born on June 5, 1895, the son of Michael and Mary (MacLellan) MacDougall, Aspy Bay. He served overseas and returned from France on June 25, 1919. He and his wife, Mary, resided in the United States. He is buried in Boston.

(John Dan MacDougall and wife, Mary, children Sandra and Jacqueline)

MacEachern, Alexander 715169

Private MacEachern served with the Canadian Expeditionary Force, 106th Overseas Battalion. He hailed from Boularderie.

MacEachern, Archibald

Archie was the son of Little Hugh and Annie (MacDonald) MacEachern, Black Point. Private MacEachern served with the 1st Depot Battalion. He and his wife, Edna, resided in the United States.

MacEachern, Murdoch 2020711

Murdoch was born on August 16, 1892, the son of Murdoch and Grace (MacDonald) MacEachern, Tarbot/North River. He enlisted in January, 1918 with the 1st Depot Battalion, British Columbia Regiment. Private MacEachern served overseas and suffered a spinal injury which caused a permanent disability. He spent one year as a patient in Camp Hill Hospital, Halifax.

He married Josie Morrison, North River. He served as postmaster and operated a general store in North River Bridge. He was an accomplished harmonica and piano player. He died on July 11, 1967, and is buried in Riverside Cemetery, North River.

MacFarlane, Neil A. 2330352

Neil was born on April 10, 1882, the son of Angus and Sarah (MacLennan) MacFarlane, Zion Road, Big Baddeck. Private MacFarlane enlisted on May 1, 1917, in Sydney and served overseas with the 2nd Forestry Reinforcing Draft from Military Depot # 6.

He married Christy Belle Stewart, Rear Baddeck Bay. He died on January 3, 1926, and is buried in Revere, Massachusetts.

MacGean, Amos

Amos was born on January 14, 1895, the son of John and Mary Jane (Donovan) MacGean, South Ingonish. Private MacGean served with the 17th Battalion Canadian Infantry. He married Pearl Hoskins and resided in Ingonish. Due to a vision impairment, he was known as 'Blind Amos.'

MacGregor, Franics M. 67564

Francis was born on September 30, 1883, the son of Farquhar and Christie (Morrison) MacGregor, Baddeck River. He joined the 94th Militia Unit (headquarters) Baddeck. He was a 1901 graduate of the Military School, Fredericton, New Brunswick, with the rank of Sergeant Major. During his youth, he worked in the Old Caledonia Mine, the Gold Brook Mine, Middle River and at hard rock mining in Cobalt, Ontario.

In Halifax on November 26, 1914, he enlisted with the 25th Battalion Canadian Expeditionary Force. Later he joined the 25th Infantry Unit. From April, 1916, to November, 1917, he served at the front and fought at Ypres, the Somme, Vimy Ridge, Hill 70 and Passchendaele. He remembered the trenches at Ypres:

" ... filled with dirty, stinking water - filling sand bags with mud and piling them on top of each other as their own protection from the enemy gunfire. Rations consisted of bully beef, hard tack and bottled water plus dry tea."

In November, 1917, Sergeant MacGregor took final leave from Flanders and was sent to the old garrison city, Halifax, to instruct in trench warfare. He was discharged on February 22, 1919.

During World War II, he served with the Military Police at the Canadian National Railway bridge in Iona for four years. He was described as

" ... an inveterate reader and he acquired a bountiful vocabulary. With his Scottish brogue to go with it, he was a master story teller, an outstanding public speaker and a wonderfully entertaining master of ceremonies."

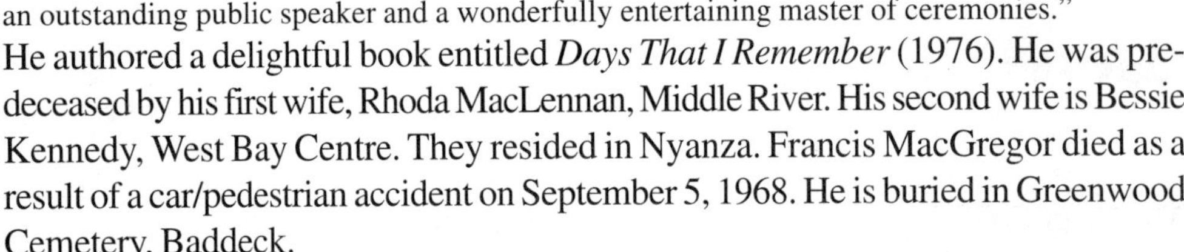

He authored a delightful book entitled *Days That I Remember* (1976). He was predeceased by his first wife, Rhoda MacLennan, Middle River. His second wife is Bessie Kennedy, West Bay Centre. They resided in Nyanza. Francis MacGregor died as a result of a car/pedestrian accident on September 5, 1968. He is buried in Greenwood Cemetery, Baddeck.

MacInnis, Dan Donald 3180011

Dannie was born on January 2, 1892, the son of John and Annie (MacDonald) MacInnis, Washabuck Bridge. He enlisted on November 27, 1917, and served with the 94th Regiment and the 1st Depot Battalion in Canada. Sergeant MacDonald was discharged on April 12, 1919. He died on June 17, 1924, and is buried in the Little Narrows Cemetery.

MacInnis, John Allan 877502

'John A.' was born on March 1, 1875 and hailed from Baddeck. At the time of his enlistment he was a miner, Dominion No. 4 in Glace Bay, Nova Scotia. He served with the 185th Battalion, Cape Breton Highlanders.

MacInnis, John Francis

'John F.' was born on March 3, 1899, the son of John and Annie (MacNeil) MacInnis, Iona. Private MacInnis served in both World Wars. He served with the 94th Regiment during the First World War. Private MacInnis served with the North Nova Scotia Highlanders in Canada and the United Kingdom during the Second War. He married Annie Morrison, Iona. He died on June 11, 1973 and is buried in St. Columba Cemetery, Iona.

(Right - John Francis MacInnis)

MacInnis, Malcolm Angus 877491

Malcolm was born on December 28, 1891, the son of Neil and Jessie (MacAulay) MacInnis, South Cove. He enlisted on March 22, 1916, in Glace Bay in the Canadian Expeditionary Force - Royal Canadian Regiment. He served in Canada, Britain and France. He was killed in action on September 28, 1918, in Cambrai, France. He is buried in Raillencourt Community Cemetery Extension, France. His widow, Christine Ann (MacInnis) MacInnis, Indian Brook and young son, Clarence (World War II), resided in Indian Brook. Private MacInnis wrote the following letters to his brother Rev. Angus John MacInnis:

France May 27th, 1918

Rev. A.J. MacInnis
My Dear Brother:
Here goes once more to write you a short letter in hopes that you get time to answer it. I am fairly well hoping the arrival of this will find you the same. I had a letter from Mary and she said that you had written to me but your letter was returned. It is too bad but things like that will happen. I heard a short time ago that you were married. Well I wish you all good luck. You must know that it is pretty hard to write an interesting letter to anyone from France for we can say so very little about it even if it is the most beautiful country that I have ever seen but don't say much. We are not far from Belgium now. A person could easily walk it in about four hours. You can have a fair idea even if you are not used to walking for a soldier walks about four miles per hour.

The farming around here is a lot ahead of anything I have ever seen in Canada. The Rye is about four feet tall. You can only see the head of a man when he is walking through it. We are having the most beautiful weather here that I ever saw and the sun is a bit too hot some days. When you write to me my address will be 877491 Ptd Malcolm McInnis, 7 Platoon B, (leay?), RCR Batt, BEF, France.

I have not much news for this time but will write soon again. Good bye with my best wishes to both of you. From you loving Brother

Malcolm McInnis

France Aug 26th, 1918

Rev. A.J. McInnis

My Dear Brother:

I received your most kind and always welcome letter a few days ago in which you sayed that both you and your wife were well as I can say the same in regards to my own health.

I would have written to you before only we were shifting about so much and we do not get much time. I have had great fun two weeks ago chasing Heinies across the --?--. All together in that drive we captured over 40,000 prisoners since (erased by censor) there have been 15,000 captured (erased by censor) months like that and all his reserves will be used up. When it will --?-- we'll begin to talk of peace. He can not stand much more of it. It is my opinion that there will be peace before 1919. What do you think. I have had letters from all the folks. They are all fine. Well I expect to be home before nine months time. I have no more to say for this time so I will say good bye for this time. Hoping to hear from you soon again, with best regards from your loving

Brother

M. McInnis

Neil MacInnis, father of Private Malcolm MacInnis, wrote the following poignant letter to his other son, Rev. A.J. MacInnis:

South Cove Grant *Oct. 21st, 1918*

Mr. A.J. McInnis

Dear Son

With a sad heart I have to relate to you that your brother Malcolm was killed in action on the 28 of September. We got a telegram on the nineteenth. You know that he was our hope and support but we must look to a higher support and that is God.

Yours truly
Neil McInnis

MacInnis, Malcolm John 442156

'Malcolm J.' was born on August 13, 1890, the son of Neil and Margaret (MacAskill) MacInnis, Humes Rear. Private MacInnis enlisted on July 4, 1915, at Vernon, British Columbia and served overseas with the 54th Battalion.

MacInnis, Robert Lawrence 715445

Robert was born on April 2, 1896, the son of John and Ester (Jobe) MacInnis, Sugar Loaf. Prior to enlistment, he had been a member of the 94th Argyle Highlanders. He was assigned to the 106th Battalion, Nova Scotia Rifles. He departed on the SS *Empress of Britain* with the 25th Battalion. Private MacInnis was killed in action around La Folie Section, Vimy Ridge on March 5, 1917. He is buried in Ecoivres Military Cemetery, Mont-St.-Eloi, France.

MacIntosh, Duncan

Duncan was the son of Robert and Annie (MacPherson) MacIntosh, Bay St. Lawrence. Private MacIntosh served with the American Navy. He was killed during the war. He is buried in MacIntosh Cemetery, Bay St. Lawrence.

MacIntyre, Bernard

Bernard's name appears in the nominal enlistment roll for the parish of Iona. Private MacIntyre served with the 185th Battalion Canadian Infantry. He was wounded in action.

MacIver, A.

A. MacIver's name is inscribed on the war monument in Little Narrows. Major MacIver served during the war.

MacIver, Angus Henry 438922

'Angus H.' was born on November 30, 1892, the son of John and Alena (MacMillan) MacIver, Nyanza. He enlisted on December 24, 1914, in Dryden, Ontario and served with the 52nd and 12th Battalions, Canadian Expeditionary Force. He was severely wounded in France at the Battle of the Somme in 1916. On demobilization, Corporal MacIver was discharged on February 14, 1919. His wife, Katie, hailed from Scotland. He died in Florida.

MacIver, Angus John 222268

Angus John was born on February 22, 1898, the son of John E. and Mary (Gillis) MacIver, South Cove. He served with the 85th Battalion No. 16 Platoon, Highland Brigade. Private MacIver was killed in action on April 9, 1917, at Vimy Ridge, France. He is buried in the Canadian Cemetery # 2 Neuville St. Vaast.

MacIver, Arthur P. 111305

Arthur was born on August 1, 1894, the son of Murdoch and Jane (Buchanan) MacIver, Port Bevis. He served with the 5th Mounted Rifles Canadian Expeditionary Force. He was killed in action at Mount Sorrel, Ypres on June 2, 1916. His name is inscribed on the Menin Gate Memorial, Belgium.

Trooper MacIver was unmarried at the time of his death. He had interrupted his divinity studies at Pine Hill Presbyterian College to serve his country.

MacIver, Daniel John 1030799

Dan was born in June, 1897, the son of Henry and Mary MacIver, Washabuck. Private MacIver served with the 42nd Unit. While fighting at Vimy Ridge with the 236th Battalion, he was killed in action on August 12, 1918. His name in inscribed on the Vimy Memorial. When Dan was four years of age, his widowed mother, along with her children, moved to Baddeck. His mother later married Neil D. MacLennan. Prior to his enlistment, twenty-two year old MacIver had been in the field of dentistry in Boston.

MacIver, Daniel John 3206299

Daniel was born on January 24, 1891, the son of Malcolm and Willena (MacKenzie) MacIver, Indian Brook. Private MacIver served with the 1st Dispatch Battalion. He was discharged in Calgary. He worked with the original Peace River Survey crew in Alberta. He returned to Indian Brook circa 1950. Unmarried, he died on February 29, 1980, and is buried in Pine Hill Cemetery, River Bennett.

MacIver, James Neil 3188884

James was born on December 29, 1896, the son of Peter and Isabelle (MacKenzie) MacIver, Cain's Mountain. Private MacIver enlisted on June 12, 1918, and served with the 17th Reserve Battalion, Canadian Infantry, 1st Depot N.S. Regiment. He died on August 19, 1918, aboard ship. He is buried in Aldershot Military Cemetery, Hampshire, England.

MacIver, John Angus 841548

John Angus' name is inscribed on the war monument in Little Narrows. He served in the 24th and 148th Battalions. Corporal MacIver was killed in action and is buried in Aubegny Community Cemetery, Aubigny en Artois, France.

MacIver, John Charles 222267

John Charles was born on February 14, 1896, the son of John and Alena (MacMillan) MacIver, Nyanza. He enlisted in 1915 and served in the Canadian Infantry - Manitoba Regiment. Private MacIver was killed in action on April 9, 1917, at Vimy Ridge. The bullet pierced through his Bible which he kept in his breast pocket. The Bible was returned with his belongings. His mother treasured it and would sit by her window and read from it. Private MacIver is buried in Pas de Calais, France - Canadian Cemetery # 2 Nouville St. Vaast.

MacIver, John M.

'John M.' was born on October 3, 1890, the son of John and Christie (MacLeod) MacIver, Baddeck Bay. John served overseas in the army during the war. After the war, he went to the United States and worked for the Goodyear Leather Company in Akron, Ohio. He fell from a scaffolding and was killed in February, 1920. His remains were sent home to Baddeck Bay and he is buried in the MacIver Cemetery, Baddeck Bay.

MacIver, Joseph Hartley

'J.H.' was born on October 26, 1893, the only son of James H. and Rose (Crowdis) MacIver, West Side Baddeck, Big Baddeck. Lieutenant MacIver served overseas with the 25th Battalion. He died of wounds on August 10, 1918. He is buried in Villers-Bretonneux Military Cemetery, Fouilloy, France. He was survived by his widow, a daughter of Mr. and Mrs. M.J. Ross, North Sydney.

MacIver, Joseph Lloyd

'Joe Dolly Henry' was born on January 12, 1899,the son of 'Dan Dolly Henry' and Margaret (Matheson) MacIver, Upper Washabuck. He served during the war. He married Mary MacInnis, South Cove. In 1925, he went to work in Chicago and returned home for a few years. Then they relocated to Malden, Massachusetts. He died there on December 24, 1972, and is buried in Little Narrows Cemetery.

MacIver, Norena

Norena was born on March 10, 1882, the daughter of Malcolm and Margaret (MacIver) MacIver, South Cove. Nursing Sister MacIver served during the war. She died in 1970 and is buried in Little Narrows Cemetery.

MacIver, William Ross 2001285

William was born on May 14, 1898, the son of John and Alena (MacMillan) MacIver, Nyanza. Private MacIver enlisted in Halifax on November 20, 1916, and served in the army - 4th Canadian Division Canadian Expeditionary Force. He served in France and was discharged on demobilization in Halifax on February 26, 1919. He died in Florida. This MacIver family lived in Bucklaw where their children were born. They later moved to Nyanza where their father operated a blacksmith shop, store and, on occasion, the post office.

MacKay, Alexander Henry

Alexander's name is inscribed on the war monument in Little Narrows. Lieutenant MacKay served overseas with the 5th Battalion. He was killed in action on May 22, 1915, and his name is inscribed on the Vimy Memorial, France.

MacKay, Hugh N. 878399

Hugh was born on June 1, 1898, the son of Dan and Mrs. MacKay, Englishtown. He enlisted on June 5, 1916, in Aldershot and served overseas with the 185th Battalion # 2 Platoon. Private MacKay was discharged on December 12, 1918. He was unmarried and resided in the United States.

MacKay, J.C.

'J.C.' has his name inscribed on the war monument in Little Narrows. Private MacKay served during the war.

MacKay, James Wilson 415002

Wilson was born on December 23, 1894, the son of Edward and Jessie Amelia (Fraser) MacKay, Baddeck. He enlisted out of college on March 14, 1915, and joined the Canadian Expeditionary Force. He became the youngest quartermaster sergeant of the 40th Battalion Canadian Independent Force. Later he transferred to the Royal Canadian Flying Corps. Lieutenant MacKay was discharged on demobilization.

He married Ann F. Inglis. He was an employee of the Royal Bank of Canada in Sydney and later moved to the United States. He retired from an executive position in banking in 1959. He died on January 11, 1962.

MacKay, Libby Garfield R.N.

Passport photo

Garfield was born on January 16, 1892, a sister to Kenneth John MacKay, merchant and partner of the 'MacKay and MacAskill Store,' Baddeck.

Garfield MacKay was a graduate of Newport Hospital, Rhode Island. She carried on her nursing career in Public Health in the slums of New York City. She wrote a detailed account of health conditions and practices in New York during the early part of the century. She attended Mount Allison University and completed a librarian course at Acadia University. Nursing Sister MacKay served as a member of the post nursing unit to the front in Europe. For her wartime services she was twice decorated by the Romanian government and twice by the government of France. After the war she worked with Madam Curie in France. Upon her return to Baddeck she served as librarian for twenty years. She died on November 15, 1974, and is buried in Greenwood Cemetery, Baddeck.

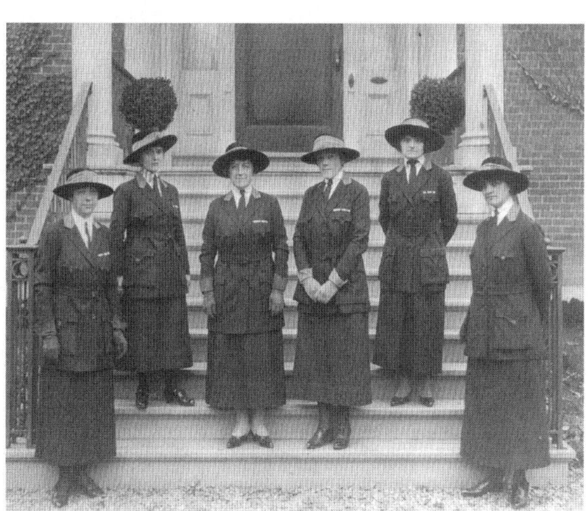

(Canadian Nursing Sisters left to right: Helen Kendell, Sydney; Ethel Carter; Olive Fitzgerald; Dorothy Cotton; Garfield MacKay, Baddeck; and Irene Savage)

MacKay, Malcolm A. 878335

Malcolm was born on April 23, 1883, the son of John (Coddy) and Jessie (MacLeod) MacKay, Baddeck. He enlisted on April 2, 1916 and served with the 185th Canadian Infantry Battalion and the 246th Battalion. It is believed that he never recovered from the effects of the war. He died in 1930 and is buried in Greenwood Cemetery, Baddeck.

MacKay, Neil 3188886

Neil was born on February 9, 1896, the son of Daniel and Margaret (MacLeod) MacKay, Big Baddeck. He served overseas as a private with the 14th Canadian Grenadier Guards from June 13, 1918, to September 16, 1919. He married Jessie Ann MacLean, Big Baddeck. He farmed in Big Baddeck. He died in 1968 and is buried in St. Andrew's Cemetery, Baddeck Forks.

MacKay, Neil Allan 878341

'Neil A.' was born on January 10, 1895, the son of Dan and Mrs. MacKay, Englishtown.

He enlisted on April 1, 1916, in Sydney and served overseas with the 185th Battalion # 2 Platoon. Private MacKay was discharged in Halifax on March 4, 1919. He married Mae Shoebridge of Alberta and resided there.

MacKeen, Dr. George Wilbert, M.D.

George was born on March 27, 1871, the son of Dr. S.G.A. and Rebecca J. (Hadley) MacKeen, Baddeck. Dr. MacKeen was a graduate of Harvard University Medical School. Captain MacKeen, M.D., served with the Canadian Forces as a medical officer in France and England during the war.

He married Elizabeth Flagler, Georgia, USA. In 1920, he established his medical practice in Baddeck. Previously he had practised in Neil's Harbour. His sister married the renowned American poet, Robert Norwood. He died in 1928 and is buried in the Auld Kirk Cemetery, Baddeck.

MacKenzie, Alexander

Alex was born on April 4, 1882, the son of John and May (MacLeod) MacKenzie, Murray Road, North River. He served overseas. He married Tena MacDonald Hart, North River/Baddeck. He died on February 4, 1957, and is buried in Riverside Cemetery, North River.

MacKenzie, Alexander R.

Alexander was born on December 22, 1879, the son of Donald F. and Isabella (Morrison) MacKenzie, Baddeck. He served during the war. He married Sadie MacQueen, Plaister Mines. They resided in Baddeck. Alexander MacKenzie operated a barber shop in the village.

MacKenzie, Alexander William

Alexander was born on October 31, 1889, the son of Roderick Fraser and Bella (MacKenzie) MacKenzie, Kempt Head. He served overseas and the night the armistice was declared, he was in the trenches. Unmarried, he died on November 5, 1955, and is buried in Man O' War Cemetery, Boularderie.

MacKenzie, Angus Norman

'Angus N.' was born on October 15, 1882, the son of Donald F. and Isabella (Morrison) MacKenzie, Baddeck. He served with the 94th Regiment, Argyle Highlanders. He enlisted on June 8, 1914, as a Lieutenant. Captain MacKenzie was discharged on June 30, 1918. He operated a meat market at the site of the present day post office. He served as superintendent of Sunday school and Clerk of Session at Knox Church. He was predeceased by his first wife, Margaret MacDonald. He later married Mina Hart, Baddeck. Angus N. MacKenzie died in 1956 and is buried in Greenwood Cemetery, Baddeck.

MacKenzie, Charles Dawson 3189190

Charles was born on October 30, 1889, the son of Donald F. and Isabella (Morrison) MacKenzie, Baddeck. He enlisted in the 1st Depot Battalion, Nova Scotia Regiment in Aldershot on June 4, 1918. He served with the 17th Reserve Battalion in England. He was discharged July 18, 1919.

He married Julia Ann Morrison, Big Baddeck. He was a Royal Canadian Mounted Police officer. He died on April 14, 1968, in New Glasgow.

MacKenzie, Christine Mary R.N.

Christine was born on July 21, 1881, the daughter of Christopher and Annie (MacDonald) MacKenzie, Yankee Line. Registered Nurse MacKenzie enlisted on May 8, 1916, in Halifax. Nursing Sister MacKenzie served with the Canadian Army Medical Service in England and France - # 9 Stationary Hospital. She died on October 10, 1967, and is buried in the Middle River Cemetery.

MacKenzie, Daniel 222579

Dan was the adopted son of William and Hannah (Gunn) MacKenzie, New Harris. Private MacKenzie served overseas with the 85th Battalion # 15 Platoon. He was killed in action on January 29, 1917. He is buried in Maroc British Cemetery, Grenay, France.

MacKenzie, Daniel John Angus

Dan was born on April 13, 1893, the son of Charles and Mary (MacNaughton) MacKenzie, Nyanza. He was a graduate of the School of Infantry in Halifax. He qualified for the rank of Sergeant on February 15, 1913, and qualified for rank of Lieutenant on August 16, 1915. He enlisted with the 6th Battalion, Canadian Garrison Regiment, Canadian Expeditionary Force. Lieutenant Colonel MacKenzie served in Canada. He was discharged on December 31, 1918. He resided in Nyanza. He died on November 7, 1980, and is buried in Middle River Cemetery.

MacKenzie, Daniel Kenneth

Dan was born on December 7, 1895, the son of Sea Captain William D. and Catherine (MacRae) MacKenzie, Big Baddeck. He served overseas and was wounded while serving in France. He was reported missing in action. He had been shot in the leg and unable to walk. The Salvation Army located him and throughout his life, he never missed an opportunity to support their works. He married Catherine MacKenzie from Scotland on April 23, 1919. On December 5, 1959, at the age of sixty-three years, he died in Boston, Massachusetts.

MacKenzie, Duncan Alexander 877427

Duncan 'Heckadec' (Gaelic - Hector) was born on May 22, 1890, the son of Hector and Mary (MacAulay) MacKenzie, Backlands, off Church Road, Boularderie.

Duncan served overseas in the 185th Battalion, Canadian Expeditionary Force. He enlisted on March 9, 1916, and served in France and Belgium. He was wounded in battle and suffered a leg amputation. He was discharged in Toronto on December 31, 1917.

He married Johanna MacAulay, Black Rock. They were light keepers in Black Rock. Duncan is buried in the Black Rock Cemetery. An older brother, Kenneth MacKenzie, served during the Spanish American War.

MacKenzie, George Hugh 222269

'George H.' was born on July 18, 1892, the son of Murdoch Hugh and Maude (Dunlop) MacKenzie, Baddeck. He served with the 85th Battalion. He was invalided out of the service and died from tuberculosis on June 5, 1921. He is buried in Long Beach Sunnyside Cemetery, California.

The decorations and medals of the three MacKenzie brothers - Captain Ross, Lieutenant J.D. and George H. - became the property of their only sister, Catherine, Mrs. Edward Hale of Bierstadt, New York. She was the Parent Child editor of the *New York Times* at the time of her death. She bequested that the medals be dropped in the waters of the Bras d'Or Lakes. On November 11, 1957, six veterans committed the memorials to the waters off Kidston's Island, Baddeck.

MacKenzie, John David, M.C. 878358

'J.D.' was born on June 1, 1888, the son of Murdoch Hugh and Maude (Dunlop) MacKenzie, Baddeck. Dr. MacKenzie, PhD (gold medallist - Massachusetts Institute of Technology), was a well-known geologist and a director of the British Columbia Division of the Geological Survey of Canada.

He enlisted on April 4, 1916, and joined the 185th Battalion in Aldershot on July 5, 1916. Bombing Officer Lieutenant MacKenzie joined the 85th Battalion on May 18, 1918. On September 2, 1918, in Arras, he sustained serious wounds when splinters from an exploding shell penetrated his chest. Lieutenant MacKenzie was awarded the **MILITARY CROSS** at Amiens
"... for conspicuous gallantry and good leadership. During the first phase of the attack he led his platoon to the final objective under heavy machine gun fire. Two days later, when his company commander became a casualty, he took command, leading his men against machine gun nests, and saving a critical situation on his left by forming a defensive flank. He was untiring in encouraging his men." *London Gazette*.

He died in December, 1922, in St. Anne de Bellevue Hospital as a result of wounds sustained during combat. He was the third son to die as a result of the war. Lt. John D. MacKenzie's father, Murdoch Hugh MacKenzie, was profiled in *The Canadian Album - Men of Canada or Success by Example* (published in 1895). He was a Baddeck merchant, Justice of the Peace, Warden of Victoria County and had served as a captain in the 94th Battalion since 1891.

MacKenzie, John Hector 715987

Jack was born on May 26, 1896, the son of Hector and Mary (MacAulay) MacKenzie, Backlands off Church Road, Boularderie.

He enlisted while he was underage and was taken out of the service by his father. He re-enlisted and went overseas with the 26th Canadian Battalion. While serving in France, he was killed in action. On March 15, 1917, he gave his life for his country. He is buried at Aub'gry Communal Cemetery Plot I, Row H, Grave 18. His monument in the family plot at Man O' War Cemetery bears the following inscription:

"Soldier lay thy weapon down
quit the sword and take the crown, triumph
All thy foes are vanished
Death is slain and earth has vanished."

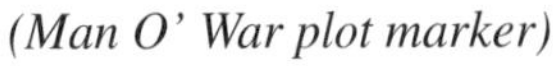

(Man O' War plot marker)

(Aub'gry plot marker)

MacKenzie, John Phillip 1258247

Jack was born on April 6, 1887, the son of Rory and Margaret (MacLeod) MacKenzie, Plaister Mines.He enlisted in June, 1917, and served as a gunner with the 10 Siege Battalion. He served in England and Continental Europe. He was discharged in June, 1919. During World War II, he was a member of the Veteran's Guard. He was posted to the bridge at Iona.

He married Catherine MacQueen, Plaister Mines where they resided. He died in October, 1949, and is buried in Highland Cemetery, Baddeck Bay.

MacKenzie, John Stephen

John was born on July 4, 1895, the son of Charles and Ann (MacNeil) MacKenzie, Washabuck Bridge. Private MacKenzie served with the 94th Battalion Canadian Infantry.

He married Mary Ann Deveaux, Washabuck. His four sons were accomplished fiddlers, one son being Carl MacKenzie. They were also the grandparents of members of the musical groups the Barra MacNeils and Slàinte Mhath. He died on September 7, 1945, and is buried in Holy Rosary Cemetery, Washabuck.

MacKenzie, Margaret Eliza R.N.

Margaret was born on May 24, 1883, the daughter of Christopher and Annie (MacDonald) MacKenzie, Yankee Line.

She was a graduate of the Victoria General School of Nursing, Halifax. Nursing Sister MacKenzie served with the Canadian Army medical service in England and France. She served in public health nursing in Nova Scotia from 1920 until her retirement in 1950. At the time of her retirement, she was Director of Public Health Nursing. She served as president of the Nova Scotia Nurses' Society when its name changed (1931) to the Registered Nurses Association of Nova Scotia. She died on December 12, 1969, and is buried in Middle River Cemetery.

MacKenzie, Minnie Hannah R.N.

Minnie was born on November 26, 1888, the daughter of Christopher and Annie (MacDonald) MacKenzie, Yankee Line.

Minnie was a Registered Nurse. Nursing Sister MacKenzie served overseas in England and France. She married Cecil Mayhew. They resided in Ontario. She retired to Chester and died in 1972. There is a marker in her memory in the Middle River Cemetery.

MacKenzie, Roderick Irving 478538

Roddie was born on July 5, 1897, the son of Rory and Hannah (MacKenzie) MacKenzie, St. Patrick's Channel. He served for two years with the 94th Regiment. He enlisted on September 17, 1915 with the Royal Canadian Regiment. He served in Canada, France and Belgium. He received shrapnel wounds to his face and eyes. Private MacKenzie was discharged on April 20, 1919, on demobilization.

Roddie's parents died when they were quite young, leaving four young boys. Roddie lived with relatives in Margaree. Following the war, he moved to Western Canada.

MacKenzie, Ross MacAulay 222504

Ross was born on January 29, 1891, the son of Murdoch Hugh and Maude (Dunlop) MacKenzie, Baddeck.

"The outstanding phase of the battle of Passchendaele was the re-capturing of the front line by "D" Company (Cape Bretoners) commanded by Captain Ross M. MacKenzie. Another 'saving of the day' was at Vimy by the 85th Battalion. Then it was that the ancient fighting spirit of his Gaelic ancestors shone brilliantly in Captain MacKenzie and he became the Gaelic Hero Cuchallain in the fight and in death. Riddled with machine gun bullets, he fell. But he struggled to his feet and kept on with his company, bleeding to death, and commanded his men, encouraging them, until he dropped exhausted into a shell hole. Even then, though undone, he would not be attended to, but kept encouraging his company. Eventually he permitted himself to be placed on a stretcher and while being borne away, he died - like Cuchallain too, unconquerable in death."

He was killed in action on October 28, 1917. His name is inscribed on the Menin Gate Memorial, Belgium.

The following letter was written by Ross MacKenzie's aunt, Annie MacKenzie, to her niece (Ross's sister), Catherine MacKenzie, Baddeck.

Allinges - Messniges
Haute Savoie, France
March 1918

My dear Catherine,

Your sweet photograph has just come but dear I cannot find one trace of my former baby girl in your face. How grown up you are an let me also say how beautiful too. I look at your face as I write and think of Ross. He wrote me about what a good looking sister he had. He was very proud of you dear and am sure you loved him dearly. His loss has been a severe blow to us all but read this little clipping "There is no death but forgetfulness; everything that has loved and has loved to the end will meet again." I did not write you at the time of his death dear as I knew you suffered too much for me to say anything but don't imagine I did not mourn with you in your grief - your first real grief. He was a dear brother, a good soldier, brave and courageous officer and died a hero, having done his duty fearlessly. How grand to feel he was your brother. I have lost my favourite relative. Since he was a baby I loved him and how well I remember his little ways - always so happy. When he was in Boston before going West, he was so friendly to me. No matter where I was working he came regularly to see me. And when he left for Regina, I bought him a gold watch and he wished my name to be inside the case with his own. He was only a big boy then 17 but I feel he did not change by his letters from France. How I had hoped to see him here one day but that was not to be. Yet Catherine dear we have only the sorrow and loss of thousands to share. I had such a dear boy friend killed April 14, 17 his first day at the front. He was French but spoke English perfectly and wrote it too. He looked like Ross and I think that was why I cared so much for him. His mother wrote me such lovely letters full of hope for her boy but alas poor Jean was killed the first day. He was an only son, his sister of 16 is broken hearted. They live in Nice where I met them.

Formerly they lived in Montreal but being French came to France when the war broke out.

Do you read French or would you like some simple books or newspapers to read? Here everyone speaks English to me and I have not much opportunity to learn the language grammatically but can do well enough to run the house. The servants of course can't speak a word of English and I have a time of it - sometimes trying to make them understand me.

Now we are having a dose of fine weather after 2 months of severe cold and the lilies are budding and the roses are forming leaves. I am very grateful to you all for the papers you have sent me and the Victoria news especially.

Kindest love to mamma and George and sincerely sharing your young hearts sorrow

Affectionately,
Aunt Annie

MacKenzie, William Walter

William was born on June 9, 1893, the son of Roderick Fraser and Bella (MacKenzie) MacKenzie, Kempt Head. He enlisted with the Canadian Overseas Expeditionary Force on June 4, 1918. Private MacKenzie served with the 1st Depot Battalion Nova Scotia Regiment. He served in the Reserve/Glace Bay area. He was discharged on January 16, 1919.

He married Mae Campbell, Lake Ainslie. He died on February 1, 1963, and is buried in the United States.

MacKinnon, Angus

Angus was born on May 6, 1895, the son of Rory and Catherine (MacDonald) MacKinnon, Washabuck. He served with the 94th Battalion in Canada. He married Catherine Jane Gillis, Inverness County. He died in 1961 in Long Island, New York.

MacKinnon, Archibald D. 877621

Archie was the son of Donald and Annie (Fraser) MacKinnon, Black Point. He served with the 185th Canadian Infantry Battalion. He married Helen MacDonald.

MacKinnon, Daniel Francis

Dan Francis was born on January 10, 1900, the son of Ambrose and Mary (MacEachern) MacKinnon, MacKinnon's Harbour. Private MacKinnon served with the 1st Depot Battalion. He married Mary Curry, Boisdale. They resided in Sydney.

MacKinnon, Donald John

'Big Donnie' was born on September 17, 1891, the son of Donald and Alexis (MacLeod) MacKinnon, Ingonish Harbour. He served in the military police in the American Army. He married Mary MacDonald, Ingonish. He was a carpenter, farmer and light keeper at the entrance to Ingonish Harbour. He was a boxer and participated in many tournaments. He sparred with the great Jack Dempsey. He died on April 14, 1971, and is buried in the United Church Cemetery, Ingonish Ferry.

MacKinnon, Hector

Hector was born on January 12, 1897, the son of Dan and Catherine (MacKenzie) MacKinnon, Washabuck/ Cain's Mountain. Private MacKinnon served with the 1st Depot Battalion, Canadian Army Medical Corps, Canadian Expeditionary Force and with the 17th Reserve Battalion. He was a master carpenter and cabinet maker. He was a talented fiddler and step dancer who continued to play and dance well into his advanced years. Unmarried, he was laid to rest on his ninety-eighth birthday, January 12, 1995, in Holy Rosary Cemetery, Washabuck.

MacKinnon, John D.

John was born on December 2, 1885, the son of Neil and Catherine (MacLeod) MacKinnon, Glen Nevis. He served during the war. He married Ellen Ayers, U.S.A. He is buried in Weymouth, Massachusetts.

MacKinnon, John James

James was born on January 18, 1898, the son of Norman and Catherine (MacNeil) MacKinnon, Highland Hill. Private MacKinnon served in the 106th Battalion Canadian Infantry.

World War II

MacKinnon, John Malcolm

John Malcolm was born on October 15, 1893, the son of Kenneth and Rachel (MacDonald) MacKinnon, Glen Nevis, Cape North. He served in both World Wars.

He worked in the silver mines in Ontario and as a tractor operator in Saskatchewan. He maintained a family farm in Red River, Pleasant Bay. He married Kezziah Strickland, Neil's Harbour, and they resided in Pleasant Bay. He died on April 18, 1979, and is buried in St. Andrew's Cemetery, Pleasant Bay.

World War I

MacKinnon, John Murdoch 301272

John Murdoch was born on December 28, 1895, the son of Stephen J. and Catherine (MacNeil) MacKinnon, McKinnons Harbour. Driver MacKinnon served with the 94th Non-Permanent Active Militia and the 36th Battalion, Canadian Field Artillery, in Canada, England and France (1914 - 1919).

He married Angela MacIntyre, Big Pond. He is buried in Sacred Heart Cemetery, McKinnons Harbour.

MacKinnon, John P. 3187627

'John P.' was born on April 30, 1893, the son of Paul and Catherine (MacNeil) MacKinnon. Private MacKinnon served with the 1st Depot Battalion, Canadian Infantry (1918 - 1919). He married Veronica MacLean, Gillis Point. He died in 1951 and is buried in St. Columba Cemetery, Iona.

MacKinnon, John Patfield

John Patfield was the adopted son of John J. and Mary (MacNeil) MacKinnon, McKinnons Harbour. Sixteen year old Private MacKinnon served with the 94th Battalion Canadian Infantry. He was drowned off North Sydney on July 25, 1917 and is buried in St. Columba Cemetery, Iona.

MacKinnon, John Vincent

John Vincent was the son of Neil S. and Mary Sarah (MacNeil) MacKinnon, MacKinnon's Harbour. Private MacKinnon served with the 94th Regiment. Unmarried, he died on April 25, 1973, and is buried in Sacred Heart Cemetery, MacKinnon's Harbour.

MacKinnon, Malcolm Joseph 478544

Malcolm Joseph was born on September 22, 1882, the son of John A. and Margaret (MacNeil) MacKinnon, MacKinnon Settlement.

Private MacKinnon served with the Royal Canadian Regiment - Canadian Infantry. Twenty-four year old MacKinnon was killed in Courcelette on October 8, 1916. His name is inscribed on the Vimy Memorial. His mother never gave up hope that her son would return. She felt that he could be an amnesia victim who may have drifted around Europe. During World War II, as the young men from the community readied for overseas, they would pay a visit to Mrs. MacKinnon. She always made the request, "Please watch for my son and try to get him to come home." When the returning soldiers would visit, she would make the usual inquiry, "Did you see any sign of Malcolm Joseph?"

In 1948, a comrade of Malcolm Joseph came to the area and was inquiring about the MacKinnon family. He was told about Malcolm's mother and her steadfast belief that he was alive. The comrade slowly responded, "There is no need to hope. I saw an enemy shell fall on Malcolm and two others and they were killed instantly." No one could bear to share this eye witness account with Mrs. MacKinnon and felt it was kinder to let her live with her hope.

MacKinnon, Murdoch

Murdoch was born on May 6, 1898, the son of Dan and Catherine (MacKenzie) MacKinnon, Washabuck/Cain's Mountain. Private MacKinnon served with the Royal Canadian Regiment, Canadian Infantry and 1st Depot Battalion. He also served during World War II.

MacKinnon, Murdock

Murdock was the son of John A. and Sarah (MacNeil) MacKinnon, MacKinnon Settlement. Private MacKinnon served with the 1st Depot Battalion in Canada. He died on May 8, 1974, and is buried in St. Columba Cemetery, Iona.

MacKinnon, Roderick 878274

Roderick served with the 185th Canadian Infantry Battalion. His birthplace is given as Boularderie.

MacKinnon, Thomas

Tom was born on May 11, 1872, the son of Malcolm and Effie (MacNeil) MacKinnon, MacKinnon Settlement. Private MacKinnon served with the 94th Regiment. He is buried in St. Columba Cemetery, Iona.

MacLean, Angus 877677

Angus was born on August 15, 1889, and he hailed from Iona. At the time of his enlistment he was a brakeman. Private MacLean served with the 185th Battalion Canadian Infantry.

MacLean, Charles

Charles was the son of John and Jessie (Gillis) MacLean, Ingonish. Charles MacLean was killed in action.

MacLean, Charles J.

Charles was born on October 15, 1886, the son of Michael C. (hotel keeper) and Effie (Nicholson) MacLean, Baddeck.

He served overseas in England and France with the 25th Battalion Canadian Expeditionary Force. He was in the service for four years and was discharged with the rank of Sergeant.

He married Rose Binns, Prince Edward Island. He was an historian and a noteworthy composer of poetry. Their five children served in the Second World War. Arthur, their eldest son, made the supreme sacrifice when he went down with the SS *Andorra Star* when she was torpedoed by the enemy.

Charles MacLean died on November 25, 1947, and was buried with military honours. He is buried in St. Michaels Cemetery, Baddeck.

The following is a poem written by Sergeant MacLean, dated Armistice Day, 1932.

"Do You Remember?"

I see by the news in this morning's papers
The God of War is again cutting capers.
The nations, we're told, are all ready for battle;
At the drop of a hat the sabers will rattle;
But before we'll enlist, and our knapsacks stow
Let's see what happened just a few years ago.
A prince or a pauper was shot in fourteen.
At that time the blood was just a small stream;
From that to a river, then to a cascade
And for four bloody years not a whit did it fade.
Remember Ypres, that line with a curve?
In that salient plenty died, their country to serve.
And Mons, the battle, that was a retreat!;
Some called it victory, some others defeat.
It was not for us to decide who was right;
We were just there for one thing, and that was to fight
And while in that sector don't forget Sillibeck
Where death stood by and with fingers did beck.
He collected his thousands at bleak St. Eloi;
Passchendale and Kemmel must have filled him with joy.
He gathered his full quota at old Dicie Bouche,
Before, after, and at the time of the push.

Remember Cloth Hall and torn Ypres Square
That you crossed by good luck, or maybe a prayer?
Then Hell Fire Corner was your destination;
Will you ever forget there that field dressing station
That you passed so swiftly, just holding your breath,
For to stop there an instant was almost sure death?
But move farther south and of time make a bridge;
Let's see what happened around Vimy Ridge.
White crosses bear evidence of that awful slaughter;
Why, blood was so plenty, it ran just like water.
And Crucifix Corner, far up on the way
To the saving Victim you had this to say,

"Open wide the Gate of Heaven to us below
Thy aid supply, Thy strength bestow."
Did you forget the fronts ahead of Bruay,
Boveeney, Hersin Compeeniee, and Ester Cushay,
Lens, Arras, Mericourt and Bethune,
Monchy, Carency, not forgetting Bapune?
This was no Gettysburg, nor yet Waterloo,
But a continuous battle, all the way through.
Now, let's stop at Amiens, that city so fair
And ponder awhile on those buried there;
The flower of youth who was so impatient
To lay down his life for his very own nation;
For Democracy to guard, and always to keep.
I don't know whether to laugh ... or ... to weep.

Now on to the Somme, and to Courselette;
Things happened there you'll never forget.
Remember the town Albert, with just a few people,
And the Virgin bent over the old church steeple?
With outstretched arms she watched you go by
As if praying for those about to die.
And maybe, as they looked far above,
Said, "Touch my spirit, O Fountain of Love."
After the battle you passed on that street.
There she was, lying down at your feet,
All covered with mud, battered and broken;
A piece in your pocket you took for a token.
Of course you picture with some alarm
The remains of your buddies at Molke's farm.
If your mind is clear and can still bear the load,
Just think of the dead along Sunken Road.
And the sugar refinery that once was so sweet,
Where the flies started on sugar, but ended with meat.
In those battles we thought we were awful good,
But the Yanks did the same down Belleau Wood.
Now down in that sector I am not familiar,
But you can take it from me it was just similar.
With valor and courage they fought Chateau Thiery;

That they won the battle is still the old theory.
If you ask my opinion no battle is won
With bombs or sabres, cannon or gun;
For it's got to be finished by those left behind,
The nerve broken vets, the lame and the blind.

A million lie dead down in Verdun;
They called it a victory and a fight well done.
If that is the case, to that I retort,
"Bring back my buddies, you take the fort!"
But what's the use of talking and taking your time?
There are as many heroes across on the Rhine;
And in Austria, Russia, and Turkey too;
In Italy, Spain, and down in Peru.
What we were fighting for, excuse the pun,
We were not mad with Austrian, Turk, or Hun.
Just because a prince got rubbed out with some lead
They crippled and maimed and left five million dead.
Now before I finish let me you remind
Of the trenches, the vermin, the gas and the grind;
The funkholes, the sunkholes, the shellholes and craters,
Also the liquid fires that were merely crematers.
The lousy dugout, the miner's wet sap,
The listening post by the wire just out at the gap,
Where you lay there and shivered without even a grumble,
If you'd anything to shoot at, the chance is you'd fumble.
Do you remember the mud, the muck and the rain --
Number nines from the doctor to cure all your pain?
Just listen to me - war' not what it's painted --
The rations were bad, the water was tainted.
Can't you hear still the scream of the big shells,
As your hair stood on end and your blood it did jell?
The rattle of machine guns, the crump of the motor,
The cry of the wounded just pleading for water.
What about the coal boxes, the fish tails and stokes,
With a number on them for some of the blokes?
The swish of the whiz bang, the moan of the dying --
You were there, Buddy, you know I'm not lying.

Now about the wounded still walking our streets;
Maybe to some life is still sweet.
To others life, I know, must be near zero.
Well, what do you expect? You're just a live hero --
Don't you remember at the end of the war,
You got a gold medal, and also a bar?
For the others, I mean the ones that are dead,
Will give you a requiem of sights, and tears that are shed
By mothers, and sisters, or maybe a wife,
Sweetheart, brother, or dad, bet your life.
So you thought you're a hero! For crying out loud!
Why, you old sap, you're just one of the crowd!
Don't talk war to me; just hold your whist.
Let's stow our knapsacks. What say we enlist?

Armistice Day, 1932 — *Sgt. C.J. MacLean*
25th Infantry, C.E.F.

MacLean, Daniel C. 878077

'Daniel C.' was born on February 15, 1872, and is believed to be the son of Donald and Mary MacLean of North Shore/Englishtown.

Private MacLean enlisted in Broughton and served overseas with the 185th Canadian Infantry Battalion, Transport Division. Private MacLean was a wounded casualty and was discharged on April 9, 1917.

He died on January 26, 1920. His sister, Mrs. Dan. A. Ferguson, Murphy's Lane, Glace Bay, was listed as his next of kin. In civilian life he had been a tailor.

MacLean, Donald Murray 877181

'Donald M.' was born on March 2, 1889, the son of Donald and Kate (Buchanan) MacLean, Oregon, North River. Members of this family moved to Grand Lake Road, Sydney. Lance Corporal MacLean served overseas with the 185th Battalion, Canadian Infantry (Transport Division and Pioneers). While in England he suffered a severe eye injury as the result of being kicked by a horse. He was a lineman for the telephone company. He married Ann Johnston, Dominion. They moved from Sydney to Ontario. He died on April 9, 1952, and is buried in London, Ontario.

MacLean, Francis Alexander

Francis was born on July 1, 1895, the son of Neil P.S. and Elizabeth (MacNeil) MacLean, Washabuck. Gunner MacLean served with the 7th Battalion Canadian Field Artillery. Unmarried, he died in 1938 in Detroit and is buried there.

MacLean, Hugh 3206152

Hugh was born on December 11, 1896, the son of Torquil and Sarah (MacLean) MacLean, Englishtown. He served in Siberia with the 260th Battalion, Canadian Rifles. Hugh MacLean was working in the coal mining industry in Pocahontas (approximately 45 km east of Jasper), Alberta prior to his military service. He wrote the following letter to his mother in Englishtown on November 29, 1917.

Pocahontas
Nov. 29th / 1917

Dear Mother,

Just a few lines to let you know I am well. Hope you are all very well. I suppose you were expecting to hear from me before but I was to town last week to report for medical examination. I passed O.K. I don't suppose it will be long before I am called up. Dan MacAulay passed the examination too. Danie was in town for exemption the day I was there but I left before he got finished so I don't know how he got along.

I hear we will be called up on the 10th of December to drill in Calgary. I believe Danie will get exempted on account of his leg. How did Allan make out? Well things are beginning to look very much like winter here now so I would just as soon be a soldier as drive a team. There was a MacLeod fellow from Springhill killed in the mine yesterday. He was gassed. Also a McAulay fellow from Springhill a few days before and McPherson from Pictou drowned in the river on Sunday. He was in France for over a year. So a fellow is in danger without going to the trenches. Do you hear from Jack or Kenny? Are they going home this winter? There was a Carmichael from Big Harbour that was working here went home a week or two ago. His brother was killed at the front.

Well have no news to write you this time. I am writing to Allan soon.

Regards to all,
Hughie

He returned to America following the war. His last known whereabouts was in New York where he and his brother Jack had made contact. They had arranged to meet at a certain place but Hugh MacLean failed to appear and, sadly, was never heard of again.

MacLean, John Druhan 3180474/F54917

'John D.' was born on October 18, 1895, the son of Neil P. and Marjorie (Druhan) MacLean, Washabuck Centre. Private MacLean served with the 1st Depot Battalion. Sergeant Major MacLean served with the Cape Breton Highlanders in World War II.

He married Eva Pearl, Kentville. He died on October 14, 1961, and is buried in Holy Rosary Cemetery, Washabuck. His medals have been donated to the Highland Village, Iona.

MacLean, John Hector 222652

'John H.' was born on May 15, 1877, the son of Michael Charlie and Effie (Nicholson) MacLean, Baddeck. He enlisted on October 5, 1915 and served with the 85th Battalion, No. 14 Platoon. Private MacLean served as a ferrier in France. He contracted an illness and died on September 5, 1918. He is buried in Terlmethon British Cemetery, Wimille. Following his death his widow, Margaret, and their large family moved to New Glasgow, Nova Scotia.

MacLean, John Jay 469662

John Jay was born on January 1, 1896, the son of John and Bessie (MacNeil) MacLean, Washabuck Centre. Private MacLean served with the 85th and 64th Battalions, Canadian Infantry. He was wounded while serving with the 26th Battalion (New Brunswick Regiment) and died of wounds on August 11, 1918. He is buried in Villens-Bretonneux Military Cemetery, Fouilloy.

MacLean, John Joseph 482017

'John J.' was born on December 24, 1898, the son of Neil P.S. and Elizabeth (MacNeil) MacLean, Washabuck. Private MacLean served with the 40th Battalion. He was taken on strength in Sydney on August 13, 1915. He married and resided in Detroit and is buried there.

MacLean, Joseph Sutherland

'Joseph S.' was born on December 11, 1860, the son of William and Georgina (Fraser) MacLean, Bay Road, Baddeck. Captain MacLean served as a field officer with the 94th Regiment Argyle Highlanders (Aldershot - 1903). He was promoted to Major on June 12, 1905 and transferred to Recruiting Officer on April 14, 1911 and continued to serve in this capacity during World War I. His son W. Murray MacLean served overseas during World War I.

He was predeceased by his first wife Ada Plant, North Sydney. He later married Katherine Morrison, North Gut. He was a crown land surveyor and draftsman for over fifty years. He died on May 9, 1935, and is buried in Knox Auld Kirk Cemetery, Bay Road, Baddeck.

MacLean, Malcolm 3181979

Malcolm MacLean, Baddeck, served during the war from April 27, 1918, to January 8, 1919.

MacLean, Malcolm 222855

Malcolm MacLean hailed from Washabuck. Sergeant Major MacLean served with the 185th Battalion A Corps. He also served in World War II and it is believed that he was involved with training recruits.

MacLean, Michael Donald 878339

'Michael D.' was born on October 13, 1890, the son of Neil Stephen and Christina (Campbell) MacLean, Baddeck. Lance Corporal MacLean, while serving with His Majesty's Forces, Canadian Expeditionary Force, was killed in action on August 26, 1918, in Monchi near Arras, France. His name is inscribed on the Vimy Memorial, France.

The following is a letter to his mother, Mrs. James MacIntyre, from his chaplain with particulars of her son's death.

"R.C.R., B.E.F., France October 3, 1918
Mrs. James MacIntyre, Baddeck, Nova Scotia
Dear Mrs. MacIntyre - This letter of information has been delayed by the continuous service of the Canadian Corps the past two months. I take the first opportunity of writing to give you such particulars as are at hand about your son, L.C., M.D. McLean, missing since August 26th last and to extend to you the sympathy of his comrades in the great anxiety under which you suffer. Your son took part in the great battle of Arras which began on the above date, and in the attack on Monchy as his company passed through the village, on which heavy enemy shells fell like hail, he was missed and no trace has been found of him since.

One is forced to the conclusion that your brave son is numbered among those who have proved their patriotism by giving their lives for their homes, their country and their God. Surely such men do rest in peace.

With sincere sympathy, I am yours very faithfully,
A.E. Andrew, Chaplain."

Michael D. MacLean was a brother to the colorful Alex D. MacLean, author of an unpublished manuscript entitled *History of Victoria County (1949).*

MacLean, Michael John

Michael was born on June 10, 1894, the son of Rory and Flora (MacNeil) MacLean, MacKinnon's Harbour. Private MacLean served with the 40th Battalion, Canadian Infantry in Canada, United Kingdom and France.

(Standing - Michael John MacLean)

MacLean, Neil 877294

Neil was born on June 1, 1894, the son of Big John and Margaret (MacLeod) MacLean, Big Baddeck. Sergeant MacLean served with the 185th Canadian Infantry Battalion. He married Norma MacLean, Hunters' Mountain and worked in the United States for many years. He died on July 1, 1975, and interment was in the Middle River Cemetery.

MacLean, Neil Stephen 877296

'Neil S.' was born on December 17, 1896, the son of Allan and Mary Ann (MacNeil) MacLean, Washabuck Centre. Private MacLean served with the 185th Battalion, Canadian Infantry. He was wounded in action.

MacLean, Peter A. 877279

'Peter A.' was born on January 8, 1895, the son of Allan and Mary Ann (MacNeil) MacLean, Washabuck Centre. Private MacLean served in the 185th Battalion, Canadian Infantry. He lost his life in a flood in Florida.

MacLean, Peter Neil 3181750

Peter Neil was born on September 23, 1898, the son of Neil P.S. and Elizabeth MacLean, Washabuck. Private MacLean served in the 1st Depot Battalion, Nova Scotia Regiment, Canadian Expeditionary Force. Unmarried, he died on January 17, 1921, from the effects of gas poisoning which he was exposed to in the trenches and is buried in Holy Rosary Cemetery, Washabuck.

MacLean, Roderick Charles 222409

Rod was born on February 18, 1896, the son of Dan Rory and Flora (MacLean) MacLean, Hunter's Mountain. He enlisted on October 14, 1915, and served with the Nova Scotia Highlanders, 16 Platoon, 85th Battalion. He served in Canada, England and France. He was wounded in the Battle of Vimy Ridge on April 9, 1917. Sergeant MacLean was discharged on July 4, 1919. He married Ethel MacLean, Orangedale. He died in 1964 and is buried in Middle River Cemetery.

(Seated - Rod C. MacLean)

MacLean, Roderick James 878336

'Rory' was born on December 11, 1898, the son of Allan and Mary Ann (MacNeil) MacLean, Washabuck Centre. Private MacLean enlisted on April 1, 1916, in Sydney and served in the 185th Battalion. He was wounded in action. He married Maude Boutilier, Sydney.

MacLean, Roderick Joseph

'R.J.' was born the son of Peter and Flora (Gillis) MacLean, Ottawa Brook. Private MacLean served in the 1st Depot Battalion, Canadian Infantry and with the 17th Reserve Battalion in England (1918 - 1919). He married Katie MacDonald. He died on January 20, 1974, and is buried in Sacred Heart Cemetery, McKinnons Harbour.

MacLean, Wilfred Murray 501225

Murray was born on January 8, 1897, the son of surveyor Joseph S. and Ada (Plant) MacLean, Baddeck Bay. Trooper MacLean enlisted on September 27, 1915 in Sydney and served overseas with # 1 Tunnelling Company. Murray MacLean was an employee of the bank. He died on November 19, 1924, in Oil City, Peru. His name is inscribed on the family marker in Knox Auld Kirk Cemetery, Bay Road, Baddeck.

MacLennan, Alexander Donald 31888891

'Sandy Neil Rory' was born on May 24, 1896, the son of Neil and Isabella (MacRae) MacLennan, Gold Brook. He enlisted on June 12, 1918. Private MacLennan served with the 1st Depot Battalion, Nova Scotia Regiment, Canadian Expeditionary Force in Canada and England. He was discharged on demobilization on August 2, 1919. He resided in Middle River. He died in 1956 and is buried in Middle River Cemetery.

MacLennan, Hector Alexander 154180

Hector was born on February 14, 1871, the son of Kenneth and Ann (Campbell) MacLennan, West Side Middle River. He served for six years with the 94th Argyle Highlanders. He enlisted in Victoria, British Columbia on September 22, 1915. He served as a sapper with the 1st Canadian Pioneer Battalion. Prior to the war his civilian trade was that of bridge builder. He resided in the United States.

MacLennan, Norman

Norman was the son of John and Lizzie (MacDonald) MacLennan, Big Intervale. Private MacLennan served overseas and was killed in action. His name is engraved on the cenotaph at Cape North.

MacLennan, Norman 427017

Norman was born on June 29, 1876, the son of Peter and Catherine (Buchanan) MacLennan, Baddeck.

Private MacLennan was taken on strength in Regina on May 22 1915 and served with the 46th Battalion. He was killed in action on September 26, 1916 and his name is engraved on the Vimy Memorial, France.

Farquhar MacLennan, Norman's brother, was born on August 26, 1885.

The following is an undated excerpt from a local newspaper:

"Young 'Fred' McLennan left home about two years ago and since that time has worked in different parts of Western Canada. He was a splendid specimen of the Cape Breton Highlander standing more than six feet, erect, well proportioned, a physique that would attract attention anywhere. While home he took a deep interest in military affairs and was an officer of the 94th Regiment. He was possessed of an open, affable, generous nature and had many friends. He was deeply attached to his home and his parents were looking forward with pleasure to his promised visit next summer. It is indeed a terrible shock to learn by telegram on Thursday that death had claimed their beloved son."

Farquhar MacLennan was a member of Gunn's Hydrographical Survey party who left camp with a load of supplies in a canoe. He and three others drowned in Grand Rapids, Manitoba.

MacLennan, Peter Malcolm 715535

Peter was born on July 25, 1887, the son of Peter and Catherine (Buchanan) MacLennan, Baddeck. He served as a Sergeant with the 106th Overseas Battalion, Canadian Expeditionary Force. He married Florence Robinson, Alba, Inverness County. For many years they tended the lighthouse on St. Paul's Island and later in Money Point. Their three sons served in World War II and two of them failed to return. Peter MacLennan died on May 24, 1969, and is buried in Greenwood Cemetery, Baddeck.

MacLeod, Abraham

Abraham was born circa 1892, the son of Murdoch Hugh and Christy (MacInnis) MacLeod, Plaister Road, Baddeck Bay. He served on guard duty at the Marconi Towers in Sydney. Due to a broken foot he was unable to serve overseas. He married Margaret MacDonald, North River. They resided in Florence, Cape Breton. He was a miner in the old Florence Colliery. He died on December 24, 1983, and is buried in Brookside Cemetery, Sydney Mines.

MacLeod, Alexander

(Right -Alexander MacLeod and Left - Pat MacLeod)

Alexander was born on May 6, 1897, the son of Kenneth and Mary (Meade) MacLeod, Indian Brook. He enlisted three months short of the legal entry age. Hence, his brother reported this and he was discharged out of the service. When he reached legal age, he re-enlisted and served overseas. He married Jessie Belle MacGregor, North River. They moved to the United States where he worked as a railroad foreman and as a contract carpenter. He died in Maine and is buried in Wells, Maine.

MacLeod, Alexander Albert 877325

'A.A.' was born on April 2, 1902, the son of Malcolm 'Gold' and Mary (MacKenzie) MacLeod, Black Rock, Boularderie.

As a fourteen year old lad, he served overseas with the 185th Battalion, Cape Breton Highlanders. He was educated in Sydney Mines and Windsor, Nova Scotia, and at the Maritime Business College in Halifax. Twice married, his first wife was Annie Hicks, Dalhousie, New Brunswick. After her tragic death he married Virginia K. MacLean, North Sydney. In 1943 he was elected to the Ontario Provincial Parliament for Toronto-Bellwoods and was re-elected in 1945. He was an advisor and editor for the Ontario Human Rights Commission. He was the driving force behind the restoration of St. Andrews Cemetery, Sydney Mines. A marker at the site bears this inscription: "A native son who loved Cape Breton, Its history and Its people."

His nephew, Floyd Williston, in 1996, published the book *Through Footless Halls of Air*. It is about six Atlantic airmen who failed to return.

He died in Toronto on March 13, 1970, and is buried in Prospect Cemetery, Toronto.

MacLeod, Alexander Kenneth 877171

'A.K.' was born on October 29, 1892, the son of Alexander Kenneth and Sarah (Nicholson) MacLeod, Hunter's Mountain. The MacLeod family moved from Hunter's Mountain to Whitney Pier. Corporal MacLeod served in Canada and overseas with the 185th Battalion. He died on March 13, 1918, as a result of tuberculosis. He is buried in Eastmount Cemetery, Whitney Pier.

MacLeod, Alexander Myles 878346

'Alex Miley' was born on October 27, 1898, the son of Myles and Flora (MacCalder) MacLeod, North Gut, St. Ann's. Private MacLeod enlisted on April 19, 1916, and served overseas with the 185th Battalion, # 2 Platoon. He joined the Veterans Guard of Canada during World War II. He served as a guard in the prison camp in Montrith, Ontario. He married Catherine Stowe, South Gut. They resided in Glen Tosh. He died on June 14, 1965, and is buried in Harbourview Cemetery, South Haven.

The following is a letter he sent to his little daughter Lucy:

No 97384
No 5 Platoon
No 8 Cpy V.G.O.C.
Camp 23
Montrith, Ontario

Sunday 15th

Dear Lucy:

I am away up in the woods guarding a German prison camp. Feeling fine. Fed on the best. Putting on flesh like a pig.

I did not hear from home yet. I sent them four letters from Halifax and three from here. Will not get home until August. Have no news. Write and give all the news.

Love Daddy

MacLeod, Alexander Norman 3181753

'Alex Governor' was born on April 3, 1899, the son of Norman and Catherine (MacLeod) MacLeod, Munroe's Point. He enlisted on June 11, 1917. He served with the 94th Regiment and transferred to "B" Company, 6th Battalion, Canadian Railway Corps, Canadian Expeditionary Force. He served overseas. Private MacLeod was discharged on December 31, 1918, in North Sydney. On October 3, 1940, he enlisted with the 18 Company Veterans Guard and served until he returned to civilian life on demobilization.

He married Margaret Buchanan, Munroe's Point and they resided in Munroe's Point. He died on March 25, 1970, and is buried in Goose Cove Cemetery, St. Ann's.

MacLeod, Angus

Angus was born on March 15, 1867, the son of Donald (Dan) and Annie Christy (Buchanan) MacLeod, Tarbotvale. He served overseas. He married Hannah MacDonald, Tarbot. He and his wife moved to Winnipeg. Angus died in Texas.

MacLeod, Angus B. 2005243

'Angus B.' was born on May 7, 1879, the son of Donald and Mary (Morrison) MacLeod, Wreck Cove. He began his career as a school master. In 1907 he entered Dalhousie University and studied civil engineering. He enlisted on July 12, 1916 and served overseas in France with the Canadian Engineers. Lieutenant MacLeod was discharged in September, 1919.

He married Jessie Buchanan, South Gut. He was a survey engineer. The family home was destroyed in the forest fire of 1968 that swept Smokey Mountain and beyond. Angus B. died in 1963 and is buried in Harbourview Cemetery, South Haven.

MacLeod, Angus Daniel 414333

Angus was born on November 30, 1893, the son of Malcolm and Annabel (MacAskill) MacLeod, Black Head. Private MacLeod enlisted in Halifax and served overseas with the 2nd Canadian Mounted Rifles - 1st Ontario Rifles - 40th Battalion. He was reported missing in action on October 30, 1917, and his name is inscribed on the Menin Gate Memorial, Belgium.

MacLeod, Angus George

Angus George was born on May 5, 1887, the son of Daniel J. and Christie Annie (Stewart) MacLeod, Peter's Brook/Whitney Pier. He served overseas with the American Air Force. He was a member of the Lafayette Escadrille Team - The Flying Aces. He married a schoolteacher, Florence Matheson, Whitney Pier. They resided in San Francisco. He prospected in the gold fields of Alaska. He died on January 24, 1976, in San Francisco, California.

MacLeod, Archie 2020914

Archie was born on May 28, 1884, the son of Roderick and Jane (Buchanan) MacLeod, Birch Plain. Private MacLeod enlisted on January 14, 1918 in Vancouver, British Columbia. He served in the 1st Unit of the Canadian Infantry in Canada, England and France. He was discharged on July 17, 1919 in Halifax. He married Sadie A. Morrison, Goose Cove, and they resided in British Columbia. He worked as a ship builder. He died in Burnaby, British Columbia, in 1954.

MacLeod, Charles Tupper 111310

Charlie was born on February 16, 1891, the son of (general merchant) Hector and Catherine (Hellen) MacLeod, New Haven. Trooper MacLeod served overseas with the 6th Regiment Canadian Mounted Rifles (1914 to 1918). He was heavily gassed several times during combat and as a result, he suffered from ill health for the rest of his life.

He married Gladys Fader, R.N., Quincy, Massachusetts (she was a descendant of Charles A. Fader, Englishtown). He was a graduate of Dalhousie Law School (BA and LLB - 1919). He practiced law in Sydney and then moved to Massachusetts and to Chicago where he died on April 8, 1954.

MacLeod, Daniel 78504

'Danny Drover' was born on October 12, 1894, the son of Donald and Peggy (MacLeod) MacLeod, Port Bevis. He joined the 94th Argyle Highlanders and then the 185th. He enlisted in April, 1915, and Private MacLeod served until he was discharged in October, 1918.

He married Sarah Ann MacAskill, Indian Brook. He was a marine engineer and worked as an engineer on *Ross Ferry* for many years. He died in 1971 and is buried in Harbourview Cemetery, South Haven.

MacLeod, Daniel N.

Dan was born on August 15, 1895, the son of Daniel and Mary (Morrison) MacLeod, Glen Tosh. He served overseas including Siberia. He married Jessie MacLeod, Broughton, Cape Breton. They resided in Massachusetts but each summer returned to Glen Tosh where they operated tourist cabins.

MacLeod, Donald Frank 111376

'Donnie John C.' was born on March 22, 1895, the son of John C. and Mary Jane (Morrison) MacLeod, South Gut. Trooper MacLeod served overseas with the 6th Regiment Canadian Mounted Rifles. Prior to enlisting, he was a well respected local school master. He returned from the war feeling very distraught from his experiences. He settled in Falun, Alberta where he was engaged in farming and teaching school. He married Myrtle Morrison, Debert. He died on October 11, 1982, in White Rock, British Columbia.

MacLeod, Donald M. 222412

'Donald M.' was born on May 11, 1895, the son of John A. and Catherine (MacLeod) MacLeod, Baddeck. He was raised in the home of Donald Tailor MacDonald, South Cove. He served overseas with the 85th Battalion, # 16 Platoon. He was shot through the ankle at Vimy on April 9, 1917. He was discharged with the rank of Sergeant Major. Donald married and resided in Richmond, Virginia.

MacLeod, Duncan David 877302

Duncan was born on April 8, 1895, the son of Malcolm and Annabel (MacAskill) MacLeod, Black Head. He enlisted on March 13, 1916 in Sydney Mines with the 185th Battalion. Due to medical reasons, he was discharged in Aldershot on July 4, 1916. He married Jennie Ferguson, Glace Bay. They lived in Englishtown for a time and then moved to Glace Bay. His occupation was a mine examiner. He died on July 19, 1940 and is buried in Bayview Cemetery, Englishtown.

MacLeod, Duncan John 688252

'D.J.' was born on January 13, 1892, the son of Daniel and Christie Annie (Stewart) MacLeod, Peter's Brook (this family moved to Whitney Pier).

Private MacLeod served overseas with the 16th Machine Gun Company - 172nd Battalion. He was killed in action on October 30, 1917. His name is inscribed on the Menin Gate Memorial, Belgium. His name is also inscribed on the family marker located in the Stewart Cemetery, Peter's Brook.

MacLeod, Duncan Morrison

'Duncan John C.' was born on January 26, 1890, the son of John C. and Mary Jane (Morrison) MacLeod, South Gut. He served overseas in active combat. After the war, he went to the mines in Ontario. Eventually, he was part owner of Nickel and Silver Mines in Northern Ontario. Unmarried, he died on July 14, 1963, in Cobalt, Ontario. He is buried in Harbourview Cemetery, South Haven.

MacLeod, G. Dewey

'Dewey' was born in Lewis Mountain, Inverness County. He was raised in the home of Malcolm and Catherine (MacAulay) MacIvor, MacIver's Point. Private MacLeod served during the war. Post war he may have gone to Alaska.

MacLeod, Hector

Hector was born on October 31, 1897, the son of Malcolm and Agnes (Corbett) MacLeod, Boularderie. He served during the war. After the war he served on the Halifax Police Force.

MacLeod, Hector 877624

Private MacLeod, Baddeck, served with the 185th Overseas Battalion, Nova Scotia Overseas Highland Brigade.

MacLeod, Hector Allister 480796

Allister was born on January 20, 1900, the son of general merchant Hector and Catherine (Hellen) MacLeod, New Haven. He interrupted his studies at Mount Allison University and, underage, he enlisted for war service. Sergeant MacLeod served overseas with the North Nova Scotia Highlanders and fought at Vimy Ridge.

Until 1932 he was a partner with his brother John J. in the MacLeod family fish business in New Haven. He married Mary Frances MacLeod, Ingonish. They were proprietors of the tourist resort 'The Point' in Ingonish. During the 1930's he ran for a seat in the provincial legislature, but Casey Baldwin became the successful candidate. He died on October 24, 1981, and is buried in St. Peter's Cemetery, Neil's Harbour.

MacLeod, James

Jim was born on October 28, 1900, the son of John A. and Catherine (MacLeod) MacLeod, Baddeck. He was raised in the home of Donald Tailor MacDonald, South Cove. Private MacLeod served during the war. After the war he resided in Cambridge, Massachusetts but later moved elsewhere.

MacLeod, Rev. John Donald 282098

'John Dan' was born on February 6, 1894, the son of John and Catherine (MacDonald) MacLeod, Baddeck. He served as a combatant in France with the 219th Overseas Battalion, Nova Scotia Overseas Highland Brigade during World War I. He served as a chaplain during World War II.

He was educated at Dalhousie University and Pine Hill Divinity Hall, Halifax. He was granted his Doctor of Divinity Degree by Pine Hill in 1958. He was predeceased by his first wife, Annie Porter. His second wife was Blanche Reid of Green Hill, Pictou County. He and his wife retired to Greenhill and Rev. MacLeod died on December 26, 1971 and is buried in Fairview Cemetery, Halifax.

MacLeod, John Hugh 415735

'John Hughie' was born circa 1888, the son of Murdoch Hugh and Christy (MacInnis) MacLeod, Plaister Road, Baddeck Bay. Private MacLeod enlisted on August 13, 1915, in Sydney and served overseas with the 40th Battalion (1915 to 1918). He married Etta MacLeod, Port Bevis and they moved to Pictou County.

MacLeod, John Murdoch

John Murdoch was born on March 19, 1895, the son of Angus B. 'Ford' and Christy (Morrison) MacLeod, North Shore. He served overseas.

He returned to work in the lumber woods at North River. He sustained severe injuries while working on the construction of a dam site located considerable distance up the North River. He was transported by horse and wagon to Murray. There he remained overnight and was placed aboard the *Aspy* the next day and taken to North Sydney. He died as the *Aspy* docked at the North Sydney Pier (circa 1920). He was unmarried. He is buried in Pine Hill Cemetery, River Bennett.

MacLeod, John William 877317

John William was born on May 10, 1880, the son of John and Catherine MacLeod, Ross Ferry. He served overseas with the 185th Canadian Infantry Battalion. He married Sarah MacNeil, Millville. After the war, he worked in the coal mines. They resided in Florence. He died in Ontario and is buried there.

MacLeod, Joseph

Joseph was born on May 10, 1892, the son of Norman and Ann (MacMillan) MacLeod, Upper Baddeck River. He served with the Canadian Expeditionary Force in England and Continental Europe. He enlisted on May 15, 1918 and was discharged on July 11, 1919 in Halifax.

He married Alma A. Dundas in Thorold, Ontario on March 13, 1921. He died on June 1, 1966 in Edmonton, Alberta.

MacLeod, Kenneth

Kenneth was born on April 26, 1896, the son of Kenneth and Mary (Meade) MacLeod, Indian Brook.

He entered military training at the Royal School of Infantry Training, Halifax. On the morning of December 6, 1917 he was in his barracks during the Halifax Explosion. Later he directed men in the rescue operations in the north end of the city. They recovered all whom were alive and then dealt with the bodies of the dead. A severe blizzard struck that night compounding the hardships. He remembered cleaning the faces of the dead so that they could be identified "and there were some awful sights." Sergeant MacLeod served with the 206th Battalion, Canadian Expeditionary Force. He served in active combat in Siberia until April 1919. Company-Sergeant-Major MacLeod was called up at the outbreak of World War II and again served his country.

He was predeceased by his wife Margaret MacIntosh and his second wife Katie Johnson Curtis. In civilian life he was a carpenter. He died on March 10, 1988, and is buried in Indian Brook Cemetery.

MacLeod, Kenneth Angus

'Kennie George' was born on December 4, 1897, the son of George and Elizabeth (Stewart) MacLeod, Peter's Brook/Baddeck Bay.

He enlisted, but, he contracted measles and before he was released from quarantine the war had ended. He was predeceased by his first wife Armenia Rice, Big Baddeck. His second wife was Vera Smith from Inverness. He and his wife resided in Baddeck Bay. He died on September 24, 1985, and is buried in Highland Cemetery, Baddeck Bay.

(Left-Kenneth MacLeod, Right-Dan Stewart)

MacLeod, Rev. MacIntosh

(W.W. I)
(W.W. II)

'Tosh' was born on October 23, 1890, the son of Angus and Mary (Gunn) MacLeod, Baddeck.

He interrupted his studies at Dalhousie University to enlist in March, 1915. He was attached to the 40th Battalion, Canadian Overseas Expeditionary Force and then with the 5th Canadian Mounted Rifles. He was wounded in France on October 18, 1916. He returned to the front and remained in France until 1919.

Lieutenant MacLeod was honoured in March, 1919 by the British government. He is **MENTIONED IN DISPATCHES** "... for gallant and distinguished service in the field" signed by the then Secretary of State Winston Churchill.

He resumed his studies and received his Bachelor of Divinity degree in 1921. He became an ordained Presbyterian minister.

He served during World War II as a training instructor in the army and later as a chaplain in the Royal Canadian Air Force. His postings were in Nova Scotia and Toronto. He was demobilized in August, 1945.

He married Gladys Baird and they resided in Wolfville, Nova Scotia. He worked in the public service until his retirement. Rev. MacIntosh MacLeod died in Camp Hill Hospital on November 11, 1972.

MacLeod, Malcolm

Malcolm was born in 1865, the son of Donald (Dan) and Annie Christy (Buchanan) MacLeod, Tarbotvale. He served overseas. He married Margaret Smith, Indian Brook. They moved to British Columbia and he died there.

MacLeod, Malcolm

'Malcolm Billy' was born on September 23, 1892, the son of William and Christy (MacMillan) MacLeod, Plaister Mines.

He interrupted his medical studies to serve his country. He served overseas but the effects of the war had taken a great toll. Afterwards, he was unable to continue at university. He died on December 31, 1938, and is buried in Highland Cemetery, Baddeck Bay.

MacLeod, Malcolm 301190

'Malcolm Mason' was born on August 10, 1888, the son of John and Catherine (MacDonald) MacLeod, Baddeck. He worked for a number of years in the mining community of New Waterford. It was there that he enlisted with the Canadian Army on September 10, 1915. He served with the 27th Battery, Canadian Field Artillery. He was wounded in France in the spring of 1918, and later returned to the front. He was discharged on June 8, 1919. Following his return he moved to Western Canada where he was employed as an Indian Agent on their native reserves. He married Sophie MacLennan, South Bar. They retired to Baddeck in 1953. He died on January 28, 1973, and is buried in Greenwood Cemetery, Baddeck.

MacLeod, Malcolm A.

'Malcolm J.P.' was born on August 20, 1878, the son of John P. and Christie Ann (Matheson) MacLeod, Baddeck. He was a bandmaster and served with the 85th Battalion. He was a partner in the firm J.P. MacLeod & Sons est. 1874 (General Store). He married Mabel Kenny, New Brunswick. He died in 1924 and is buried in Greenwood Cemetery, Baddeck.

MacLeod, Malcolm Angus

Malcolm was born on September 20, 1897, the son of John and Jessie (MacLeod) MacLeod, Tarbotvale. He served in Canada. He was prepared to disembark for overseas when he caught the measles. The war ended before he was out of quarantine so he did not go overseas. He resided at Tarbotvale. Unmarried, he died on May 3, 1984, and is buried at Pine Hill Cemetery, River Bennett.

MacLeod, Malcolm John 222428

Malcolm was born on March 21, 1886, the son of Alexander and Sarah (Nicholson) MacLeod, Hunter's Mountain. Private MacLeod served overseas with the 246th and the 85th Battalions. He was wounded on March 16, 1918. He married J. Christine Campbell, Scotland.

MacLeod, Margaret S., R.N.

Margaret was born on August 7, 1892, the daughter of George and Elizabeth (Stewart) MacLeod, Peter's Brook. A Registered Nurse, Nursing Sister MacLeod served with the American Army. She was discharged on September 8, 1919. She married a Mr. Allen and they resided in the United States.

MacLeod, Murdoch 1006070

Murdoch was the son of John and Annie (Stewart) MacLeod, New Harris. As a young lad, he served in the Boer War and he served overseas in the Great War. Private MacLeod enlisted on April 3, 1916, in Porcupine, Ontario and served overseas with the 228th Battalion. After the war he went to the 'gold fields' in Ontario. Unmarried, he never returned home but over the years kept in contact with his sister, Alice MacLeod.

MacLeod, Murdoch Daniel 878067

'Murdoch Robert' was born on August 28, 1896, the son of Robert and Jessie (Nicholson / MacDonald) MacLeod, South Gut. He served in both World Wars. He served overseas with the 185th Canadian Infantry Battalion in Canada, England and France. He suffered a shoulder wound in combat. He served with the Veterans Guard of Canada in Debert during World War II. He married Catherine MacFarlane, Baddeck. They resided in South Haven. He died on January 10, 1965, and is buried in Harbourview Cemetery, South Haven.

MacLeod, Murdoch Edward 2552304

'Murdoch E.' was born on September 11, 1896, the son of Kenneth and Sarah (MacLeod) MacLeod, Black Head. He served in the 27th Battery, Canadian Field Artillery in France from 1917 to 1919.

He married Catherine C. Fraser, Sydney Mines and lived in North Sydney until 1932 when they moved to Halifax. He was a purser with the White Star Shipping Line. He died on September 7, 1986, and is buried in Fairview Cemetery, Halifax.

MacLeod, Neil Benjamin 715466

Neil was born on May 6, 1888, son of Matilda MacPhee, Big Baddeck/North Gut. He enlisted on December 13, 1915, in Sydney. He served with the 106th Overseas Battalion and the 26th Battalion. He served in Canada, Britain and France. Lance Corporal MacLeod was killed in action on August 8, 1918, while serving with the 26th Battalion. He is buried in Villers-Bretonneux Military Cemetery, Fouilloy, France.

MacLeod, Peter Clarke

Peter was the son of Angus and Ann (MacAskill) MacLeod, Cape North. He moved to Boston in 1894 and became a stone cutter in Quincy and later carried on his trade in Barre, Vermont. Circa 1912 he moved to San Francisco. He enlisted in 1916 and served overseas during the war. As they were passing Cape Breton going and returning from war, he could plainly see from the troopship his old home in Aspy Bay. A few years later he was stricken with stone cutter's lung disease and passed away at his brother Murdock's home in Centuria, United States.

MacLeod, Phillip A. 715826

Phillip was born on January 10, 1897, the son of John A. and Catherine (MacLeod) MacLeod, Baddeck. He was raised in the home of Peter MacRitchie in South Side Whycocomagh.

He was stationed in Truro when his chum, Harold Robbins (World War I), was drowned. He served with the 106th and the 85th Battalions. Private MacLeod joined the 85th Battalion on August 15, 1918, and was killed in action from shrapnel wounds on September 2, 1918. He is buried in Dury Mill British Cemetery, France.

MacLeod, Richard

Richard was born on October 7, 1894, and was raised by Donald and Ann (Matheson) MacLeod, Cain's Mountain. Private MacLeod served overseas and was wounded in action. He married Mabel MacSween, Lake Ainslie. They resided in Sydney. He is buried in Sydney.

(left to right - Richard MacLeod, Ann and Donald MacLeod)

MacLeod, Robert Neil

'Robbie Neily' was born on February 4, 1896, the son of Neil and Annie (Morrison) MacLeod, Cape North. He served in the war in 1918. He married Mary Catherine Shaw, Framboise. In his latter years he moved to Milford and resided with his son. He died on August 3, 1990, and is buried in Hants County, Nova Scotia.

MacLeod, Roderick William 878342

'Roddy Danny' was born on August 11, 1890, the son of Dan and Mary (Morrison) MacLeod, Glen Tosh. Private MacLeod enlisted on April 2, 1916, and served with the 185th Battalion, # 2 Platoon. He married Rena White Munro, Canso. They resided in Everett, Massachusetts.

MacLeod, Sadie R.N.

Sadie was born on December 17, 1891, the daughter of Angus and Mary (Gunn) MacLeod, Baddeck. She was a graduate of the Victoria General Hospital School of Nursing, Halifax. Nursing Sister Sadie MacLeod served in the Canadian Army Medical Corps, Canadian Expeditionary Force. She enlisted on October 28, 1915, and was attached to the Dalhousie Unit. She served in Canada, England and France with the # 7 Stationary Hospital, No. 4 Casualty Clearing Station, C.A.M.C. Depot, Kings Canadian Red Cross Hospital and Moxham Hospital. She was discharged on May 30, 1919.

She married Dr. James A. Currie, M.D. Mrs. Currie served as a Nursing Sister at Camp Hill Hospital, Halifax from 1942 to 1945 until two weeks before her death in April, 1945. Interment was in Greenwood Cemetery, Baddeck.

MacLeod, Sarah Isobel R.N.

Sadie was born on October 25, 1889, the daughter of general merchant Hector and Catherine (Hellen) MacLeod, New Haven. She was a graduate of the Winnipeg Hospital School of Nursing. Nursing Sister MacLeod served overseas with the Dalhousie Medical Unit during the war.

She resided in Chicago, United States. She and her sister, Ida, retired to Truro, Nova Scotia. She died on January 19, 1968, and is buried in St. Peter's Cemetery, Neil's Harbour.

MacLeod, Thomas 715524

Thomas was born on July 2, 1896 in Big Bras d'Or. He served with the 106th Overseas Battalion, Canadian Expeditionary Force. He enlisted on February 25, 1916, in Truro, Nova Scotia. Private MacLeod served in Canada, Britain and France. He was discharged on July 4, 1919, in Quebec.

MacLeod, William Donald 415077

Billy was born on June 22, 1884, the son of John D. and Annie (MacLeod) MacLeod, Fife's Hill, Big Bras d'Or. Private MacLeod enlisted on March 31, 1915 in Sydney and served with the 40th Battalion. He was a member of the Military Police in England. He was wounded while serving in England. The telegram read: "June 17, 1916. Shrapnel to head, severe wound - survived". He was discharged at the end of the war in 1918.

He married Katie MacLennan, New Campbellton. They resided on Bird Island and later in Fife's Hill. He died on July 2, 1976, and is buried in St. James Cemetery, Big Bras d'Or.

MacMillan, Joseph 877293

Joseph was born on March 14, 1893, the son of Samuel and Christy (Campbell) MacMillan, Big Baddeck. Private MacMillan served overseas with the 185th Canadian Infantry Battalion. He had been serving with the 25th Battalion Unit when he died of wounds on August 11, 1918. He is buried in Crovy British Cemetery.

His family moved from Big Baddeck to Sydney, Nova Scotia. He was unmarried. A family member is still in possession of his rifle.

MacMillan, Malcolm 3189290

Malcolm was born on November 3, 1894, the son of Malcolm and Jane (MacKenzie) MacMillan, Big Harbour.

Private MacMillan served with the 85th in France. Unmarried, he died on September 21, 1925, in Alberta. He is buried in the little roadside cemetery (by Trans Canada Highway), Port Bevis.

MacMillan, Murdoch

Murdoch was born on June 24, 1895, the son of Neil and Flora (MacKenzie) MacMillan, Big Baddeck/ North River. He served overseas and was wounded at Vimy Ridge. As a result, he suffered permanent lameness. He enlisted in Alberta and was discharged there. He married and settled in Pennsylvania where he was advertising manager of *Times Leading News*.

MacNaughton, D.

Private MacNaughton's name is inscribed on the war monument in Little Narrows. He served during the war.

MacNeil, Alexander Roderick

'Alex Rory' was born on January 10, 1898, the son of Rory G. and Margaret Anne (MacKinnon) MacNeil, Iona Rear. Sergeant MacNeil served in the 94th Battalion, Canadian Infantry. He married Ella Copps, Ontario. He died in Toronto.

MacNeil, Allan

Allan was the son of Peter S. and Bessie (MacNeil) MacNeil, Gillis Point. Gunner MacNeil served in the 7th Battery, Canadian Field Artillery.

MacNeil, Allan Austin

'Allan A.' was the son of Roderick N. and Mary (MacNeil) MacNeil, Washabuck. Sergeant MacNeil served in the 94th Regiment. He married Sadie MacNeil and they resided in Gillis Point. He died on July 20, 1969, and is buried in St. Columba Cemetery, Iona.

MacNeil, Ambrose

Ambrose was the son of Alex P. and Catherine (MacNeil) MacNeil, Gillis Point. Sergeant MacNeil served in the 94th Regiment. He married Ann MacDougall, Creignish, and they lived in Creignish.

MacNeil, Angus

Angus was the son of Michael and Christy (MacNeil) MacNeil, Iona Rear. Private MacNeil served in the 25th Battalion, Canadian Infantry. He was wounded in action. Unmarried, he was killed in a train accident. He is buried in St. Columba Cemetery, Iona.

MacNeil, Angus J.

'Angus J.' was born in 1867, the son of John and Mary (MacLean) MacNeil, Gillis Point. Captain MacNeil served with the 94th Regiment and the Canadian Garrison Regiment, 6th Battalion. He served as a piper and instructed piping while in the army. He died while in active service on October 7, 1917, a victim of the Spanish influenza. He is buried in St. Columba Cemetery, Iona.

MacNeil, Charles Grant

Grant was born circa 1890, the son of Rev. John and Annie (Drummond) MacNeil, Baddeck Forks.

He was residing in Western Canada at the time of his enlistment. Corporal MacNeil, a machine gunner, was wounded in the trenches somewhere in France.

'The following address was made at the reception in honor of Grant McNeil, a returned wounded soldier, which was held in St. Andrew's Church, Baddeck Forks, on February 25th, 1917:

"Mr. Chairman, Ladies and Gentlemen.

We read fiction with great interest and sometimes with wonder. We trace the ideal characters described. We search for the hero.

But the saying that fact is stronger than fiction is proved to be true to-night, for we have as our guest of honor a real hero. Not one portrayed on paper, but a man with brawn and muscle, who left the comforts and loves of home and went down into the depths of hell to defend us from a tyranny that would overthrow that sacred altar, to defend us from a despotism that would despoil our homes.

Jesus Christ put some backbone in the Christian religion when he said "He that hath no sword let him sell his garment and buy one." He taught the rash Peter that there was a time to sheath the sword, but he also taught him, to draw the sword.

Under the inspiration of these words of Jesus Christ, Garibaldi Italian patriot fought for the liberation of Italy.

Under the inspiration of these words of Jesus Christ, Oliver Cromwell and his Ironsides rose from their knees, to cleanse the English Parliament - to cleanse the English state. And under the inspiration of these same words, the Barons at Runny-mead wrested the Magna Charta, from the tyrant King John. And perhaps there is no more inspiring page in British History than that which gives an account of it. And when afterwards when the Tyrant king recanted, and asked those same Barons "By what right they held their lands and their liberties," and with drawn swords they answered him, "By these we have won them, and by these we hold them."

That Heritage of Freedom which our grand-sires bought with their blood - bought with their lives, has been handed down to us to guard and keep.

It is a sacred trust, and now that a monstrous modern tyrant is trying to deprive us of them, our brave boys under the inspiration of these words of Jesus Christ are answering him on the battle field of France.

"By these we will hold them."

We came here to honor Grant McNeil and now we must confess we envy him, envy him for the wounds he received while battling for civilization, for Righteousness, for God."

From 1918 to 1925, Grant MacNeil served as the national secretary-treasurer of the Great War Veterans Association which sought to further the cause of ex-servicemen and their dependents. This organization later merged to become the Canadian Legion. He was elected as the C.C.F. member in 1935 from North Vancouver to the House of Commons. He later became the C.C.F. Dominion organizer.

MacNeil, Daniel Allan 878338

'Dan A.' was born on January 10, 1891, the son of Hector P. and Annie (MacNeil) MacNeil, Baddeck. Lance Corporal MacNeil served overseas with the 185th Canadian Infantry, Battalion # 2 Platoon. He was wounded in action. He married Mary MacKinnon, Barrachois. He lived in Washington, U.S.A., where he worked for the Beinn Bhreagh Bell families.

MacNeil, Daniel G.

'Dan G.' was the son of Neil and Annie (MacNeil) MacNeil, MacNeil's Vale. Sergeant MacNeil served in the 94th Regiment. He married Mary MacNeil. He is buried in St. Columba Cemetery, Iona.

MacNeil, Daniel J.

'Dan J.' was born on April 26, 1889, the son of John Hector and Margaret (MacNeil) MacNeil, MacNeil's Vale. Sergeant MacNeil served in the 94th Regiment. He married and resided in the United States.

MacNeil, Daniel J.D. 3188342

'Danny John D.' was the son of John D. and Mary Ann (MacNeil) MacNeil, Gillis Point/Grass Cove. Private MacNeil served in the 1st Depot Battalion, Canadian Machine Gun Corps. He married Marion Edith Peterson, Detriot. He died on December 18, 1973, and is buried in St. Columba Cemetery, Iona.

MacNeil, Daniel Joseph 877156

'Dan J.' was born the son of Jonathan and Margaret (Campbell) MacNeil, MacNeil's Vale. Private Dan J. served in the 94th Regiment. He married Mary MacLean.

MacNeil, Daniel Joseph 878156

'Dan Joe' was born on April 26, 1890, the son of Francis X.H. and Mary (MacNeil) MacNeil, Iona. Corporal MacNeil served overseas in the 185th Battalion, Canadian Infantry. He was one of five MacNeil brothers to serve their country. He married Catherine MacNeil, Iona. He died on May 13, 1931.

MacNeil, Daniel Roderick

'Dan Rory' was born on January 5, 1894, the son of Daniel and Mary (Beaton) MacNeil, Iona. Private MacNeil served in the Royal Canadian Regiment, Canadian Infantry. He was wounded twice. He married in England and remained there after the war.

MacNeil, Gordon Michael, M.C.

Gordon was born on January 6, 1892, the son of Captain John P. (section foreman of the C.G.R., Iona) and Mary (MacDonald) MacNeil, Iona. From *The Chronicle*, Halifax, December 1918:

"He is the only one of the original officers who left Halifax on May 20th, 1915 with the 25th Nova Scotia Battalion who is still with the famous fighting battalion of which all Nova Scotia is proud. Lieut. MacNeil has been with the 25th through its whole campaign and at the last report was in Germany with its battalion. To him fell the honor of carrying the battalion colors into Germany at 10:05 am on December 5th. He writes that the pipe band played 'A Highland Soldier' coming up to the frontier, and when we were crossing they played 'The Bonnie Blue Bonnets Are Over the Border.'"

Lieutenant MacNeil served in the 25th Battalion Canadian Infantry. He was twice wounded. He was awarded the **MILITARY CROSS**

" .. for marked gallantry and good work during an attack on the enemy outpost line southeast of Inchy-en-Artois on the night of 23rd - 24th September and during the 25th September, 1918. He was in command of a company ordered to establish a post in the enemy outpost line. The post was entered, all the enemy killed, and a machine gun captured, without a casualty. By skillful consolidation this post was held against seven counter-attacks during thirty-six hours. He personally killed several of the enemy."

When World War II broke out, he went overseas again as second in command of the Cape Breton Highlanders.

He married Annie Laurie MacNeil, Mabou. A generation later their son, Gordon MacNeil (World War II), was the recipient of the **MILITARY CROSS**. Lieutenant MacNeil died on January 9, 1954, at sixty-two years of age and is buried in St. Columba Cemetery, Iona.

MacNeil, Hector 715532

Hector was the son of John Hector and Margaret (MacNeil) MacNeil, MacNeil's Vale. Private MacNeil served in the 106th Battalion Canadian Infantry. A bullet or shrapnel penetrated and lodged in the prayer book which he kept in his breast pocket, thereby saving his life. He married Annabel Chisholm, Antigonish.

MacNeil, Hector

Hector was born on November 15, 1895, the son of Francis X.H. and Mary (MacNeil) MacNeil, Iona. Private MacNeil served in the Royal Canadian Regiment, Canadian Infantry. He married Mary Anne MacMullin. He died on July 20, 1967.

MacNeil, Hugh Daniel

Hugh Dan was born on January 24, 1895, the son of Neil H. and Mary (Nash) MacNeil, Barra Glen. Private MacNeil served in the 1st Depot Battalion in Canada, United Kingdom, France and Belgium. He died in Detroit, Michigan.

MacNeil, J.W. 878155

'J.W.' MacNeil hailed from Gillis Point. Private MacNeil served overseas with the 185th Battalion.

MacNeil, James

James MacNeil is on the nominal enlistment roll for the parish of Iona. Private MacNeil served in the 94th Regiment.

MacNeil, James C.

'James C.' was born on January 13, 1865, the son of John and Mary (MacLean) MacNeil, Gillis Point. Sergeant MacNeil served in the 94th Regiment. He married Jane Campbell. He is buried in St. Columba Cemetery, Iona.

MacNeil, James Hugh

'James H.' was born on December 5, 1890, the son of Stephen A. and Catherine (MacNeil) MacNeil, Grass Cove. Sergeant MacNeil served in the 94th Regiment and the 85th Battalion in Canada.

He married Elizabeth MacLean, Middle Cape. His name is on the honour roll of St. Francis Xavier University, Antigonish. He was the chief accountant for The Dominion Steel Company in Nova Scotia, New Brunswick and Newfoundland. He died in August, 1956, and is buried in Holy Cross Cemetery, Sydney.

MacNeil, James J.D.

'Jimmy John D.' was the son of John D. and Mary Anne (MacNeil) MacNeil, Grass Cove. Sergeant MacNeil served in the 94th Regiment. He married Lucy MacNeil, Gillis Point and they resided in Grass Cove. They are grandparents of members of the musical groups The Barra MacNeils and Slàinte Mhath.

MacNeil, James S.

'James S.' was born in 1889, the son of Alexander J. and Annie (MacLean) MacNeil, St. Margaret's Village. Sailor MacNeil served in the Merchant Navy aboard the HMCS *Niobe*. He is buried in St. Margaret's Village Cemetery.

MacNeil, John A.

'John A.' was the son of Captain John P. and Mary Catherine (MacDonald) MacNeil, Iona. He served with the 94th Regiment during World War I. Private MacNeil served with the West Nova Scotia Regiment in Canada, the United Kingdom, Italy and Northwest Europe during World War II. He married Margaret Burns. They resided in Toronto where he was an accountant with the firm of H.W. Bacon Ltd. He died in Sunnybrook Hospital in August 1967 and is buried in St. Columba Cemetery, Iona.

MacNeil, John A. J.

'John A.J.' was born in 1870, the son of John and Annie (MacKinnon) MacNeil, Barra Glen. Private MacNeil served with the 94th Regiment. He married Mary MacNeil, Benacadie. He died in 1956 and is buried in St. Columba Cemetery, Iona.

MacNeil, John Alexander

John Alexander was born in 1888, the son of Michael and Bessie (MacNeil) MacNeil, Gillis Point. Sergeant MacNeil served with the 94th Regiment. He was an accomplished fiddler. Unmarried, he died on December 19, 1957 and is buried in St. Columba Cemetery, Iona.

MacNeil, John Allan 67870

John Allan was the son of Michael N. and Christy (MacNeil) MacNeil, Iona Rear. Private MacNeil served in Canada, United Kingdom and Northwest Europe. He sailed for Britain on the *Saxonia* on May 20, 1915 and arrived nine days later. He served with the 25th Battalion. He was taken on strength with the 3rd Canadian Tunnelling Company on November 17, 1915. Twenty-seven year old Private MacNeil was killed in action in Fresnoy on April 28, 1917. His name is inscribed on the Vimy Memorial, France. He was survived by his young widow, née Veronica Farmer.

MacNeil, John Allan

John Allan was born in 1893, the son of Michael and Bessie (MacNeil) MacNeil, Gillis Point. Private MacNeil served in the 94th Regiment. Unmarried, he died on December 29, 1950, and is buried in St. Columba Cemetery, Iona.

MacNeil, John C.

'John C.' was the son of Malcolm and Mary Ann (MacNeil) MacNeil, Gillis Point. He was adopted by his uncle and aunt, Alex S. and Anastasia MacNeil. Sergeant MacNeil served in the 94th Regiment. He married in Boston.

MacNeil, John D.

'J.D.' was the son of Donald and Katie (MacKinnon) MacNeil, MacKinnon's Harbour. Prior to the First Great War, he served in the South African War. Captain MacNeil was wounded twice during the First Great War and returned home having lost his left leg. This is believed to have happened while he was serving with the 25th Battalion during the capture of Courcellette on September 15, 1916.

He was affectionately known as 'South African Jack'. He was predeceased by his first wife. His second wife was Mary MacNeil. He died in July, 1957 and was buried with full military honours in Christmas Island.

MacNeil, John Daniel 222432

'John D.' was born on January 25, 1894, the son of Hector P. and Annie (MacNeil) MacNeil, Baddeck.

Corporal John D. MacNeil served overseas with the 85th Battalion Canadian Infantry. Sergeant MacNeil was awarded the **MILITARY MEDAL** " ... for conspicuous gallantry in action on Passchendaele Ridge between 28 and 30th October, 1917. While in support trenches he rushed out under heavy shell fire, dressing and carrying in wounded. Later during the advance, when his platoon commander became a casualty, he rallied his platoon, led them gallantly forward, capturing a strong point and going on to the objective, where he used excellent judgment and skill in re-organizing, consolidating and arranging the posts." Authority - Veteran Affairs, Honors and Awards: *London Gazette* # 30573 - March 13, 1918.

He married Freda Casey, Glace Bay. They resided in Baddeck where he served as collector of customs for many years. He died in 1966 and is buried in St. Michael's Cemetery, Baddeck.

MacNeil, John Hector

John Hector was the son of Dan S. and Katie (MacDonald) MacNeil, MacNeil's Vale. Sergeant MacNeil served with the 7th Canadian Siege Battery. He served in Canada, the United Kingdom and France, and was at Vimy on Easter Monday, 1917. He was wounded during the war. He again served during World War II with the Cape Breton Highlanders. He married Mary Francis MacNeil, Iona. He was a manager of a Nova Scotia Liquor Store in Dartmouth.

MacNeil, John Hugh

'John H.' was the son of Rory and Elizabeth (MacNeil) MacNeil, Gillis Point. Private MacNeil served in the 1st Depot Battalion and other battalions in Canada, United Kingdom and Northwest Europe. He is buried in St. Columba Cemetery, Iona.

MacNeil, John J.

'John J.' was the son of Jonathan and Margaret (Campbell) MacNeil, MacNeil's Vale. Private MacNeil served with the 85th Battalion, Canadian Infantry. He is buried in St. Columba Cemetery, Iona.

MacNeil, John James

John James was the son of John A.J. and Mary MacNeil, Barra Glen. Private MacNeil served in the 94th Regiment.

MacNeil, John M. 877623

'John M.' was born on November 25, 1894, the son of Peter S. and Bessie (MacNeil) MacNeil, Gillis Point. Lance Corporal MacNeil served in the 185th Battalion, Canadian Infantry. He was wounded in action.

MacNeil, John M.

'John M.' MacNeil hailed from Iona. Gunner MacNeil served in the 36th Battery Canadian Field Artillery. He was wounded in action.

MacNeil, John M.

'John M.' was the son of Roderick and Elizabeth (MacDonald) MacNeil, St. Columba. Corporal MacNeil served in the 94th Regiment. He married Tena Deveaux, Washabuck. He is buried in St. Columba Cemetery, Iona.

MacNeil, John Malcolm 878427

John Malcolm was born on June 7, 1897, the son of Francis X.H. and Mary (MacNeil) MacNeil, Iona. Private MacNeil served in the 185th, 85th and 73rd Battalions in Canada, the United Kingdom and France. He served from October 5, 1916, to July 10, 1919. He was wounded at Vimy on May 26, 1917. He served with the Veterans Guard of Canada from January, 1941, to July, 1942, during the Second World War. He was one of five brothers who served during World War I. He married Elizabeth MacNeil. They resided in New Waterford where he worked in the coal mines.

MacNeil, John Michael

'John M.' was the son of Michael and Jane (MacNeil) MacNeil, Iona Rear. Private MacNeil served in the 94th Regiment. He married Christy MacDonald, Ottawa Brook. He is buried in St. Columba Cemetery, Iona.

MacNeil, John Murdoch 67630

Murdoch was born on April 26, 1895, the son of John and Catherine (MacNeil) MacNeil. He was born in Boston and raised by his grandparents, Michael Eoin and Lucy MacNeil, Washabuck Centre.

The following is an undated exerpt from a local newspaper:

He commenced military life in North Sydney in the old Cape Breton Regiment - the 94th. In the fall of 1914, he left with the first batch for overseas and served with the 25th Battalion Canadian Infantry. Twenty-one year old Private MacNeil boldly left the ranks during a deadly hail of fire and shrapnel from the enemies' guns and rescued a wounded officer of his company who had fallen on the field of battle. It was a feat that none but a brave son of the good old Highland stock would attempt. Not only did he reach the side of his fallen superior in safety, but MacNeil cooly proceeded to render what aid possible to alleviate the officer's suffering before he started to carry the latter to the rear. During all this, the Cape Bretoner remained perfectly cool and succeeded in conveying his charge to a place of safety at the rear. It was admittedly one of the bravest feats so far recorded and was promptly recognized by Headquarters when MacNeil was recommended for the **VICTORIA CROSS**. (undated).

However, the **VICTORIA CROSS** was never awarded to him.

He had been a student in St. Francis Xavier College, Antigonish - " .. one of its brightest scholars and best athletics whoever left the Cathedral Town".

Private MacNeil was killed in the second battle of Ypres on June 10, 1916. His name is inscribed on the Menin Gate Memorial, Belgium.

MacNeil, John Neil

'John N.' was born circa 1896, the son of Rev. John and Annie (Drummond) MacNeil, Baddeck Forks. Twice he enlisted in the Canadian Expeditionary Force. First he enlisted with the 85th Nova Scotia Highlanders from which he was invalided home. He then enlisted in the 8th Siege Battery Canadian Garrison Artillery where he served in France and Flanders.

Despite his studies being interrupted, he graduated from Dalhousie University in 1922 with a Master of Arts degree. Later he graduated from Springfield College, USA, with a degree in Physical Education. He became a teacher of mathematics and physical education. For two years he taught at the Presbyterian Church mission school in British Guiana.

In 1940, he served as a Lieutenant in the 2nd Battalion, Cameron Highlanders, Ottawa. He felt that it was his duty to make his teaching experience available to younger comrades. While on staff at the Ottawa Glebe Collegiate School, he took a leave of absence to join the overseas educational staff of the Canadian Legion War Services. En route overseas, aboard the *Nerissa*, John N. MacNeil was among the 122 passengers who were reported missing "as a result of enemy action." The *Nerissa* was fifty-five miles off the coast of Ireland when he was lost at sea on May 7, 1941. He was survived by his widow and three young children.

MacNeil, John Neil

John Neil was born on August 26, 1894, the son of James and Annie (MacNeil) MacNeil, Gillis Point. Private MacNeil served in the 94th Regiment in Canada. He married Genevieve MacNeil, Iona. He is buried in St. Columba Cemetery, Iona.

MacNeil, John Neil 878146

John Neil was the son of Hector and Mary (MacDonald) MacNeil, Gillis Point East. Private MacNeil served in the 185th and the 119th Battalions, Canadian Machine Gun Corps. He is buried in St. Columba Cemetery, Iona.

MacNeil, Joseph R.

'Joseph R.' was born on May 26, 1894, the son of Michael D. and Mary Jane (Cash) MacNeil, Iona. Private MacNeil served with the 94th Regiment in Canada. He married twice. He died on March 16, 1972, and is buried in St. Columba Cemetery, Iona.

MacNeil, Leo 877274

Leo was born on June 27, 1895, the son of Dan S. and Katie Ann (MacDonald) MacNeil, MacNeil's Vale. Private MacNeil served in the 185th Battalion Canadian Infantry. Twenty-one year old MacNeil was killed in action while serving with the 73rd Battalion on February 25, 1917. He is buried in Villers Station Cemetery, Villers-au-Bois, France.

MacNeil, Malcolm

Malcolm was born on September 5, 1883, the son of Angus and Sarah (MacNeil) MacNeil, Iona Rear. Private MacNeil served with the 94th Regiment in Canada. He married Mary Lizzie MacLean, Gillis Point. He is buried in St. Columba Cemetery, Iona.

MacNeil, Malcolm J.

'Malcolm J.' was born on January 5, 1895, the son of John J. and Margaret (MacNeil) MacNeil, Iona. Corporal MacNeil served with the 94th Regiment. He is buried in St. Columba Cemetery, Iona.

MacNeil, Michael 877522

Michael was born on February 10, 1897, the son of Francis X.H. and Mary (MacNeil) MacNeil, Iona. Private MacNeil served in the 185th Battalion Canadian Infantry. He died on December 14, 1926, as a result of a mining accident in New Waterford.

MacNeil, Michael Ambrose

Michael was the son of Rory and Elizabeth (MacNeil) MacNeil, Gillis Point. Private MacNeil served in the 94th and 85th Battalions. He was wounded in action. He married Flora MacInnis and they resided in Industrial Cape Breton.

MacNeil, Michael Daniel F55069

Michael Dan was the son of Murdoch and Mary (MacNeil) MacNeil, Jamesville. He served during both World Wars. He served with the 94th Regiment during World War I. He served with the Cape Breton Highlanders during World War II (F55069). He married Helen MacNeil, Point Tupper. He and his wife resided in Jamesville. He died on February 19, 1976, and is buried in St. Columba Cemetery.

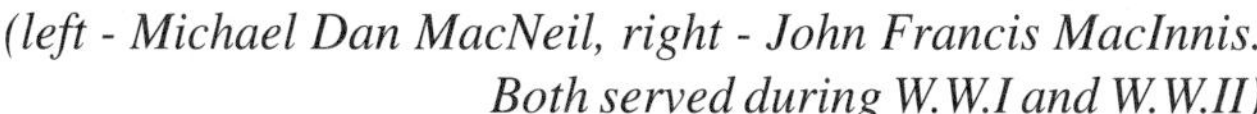

(left - Michael Dan MacNeil, right - John Francis MacInnis. Both served during W.W.I and W.W.II)

MacNeil, Michael J.

Michael was the son of Peter and Mary (MacNeil) MacNeil, Gillis Point. Private MacNeil served in the 94th Regiment. He married and resided in the United States.

MacNeil, Murdoch

Murdoch was born on May 8, 1884, the son of Francis X.H. and Mary (MacNeil) MacNeil, Iona. Private MacNeil served in the 94th Regiment. He married Theresa Corrigan. He died on April 19, 1958.

MacNeil, Murdock A. 67623

Murdock was born in 1886, the son of Alex P. and Catherine (MacNeil) MacNeil, Gillis Point East. He served in both World Wars. He enlisted on November 26, 1914, in Halifax. Sergeant MacNeil served in the 25th Battalion Canadian Infantry in Canada, the United Kingdom and Northwest Europe. He was wounded three times. He served during World War II with the Cape Breton Highlanders in Canada and the United Kingdom. He is buried in St. Columba Cemetery, Iona.

MacNeil, Murdoch Allan 466527

Murdoch was born on June 2, 1893, the son of Malcolm and Jessie (MacKenzie) MacNeil, New Harris. Private MacNeil was killed in action on September 24, 1916, while serving with the 13th Battalion. His name is inscribed on the Vimy Memorial, France.

(standing - Murdoch A. MacNeil)

MacNeil, Neil A.

'Neil A.' was the son of Allan and Mary (MacNeil) MacNeil, Gillis Point. Sergeant MacNeil served in the 94th Regiment.

MacNeil, Neil Ambrose 222414

'Neil A.' was born on October 16, 1900, the son of Phillip B. and Lizzie MacNeil in Baddeck. Private N.A. MacNeil served overseas with the 85th Battalion, No. 14 Platoon. He was reported missing in action on October 10, 1918, and his name is inscribed on the Vimy Memorial, France.

MacNeil, Neil Archie

'Neil A.' was the son of Roderick and Elizabeth (MacDonald) MacNeil, St. Columba. Sergeant MacNeil served in the 94th Regiment in Canada. He was tragically killed while felling a tree. He is buried in St. Columba Cemetery, Iona.

MacNeil, Neil F.

'Neil F.' was born on February 6, 1891, the son of John A. and Catherine MacNeil. He was raised by his grandparents, Michael Eoin and Lucy MacNeil, Washabuck Centre.

Sergeant Major MacNeil served in the United States Army in charge of the trade test centre at Fort Dix. Neil MacNeil (Jr.) related an amusing story about his father. A United States government agent arrived at the *New York Times* office seeking Neil F. MacNeil indicating that they were searching everywhere for him. A staff member asked, "Have you looked in the army?" MacNeil had been born in Boston and registered there. Since he was working in New York, he re-enlisted there which explains why he was being sought as a draft dodger in Boston.

He was a graduate of St. Francis Xavier University and honoured by his alma mater in Antigonish with the degree LL.D. Honoris Causa. He married Elizabeth Quinn and resided in the United States. He served on the executive of the *New York Times* for thirty-three years and was night editor of that newspaper at the time of his death. He was the author of the delightful book about the Scottish community of Washabuck entitled *The Highland Heart in Nova Scotia*. He died on December 30, 1969, and is buried in South Hampton, New York.

MacNeil, Neil J.

'Neil J.' was the son of Michael D. and Catherine (MacNeil) MacNeil, Ottawa Brook. Private MacNeil served with the 1st Battalion in Canada, the United Kingdom and France. He married Margaret MacPhee.

MacNeil, Neil J.

'Neil J.' was born on December 6, 1890, the son of Peter S. and Bessie (MacNeil) MacNeil, Gillis Point. Private MacNeil served with the 94th Regiment.

MacNeil, Neil John

'Neil J.' was born on May 24, 1890, the son of Michael and Mary (MacNeil) MacNeil, Barra Glen. Private MacNeil served with the 94th Regiment in Canada. He resided in Sydney. Unmarried, he died there.

MacNeil, Neil Laughlin 222446

Neil Lauchie was the son of James and Bridleben (MacLean) MacNeil, MacAulay's, Upper Baddeck. He enlisted on October 19, 1915, in Halifax. Private MacNeil served overseas with the 85th Battalion, No. 14 Platoon.

MacNeil, Neil M.

'Neil M.' was the son of Michael and Jane (MacNeil) MacNeil, Iona Rear. Private MacNeil served with the 94th Regiment. He married Christy MacLean, Rear Christmas Island. He is buried in St. Columba Cemetery, Iona.

MacNeil, Roderick 715356

Rory was born on April 9, 1891, the son of Francis X.S. and Christy (MacDougall) MacNeil, Iona. Sergeant MacNeil served with the 106th Battalion Canadian Infantry. He was wounded in action. He married Mary MacNeil, Barra Glen. He is buried in St. Columba Cemetery, Iona.

MacNeil, Roderick F.

'Roddie M.D.' was born on June 19, 1899, the son of Michael D. and Mary Jane (Cash) MacNeil, Iona. He served in both World Wars. Private MacNeil served with the 94th Regiment. He served with the Royal Canadian Engineers during World War II. He married Margaret MacNeil, Ottawa Brook. He is buried in St. Columba Cemetery, Iona.

MacNeil, Roderick J. 469699

'Rod J.' hailed from Iona. Elizabeth MacNeil was listed as his next of kin. Private MacNeil was taken on strength with the 64th Battalion on September 1, 1915, in Sydney.

MacNeil, Stephen

Stephen MacNeil hailed from Iona. Private MacNeil served with the 85th Battalion, Canadian Infantry.

MacNeil, W.A. 877522

'W.A.' MacNeil hailed from Iona. Lance Corporal MacNeil served overseas with the 185th Battalion.

MacPhail, John Lauchlin 2700808

Jack was born on March 26, 1899, the son of Donald and Mary (Robinson) MacPhail, Nyanza.He enlisted in the Canadian Army in 1917 and went overseas in 1918, but he was returned during the crossing as word was received that the war had ended. During the Second World War he served as a Police Guard on the Ottawa Brook trestle.

He married Katie MacLean, Big Baddeck. He joined the Corps of Commissioners at Point Edward Naval Base and worked there until his retirement in 1964. He died on July 5, 1966, and is buried in St. Patrick's Channel Cemetery.

MacPhee, William 222417

William served overseas with the 85th Battalion # 13 Platoon. Private MacPhee's place of birth is listed as Baddeck. It is believed that he hailed from Big Baddeck.

MacPherson, Rev. Angus Gordon

Gordon was born on April 14, 1891, the son of Murdoch and Christy (MacLean) MacPherson, Bay St. Lawrence.

He enlisted in 1914 and served overseas. A 1918 newspaper article reveals that he was convalescing at a friend's home in Scotland. He was discharged in 1919. He resumed his studies upon returning to Canada. After forty years in the ministry in British Columbia and Ontario, he returned to Toronto in 1962. Rev. MacPherson received an honorary Doctor of Divinity Degree from the Presbyterian College, Montreal.

MacPherson, Charles

'Charlie Calum' was born on April 5, 1893, the adopted son of Malcolm and Julia MacPherson, South Harbour. He served in both World Wars. Private MacPherson served from 1916 to 1918 with the Royal Canadian Artillery. He served in the Veterans Guard of Canada from 1942 to 1945.

He married Mary Rambeau, Smelt Brook. He died on January 11, 1971, and is buried in Dingwall Cemetery.

MacPherson, Daniel

Danny was born on July 23, 1890, the son of Johnny and Mary (Gwynn) MacPherson, South Harbour. Private MacPherson served overseas during the war. He was killed accidentally when he fell climbing to the upper deck of a gypsum boat in Dingwall. He is buried in MacPherson Cemetery, Dingwall.

MacPherson, Donald J. 222419

Private MacPherson, Baddeck, served overseas with the 85th Battalion, No. 14 Platoon. He married Florence (J.P.) MacLeod, Baddeck.

MacPherson, John Harold 3188692

Harold was born on September 21, 1897, the son of David W. and Jessie (Morrison) MacPherson, Dingwall. Private MacPherson served with the # 1 Depot Battalion, N.S. Regiment. His date of attestation was June 11, 1918. He was discharged on September 12, 1918, for harvest leave for disposal on demobilization.'

Twenty-one year old MacPherson's pay schedule:

Daily rate of pay		$1.00
Field allowance		.10.
	30 x	$1.10 = $33/month
Deduct stoppages =		$15
Net Rate - 30 days =		$18

Paymaster E. Ferrish - Aldershot, NS

He farmed and worked at the National Gypsum Company in Dingwall. Unmarried, he died on May 30, 1992, and is buried in MacPherson Cemetery, Dingwall.

MacPherson, William

William was the son of Murdoch and Christine (MacLean) MacPherson, Bay St. Lawrence. He served during the war. He is buried in MacIntosh Cemetery, Bay St. Lawrence.

MacQuarrie, Daniel Ernest 222434

Dan was born on March 1, 1890, the son of Malcolm and Elizabeth (Finlayson) MacQuarrie, Upper Middle River. In 1907, Private MacQuarrie joined the militia and attended drill camp at Aldershot. He continued for six or seven years. The old Ross rifles that they used for drill exercises went overseas with the soldiers! He enlisted in August, 1914, and served with the 85th Battalion. He disembarked from Halifax aboard the *Olympic* and arrived in Liverpool five days later. He is featured in the *Cape Breton*

Magazine # 33. Here he gave a detailed account of the horrors and hardships endured on the battlefields and trenches in Belgium and France. Corporal MacQuarrie was discharged on demobilization in 1919. He served on guard duty during World War II.

He married Belle Carmichael, Margaree. They resided in Middle River. He died on January 12, 1988, and is buried in Middle River Cemetery.

(Dan E. MacQuarrie and his wife, Isabel)

MacQuarrie, Laughlin A.

Laughie was born on August 15, 1896, the son of Donald and Jessie (MacDonald) MacQuarrie, Middle River. He served in Canada with the home guard during the war. Laughie married Ruth MacDonald. They resided in Middle River. He worked with the Department of Highways. He died in July, 1989, and is buried in Middle River Cemetery.

MacQuarrie, Malcolm William 68274

Malcolm was born on February 13, 1885, the son of Malcolm and Elizabeth (Finlayson) MacQuarrie, Middle River. Private MacQuarrie enlisted on March 25, 1915, and served with the 25th Battalion, Canadian Expeditionary Force. Lance Corporal MacQuarrie was killed in action at the Battle of the Somme on October 1, 1916. His name is inscribed on the Vimy Memorial, France.

MacQueen, Alexander

Alexander was born on March 18, 1875, the son of Kenneth and Christy (Morrison) MacQueen, Wreck Cove.

He moved to Glace Bay in his youth and worked in the coal mines. He left the mines to serve in the 94th Regiment, Militia Unit. During the war he was stationed to guard duty in Louisbourg. He returned to the collieries, but he also operated a shoe repair business in New Waterford. He married Mary MacLeod, Indian Brook. Their twenty-three year old son, Pilot Officer Frederick MacQueen, was killed during night flight manoeuvers over England in 1943. He died in Glace Bay at eighty-four years of age.

MacQueen, Alexander Roderick, M.M. and Bar 427640

Rod was born on January 8, 1892, the son of Alexander and Christy (MacDonald) MacQueen, Plaister Mines. Lance Corporal MacQueen served overseas with the Manitoba Regiment. He was decorated for bravery under fire while serving as a stretcher bearer with the 52nd Battalion. He was awarded the **MILITARY MEDAL** on November 13, 1918, and **THE BAR** on March 13, 1919. Source - *London Gazette*.

His first wife was Georgina MacLeod, Big Hill. His second wife was Mae Kennedy, Florence. They resided in Massachusetts. He died on June 4, 1987, and was buried in Boston.

MacQueen, John

Jack was born on March 8, 1899, the son of Alexander and Christy (MacDonald) MacQueen, Plaister Mines. He served during the war. He married Laura MacKay, Englishtown. They resided in Stoneham, Massachusetts. He died on October 14, 1988.

MacRae, Alexander David

'Sandy Bentick' was born on May 6, 1868, the son of John and Willena (Ross) MacRae, Baddeck Bridge. He served as an instructor of recruits at Aldershot during the war from 1914 to 1918.

Lieutenant Colonel A.D. MacRae married Annie MacDonald, Hunter's Mountain. He died on August 5, 1950, and is buried in St. Andrew's Cemetery, Baddeck Forks.

MacRae, Alexander Donald

Donald was born on March 18, 1870, the son of Alexander and Margaret (MacKay) MacRae, Baddeck Bridge. He served as a major with the 94th Highlanders, Baddeck. On November 23, 1914, he joined the 25th Nova Scotia Battalion, 2nd Division Attached. He was wounded at Kemmell on October 8, 1915. In 1916 he served with the 17th Nova Scotia Reserve Battalion, East Sandling. He was invalided home from overseas after shell shock in May, 1916. He was placed on strength of Canadian Training Division and added to general list of officers. Lieutenant-Colonel MacRae was director of S & T; and an officer in charge of demobilization for Nova Scotia and Prince Edward Island.

Donald married Emma Payne. Her father was an engineer on the lake boat *The Blue Hill*. He and his wife moved to California. He died on February 10, 1931. His ashes were scattered over the Pacific Ocean.

MacRae, Charles Roderick 2024598

'Charlie Angus' was born on January 27, 1884, the son of Angus and Elizabeth (MacKenzie) MacRae, Big Farm, Baddeck Bridge. Private MacRae enlisted in November, 1917 in British Columbia with 1st Depot Battalion. He served in Canada.

He married Catherine May Morrison, Marion Bridge. For a time they resided in the United States and then returned to Baddeck. He died in December, 1956, and is buried in Greenwood Cemetery.

(seated - Charles R. MacRae)

MacRae, Donald Hugh 3182514

'Donald Sandy' was born on December 15, 1897, the son of Alexander D. and Janice (MacDonald) MacRae, Upper Middle River. He enlisted on April 29, 1918, in Windsor, Nova Scotia. He served with # 1 Depot Battalion, New Brunswick Regiment. Private MacRae served in Canada and he was discharged on demobilization on November 26, 1918.

Prior to war, he was employed as a section man and resided in Glace Bay. He married Ella Austin, Inverness County. He is buried in Edmonton.

MacRae, Edgar Fryer 3188896

Private MacRae, Baddeck, served in Canada with the Nova Scotia Regiment.

MacRae, John Donald

'Johnny Duncan' was born on February 15, 1859, the son of Duncan and Elizabeth (MacKenzie) MacRae, Yankee Line. Colonel J.D. MacRae was a commander with the Cape Breton Highlanders at the outbreak of World War I. He married Mary Johann MacKenzie, Iron Mines. They resided in Nyanza. In 1926, he died in a drowning accident at Ross Ferry. He is buried in Middle River Cemetery.

MacRae, Malcolm M. 68318

Malcolm was born on December 2, 1895, the son of Alexander and Johanna (Kerr) MacRae, North River Bridge. He enlisted on March 31, 1915, in Glace Bay. Private MacRae served overseas in France with the 3rd Canadian Tunnelling Company, Canadian Expeditionary Force. He was wounded on March 13, 1916. He was discharged in Halifax on June 25, 1918. He married Catherine MacLeod, Big Baddeck Centre. They resided in Massachusetts. He is buried in Mount Hope Cemetery, Boston.

MacRae, Murdoch Alexander 2014173

Murdoch was born on January 5, 1895, the son of Alexander (Sandy Gairloch) and Isabella (MacRae) MacRae, Gairloch Mountain. Some members of this family moved to Boularderie. Private MacRae served during the war.

He married Katie Belle MacKenzie, New Harris. They resided in Baddeck. At the time of his death, he was caretaker of the provincial building at Baddeck. He died in April 1950, and is buried in Greenwood Cemetery, Baddeck.

MacRae, Murdoch James 1668485

Murdoch was born on January 31, 1886, the son of Alexander and Johanna (Kerr) MacRae, North River Bridge. Sergeant MacRae (1st Class) served overseas with C Company, 301st Engineers.

He married Annie Morrison, Middle River. They resided in Massachusetts where he was a carpenter. He fell from a scaffolding and was tragically killed in 1936. He is buried in Arlington, Massachusetts.

MacRae, Murdock John 222435

(left - Murdock J. MacRae, right - Roddie MacLean)

'Murdock Farquhar' was born on November 18, 1893, the son of Farquhar and Christy "Buckles" (MacRae) MacRae, Middle River. Sergeant MacRae served in the "D" Company, 85th Overseas Battalion. He was wounded during battle. He was discharged on demobilization on January 27, 1919. He married Jessie MacLennan, Upper Middle River. He farmed in Middle River. He died in 1974 and is buried in Middle River Cemetery.

MacRae, Roland John

Roland was born on March 22, 1898, the son of Farquhar and Christy 'Buckles' (MacRae) MacRae, Middle River. He enlisted on August 4, 1914. Due to his parents' objection, he was discharged on October 30, 1914. Private MacRae was underage.

He married Margaret (Argie) MacRae, Nyanza. They resided in Middle River. Roland was a blacksmith and carpenter. He died in 1968 and is buried in Middle River Cemetery.

MacRae, William Duncan 434816

William was born on June 11, 1885, the son of Hector and Elizabeth (Morrison) MacRae, Plaister Mines. Private MacRae served in the Canadian Infantry, Alberta Regiment. He was taken on strength in Calgary on February 5, 1915 and he sailed overseas with the 50th Battalion. Unmarried, he was killed in action on October 9, 1916, in France. His name is engraved on the Vimy Memorial in France.

MacRae, William George

'Willie G.' was born on June 23, 1881, the son of Alexander and Margaret (MacKay) MacRae, Big Farm Baddeck Bridge. Colonel MacRae served with the "D" Company and was adjutant of the 85th Battalion. He was hospitalized in February, 1916, and underwent an appendectomy. He then remained in Aldershot. However, the adjutant who went overseas as his replacement was killed in action.

Colonel MacRae served as the first president of the Branch # 53, Royal Canadian Legion in Baddeck which was formed in 1937. He also served as secretary-treasurer of the Veteran's Association in the Baddeck area. He was the recipient of the Volunteer's Decoration. Willie G. MacRae married Ann Hart, Baddeck. They resided at Big Farm. He died on May 9, 1943, and is buried in St. Andrew's Cemetery, Baddeck Forks.

MacRitchie, Daniel Matison 2556

Dan was born on March 2, 1888, the son of Norman and Mary (Matheson) MacRitchie, Hazeldale. He had been homesteading in Alberta when he joined there with the Lord Strathcona's Horse. Lance Corporal MacRitchie died of wounds on April 15, 1918. He is buried in St. Sever Cemetery Extension, Rouen, France.

MacRitchie, Donald

Donald was born on June 2, 1881, son of Donald and Catherine (Graham) MacRitchie, Englishtown. He served as a signaler with the 36th Field Howitzer Artillery Battery in France (1915 - 1919). During World War II he served in Halifax in the highly sensitive and exacting position of Chief Telephone Censor.

Renowned cartoonist, Donald MacRitchie is featured in the *Canadian Who's Who 1936 - 1937.* His cartoons and illustrations appeared in numerous provincial and national newspapers. For many years he was the staff artist with the *Halifax Herald* and *The Halifax Mail*.

He married Mary Fraser, Ross Ferry. He died on November 29, 1948 and is buried in Camp Hill Cemetery.

MacRitchie, John Alexander

John was born on April 27, 1877, the son of Kenneth and Christie (Matheson) MacRitchie, Bucklaw. Private MacRitchie served during the war. He died in Phoniex, British Columbia.

MacRitchie, John James M.D.

'J.J.' was born on July 29, 1883, the son of Angus and Catherine (MacKenzie) MacRitchie, Englishtown. He was a 1911 graduate of Dalhousie Medical School, Halifax. Lieutenant MacRitchie served in the Royal Army Medical Corps in Iraq and India and aboard hospital ships out of England.

Dr. MacRitchie practiced medicine in Goldboro, Guysborough County before and after the war. This community honoured him by naming their legion "The MacRitchie Branch, 157 Royal Canadian Legion, Goldboro". He married Jessie Saunders, North Sydney. He died in September, 1960, and is buried in Bayview Cemetery, Englishtown.

Maloney, David Hamilton 301252

David was born on February 18, 1885, the son of Norman and Alice (MacDonald) Maloney, Dingwall. He enlisted with the 36th Battery in Sydney in 1915, and Gunner Maloney served overseas with the 11th Battery in France and Belgium. He served for a time under Major (later) General Crerar. He was hospitalized in Exeter, England after he was gassed in the Passchendaele Battle. Later he went to Northern Russia under General Ironsides of the Imperial Army. He returned to Canada in 1919.

He was a railroader in Nova Scotia from 1906 to 1925 with the exception of the war years. In 1957 he received his fifty year membership emblem of the Brotherhood of Railway Trainmen. He was caretaker of Hume School for twenty-two years. He died in Kootenay, British Columbia. He was survived by his wife, May Munro, and son, Cecil Maloney.

Maloney, Frank

Frank was the son of James and Mary (MacPherson) Maloney, Dingwall. He served during the war. He married and resided in Halifax. In later years he moved to Big Harbour. He is buried in Bras d'Or.

(Left - Frank Maloney, Right - Jack Maloney)

Maloney, John

Jack was the son of James and Mary (MacPherson) Maloney, Dingwall. Private Maloney served during the war. He died on November 27, 1918, and is buried in Aspy Bay Cemetery.

Maloney, John Sheppard

Sheppard was born in 1898, the son of Norman and Alice (MacDonald) Maloney, Dingwall. Private Maloney served during the war. He married Jenny Harvey, Neil's Harbour. He died in 1978 and is buried in Aspy Bay Cemetery.

Maloney, William Henderson 877749

'William H.' was born on December 13, 1888 and hailed from Aspy Bay. He served with the 185th Canadian Infantry Battalion.

Matheson, Alexander Donald Angus 469669

Alexander was born on June 24, 1894, the son of Alexander and Mary Elizabeth (MacLennan) Matheson, Boularderie Centre. Private Matheson was taken on strength with the 64th Battalion on September 1, 1915, in Sydney. He served overseas.

He married Irene Elizabeth Krouse, Chicago. By trade, he was a wood worker and house carpenter. They resided in Chicago and then returned to Liverpool, Nova Scotia. Later they lived in Montreal and London, Ontario.

Matheson, Daniel William

Dan was born on January 10, 1884, the son of Angus and Katherine (Smith) Matheson, Breton Cove. He served overseas. He married Irene Matilda Abrams. They resided in British Columbia. He died on October 16, 1969, and is buried in Valley View Memorial Gardens, New Westminister.

Matheson, Guy McLean, M.C., M.M., D.S.O. 67639

Guy McLean was born on January 18, 1892, the son of Peter and Christine (MacRae) Matheson, Inlet Baddeck. He enlisted on November 27, 1914, in Halifax. He served with the 25th Canadian Infantry Battalion, Canadian Expeditionary Force. He served in Canada, Britain and France. He was awarded the **MILITARY MEDAL**.

" ... During the bombardment of our trenches on January 14th, 1916 this non commissioned officer displayed great coolness. When the Coy-Sgt-Major had been wounded, he took the Sgt-Major's place and dressed three wounded men himself and placed them in comparative safety.

He had constantly been placed in charge of wiring parties in front of our lines owing to his great courage and coolness. His work has been excellent." Authority - *London Gazette* No. 29608 dated 3-6-1916.

He was awarded the **MILITARY CROSS**
" ... for conspicuous gallantry in action. He assumed command of his company and led it with great courage and determination. Later, he assumed command of another company. He showed marked coolness and ability throughout and set a fine example to his men." Authority - *London Gazette* No. 29824 dated 14-11-1916.

He was awarded the **DISTINGUISHED SERVICE ORDER**
" ... for conspicuous gallantry and devotion to duty. This officer led his company in the attack, and later took command of the battalion and skillfully consolidated the position gained. The following day, in directing the advance of the front line, he was severely wounded but continued on duty for twenty-four hours. His courage and coolness set a fine example." Authority - *London Gazette* No. 31043 dated 2-12-1918.

On May 4, 1920, he was appointed Lieutenant Colonel Officer commanding the Cape Breton Highlanders.

Robert the Bruce (mascot goat of the 185th) was given to Lt. Col. Matheson at the end of the war. He brought him to his home in Inlet Baddeck where he died after feasting in the garden which had been sprayed with an insecticide (probably 'Paris Green'). The goat's collar was donated to the Military Museum at the Citadel in Halifax.

Guy McLean Matheson married Flora MacDonald, Middle River. Following the war Lt. Col. Matheson went to the USA and became a business partner with his brother, Sylvester. They operated their business until the outbreak of World War II. Then he worked in a defence factory.

During World War II, he served as a Major in the Rhode Island National Guard which replaced the National Guard when it was activated for overseas duty. Guy McLean Matheson died on January 15, 1981, in Warwick, Rhode Island, USA.

Matheson, James 23412

James was the son of Kenneth and Bena (Morrison) Matheson, Breton Cove. Private Matheson was taken on strength in Valcartier, Quebec on September 18, 1915 and served with the 12th Battalion. His next of kin was listed as Norman Matheson, North Shore, St. Ann's.

Matheson, John

John was born on August 7, 1897, the son of Neil and Catherine (MacLeod) Matheson, Crescent Grove. John Matheson served during the war. His wife, Cora, had been a victim of the Halifax Explosion. This family moved to Massachusetts.

(Left - Bill Turnbull, right - John Matheson)

Matheson, Malcolm Dan

'Red Malcolm' was born on June 1, 1877, the son of Angus Matheson, Jubilee. Private Matheson served with the Royal Canadian Regiment, Canadian Expeditionary Force. For many years he tended the lighthouse in Little Narrows. He died on November 22, 1956, and is buried in Little Narrows Cemetery.

Matheson, Murdoch Alexander

Murdoch was born on January 9, 1893, the son of Alexander and Mary Elizabeth (MacLennan) Matheson, Boularderie Centre. He was a member of the first group of Canadian soldiers to serve overseas and he returned unwounded.

He married Elizabeth (Bessie) Farrell. They resided in Winnipeg where he was employed with a wholesale grocery company.

Matheson, Neil M.

Neil was born on September 15, 1887, the son of Angus and Katherine (Smith) Matheson, Breton Cove. He served overseas as a mechanic in the Royal Flying Corps. He married Violet Stead and they resided in New Westminister, British Columbia. He was employed as a fireman for thirty-three years and before he retired, he had been New Westminister's fire chief. He died on January 27, 1976.

Matheson, Norman Donald

Norman was born on February 9, 1876, the son of John ad Ann (Matheson) Matheson, Little Narrows. Private Matheson served overseas as a ferrier during the war. He married Louise Watson, Sydney. They resided in Sydney where he was a railroad engineer. He was scalded to death on April 8, 1927, when a steam engine overturned near Bathurst, New Brunswick. He is buried in Sydney, Nova Scotia.

Matheson, Wilfred Laurier 415711

Wilfred was born on July 4, 1896, the son of Alexander and Mary Elizabeth (MacLennan) Matheson, Boularderie Centre. Private Matheson was taken on strength with the 40th Battalion on August 9, 1915, in Sydney. He married Minnie Lurge, Chicago, and they resided in the Northeast United States. He and his wife were an exceptional team and the driving force behind the International Ladies' Garment Workers Union in Chicago. They were featured in a *Reader's Digest* article. He was a journalist for a unionist newspaper and was involved with amateur theatre. They were instrumental in the development of one of the first federal disaster relief plans and the formation of Wilkes College and union health plans. He died in Kingston, Pennsylvania.

Morrison, Allan D. 437099

Allan was born on December 14, 1870, the son of A.B. and Isabella (MacAulay) Morrison, Englishtown. Private Morrison enlisted on May 6, 1915 in Edmonton, Alberta. He was taken on strength with the 51st Battalion and served with the overseas troops of the 14th Battalion. Private Morrison was killed in action in France on January 17, 1917. He is buried in Boulogne Eastern Cemetery.

Morrison, Angus 222571

'Angus Aulay' was born on May 15, 1897, the son of Aulay G. and Annie Isabella (Morrison) Morrison, South Gut. He served with the 85th Battalion, No. 15 Platoon. Private Morrison was killed in action on April 28, 1917. He is buried in La Chaudiere Military Cemetery, Vimy, France.

Morrison, Charles William

Charlie was born on March 20, 1890, the son of John and Catherine (MacDonald) Morrison, Baddeck Bay. When war was declared, he was residing in Winnipeg and he enlisted there. He served overseas. He married Alice Rayner. They resided in Winnipeg. He worked for many years with the City of Winnipeg Fire Department. He died in February, 1973, and is buried in Winnipeg.

Morrison, Dan John 222394

'D.J.' was born on August 24, 1888, the son of widow Annie Morrison, New Campbellton. He enlisted on August 25, 1915, in Halifax. He joined the 85th Battalion, Canadian Expeditionary Force and served in Canada, Britain and France. While serving with the 85th Battalion, Private Morrison was killed in action on August 23, 1917. He is buried in La Chaudiere Military Cemetery, Vimy, France. His family ran the New Campbellton post office and telegraph office. His sister, Matilda Morrison, was the last postmistress in New Campbellton.

Morrison, Ernest

Ernest was a nephew to Donald (Short) Morrison, Gairloch Mountain. Private Morrison served during the war. He was discharged due to illness and died in Sydney in 1917.

Morrison, John

John Morrison served with the 94th Regiment. Private Morrison drowned on October 4, 1916, and is buried in Greenwood Cemetery, Baddeck.

Morrison, John Alexander

(Brothers John Alex Morrison - left, and Thomas Morrison - right)

John Alex was born on November 25, 1892, the son of Donald and Catherine (MacLeod) Morrison, North River Bridge. He served overseas. He married Catherine MacLean, Estmere. They lived in Mattapan, Massachusetts.

Morrison, John Angus 878337

John Angus was born on September 22, 1880, the son of Roderick Morrison, Baddeck.

He served overseas with the 185th Canadian Infantry Battalion. He was killed in action in England on April 2, 1916. Private Morrison was buried in Buckingham Cliveden War Cemetery, Taplow, Eton. Private Morrison was survived by his widow, Bessie Jane Campbell Morrison, and three daughters. In civilian life he had been a seaman.

Morrison, John Kenneth

Kenneth was born on October 11, 1895, the son of Kenneth and Annie (Morrison) Morrison, Wreck Cove. He served during the war. He married Katie Morrison, Quarry, St. Ann's. He died in Boston and is buried in Hillcrest Cemetery, Wreck Cove.

Morrison, John M. William 415050

John was born on June 7, 1891, the son of widow Annie Morrison, Baddeck. Private Morrison was taken on strength with the 40th Battalion on March 26, 1915, in Sydney.

Morrison, John Roderick

'John Rory' was the son of Donald and Katie (MacNeil) Morrison, Gillis Point. Sergeant Morrison served in the 94th Battalion, Canadian Infantry.

Morrison, Kenneth

'Kennie Aulay' was born on March 16, 1882, the son of Aulay and Annie Isabella (Morrison) Morrison, South Gut. He served overseas with the Canadian Forestry Corps. He and his war bride, Jessie King, Scotland, returned home and settled in Ontario. He died on December 2, 1939.

Morrison, Kenneth Angus, M.M. 167085

Kenneth was born on July 27, 1893, the son of Daniel and Annie (MacDonald) Morrison, MacAulay's, Big Baddeck. Private Morrison was taken on strength on October 29, 1915 in Sydney and served with the 2nd Canadian Pioneer Battalion, Canadian Expeditionary Force. He was a Company Sergeant Major and while serving with the engineers in France, he was awarded the **MILITARY MEDAL** "... for bravery on the field. This Non Commissioned Officer was in charge of a working party on October 29/30th 1917. On the way up sudden heavy shelling was encountered and the party was forced to withdraw. In spite of the darkness of the night and the extended position of the men, Sgt. Morrison with fine control collected and held his men well in hand and as soon as possible, led them to the work and maintained the supply of plank necessary at the road head. He showed great endurance and determination on the work in spite of frequent heavy shell fire. Throughout his 20 months service in the line he has continually shown marked courage and devotion to duty. (Medals and Honors Awards)."

He was summoned to be decorated by King George of England, but declined the honour saying, "Others deserved it more than I." Kenneth A. Morrison's **MILITARY MEDAL** was donated by his family to the Military Museum at the Citadel in Halifax, Nova Scotia.

He married Christine MacLean, Middle River. Their two sons, Walter and Donald, served with the United States of America Air Force during World War II. Kenneth died on April 2, 1969, in Waltham, Massachusetts. He is buried in Middle River Cemetery, Cape Breton.

Their son, Walter Kenneth Morrison, saw combat as an aerial gunner in a B-17. He was a S/Sgt in the 774th Squadron, 463rd Bomb Group in the 15th Air Force flying from Foggia, Italy.

Their son, Donald MacAulay Morrison, was a 2nd Lieutenant and co-pilot in a B-29 (super fortress). On a bombing run over Ota, Japan, on February 10, 1945, there was a mid air collision with no survivors. His ashes were buried in Arlington National Cemetery, Washington, D.C. in 1948. Posthumously, he was awarded the **PURPLE HEART**.

Morrison, Malcolm Hugh

Malcolm Hugh was born on January 20, 1880, in Little Narrows. He enlisted in Sydney on August 7, 1914, as Captain in the Canadian Army Pay Corps. He went overseas on October 13, 1916 and was appointed Regimental Paymaster of the 85th Battalion of the Nova Scotia Highlanders. He proceeded to France on February 10, 1917, and was promoted to Major on November 10, 1914. His engagements were at Vimy Ridge, Passchendaele and other operations in which the 85th Battalion participated from February 10, 1917, to January 1918.

He and his wife, Laura E., lived in Sydney. He was senior partner in the grocery firm of Morrison and MacInnis in Whitney Pier. He was associated with Burchell Agencies and the federal employment agency in Sydney. He died on November 28, 1957, and is buried in Hardwood Hill Cemetery, Sydney.

Morrison, Murdoch 715687

Murdoch was the son of Norman and Flora (MacLean) Morrison, Big Glen. In later years his family moved to Goose Cove, St. Ann's. For four years he served overseas. He suffered a head wound during action, which fortunately did not cause permanent damage.

After the war he returned home and was employed in Sydney. Foul play was suspected in his death. He had collected his pay cheque and later his body was discovered by a trapper near a brook situated above Moxam's Castle in Sydney. At the same time, this handsome young man was engaged to be married. His bride-to-be, an exceptional seamstress, had made her wedding dress. Murdoch Morrison's death occured circa 1920 and he is buried in Goose Cove Cemetery, St. Ann's.

Morrison, Murdoch D.

'M.D.' was born on January 15, 1888, the son of Aulay and Annie Isabella (Morrison) Morrison, South Gut. He served during the Great War.

He married Margaret Whidden, Reserve Mines, where they resided. He was employed as a fireman at No. 10 Colliery and then he worked on the bank head at Caledonia Colliery. He was active in sports and community affairs. He died on February 14, 1951, and is buried in Gordon Cemetery, Reserve Mines.

Morrison, Murdoch R. 2138884

Murdoch was born on March 11, 1888, the son of Phillip and Margaret (MacKenzie) Morrison, Kempt Head. He enlisted in the Canadian Army and served with the 7th Battalion, Canadian Expeditionary Force. He served in France and Belgium. He fought at Vimy. Wounded twice, gassed and shell shocked, he returned home from the war a very sick man. Unmarried, he died on December 12, 1943, in the Kentville Sanatorium. He is buried in Man O' War Cemetery, Boularderie.

Morrison, Norman

Norman was born on April 26, 1875, the son of Samuel and Catherine (Nicholson) Morrison, New Glen. He resided at the outer North Branch, New Glen, Big Baddeck. Unmarried, he eventually moved to Prince Edward Island to live with his sister, Mrs. Annie Coombs.

Morrison, Peter 1015587

Peter was the son of Hector and Barbara (MacRae) Morrison, West Side Middle River. Private Morrison was taken on strength with the Yukon Infantry Company on July 1, 1916, in Sydney.

Morrison, Roderick B. 67597

Rod was born on June 23, 1895, the son of Christopher and Margaret (MacLeod) Morrison, Big Hill.

Private Morrison served overseas in the 25th Battalion Canadian Expeditionary Force. Unmarried, he died on March 25, 1915, at Camp Hill Hospital, Halifax. He is buried in MacLeod Pioneer Cemetery, North Gut, St. Ann's.

(left - Rod D. Morrison, right - his brother, Charlie Morrison)

Morrison, Roderick Daniel 435832

'Roddie Johnny Allan' was born on April 9, 1883, the son of John Allan and Sarah (MacLean) Morrison, West Side Upper Middle River. He attended military school in Fredericton, New Brunswick. He and Francis MacGregor graduated and returned via train to Orangedale from their military training. Since there was no means of transportation from the station, they walked to their respective homes through mud and snow, a distance of thirty-five miles on March 1, 1901. Shortly after their trek, Roddie Morrison left for Alberta. On July 24, 1915, in Calgary he enlisted with the 50th Overseas Battalion. Private Morrison served in France with the 29th Overseas Battalion. He was discharged in Calgary on July 20, 1918, "... being medically unfit for further service on account of wounds received in action".

Roddie married and remained in Western Canada. He returned to Cape Breton sixty years later where he met his old friend, Francis MacGregor, on the village street in Baddeck. Both men had seen considerable war service, but in different regiments. They had not seen each other or knew of each other's whereabouts until then. Roddie Morrison died in 1971.

Morrison, Roderick Peter 3182328

Roddie was born on August 1, 1899, the son of John and Catherine (MacDonald) Morrison, Baddeck Bay. He enlisted on May 3, 1918 with the 17th Reserve Battalion and served in Canada and France. Private Morrison was discharged on July 15, 1919.

He married Nellie MacDonald, Tarbot. They resided in Baddeck Bay. In civilian life he was a land surveyor. He died on March 10, 1966, and is buried in Highland Cemetery, Baddeck Bay.

Morrison, Thomas

Thomas was a son of Donald and Catherine (MacLeod) Morrison, North River Bridge. He served overseas. He married Murdell Matheson, Estmere and they resided in the United States.

(Brothers John Alex Morrison - left, and Thomas Morrison - right)

Morrison, Wilfred Laurier 878343

Wilfred was born on February 21, 1896, the son of John G. and Mary (MacDonald) Morrison, Englishtown.

Private Morrison enlisted on April 1, 1916, in Sydney. He served with the 185th Battalion, Platoon # 2. He was killed in action on August 18, 1917, while serving with the 25th Battalion in France. He is buried in Aux-Noulette Communal Cemetery Extension, France.

Munroe, George A.

George was born on February 14, 1886, the son of David and Jane (Roberts) Munroe, Inlet Baddeck. He enlisted in 1915 and served for the duration of the war. He served with the Veteran's Guard on duty on the trestle at Ottawa Brook during the

(Standing - George Munroe)

Second World War. He married Annie Mae MacDonald, Tarbot. They resided in Baddeck and later moved to Little Narrows. He died in 1961 and is buried in Greenwood Cemetery, Baddeck.

Munroe, John Alexander 1769

Jack was born on June 26, 1873, the son of Alexander and Annabella (Kerr) Munroe, Upper Kempt Head. Forty-one year old Munroe enlisted in Ontario and served overseas with the Princess Patricia Light Infantry. He is credited as being the first Canadian soldier to land on French soil. While serving in the trenches, he was severely wounded when shot through the shoulder. He spent over one and one-half years recuperating in England and Canada; however, his famous right arm sustained permanent paralysis. Subsequently he served as a recruiting officer for Northern Ontario and a founder and first president of the War Veterans' Association.

(Jack Munroe and collie, 'Bobbie Burns')

Jack Munroe's collie dog, Bobbie, accompanied his master to war. This incredible story will move the hearts of all who read about the mascot of the Princess Infantry. On January 26, 1917, the Toronto Humane Society presented a medal to this collie dog - Presented to 'Bobbie Burns' - a collie hero of the trenches. Author Dorothy Farmiloe has masterfully captured Jack Munroe's life in his biography entitled *The Legend of Jack Munroe - A Portrait of a Canadian Hero*. Twelve year old Jack Munroe moved with his two older brothers to Montana. Besides his military service, he became a prospector, mining authority, football star, boxing champion and the 1906 challenger for the World Heavyweight Title. He founded the town of Elk Lake, Ontario, and published his autobiography entitled *Mopping Up*. He married soprano soloist Colina Craine, Toronto. He died of cancer on February 12, 1942, and is buried in Fairview Cemetery, Acton, Ontario. Posthumously, he was inducted into the Canadian Boxing Hall of Fame.

Munroe, Murdock Kenneth

Murdock Kenneth was born on November 6, 1891, the son of Angus and Isabelle (MacDonald) Munroe, Boularderie Centre. He served with the 17th Reserve Battalion, Canadian Expeditionary Force. Unmarried, he died in 1983 and is buried in Man O' War Cemetery, Boularderie.

Murphy, Harold 318018

Harold was born on June 8, 1897, the son of James and Ellen M. Murphy, Ingonish. He served overseas during the war. He married Carrie MacLean, Ingonish. They resided there and he worked at the Cape Breton Highlands National Park. He is buried in St. John's Cemetery, Ingonish.

Neal, Harry

Harry was born on April 21, 1898, the son of John and Mrs. Neal, Ingonish. He served during the war.

Nicholson, Donald Jonathan 222487

'D.J.' was born on June 2, 1894, the son of Neil and Catherine "Steele" (MacLeod) Nicholson, Gillanders Mountain. This Nicholson family moved from Gillander's Mountain to Big Baddeck. He enlisted on October 9, 1915, and was promoted to Lance Corporal on October 13, 1916. While serving with the 85th Battalion, he was shot down while piping the troops at Lens and died of wounds on June 29, 1917. He is buried in Noeux-Les-Mines Communal Cemetery, France.

Nicholson, Frank Donald, M.M. 2137449

Frank was born on December 29, 1888, the son of Jonathan and Mary Ann (MacRae) Nicholson, Middle River. In 1907, this Nicholson family moved to Big Baddeck. He enlisted in the 2nd Depot Battalion, British Columbia Regiment in Victoria, British Columbia on September 25, 1917. He transferred to the 85th Battalion. Private Nicholson served in Canada and France. He was wounded in action. On September 13, 1918, he was awarded the **MILITARY MEDAL**. (Source - *London Gazette* # 30873 - August 29, 1918) He was discharged on February 19, 1919. Following the war, he returned to British Columbia. He was injured in a logging operation in the lumber woods and died as a result of complications on June 10, 1924.
He is buried in Vancouver.

Nicholson, J.E. 223408

Private J.E. Nicholson, Baddeck, served overseas with the 85th Battalion, No. 14 Platoon.

Nicholson, James 85991

James Nicholson hailed from Ingonish. Angus Gillis was listed as his next of kin. Gunner Nicholson was taken on strength with the 6th Brigade, Canadian Field Artillery on December 22, 1914, in Fredericton.

Nicholson, John Alexander

'John A.' was born on December 20, 1896, the son of Duncan and Jane 'Steele' (MacLeod) Nicholson, Middle River Centre.

He enlisted on March 31, 1917, in Sydney. Private Nicholson served with the Canadian Expeditionary Force, 17th Field Battery. He settled in British Columbia. He died on May 26, 1974, and is buried in Vancouver.

Nicholson, John Angus 1241718

'Johnny Sam' was born on June 28, 1896, the son of Samuel and Christy (MacLean) Nicholson, West Middle River. He enlisted in December, 1917, in the United States Navy. Seaman Nicholson served on mine sweepers in the North Sea. He was discharged in September, 1921. He married Mary MacDonald, Middle River and they resided in West Middle River. A noted local historian, he served as president of the Middle River Historical Society. The book entitled *Middle River Past and Present* was dedicated to John A. Nicholson. Johnny Sam Nicholson died on March 19, 1993, and is buried in Middle River Cemetery.

Nicholson, John Neil

John Neil was born on February 27, 1884, the son of Duncan and Jane 'Steele' (MacLeod) Nicholson, Middle River Centre. Private Nicholson served during the war. He went to the Canadian West after the war. Unmarried, he died there in 1922.

Nicholson, John Norman 222436

'Jack N.' was born on January 15, 1885, the son of John A. 'Woods' and Christine (MacIver) Nicholson, 'Coire Mor,' Middle River.

He enlisted on August 10, 1914. Private Nicholson embarked for overseas with the 85th Battalion on October 16, 1915. From the files of the *Halifax Herald* and *The Halifax Mail*, October 14, 1915:

"The Sydney boys of the 85th Nova Scotia Highlanders were given a splendid send off last night. Headed by the city band they were paraded to the station as thousands of citizens thronged Charlotte Street. At the station they were met by the Glace Bay members who were under the command of Major Harrington."

Private Jack N. Nicholson was in this group. He served in Canada and France.

He married Janie Dennison MacNeil, Dennison Road. They resided in Baddeck. Jack died on July 8, 1977, and is buried in Harbourview Cemetery, South Haven.

Nicholson, Roderick Daniel 1060069

'Rory Dan' was born on November 9, 1891, the son of Neil and Catherine 'Steele' (MacLeod) Nicholson, Gillander's Mountain. This family moved from Middle River to Big Baddeck.

He enlisted on September 13, 1916, in Aldershot, Nova Scotia. Major Nicholson served as a piper with the overseas army in England and France. He served

in the 246th Reserve Battalion, Canadian Expeditionary Force, the 25th and the 185th. Pipe Major Nicholson was discharged on demobilization on May 24, 1919. 'Roddie Piper' married Mamie MacRae, Boularderie. They resided in Sydney where he was employed at the Steel Plant. Pipe Major Nicholson was an active supporter of the Gaelic College, St. Ann's, during its founding years. He served as its first piping instructor. He is buried in Brookfield - Westside Cemetery, Colchester County.

Nicholson, Roy MacLennan

Roy was born on March 6, 1892, the son of Duncan and Jane 'Steele' (MacLeod) Nicholson, Middle River Centre. Private Nicholson served during the war. He died in 1963 and is buried in Middle River Cemetery.

(Brothers John A. Nicholson - standing, and Roy M. Nicholson - seated)

Nicholson, William Wallace

'W.W.' (Willie Jonathan) was born on October 20, 1890, the son of Jonathan and Mary Ann (MacRae) Nicholson, Middle River. In 1907 his family moved to Big Baddeck. Commanding Officer Nicholson served with the 94th Regiment, the 185th and 85th and the 26th Battalions. He served in Canada, England and France. He was wounded in France. He was discharged in December, 1918.

Captain Nicholson married nursing sister Melissa Watson (World War I). They resided in Big Baddeck. Three of their children served during World War II. Captain Nicholson died on April 19, 1973, and is buried in St. Andrew's Cemetery, Big Baddeck.

Oram, Charles John, M.C. 67633

Charles Oram, Baddeck, was born on October 8, 1895. He enlisted on November 27, 1914 with the Canadian Expeditionary Force, 25th Battalion Canadian Infantry. He served in Canada, Britain and France. Lieutenant Oram was awarded the **MILITARY CROSS**. He was the recipient

" ... for conspicuous gallantry and devotion to duty. He superintended the laying of telephone lines forward, accompanying the battalion in the attack. Later, during the succeeding days, though constantly exposed to intense artillery fire, he succeeded in keeping up communication with battalion headquarters. His services were of the utmost value, and he set a splendid example to his men."

In 1921, Lieutenant Oram was serving as a signal officer with the Cape Breton Highlanders militia. Charles Oram was a grandson of Michael Charlie MacLean, Baddeck. He is buried in St. Michael's Greenwood Cemetery, Baddeck.

Peterson, Duncan D.J.

Duncan was born on December 15, 1886, the son of John and Mary (MacCharles) Peterson, Red Head. He served overseas in the American Infantry and was killed in action.

(Left - Duncan Peterson)

Petrie, Alexander

Alex was born on April 16, 1898, the adopted son of John and Mary (Dunphy) Petrie, Dingwall. He served during the war. He married and resided in Prince Edward Island.

Pritchard, Theodore

Theodore was born on November 16, 1897, the son of Arthur and Kate (Martin) Pritchard, The Chul, Hunter's Mountain. He served during the war. This family later moved to the United States.

Rice, Benjamin Russell 2138708

Benjamin was born on February 5, 1886, the son of Robert Edward and Elizabeth (Hart) Rice, Baddeck Forks. He served overseas with the 6th Battalion. He married Flora MacAskill, Cape North. They resided in Cape North. He died on August 13, 1945.

Rice, George Ernest, M.M. 204338

George was born on August 29, 1876, the son of Robert Edward and Elizabeth (Hart) Rice, Baddeck Forks. On January 15, 1913, George married Edna M. Doane, New York.

He joined the 92nd Regiment Canadian Highland Battalion. He was the recipient of the **MILITARY MEDAL**.

" ... On August 15th, (1917) Private Rice went over in the attack, and was one of those to reach the final objective. During one of the enemy's heavy counter attacks, one of their bombing parties managed to get close up to our bombing post, and was partially successful in surrounding it. Private Rice crawled out into a shell hole, and bombed them from there, inflicting many casualties on them, and the rest retired. His work throughout the operations was of the most courageous character. He showed the greatest coolness through the heavy bombing bombardment, and his work in the attack mentioned above is deserving of the greatest praise." Source - *London Gazette* 30389 November 19, 1917.

Private Rice was wounded and died of wounds October 15, 1918, in France (15th Canadian Battalion). He is buried in Duisans British Cemetery, Etrun, France.

Rice, Robert Amos 469074

Robbie was born on January 1, 1882, the son of Robert Edward and Elizabeth (Hart) Rice, Baddeck Forks. Private Rice was taken on strength on August 18, 1915, in Sussex, New Brunswick and served with the 64th Battalion, Canadian Expeditionary Force, 6907TA Company. He was promoted to Corporal while serving his battalion.

He married Constance H.K. Burt of London, England on November 6, 1918. He and his war bride settled in Big Baddeck. He died on June 11, 1942, and is buried in South Side Cemetery, Big Baddeck.

Robbins, Frank B. 715531

Frank was born in England. He was raised in the home of John Dan and his widowed mother,Margaret (MacDermid) MacRitchie (Angus), Hazeldale. He was drowned on July 10, 1916, while rescuing a comrade when they were stationed at a military training base in Truro (106th Battalion). He is buried in Little Narrows Cemetery.

(standing - Frank Robbins)

Roberts, John Garfield 488229

'John G.' was born on September 7, 1882, the son of John and Sarah Roberts, Ingonish. Private Roberts served with the Princess Patricia Canadian Light Infantry. He was killed in action on September 28, 1918, and is buried in Canada Cemetery, Cambrai, France.

Robinson, John

Jack was born on June 20, 1896, the son of William (Bill) and Mary G. (Robertson) Robinson, Ingonish. Private Robinson served with the 85th Battalion, Canadian Infantry. He married and resided in Sommerville, Massachusetts, where he was a carpenter.

Rogers, Luke 488224

Luke was born on January 12, 1879, the son of William and Mrs. Rogers, Neil's Harbour. He enlisted in the Canadian Expeditionary Force and served overseas with the 2nd Battalion, Canadian Machine Gun Corps. Private Rogers was killed in action on August 8, 1918, and his name is inscribed on the Vimy Memorial, France.

Rogers, Thomas

Thomas was born on May 13, 1888, the son of John and Rebecca (Sturgess) Rogers, New Haven. He served in the Canadian Expeditionary Force. He married and resided in Neil's Harbour. He is buried in St. Andrew's Cemetery, Neil's Harbour.

Roper, Harvey Louis 318958

Harvey was born on May 15, 1893, the son of James and Emily C. (Gillis) Roper, North Ingonish. He served overseas during the war. He married Mary MacGean. They resided in Ingonish where he was a fisherman.

Ross, Frank D.

Frank was born on October 14, 1896, the son of Harvey and Minerva (Carmichael) Ross, South Side Baddeck. He joined the militia in Kentville in 1914. Since he was his mother's sole supporter, he was sent home. Later he joined The Royal Flying Corps and served until 1919. He married Florence Richards and resided in the United States where he was employed for forty-two years with the Ford Motor Company. In 1925, he bought his first Model T car for the sum of $475. He received a $25 employee discount. He headed home to Cape Breton from Boston for his vacation and it took four days to motor over the muddy roads. He was the last surviving World War I veteran whose name is displayed on the Honour Roll at St. Andrews Church, Baddeck Forks. He died on August 25, 1992, in Wintrop, Massachusetts.

Ross, Murdoch James 105373

Murdoch was born on November 27, 1882, the son of John and Flora (MacLeod) Ross, Peter's Brook. He enlisted in Calgary with the 28th Battalion, Canadian Expeditionary Force. He was killed in action at the Somme on September 15, 1916. He is buried in Pojieres British Cemetery, Ovillers-la-Boisselle.

He was survived by his young widow, Lydia Sinclair Ross, and four children. In civilian life he had been a locomotive engineer.

Ross, Norman Angus

Norman was born on June 1, 1886, the son of John and Flora (MacLeod) Ross, Peter's Brook. Norman served overseas as a piper with the 48th Highlanders Pipe Band. He enlisted in 1915 and served in Ypres - St. Langemark, Yrestabert, Ploigstrut. In 1916 he served at Ypres, Somme, Vimy Ridge, Hill 70 and Passendaele. He married Annie MacLeod, Hunter's Mountain. They resided in Whitney Pier. He died on January 6, 1940, and is buried in Eastmount Cemetery, Whitney Pier.

Ross, Walter William

Walter was born on October 29, 1891, the son of John and Flora (MacLeod) Ross, Peter's Brook. He served overseas with the 36th Field Battery.

He married twice. His first wife was Winnifred Smorden and his second wife was Margaret Anderson. They resided in Sydney. He was a conductor with the Sydney and Louisbourg Railway. He is buried in Forest Haven Memorial Cemetery, Sydney.

Ross, William 877586

Willie was born on April 15, 1882, the son of John and Flora (MacLeod) Ross, Peter's Brook.

He enlisted on March 16, 1916, in Sydney. He served in Canada, Britain and France with the 185th Battalion, Canadian Expeditionary Force, Cape Breton Highlanders, # 16 Platoon. Lance Corporal Ross was discharged on January 8, 1919, in Halifax.

He was predeceased by his first wife Christine MacLeod, Ingonish. They were the parents of six sons who served during World War II. His second wife was Gwendolyn Went. They resided in North Gut. He died on July 7, 1966, and is buried in Harbourview Cemetery, South Haven.

The following is an excerpt from the *Cape Breton Post* in 1966 - a tribute made by Rev. A.W.R. MacKenzie (World War I), Director of the Gaelic College, St. Ann's.

"William Ross was an extraordinary man - a man of many gifts. At St. Ann's he was known as the North Gut Bard, historian and Gaelic Scholar. He had a vast knowledge of history, especially British, Canadian and American. One would think to hear him dwell on North British events that he personally was acquainted with the early army Generals, Admirals, Political leaders and the Gaelic poets and giants of English literature. Formal schooling for him was most elementary, but on many occasions he gave a most natural impression, if given the opportunity, that he would grace any University chair in the land with much ability and satisfaction.

William Ross was a master in his knowledge of sailing ships, seamanship and navigation. He was a craftsman above the average. His model of *The Margaret*, gifted to the Gaelic College and on display in the Giant MacAskill-Highland Folk Museum, will long testify to his ability as a craftsman.

William Ross was an overseas veteran of the 1st World War. He was a charter member of the Baddeck Branch of the Canadian Legion and as a worthy man-of-arms, in his departure from earthly scenes, was dressed in full Highland garb.

William Ross was for over twenty-five years a most helpful member of the Gaelic College Board of Directors. In paying tribute to his memory I honor him as one of the Gaelic College directors who made a major contribution in the early development of the Memorial Institution in its infant days."

The following undated letter written by William Ross was published in the *Post Record*, Sydney.

The Music of Bagpipes

Editor, Sydney Post Record, Sir: From time to time disparaging articles on the bagpipes have appeared in the "Round Table" section of the Post-Record. It is evident that these irresponsible scribblers have never heard the pipes in their proper setting.

"Amid the ranks of war, amid battles' magnificent stern array with the thudding thunder of distant gunfire and the eager tramp of hurrying battalions as an accompaniment a piper will continue to play," says one critic. This is correct.

Piper Kenneth MacKay of the Black Watch at Waterloo stalked out in front of the line and played the "gathering" of his regiment. With Napoleon's cavalry thundering down the slope in all the unchecked fury of a massed charge, he did not quicken his stride as he moved to the rear of the line. Not even the crash of the 2,000 muskets that smashed that charge caused him to miss a note.

Piper Findlayer of the Gordon Highlanders at Dargai Ridge had both legs broken by a bullet. His comrades propped him against a rock and he continued to play. He received the Victoria Cross for this feat. Yes, Mr. Critic the pipers will continue to play in action until the battle is won or till a soldier's death brings him face to face with "the Master of All Music and the Master of All Singing."

In the war that is now ended the troops rode in large trucks known as "troop carriers", an entire platoon with all their equipment and supplies in each truck. In the First World War the "troop carriers" were known as "Kitchener Boots." Shod with steel they weighed two or three pounds apiece. The motive power was supplied by the men who wore them. They carried all their equipment on their backs as well as 165 rounds of .303 ammunition.

And where is the "Old Sweat" who does not recall some last long weary mile? The writer vividly recalls one of these. I was in the rear platoon and the regiment swung onto a straight section of road giving a clear view of the entire right flank. The men were tired. We heard the command passed from the front to the pipe band in the centre. "The band will play." Came the preliminary roll of the drums and then "Blue Bonnets Over the Border."

Dragging feet rose higher, sagging shoulders straightened, drooping heads came to life and looked "straight to the front." An air of dejection gave way to alertness, even the colonel's horse seemed imbued with a new spirit, for the pipes were made for war and the effect is the same on any British soldier, whether he is from the East London Rifles or a private of the Seaforths from the outer Hebrides.

The passing years have brought dimness to the old soldier's vision and the color of snow to his hair, but time can not eradicate those visions of other days, for time idealizes the past.

No. Mr. Editor, the "Old Sweats" do not like those remarks and comments. They do not like them at all. We listened to some excellent pipers at the Mod held here not long ago, but alas, we heard ancient melodies in a modernized form and hardly recognizable.

With particular reference to the oldest piece of martial music in the world, "Pibroch of Domid Dhu", known in the country of Lochiel as the "Cameron's Gathering." It was composed by the chief piper of the Clan Cameron when Donald, Lord of the Isles invaded the mainland of Scotland in 1411. It was played at the Battle of Harlan in that year and has echoed over every British battlefield since the union of the Crouses.

It was played by the pipers of the Gordon Highlanders at Waterloo. Byron in his deathless verse mentions this circumstance but in a slightly different setting.

"And wild and high the Camerons' Gathering rose
The war note of Lochiel which Albyn's hill
Have heard and heard, too have her Saxon foes
How in the noon of night that pibroch thrills."

On two occasions the Germans heard it in "the noon of night," -- and fled. But the oldest marches have been modernized to suit parade ground *requirements, in other words to quicken the pace, and has lost the lilting spirit stirring swing of other days.*

I am not alone on this subject for the CBC has barred from its network those atrocious musical parodies known collectively as "modernized Gaelic music." The writer has never heard or read that impalement or boiling in oil was ever practiced in Scotland, but, I would not raise a finger to save any of those pedantic musical cranks engaged in mutilating those ancient melodies from such punishment.

I would suggest our pipers write to His Lordship, the Duke of Argyle, (Maccallanmore) for the music of "Donuil Dhu" in its original form. He is the Empire's only Gaelic-speaking Duke and is a true Hielan man and is ready and willing at all times to further anything pertaining to his country's history.

WILLIAM ROSS
St. Ann's

Samms, Edward VR1957

Edward was born on March 25, 1898, the son of John and Edith (Turner) Samms, Neil's Harbour. Ordinary Seasman served aboard the HMCS *Noibe*. He died in hospital in Halifax from the effects of influenza on April 17, 1918 and is buried in St. Peter's Cemetery, New Haven, Nova Scotia.

Shaw, John Alexander

John Alex was born on April 17, 1889, the son of Angus and Katie (Morrison) Shaw, Wreck Cove. He served overseas. After his discharge he went to work in the mines in Ontario. Eventually, 'Big' John Alex Shaw returned to the old family home in Wreck Cove. Unmarried, he died at seventy-four years of age and is buried in Birch Plain Cemetery.

Skinner, George 223279

George hailed from Iona. Private Skinner served overseas with the 85th Battalion.

Smith, Charles P.

Charlie was born on May 23, 1897, the son of John W. and Alexandra (MacDonald) Smith, Point Clear. He served overseas. He resided in the United States.

Smith, D.A.

Private Smith's name is inscribed on the war monument in Little Narrows. He served during the war.

Smith, Dan Murdock 301153

Dan Murdock was born on August 27, 1890, the son of Murdoch and Annie (MacLeod) Smith, Rear Big Hill/Port Bevis.

He enlisted on September 10, 1915 and served as a gunner with the Canadian Field Artillery, 3rd Division, 36th Battery, Canadian Expeditionary Force. He served in the United Kingdom and France. He was discharged on March 26, 1919. He married Mary MacKenzie, Rear Baddeck Bay. They resided in Port Bevis. Tragically, he died in a motor vehicle accident on May 21, 1954 and is buried in the little roadside cemetery (by the Trans Canada Highway) in Port Bevis.

Smith, Daniel John 488958

Dan John was born on July 17, 1892, the son of Murdoch and Annie (MacLeod) Smith, Rear Big Hill.

Private Smith served overseas in the infantry with the 36th Regiment. He was killed in action on April 29, 1918 (24th Battalion) and is buried in London Cemetery, Neuville-St. Vitasse, France.

Smith, Duncan Angus 255512

DUNCAN SMITH.

Duncan was born on April 27, 1870, the son of Donald and Flora (MacAulay) Smith, West Tarbot. He enlisted in Moosejaw, Saskatchewan on April 15, 1916, in the 210th Battalion, Canadian Overseas Expeditionary Force and with the 28th Battalion to France. He was injured when he fell in a shell hole in Whealey.

Prior to enlisting he had been farming in Eyebrow, Saskatchewan. He returned there and resumed farming. Unmarried, he died on May 16, 1952, in Saskatchewan.

Smith, Murdock J. 68199

'Murdock J.' was born on September 19, 1893, the son of Dan J. and Margaret (MacLeod) Smith, North River Bridge.

He enlisted in Halifax on February 11, 1915 and served overseas with the 25th Battalion, Canadian Expeditionary Force. Private Smith served in Canada, Britain and France. He died on June 5, 1916, of wounds received in action while serving with the 25th Battalion. Previously he had been wounded in September, 1915. He is buried in Lijssenthoek Military Cemetery, Belgium.

Smith, Norman Angus 2330371

Norman Smith and son

Norman was born on August 17, 1887, the son of Murdoch and Annie (MacLeod) Smith, Rear Big Hill/Port Bevis. He enlisted in 1917 and served in the Canadian Forestry Corps, Canadian Expeditionary Force. Private Smith was discharged in Halifax in 1919. He married Mary Smith, Indian Brook. They resided in North Sydney and later in Glace Bay. He operated a barber shop on Commercial Street in North Sydney. Their son, John Norman Smith, served as a flying officer/navigator during World War II. Norman Smith is buried in Greenwood Cemetery, Glace Bay.

Smith, Samuel

Sam was born on October 24, 1892, the son of John W. and Alexandra (MacDonald) Smith, Point Clear, Boularderie. He served overseas. He later resided in Glace Bay.

Smith, William 3180587

Billy was born on September 23, 1895, the son of Johnny and Roseanna (Rideout) Smith, Neil's Harbour. He enlisted on February 25, 1918, in the Canadian Army and served during the war. He was a fisherman. He is buried in St. Andrew's Cemetery, Neil's Harbour.

Stephenson, Abel

Abel was born on October 28, 1899, the son of William and Gavina (Tait) Stephenson, Black Rock. This family immigrated to Black Rock from Scotland when their children were young. The children were born in Scotland but raised in Big Bras d'Or.

Private Stephenson served in the war but due to medical reasons, he returned to Black Rock where he was a farmer. He married twice. His first wife was Agnes Reashore, Sydney Mines, and his second wife was Margaret Scott, Florence. He died on December 16, 1960, and is buried in Black Rock Cemetery, Big Bras d'Or.

Stephenson, James 877386

James was born on September 20, 1895, the son of William and Gavina (Tait) Stephenson, Black Rock. Private Stephenson served overseas with the 185th Nova Scotia Highlanders, Canadian Expeditionary Force.

He married Mary Fry, Florence. He was the light keeper in Black Rock. He died in October, 1976, and is buried in Black Rock Cemetery.

Stephenson, Thomas T. 415230

Tom was born on September 4, 1897, the son of William and Gavina (Tait) Stephenson, Black Rock. Private Stephenson (spelled Stevenson) was taken on strength on July 29, 1915, in Aldershot, Nova Scotia, and served with the 40th Battalion. He married Annie MacKay, Black Rock. He was the light keeper on St. Paul's Island. He died on February 17, 1967, and is buried in St. James Cemetery, Big Bras d'Or.

Stephenson, William 877343

Bill was born on April 5, 1894, the son of William and Gavina (Tait) Stephenson, Black Rock. He served overseas with the 85th Battalion and served as a piper in that battalion.

He married Matilda Townsley, Bras d'Or. They resided in Sydney Mines. He worked in the coal mines and was injured in the mine disaster of 1938 in Sydney Mines. He is buried in Brookside Cemetery, Sydney Mines.

Stewart, Daniel John 2101070

Dan was born on October 18, 1897, the son of William and Lena (MacLean) Stewart, Baddeck. He enlisted on April 1, 1918 and served as a gunner in the Canadian Machine Gun Pool. He served in Canada, England and France. He was discharged in July, 1919.

A carpenter by trade, he was employed with the Alexander Graham Bell estate in Beinn Bhreagh for many years. He married Mary B. MacInnis. They resided in Baddeck. Dan J. Stewart died in 1977 and is buried in Highland Cemetery, Baddeck Bay.

Stockley, Henry Herbert 68150

'Harry' was born on April 25, 1891, the son of George and Annie (Fudge) Stockley, Ingonish. Private Stockley served with the 25th Battalion in Canada. He died in Halifax on April 11, 1915, and is buried in St. John's Cemetery, Ingonish.

Stockley, William George

William was born on May 28, 1893, the son of Thomas and Josephine (Roberts) Stockley, Ingonish Centre.

He served during both World Wars. He served overseas during World War I. He served with the Veterans Guard of Canada during World War II.

He married Mary Stockley, Ingonish. He worked at the Cape Breton Highlands National Park. He is buried in St. John's Church Cemetery.

Sutherland, Andrew 415231

Andy was born on March 2, 1888, the son of Donald and Catherine (Kate) (Bain) Sutherland, New Harris. He served overseas in France with the 60th Battalion and was killed in action on April 23, 1916, while a member of the 40th Battalion. His name is inscribed on the Menin Gate Memorial, Belgium.

Sutherland, Kenneth A. 877852

Kenneth was born on October 5, 1897, in Baddeck and is believed to be the nephew of Neil MacLean, Big Baddeck. Private Sutherland served with the 185th Canadian Infantry Battalion. In civilian life he was a miner.

Theriault, John AB5097

Jack was born on April 1, 1897, the son of Frank and Susan H. (Briand) Theriault, Smelt Brook. He served during the First Great War. Private Theriault served as a prison guard during the Second World War. He married Sarah Dixon, South Harbour. He died on December 24, 1989, and is buried in St. Joseph's Cemetery, Dingwall.

Tickner, Walter

Walter was born in England and raised in the home of John G. (Bane) MacDonald in Middle River. Private Tickner served overseas and was severely wounded in 1915.

Turner, Benjamin

Ben was the son of Charles and Christina (Burton) Turner, Dingwall. Private Turner served during the war. He sailed on the American Great Lakes. He was unmarried and is buried in MacPherson Cemetery, Dingwall.

Urquhart, John Alexander

John A. was born on July 29, 1887, the son of Roderick and Catherine (MacQuarrie) Urquhart, Big Intervale, Cape North. Private Urquhart served during the war.

Warren, James George 878034

James Warren, Neil's Harbour, served in the 185th Canadian Infantry Battalion, Platoon # 8. At the time of his enlistment he was a miner and his address was stated as Dominion # 4, Glace Bay.

Warren, Matthew 488224

Matthew was born on April 4, 1890 and hailed from Neil's Harbour. Private Warren served overseas with the 85th Battalion. He was stricken with influenza and underwent surgery in England for removal of some ribs. Eventually, he returned home and tried to carry on fishing as a livelihood. He became very ill and was admitted to the Hamilton Hospital in North Sydney where he died on November 4, 1919. He is buried in St. Peter's Cemetery, Neil's Harbour.

Warren, William Lewis 437517

William was born on September 11, 1874, the son of Roby and Maria Warren, Ingonish. Private Warren was taken on strength on July 3, 1915, in Edmonton and served with the 51st Battalion.

Watson, Alexander Charles 46660

'Sandy Bay' was born on June 29, 1879, the son of Andrew Barnet (Bay) and Emily (Anderson) Watson, Baddeck Forks.

Sandy, who was unmarried, spent a number of years in California. He returned to Canada and enlisted with the 17th Battalion. While serving with the 13th Battalion Unit, he was killed in action at Ypres, June 13, 1916. His name is inscribed on the Menin Gate Memorial, Belgium.

Watson, Melissa Lydia R.N.

Melissa was born on October 25, 1892, the daughter of Edmund Ross and Alice Jane (Cranton) Watson. She taught school before entering nurses' training in Cambridge, Massachusetts. As a Registered Nurse, she joined the Harvard Unit which was recruiting nurses into the British army. Nursing Sister Melissa Watson served overseas in France.

She married Captain William Wallace Nicholson (World War I), South Side Baddeck. They resided in South Side Baddeck. She died on March 26, 1984, and is buried in St. Andrews Cemetery, Baddeck Forks.

Watson, Robert Kinney 1262019

Robbie was born on November 8, 1896, the the son of Robert and Christina (MacRae) Watson, Baddeck Forks. He was taken on strength on May 3, 1916, in Saint John, New Brunswick. Gunner Watson served overseas with the 7th Seige Battery.

Prior to the war he taught school in Baddeck Bridge. He married Annie MacKinnon, New Waterford, and they resided in Sydney Forks. He worked at the customs office in Sydney. He died on June 29, 1972, and is buried in Alfred Smith Memorial Cemetery, Sydney Forks.

Watson, Samuel Laughlan

Sam was born on January 5, 1888, the son of Robert and Christina (MacRae) Watson, Baddeck Forks. He served overseas. He married Sarah MacLeod, Dennison Road. They resided in Baddeck. He died on October 16, 1959.

Wilkie, Alexander Kenneth 1030914

Alex was born on May 3, 1895, the son of John E. and Christina (MacLeod) Wilkie, Sugar Loaf. Private Wilkie served with the 236th Battalion, Canadian Expeditionary Force.

He married Christina MacDonald, Bay St. Lawrence. He was a fisheries officer in the Cape North area. He died on August 30, 1972, and is buried in Aspy Bay Cemetery.

Wilkie, James David

Jimmy was born on October 7, 1889, the son of John E. and Christina (MacLeod) Wilkie, Sugar Loaf. He served during the war. He married Margaret MacLeod, Boularderie and resided in Halifax. During his later years, he lived in Boularderie. He died on May 4, 1966, and is buried in St. James Cemetery, Big Bras d'Or.

Young, Norman Edgar 878242

Edgar was born on June 5, 1884, the son of Anthony and Margaret (MacPherson) Young, Dingwall. He served with the 185th Canadian Infantry Battalion. During his younger years he was a school teacher. He was an accomplished portrait and landscape artist. He died on February 28, 1972, and is buried in MacPherson Cemetery, Dingwall.

Young, William A. 415341

Willie was born on January 21, 1899, the son of James and Annie (MacLean) Young, Aspy Bay. Private Young served overseas with the 5th Canadian Mounted Rifles. Private Young was killed in action on October 31, 1917, while serving with the 40th Battalion. He is buried in Tyne Cot Cemetery, Passchendaele, Belgium.

Zwicker, William

William Zwicker hailed from Bay St. Lawrence. Private Zwicker served during the war. He is buried in St. Margaret's Village Cemetery.

ANTHEM FOR THE U.N.

(Written by Rev. A.W.R. MacKenzie March 1942)

(Tune: same as for "My Country, 'Tis of Thee")

FREEDOM'S VICTORY

"The United Nations bless,

With strength and steadfastness,

in right and thee.

Let freedom's victory clear,

all lands, the seas, the air

of every tyrant foe

for ever more."

Gallantry Medals

The Most Excellent Order of the British Empire

Terms: The CIVIL DIVISION is awarded by the British Government for services to the Empire (Commonwealth) at home, India and in the Dominions and Colonies. The MILITARY DIVISION is awarded for services in the field or before the enemy or for services to the Empire (Commonwealth).

Distinguished Service Order

Terms: Established for rewarding individual instances of meritorious or distinguished service in war. This is a purely military order and is only given to officers whose service has been marked by the special mention of his name in despatches for "distinguished services under fire, or under conditions equivalent to service in actual combat with the enemy."

Distinguished Service Cross

Terms: Awarded to Naval and Marine Officers, Commanders or below, including Warrant Officers (or equivalent), for meritorious or distinguished services before the enemy. Members of the Air Force and Army serving with the fleet were also eligible.

Military Cross

Terms: Awarded to Officers of the rank of Captain or lower including Warrant Officers, for gallant and distinguished services in action.

Military Medal

Terms: Awarded to Warrant Officers, NCOs and Men for individual or associated acts of bravery and devotion under fire on the recommendation of a Commander-in-Chief in the Field.

Distinguished Flying Cross

Terms: Awarded to Officers and Warrant Officers for an act or acts of valour, courage or devotion to duty performed whilst flying in active operations against the enemy.

Distinguished Conduct Medal

Terms: Awarded to Warrant Officers, NCOs and men who have performed service of a distinctly gallant and distinguished nature in action in the field.

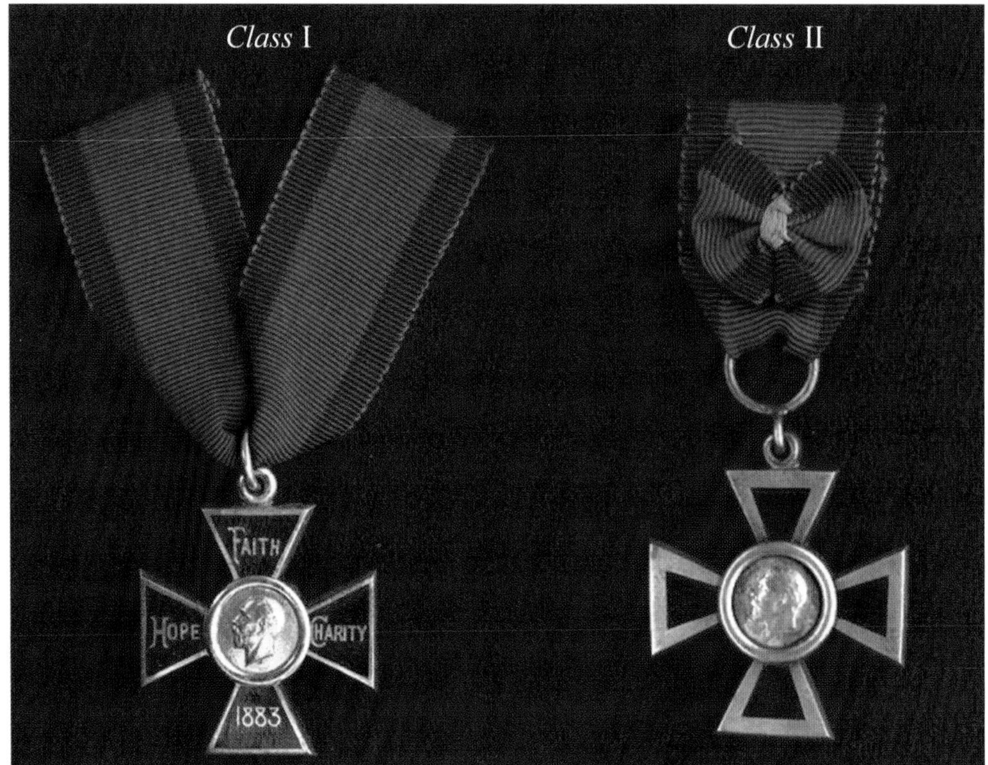

Royal Red Cross

Terms: CLASS I: Awarded to a fully trained Nurse of the official Nursing Services who has performed an exceptional act of bravery and devotion to her post of duty. First class members are called Members. Class I is limited to 2% of establishment.

CLASS II: Awarded as above except it includes Nurses and Nurses Aides and Volunteers. Class II membership is limited to 5% of establishment and members are called Associates and use the initials A.R.R.C.

Campaign Medals 1st World War

British War Medal

Terms: Awarded to all ranks of the Overseas Military Forces of Canada who came overseas from Canada between 5 August 1914 and 11 November 1918 or who have served in a theatre of war. Those who enlisted in the O.M.F.C. in the United Kingdom and have not served in a theatre of war are not entitled to this medal. The R.A.F. requirement was the same as the Army but the personnel of the naval forces required 28 days of mobilized service or if they lost their lives before the service period was complete. Seamen of the Canadian Merchant Marine who served at sea not less than 6 months and crews of Dominion Government Ships and the Canadian Merchantile Marine were also eligible.

Victory Medal

Terms: Awarded to all officers, warrant officers, NCOs and men of the fighting forces and civilians under contract, and others employed with military hospitals who actually served on the establishment of a unit in a theatre of war between 5 August 1914 and midnight 11/12 November 1918. (It was also issued to members of a British Naval mission to Russia 1919-1920 and for mine clearance in the North Sea between 11 November 1918 and 30 November 1919). This medal is never issued alone but is always issued with the British War Medal.

1914 Star

Terms: Awarded to all officers, non-commissioned officers and men of the British and Indian Expeditionary Forces including civilian medical practitioners, nursing sisters, nurses and others employed with military hospitals, who actually served in France or Belgium on the establishment of a unit of the British Expeditionary Forces, between 5 August 1914 and midnight of the 22/23 November 1914. Not awarded for service afloat. It is often called the 'Mons Star.'

1914-1915 Star

Terms: Awarded to all who saw service in any theatre of war against the central powers between 5th August, 1914 and 31 December 1915 except those eligible for the 1914 Star. Canada considered "overseas" to be service beyond the three mile limit and consequently many RCN small ships were entitled to this star.

The Merchantile Marine War Medal

Terms: Awarded to men who received the British War Medal and in addition served at sea on at least one voyage through a danger zone. It was also given to those who had served at sea for not less than six months between the 4 August 1914 and 11 November 1918. No bars.

Campaign Medals 2nd World War

1939-1945 Star

Terms: Six months service on active operations. (Two months for active aircrew), between 2 September 1939 and 9 May 1945 for Europe or 2 September 1945 for the Pacific.

The Atlantic Star

Terms: Six months service afloat between 3 September 1939 and 8 May 1945.

The Air Crew Europe Star

Terms: Two months operational flying from the United Kingdom over Europe, between 3 September, 1939 and 5 June, 1944 (not awarded after D-Day).

The Africa Star

Terms: Awarded for entry into an operational area of North Africa between 10 June, 1940 and 12 May, 1943. (one or more days service)

The Pacific Star

Terms: Awarded for operational service in the Pacific between 8 December, 1941 and 2 September, 1945.

The Burma Star

Terms: Awarded for operational service in the Burma campaign between 11 December, 1941 and 2 September, 1945.

The Italy Star

Terms: Awarded for operational service in Sicily or Italy between 11 June, 1943 and 8 May, 1945.

The France-Germany Star

Terms: Awarded for service in France, Belgium, Holland or Germany between 6 June, 1944 (D-Day) and 8 May, 1945.

The Defence Medal

Terms: Awarded to Canadians for six months service in Britain between 3 September, 1939 and 2 September, 1945.

Canadian Volunteer Service Medal

Terms: Awarded to Canadians for 18 months voluntary service between 2 September, 1939 and 2 September, 1945 or for any voluntary service outside Canada.

The 1939-1945 War Medal

Terms: Awarded to all full-time personnel of the armed forces for 28 days service between 3 September, 1939 and 2 September, 1945. (also Merchant Navy).

World War II

Allison, Michael Francis F36064

Michael was born on August 29, 1925, the son of Mary Allison, Aspy Bay. Private Allison enlisted in September 1943 and served in the Infantry Corps in Canada. He married Angeline Dykens, Wolfville. They settled in the Annapolis Valley where he was actively involved in farming. He was predeceased by his wife, and he presently resides in Medford, Kings County, Nova Scotia.

Anderson, Clifford F33018

Clifford was born on November 20, 1908, the son of George and Ada (Archibald) Anderson, Inlet Baddeck. He enlisted on February 16, 1943 and served overseas with the West Nova Scotia Regiment. Private Anderson was discharged on November 10, 1945. He served in Canada, United Kingdom, Central Mediterranean area and Continental Europe.

He married Mary Hutchison, Inlet. They resided at Shore Road, Baddeck. He died on March 24, 1987 and is buried in Greenwood Cemetery.

Anderson, George Alexander

George was born on January 5, 1907, the son of George and Ada (Archibald) Anderson, Inlet Baddeck. He served in the Royal Canadian Air Force during the war. He married Dorothy Dennison, Kentville. He held an executive position with the head office of the Royal Bank of Canada in New York. He died on November 27, 1985, and is buried in New York.

Andrews, Alexander John

Alex was born on June 26, 1921, the son of Joshua and Christine (MacDonald) Andrews, North River. He served in the Royal Canadian Navy. He was a schoolteacher in Niagara Falls, Ontario. He married Charlotte White, Niagara Falls. He and his wife reside in Niagara Falls, Ontario.

Andrews, Joseph Malcolm

Joe was born on July 25, 1912, the son of Joshua and Christine (MacDonald) Andrews, North River. He served in the Royal Canadian Air Force in Canada and Newfoundland.

His career with the postal department in the City of Sydney spanned thirty-five years. He married Ann MacIntyre, Gabarus. He and his wife resided in Sydney. He died on December 19, 1989, and is buried in Forest Haven Cemetery, Sydney.

Andrews, Murray John

Murray was born on May 2, 1908, the son of Joshua and Christine (MacDonald) Andrews, North River. He served in the Royal Canadian Navy. He was a Registered Nurse and a graduate of the Nova Scotia Hospital School of Nursing, Dartmouth. He worked at the Christie Street Hospital in Ontario and as an industrial nurse with the Ford Motor Company, Windsor. He married Aleda Moore, R.N., Collingwood, Ontario. He and his wife resided in Windsor, Ontario. He died on October 31, 1988, and is buried in Windsor, Ontario.

Andrews, William James

Bill was born on September 29, 1913, the son of Joshua and Christine (MacDonald) Andrews, North River.

He served with the Royal Canadian Navy, crossing the Atlantic on the destroyer *Kootenay* forty-eight times. For thirty years he worked as a stationary engineer in the coal mining industry in Industrial Cape Breton. He married Isobel Graham, Florence. He and his wife resided in Sydney Mines. He died on November 5, 1998, and is buried in Brookside Cemetery, Sydney Mines.

Asaph, Elmer William F21145

Elmer was born on June 11, 1921, the son of Francis and Annie (Carmichael) Asaph of Big Baddeck. He served overseas. Following the war he became a clergyman. He died on May 4, 1991, and is buried in Southside Baddeck Cemetery, Big Baddeck.

Asaph, John Kenney F10953

John, a brother of Elmer, was born to Francis and Annie (Carmichael) Asaph on July 11, 1924, in Big Baddeck. He served overseas in the Signal Corps Division and remained there with the occupation army for six months following the war. He died on September 4, 1994, and is buried in Southside Baddeck Cemetery, Big Baddeck.

Asseff, Joseph Omar

Omar was born on October 23, 1918, the son of merchant Joseph and Mary (Fitzgerald) Asseff, South Harbour. Private Asseff was in basic training when he fell ill. He died on April 12, 1941, and is buried in St. Joseph's Cemetery, Dingwall.

Bain, Leslie Archibald R176946

Leslie was born on July 21, 1914, the son of Archibald and Helen (Carey) Bain, New Campbellton. He enlisted on September 2, 1942, AC2 with the Royal Canadian Air Force. He took his basic training at Edmunston, New Brunswick and Lachine, Quebec. In January, 1944, Leading Air Craftsman Bain went overseas and served in England, France, Belgium and Germany. He was discharged on September 18, 1945.

He married Ethel MacInnis, North Shore. They

operated a general store at Big Bras d'Or which continues to be administered by his family. Leslie died on April 13, 1982, and is buried in St. James Cemetery, Big Bras d'Or.

Baldwin, Patrick Alexander Graham Bell

Patrick was a son of Frederick W. Casey and Kathleen (Parmenter) Baldwin, Beinn Bhreagh. He volunteered for duty in the Royal Canadian Navy Reserves in 1939 and served four years in motor gun boats and motor torpedo boats in the English Channel against German E Boats. He took the helm of two early hydrofoils, the *Massawippi* and the *KC-B*. Those prototypes led to one that was once the world's fastest warship, the *Bras d'Or*. He joined the Royal Canadian Navy full time in 1946. He was a keen recreational sailor and marine artist. At fourteen years of age, he crossed the Atlantic on the original *Bluenose* on its only trans-Atlantic crossing. He resided in Halifax and died in June, 1984.

Baldwin, Robert B.

Left -Robert Baldwin

Bobby was a son of Frederick W. Casey and Kathleen (Parmenter) Baldwin, Beinn Bhreagh. He was a graduate of Dalhousie Law School.

He served in the Royal Canadian Naval Volunteer Reserve and was First Lieutenant on the Canadian corvette *Rimouski*. Bobby and Patrick Baldwin were the sons of Casey Baldwin, M.L.A., the first British subject to fly a plane. They were also the great grandson of Sir Robert Baldwin, a pre-Confederation premier of Upper Canada.

Barron, Alexander F9210

Alex was born on January 17, 1912, the son of Mike and Priscilla (Donovan) Barron, Ingonish Harbour. Gunner Barron served in the Royal Canadian Artillery in Canada, United Kingdom and Continental Europe (1942 to 1946). He returned home with his war bride, Cornella Iske, Holland. He worked at the Cape Breton Highlands National Park. He died January 13, 1989, and is buried in St. Peter's Parish Cemetery.

The following is an article which appeared in the *Cape Breton Post*, an interview done by Maureen Scobie with Ella Barron.

(Alex Barron and wife, Ella)

'Ingonish Beach - Two long-ago memories remain vivid; clear as yesterday in Ella Barron's mind.

It was just after World War II in 1945, she recalls, and the Canadian forces had started to hold dances in Holland.

"At one particular dance, the moment we walked through the door we noticed bowls of fresh fruit," she says, "and I remember my cousin and I were quite greedy."

Impressed though she was by these rare delicacies, it was a tall, skinny soldier she met that night who more than impressed - the Canadian soldier captured Ella's heart.

Six months later, on January 24, 1946 Ella and Alex Barron were married in Amsterdam, Holland.

By the following May, she had said her goodbyes to family and country; joined other war brides on the voyage to London, where they embarked on the Queen Mary to join their husbands in Canada - and Ella Barron was on her way to her new home in Ingonish Beach.

"It was a very emotional time," she says, "especially for the English war brides, many with children, who were saying goodbye to their families and friends ... very emotional."

"Most of the English war brides were wearing fur coats and I remember wondering if there was snow in Canada in June."

When the train left Halifax, "I found I was the only war bride going to Cape Breton," she says. In those days there was no causeway; the train was ferried to Cape Breton. "And coming over Smokey - not a bit like today - a narrow dirt road. I think I closed my eyes most of the way" she says.

"I looked forward to arriving in North Sydney where Alex was to meet me," she says, "but when I arrived, no Alex. Here I was, expecting our first baby. I couldn't speak a word of English and I thought my new husband had deserted me. I just wanted to turn around and go home."

"Fortunately," she says, "I had his sister's address in North Sydney. I showed it to a kindly taxi driver who, drove me there, where Alex was waiting. It turned out I had arrived a day earlier than I was supposed to."

"Alex was a fisherman in those days," Ella continues. "There was no unemployment insurance. We got our groceries from a store on the hill. They were good people," she says. "We were in their books all winter and in spring the first earnings went to pay off the winter bill. It was very hard during those early years - you never caught up and so much depended on a good fishing catch."

"Alex suffered from emphysema," she said, "from sleeping in the bottom of those tanks. He never really got better and died January 13, 1990."

"He was a kind and thoughtful man" she recalls. "When I first came, everyone was making bread - something I had never done. I couldn't even cook the meals they were used to, so at first Alex did most of the cooking," she says.

"It was like living on a different planet. I was used to the city and getting used to peoples' ways and them getting used to mine was hard at first, but communicating was most difficult."

"I remember I couldn't wait for Ann Terry to come on the radio. It was Ann Terry who taught me English over the years," she says. "She was so wonderful."

Now, almost half a century later and fluent in English, Ella Barron finds it is Holland that is a bit strange when she visits her family there. Houses are birch and distances are short. And it is always nice to visit, she says, but "I'm always glad to return to my Ingonish home" - her nine children and twelve grand-children.'

Barron, Andrew

Andrew was the son of John and Bessie (Hawley) Barron, Ingonish Harbour. He served in Canada. He married and moved to the Alder Point area and he is buried there.

Barron, Godfrey

'Dots' was born on October 30, 1916, the son of Michael and Priscilla (Donovan) Barron. He served with the Cape Breton Highlanders in Bermuda. He married Mae MacIntyre. He worked at the Cape Breton Highlands National Park. He died on May 6, 1981, and is buried in St. Peter's Parish Cemetery, Ingonish.

Barron, Joseph

'Dode' was the son of Michael T. and Bridget (Hanrahan) Barron, Ingonish. He served overseas during the war. He worked at the Cape Breton Highlands National Park. He was unmarried and is buried in St. Peter's Parish Cemetery, Ingonish.

(Left - Joseph 'Dode' Barron, right - Sylvester Barron).

Barron, Percy Andrew

Percy was the son of George and Bridget (Whitty) Barron, Ingonish Harbour. He served in the navy during the war. He was a fisherman. He was predeceased by his wife, Jean Forgeron. He and his wife resided in Arichat.

(Right - Percy Barron)

Barron, Sylvester F97725

Sylvester is the son of George and Bridget (Whitty) Barron, Ingonish Harbour. Private Barron served in the Canadian Army in Canada. He married Ruby Dupe, Ingonish. He worked at the Cape Breton Highlands National Park. He and his wife reside at the Beach Crossing, Ingonish.

(left - Sylvester Barron, right - Percy Barron)

Barron, Theodore Francis

'Teed' was the son of John and Bessie (Hawley) Barron, Ingonish.He served in the army in Canada. He married and worked with the maintenance department at Sydney Academy.

Beaton, Edward

Edward was born in 1901, the son of Rev. Lauchlin Beaton and Margaret (MacMillan) Beaton, Boularderie/ Cape North. He served overseas in the Royal Canadian Air Force as a wing commander.

He and Mrs. Beaton were presented to the King and Queen of England. Mrs. Beaton was the former Margaret E. MacLeod, Baddeck. Prior to the war, Mr. Beaton operated a drug store in Baddeck. This establishment was destroyed by the fire of 1926 that ravaged so much of the village. He died on July 5, 1961, in Moncton and is buried in Greenwood Cemetery, Baddeck.

Bedwin, Albert Field F16185

Albert was born in October,1909, the son of William Field and Ella Louise Bedwin, Baddeck Bay. Private Bedwin served overseas with the North Nova Scotia Highlanders, Royal Canadian Infantry Corps. Thirty-five year old Private Bedwin was killed in action on February 14, 1945. He is buried in Groesbeek Canadian War Cemetery, Netherlands.

Besides his parents, he was survived by a young widow, Norma Collins Bedwin, of Grimshaw, Alberta. His widow and three young children were residing in Truro at the time of his death. Albert's father, William Bedwin, was a laboratory superintendent with Dr. Alexander Graham Bell, Beinn Bhreagh.

Bernard, Frank Larry

Frank hailed from Wagmatcook. Privatc Bernard served in Canada.

Bernard, Stephen

Stephen hailed from Wagmatcook. Private Bernard served during the war.

Bernard, William

William hailed from Wagmatcook. Private Bernard served during the war.

Bethune, Dr. Clarence Melville, M.D., B.Sc., C.M., M.B., M.B.E., F.R.C.P., D.C.L.

'Tabby' was born on March 22, 1903, the son of Dr. John L. (M.D.) and Mary (Jones) Bethune, Baddeck.

Dr. Bethune graduated from Dalhousie Medical School in 1931. During the war he served in Canada, England, France, Belgium and Germany from 1939 to 1945. He served as the Registrar of Halifax Military Hospital, D.A.D.M.S. Canadian Sec. 21 Army Group, and Registrar of No. 7 Canadian General Hospital which was set up in England on the estate of Lord and Lady Astor. On January 1, 1949, he received the **Order of the British Empire** from H.M. King George VI at Buckingham Palace for his operation of the # 7 General Hospital. He received the **Order of Canada** in 1976 at Government House, Ottawa.

Dr. Bethune was superintendent of the Victoria General Hospital in Halifax for many years. He died on October 13, 1993, and is buried in St. John St. Peter Anglican Cemetery, Baddeck.

Bethune, Dr. Gordon Wallace M.D.,C.M., F.R.C.S., (C) F.A.C.S.

Gordon was born in 1919, the son of John H. Gordon (World War I) and Mabel (Hickey) Bethune, Baddeck.

He graduated from Acadia University in 1939 with his B.Sc. degree. In 1943, he graduated as a licensed physician from Dalhousie Medical School. Dr. Bethune served as a medical officer in the Royal Canadian Army Medical Corps. Captain Bethune served in Italy, France and Germany until demobilization in 1946.

In 1950 he received his fellowship of the Royal College of Physicians and Surgeons of Canada. For many years he was Professor and Chief of Surgery at Dalhousie University and the Victoria General Hospital, Halifax. A tribute from the *Chronicle Herald* on April 29, 1998 reads in part - "A dedicated physician and accomplished surgeon, teacher and administrator, Dr. Bethune helped bring medicine in Nova Scotia to the mature stature which now it enjoys."

Dr. Bethune married Helen Lorraine Daley, Halifax. He died on April 26, 1998.

Bird, Charles F8828

Charlie was born on October 28, 1914, the son of Richard and Rachael (Williams) Bird, Neil's Harbour. He enlisted in the Canadian Army on March 17, 1943, and saw active duty in Continental Europe. He married Muriel Heaney and eventually they retired to Prince Edward Island.

Bird, Cyril F3964

Cyril was born on April 14, 1911, the son of Richard and Rachael (Williams) Bird of Neil's Harbour. He enlisted in the Canadian Army on November 11, 1942, and served overseas. After the war, he and his wife settled in Glace Bay. He was a fisherman. He died on June 20, 1984, and is buried in Glace Bay.

Bonaparte, Angus Lewis

Angus was the son of Seward and Sadie (MacDonald) Bonaparte, McKinnons Harbour. He served with the Canadian Provost Corps in Canada.

He married Josephine Northen, Ottawa Brook. They resided in Sydney where he worked at the Steel Plant. He is buried in Resurrection Cemetery, Sydney.

Bonaparte, Charles Lewis F10581

Charlie was the son of Joseph and Mary (Mombourquette) Bonaparte, McKinnons Harbour. Gunner Bonaparte served in the Canadian Army in Canada from 1943 to 1946.

He married Margaret MacDonald, Dominion. He is retired from the Canadian National Railway. He died on September 17, 1998, and is buried in Sacred Heart Cemetery, McKinnons Harbour.

Bonaparte, Michael Charles

'Michael Charlie' was the son of Seward and Sadie (MacDonald) Bonaparte, McKinnons Harbour.

He served with the Cape Breton Highlanders and the Royal Canadian Army in Canada and Newfoundland. He married Margaret Seddon. He worked at the Sydney Steel Plant. He died in February, 1966, and is buried in Sydney.

Bonaparte, Nora W6634

Nora is the daughter of Joseph and Mary (Mombourquette) Bonaparte, McKinnons Harbour. Private Bonaparte served with the Canadian Women's Army Corps in Canada for three years. She married Maurice Gagne, Quebec. She is retired and living in Ottawa Brook.

Bonaparte, Roderick James F77499

Rod was the son of Seward and Sadie (MacDonald) Bonaparte, McKinnons Harbour. He served with the Royal Canadian Army in Canada and the United Kingdom. He married Daphne Muldoon, England. He was tragically killed in a drowning accident while tending his fishing nets.

Bonaparte, Seward

Seward was the son of Seward and Sadie (MacDonald) Bonaparte, McKinnons Harbour. He served in Canada. He married Mary MacKenzie, Sydney. He worked at the Steel Plant in Sydney. He is buried in Resurrection Cemetery, Sydney.

Boulter, Joseph

Joe was born in 1917, the son of Swinburn and Christena (Devoe) Boulter, Sydney Mines. His mother died in childbirth. He was raised by John and Charlotte (MacDonald) Matheson, Cain's Mountain.

He served during the war. He married Violet Holmes, Brighton, England and they resided in Cain's Mountain. He died in 1974 and is buried in the Little Narrows Cemetery.

Brewer, Gordon Thomas F86162

Gordon was born on October 26, 1923, the son of Wallace Alonzo and Mary Ellen Brewer, Ingonish Centre. Private Brewer served with the Essex Scottish Regiment, Royal Canadian Infantry Corps. He was killed in action on October 25, 1944, and is buried in Bergen-Op-Zoom Cemetery, Netherlands.

Brewer, Henry Courtney F87799

Henry was born on December 30, 1919, the son of Michael and Charlotte (Stockley) Brewer, Ingonish. He enlisted on August 16, 1941, and served as a Heavy Artillery Bombardier. He went overseas on July 24, 1942. His ship was torpedoed. During combat in Germany, he suffered shrapnel wounds to his left shoulder and lower lip. He was discharged on February 2, 1946.

He married Marion MacArthur, Cape Breton County. He died on January 11, 1983, and is buried in Hardwood Hill Cemetery, Sydney.

Brewer, James Thomas F3448

Jim was born on April 2, 1913, the son of James G. and Minnie Brewer, South Ingonish. Gunner Brewer served in Canada, United Kingdom and Continental Europe (1942 to 1945). He married Molly MacGean, Ingonish. He worked at the Cape Breton Highlands National Park. He died January 31, 1960, and is buried in St. Peter's Parish Cemetery, Ingonish.

Brewer, Thomas William

Tom was born on November 7, 1914, the son of William Christopher and Elizabeth Brewer, North Ingonish. He served during the war. He married Eunice Dupe, Ingonish. He was a fisherman. He died on March 22, 1985.

Brewer, William Dugan

Billy was born on September 12, 1921, in the United States. He was raised by Mrs. Annie Brewer, River Bennet. He served in the United States Merchant Marine. His wife hailed from Prince Edward Island and they resided in the United States. In civilian life, he worked as a crane operator and as a seaman on the Great Lakes. He died on June 1, 1992, and is buried in the United States.

Briand, Ernest F97103

Ernest was born in 1917, the son of William and Martha (Dixon) Briand, Smelt Brook. Private Briand served with the Cape Breton Highlanders. He married Jeannette Harris, Newfoundland. He worked at the gypsum plant in Dingwall. He died on May 22, 1995, and is buried in St. Joseph's Cemetery, Dingwall.

Briand, James F55184

Jimmy was the son of William and Martha (Dixon) Briand, Smelt Brook. Private Briand served with the North Nova Scotia Highlanders in the United Kingdom. One of four brothers to serve his country, he was wounded in action. He now resides in Ontario.

Briand, John F55280

Jack was born on March 2, 1914, the son of William and Martha (Dixon) Briand, Smelt Brook. Private Briand served with the North Nova Scotia Highlanders. He enlisted on June 13, 1940, and served until June 16, 1941. He sustained a severe elbow injury while jumping to avoid an oncoming train. He married Margaret Fitzgerald, White Point. He worked at the National Gypsum Plant, Dingwall. He died on November 23, 1984, and is buried in St. Joseph's Cemetery, Dingwall.

Briand, William M. F55295

'Billy Mike' was the son of William and Martha (Dixon) Briand, Smelt Brook. Private Briand served with the North Nova Scotia Highlanders. He married and resided in Amherst. He was killed in a motor vehicle accident and is buried in Amherst.

Brown, Alexander

Alex was the son of Peter and Cecilia (Smith) Brown, Bay St. Lawrence. Private Brown served in the Royal Canadian Engineers 5th Division. He was one of four brothers who served his country, and two of them made the supreme sacrifice. When he returned from the war, he went to work in the mines in Ontario. He was killed in a mining accident and it was months before his parents were aware of his death.

Brown, Lauchlin Benedict F89471

Lauchie was born on April 20, 1919, the son of Peter and Cecilia (Smith) Brown, Bay St. Lawrence. Private Brown served with the Cape Breton Highlanders in Italy, France and Germany (1941 to 1946). He worked for the National Gypsum Company in Dingwall. Later he moved away, but returned to care for his aged parents. Unmarried, he died on January 28, 1992, and is buried in St. Margaret's Village Cemetery.

Brown, Michael Joseph

Michael was the son of Jack and Jane (Burton) Brown, Bay St. Lawrence. Sapper Brown served with the Royal Canadian Engineers in Canada and the United Kingdom. He died on August 12, 1987, in Glace Bay and is buried in St. Margaret's Village Cemetery.

Brown, Michael Joseph F3002

Michael was born on February 25, 1913, the son of Neil and Julia (Pettipas) Brown, St. Margaret's Village. 'Sapper' Brown served with the Canadian Army in Canada from 1942 to 1946.

He died on October 31, 1992, and is buried in St. Margaret's Village Cemetery.

Brown, Michael Peter F32380

Michael was the son of Peter and Cecilia (Smith) Brown, Bay St. Lawrence. Corporal Brown served with The Black Watch (Royal Highland Regiment) of Canada, Royal Canadian Infantry Corps. Thirty-one year old Corporal Brown was killed in action on April 5, 1945. He is

buried in Holten Canadian War Cemetery, Netherlands. Besides his parents, Corporal Brown was survived by his young widow, Lillian May Brown.

Brown, Murdoch Lawrence F55587

Murdoch was a son of Peter and Cecilia (Smith) Brown, Bay St. Lawrence. Private Brown served with the Cape Breton Highlanders, Royal Canadian Infantry Corps. Twenty-three year old Private Brown was killed in active service in Sydney, on November 19, 1940. He is buried in St. Margaret's Cemetery, St. Margaret's Village.

Buchanan, Alexander Graham

Alexander Graham Buchanan was born on June 1, 1913, the son of Duncan and Isobel (MacRae) Buchanan in Big Baddeck. He served with the Royal Canadian Army Service Corps. He was a graduate of the Nova Scotia Agricultural College in Truro. He died at Soldiers Memorial Hospital in Middleton, Nova Scotia, on May 31, 1994.

Buchanan, Angus

Angus was born on April 18, 1928, the son of Everett and Margaret (MacLeod) Buchanan, Cape North. Private Buchanan served in the American Army. He worked for the Canadian National Institute for the Blind in Ontario. He is retired in Calgary.

Buchanan, Daniel Alexander

Dan Alex was born on September 13, 1916, the son of Murdoch and Annie (Morrison) Buchanan, Indian Brook. He enlisted on November 23, 1942, in Halifax and served with the West Nova Scotia Regiment in Canada and the Central Mediterranean. Private Buchanan was discharged in Halifax on June 16, 1945.

He married Sally Liddle, and he and his war bride returned to Cape Breton. They resided in Westmount. He is a retired steelworker from the Sydney Steel Plant.

Buchanan, Daniel Allan

Daniel Allan was born on September 16, 1907, to Farquhar and Jessie (Matheson) Buchanan of Big Baddeck.

He taught school at Upper Baddeck prior to serving overseas. Following the war, he settled in Quebec and was employed in the mining industry. He died in Asbestos, Quebec on September 2, 1994. His ashes were committed in St. Andrews Cemetery, Baddeck Forks.

Buchanan, Douglas Lloyd

(Back row, left to right - 3rd, Douglas Buchanan. Front row, left to right - 3rd, Harold Hanam.)

Douglas was born in 1913, the son of merchant Angus A. and Mary (MacLeod) Buchanan, Neil's Harbour. He served in the Royal Canadian Navy. He was employed in Stellarton with the Nova Scotia Power Commission. His family home was turned into a cottage hospital, the Buchanan Memorial Hospital at Neil's Harbour. Unmarried, he died in 1978.

Buchanan, George

George was the son of Malcolm and Bella (Smith) Buchanan, Jersey Cove. He served in the Merchant Marine. For a short time he was married to Edie Myers. He worked as an engineer on the Englishtown Ferry. He died in Englishtown and is buried in Pine Hill Cemetery, River Bennett.

Buchanan, Henry Taylor

Henry was born on February 28, 1922, the son of Dan Neil and Euphemia (Taylor) Buchanan, Goose Cove. He served in Canada with the Canadian Army. He married and he and his wife reside in Saskatchewan.

Buchanan, John K.

'John K.' was a son of Malcolm and Bella (Smith) Buchanan, Jersey Cove. Trimmer Buchanan served in the Merchant Navy. His ship went down off the coast of Spain and he was lost at sea on December 2, 1941. His medal from King George V is extant. It reads: John K. Buchanan *"SS Floyd."*

Buchanan, Kenneth John F1555

'Black Kenny' was born in 1908, the son of Kenneth and Catherine (MacDonald) Buchanan, Baddeck. He enlisted on August 2, 1942 in the Canadian Army. He served in Canada as a postal carrier. He was discharged on April 16, 1946. Unmarried, he died in 1976 and is buried in St. Patrick's Channel Cemetery.

Buchanan, Norman

'Norman Bella' was a son of Malcolm and Bella (Smith) Buchanan, Jersey Cove. He served in the Canadian Army. He worked in No. 24 Colliery, Glace Bay and with the Department of Transportation. Unmarried, he died on March 8, 1993 and is buried in Pine Hill Cemetery, River Bennett.

Buchanan, Norman D.

Norman was born on February 14, 1918, the son of Dan Neil and Euphemia (Taylor) Buchanan, Goose Cove. He enlisted with the New Brunswick Rangers. He served in England, Germany and Holland. He married Mary Carmichael, Goose Cove. He died in Ontario in January, 1966.

Buchanan, Sylvia

Sylvia is the daughter of George and Katie (MacLean) Buchanan, Ingonish. She served in the army during the war and now resides in Toronto, Ontario.

Budge, George Frederick F23031

Freddie was born on December 25, 1916, the son of George and Fanny (Waye) Budge, Neil's Harbour. He enlisted in the Canadian Army on August 6, 1942. He was wounded overseas while serving with the Black Watch Regiment. He recovered in a hospital in Amiens, France. He married Edith Petrie, Neil's Harbour. He was a lighthouse keeper on St. Paul's Island. He and his wife retired to Neil's Harbour.

(Left to right - second, George Budge)

Budge, James F2948

James was born on February 22, 1918, the son of Charles and Ada (Hardy) Budge, New Haven. He enlisted in 1942 in the Canadian Army and served overseas as a vehicle mechanic. He married Theresa Fricker, Neil's Harbour. In civilian life, he was a mechanic and worked at the gypsum plant in Milford. He died in 1996 and is buried in Milford, Nova Scotia.

Budge, Robert W. F32677

Robert was born on February 1, 1918, the son of Alfred and Anna (Chislett) Budge, New Haven. He enlisted on November 27, 1942, in the Canadian Army. After the war, he resided in Glace Bay where he was employed at a fish plant. He retired to New Haven.

(Left, Robert Budge)

Budge, Walter F32678

Walter was born on December 12, 1922, the son of George and Fanny (Waye) Budge. He enlisted on November 27, 1942, in the Canadian Army and served overseas. He married Ethel Fricker, Neil's Harbour. He worked for Cape Breton Highlands National Park. They retired to New Haven. He died on August 21, 1996 and is buried in St. Peter's Cemetery, Neil's Harbour.

Buffett, Charles

Charlie was born in 1900, the son of Matthew and Elizabeth (Buffett) Buffett, Neil's Harbour. He served in the Merchant Navy. He was a sailor and he retired to Neil's Harbour. He died in 1960 and is buried in St. Andrew's Cemetery, Neil's Harbour.

Buffett, Harold W. F32679

Harold was born on December 18, 1923, the son of Charles and Elizabeth Buffett, White Point. He joined the Canadian Army in 1942 and served overseas. He married Judy Burton, Cape North. After the war he rejoined the Canadian Armed Forces where he served as a cook in the army. He and his wife retired to Oromocto, New Brunswick. He died in 1996.

Buffett, James Henry F31983

James Henry was born on April 24, 1922, the son of Luke and Susan (Warren) Buffett, Neil's Harbour. He enlisted in the Canadian Army on July 23, 1942, and served overseas. He married Gwenlyn Askay and they resided in Hamilton, Ontario where he worked as a bricklayer.

(Left - Jim Buffet)

Buffett, John

Johnnie was born on December 9, 1914, the son of Charles and Elizabeth Buffett, White Point. Third Officer Buffett joined the Merchant Navy in 1942 and served on the North Atlantic and Indian Oceans. He resided in Hamilton, Ontario, where he was a steelworker. He died in 1982.

Buffett, Leslie F2053

Leslie was born on May 2, 1924, the son of Luke and Susan (Warren) Buffett, Neil's Harbour. He enlisted on July 23, 1943, in the Canadian Army. He served overseas as an orderly aboard the Canadian hospital ship, *Lady Nelson*. He married Elizabeth Dowling, Neil's Harbour. He worked for Babcock Company, Ontario, and later as an orderly at Camp Hill Veterans' Hospital, Halifax. He moved back to Neil's Harbour where he worked with the maintenance department at Buchanan Memorial Hospital. He is retired and living in Neil's Harbour. He is a dedicated volunteer researcher who contributed greatly to this book.

Buffett, Robert Roger F89404

Robert was born on February 22, 1918, the son of Luke and Susan (Warren) Buffett, Neil's Harbour. Gunner Buffett enlisted on July 21, 1944, in the Canadian Army and served overseas. He was wounded at Caen, France. He married Beatrice Warr. He worked with a construction company in Halifax. They retired to Glace Bay where he died on March 21, 1998. He is buried in St. Andrew's Cemetery, Neil's Harbour.

Burt, Lawrence Whitney Eastman

Laurie was born on March 18, 1925, the son of Gladys Burt, Baddeck. Petty Officer Burt served in the Royal Canadian Naval Reserve in the North Atlantic. He was a former merchant seaman in the navy. He married and he and his wife reside in British Columbia.

Burt, William Thomas F89198

William was born on September 3, 1911, the son of Andrew and Margaret Elizabeth (Lamond) Burt, Baddeck. He served overseas with the Cape Breton Highlanders for the duration of the war. He married Katherine MacAskill, Red Head. They moved to Sydney. He then resided in Toronto for many years and eventually returned to Englishtown. He died on December 25, 1977, and is buried in North Sydney.

Burton, Alexander F97411

Alex was born on March 20, 1914, the son of Peter J. and Margaret (Kavanaugh) Burton, St. Margaret's Village. He enlisted on February 28, 1942, and served in the Royal Hamilton Light Infantry. Corporal Burton's theatres of service were in France, Belgium, Holland and Germany. He married Mary Stewart, Inverness County. They resided at St. Margaret's Village where he was a fisherman. He died onAugust 26, 1995, and is buried in St. Margaret's Village Cemetery.

Burton, Allan F60717

Allan was born on September 6, 1920, the son of Peter J. and Margaret (Kavanaugh) Burton, St. Margaret's Village. Private Burton enlisted on October 28, 1942 and served in the Royal Canadian Army Service Corps. He was discharged on March 20, 1946. He married Catherine Robinson. He is a retired fisherman and resides in St. Margaret's Village.

Burton, Angus

Angus was born on May 22, 1911, the son of Henry and Hannah (MacMillan) Burton, Bay St. Lawrence. Private Burton served with the Royal Canadian Engineers. He married Catherine Donahue, Bay St. Lawrence. He died in 1944 in Ontario.

Burton, Annabel

Annabel was the daughter of Allan and Grace (MacLeod) Burton, South Harbour. She served in the Canadian Women's Army Corps. Her married surname is Smith. She resides in Florida.

Burton, Ernest F37839

Ernie was born on August 21, 1926, the son of Peter J. and Margaret (Kavanaugh) Burton, St. Margaret's Village. Private Burton served in the Canadian Infantry Corps from 1944 to 1945. He and his wife, Mary MacDonald, reside in Dingwall. He was a fisherman.

Burton, Gordon

Gordon was the son of John and Mary (MacDonald) Burton, Glen Nevis. He served during the war. He is buried in MacPherson Cemetery, Cape North.

Burton, James C.

'Jim Henry' was the son of Henry and Catherine (Young) Burton, Bay St. Lawrence. Private Burton served with the Cape Breton Highlanders in England and Italy. He married Julia Catherine MacNeil, Bay St. Lawrence. He was a fisherman. He is buried in St. Margaret's Village Cemetery.

Burton, John F32631

Jack was born on June 10, 1915, the son of Peter J. and Margaret (Kavanaugh) Burton, St. Margaret's Village. He enlisted on November 17, 1942, and served in the Royal Canadian Army Signal Corps. Private Burton was discharged on February 24, 1947. He married Lorna Kenefick. He died on July 1, 1991, and is buried in Halifax. He was one of four Burton brothers who served his country during the Second World War.

Burton, Joseph

'Little Joe' was the son of George and Effie (Hellen) Burton, Cape North. Able Seaman Burton served in the Canadian Merchant Navy. The doors of his ship were jammed shut when his vessel was torpedoed while in port. He and his shipmate perished on October 19, 1940.

Burton, Norman Murdock

Norman was the son of Allan and Grace (MacLeod) Burton, South Harbour. He enlisted in 1941 in the United States Navy 82nd Airborne 13 Division. He married Blanche Falconer, Sydney. He died on January 10, 1997, and is buried in MacPherson Cemetery, Dingwall.

Burton, Ruth Ann

Ruth was born on January 30, 1924, the daughter of William H. and Catherine (Young) Burton, Bay St. Lawrence. Private Burton served in the Canadian Women's Army Corps. She married Ralph Pompe and lived in the United States. She died on February 20, 1991.

Burton, William T. F56206

Willie was born on July 31, 1921, the son of James I. (World War I and World War II) and Susan (Young) Burton, Bay St. Lawrence. He enlisted on January 20, 1943, and served during the war. He married Mary Margaret MacNeil. He was light keeper at Money Point and they operated the Bay St. Lawrence Post Office. He died on January 22, 1976, and is buried in St. Margaret's Village Cemetery.

Burton, Wilson Angus F97840

Wilson Angus was born on November 7, 1921, the son of Angus and Effie Kate (Petrie) Burton, Cape North. He enlisted on May 18, 1942. Private Burton served in Canada. He was discharged on December 4, 1942. He married Alena Agnes Cummings, Point Edward. He died on September 9, 1976, and is buried in Ontario.

Buzzan, George

George was the son of Mary (Campbell) Buzzan. He was raised by his uncle and aunt, Alex and Christy (MacNeil) Campbell, Red Point. He served in the American Army. His older brother was a bugler during World War I. He died in July, 1997, and is buried in St. Columba Cemetery, Iona.

Cameron, Ernest J. F88326

Ernie was born on August 15, 1918, the son of Donald and Catherine (Cameron) Cameron, Sugar Loaf. Private Cameron served with the Nova Scotia Highlanders, Royal Canadian Infantry Corps. He was later taken prisoner of war in June, 1944 during the invasion of France. While on "the death march" he was unable to continue and was shot by the enemy on February 10, 1945. He is buried in Prague War Cemetery, Czechoslovakia.

Cameron, John Angus

'John A.' was the son of Mark and Tena (Burton) Cameron, Dingwall. Private Cameron served overseas during the war. He resides in Ontario.

Campbell, Dr. Angus, M.D.

Angus was the son of Malcolm R. (World War I) and Elizabeth (MacKenzie) Campbell, St. Columba. Private Campbell served in Canada. He married and he and his wife lived in Halifax and Bridgewater. He is a retired radiologist.

Campbell, Angus Hector

Angus was born on July 26, 1907, the son of Captain Daniel J. and Barbara (Livingstone) Campbell, Big Bras d'Or. His family resided on Bird Island for many years. On June 20, 1940, Officer Campbell was serving as second mate on the oil tanker *S.S. James McGee* when she triggered a magnetic mine which exploded and sank her.

On August 1, 1940, he joined the navy as a sub-lieutenant and was discharged as a skipper lieutenant. He received two mentions in dispatches for his actions in helping save a floundering ship, the *S.S. Matthew Lukenbach*.

Captain Campbell is featured in the book *Running the Gauntlet* by Mike Parker. He married Beryl

Collins, R.N., Collingwood, Ontario. They resided in Halifax. Master Mariner Campbell died on April 9, 1998, and his ashes were scattered at sea off Bird Island.

Campbell, Archibald Albert V84262

Bert was born on April 7, 1926, the son of Daniel and Barbara (Livingstone) Campbell, Big Bras d'Or. He served with the Royal Canadian Naval Volunteer Reserve from 1944 to 1946. He married Marilyn MacDonald. He worked as a foreman with the Department of Transport. He and his wife reside in Sydney River.

Campbell, Christine Isobel W309013

Christine was born on May 2, 1922, the daughter of Phillip and Mary (MacIver) Campbell, Hunters' Mountain. She enlisted on November 14, 1942, with the Royal Canadian Air Force (Women's Division). She took basic training at Rockcliff, Ontario and was then posted to Headquarters in Ottawa. Later she served at Sydney Reserve Airport and in Halifax. Corporal Campbell was discharged on January 26, 1946. She was a dental assistant in civilian life. She married Edward G. Lundrigan. They reside in Whitney Pier.

Campbell, Daniel John A4989

Daniel John was born at Ciboux Island on August 29, 1916, the son of Daniel and Barbara (Livingstone) Campbell, Big Bras d'Or.

He enlisted on August 18, 1941, and he served with the Royal Canadian Navy. Leading Seaman Campbell served in the Atlantic, Caribbean, Arctic and off the coast of France. He was serving in the Channel on D-Day. He was discharged on June 11, 1945.

He married Lelia Grant and he worked for Atlantic Pilotage Authority. He died on January 3, 1991, and is buried in St. James Cemetery, Big Bras d'Or.

Campbell, Daniel Joseph

Dan Joe was the son of Dan and Sarah (MacNeil) Campbell, Jamesville. He served in the Canadian Army. His three half brothers - Jerry, Hugh and Angus Campbell (Grand Narrows) - also served during World War II.

Campbell, Donald Alexander A2840

Donnie was born on May 7, 1919, the son of John and Grace (MacKinnon) Campbell, Big Bras d'Or. He enlisted on October 3, 1940, with the Royal Canadian Naval Reserve. He was discharged on July 23, 1945.

He married Norma Morrison, Rear Little River, North Shore. He worked on Ross Ferry and then as Captain on the Big Bras d'Or Ferry. He died on April 29, 1986, and is buried in St. James Cemetery, Big Bras d'Or.

Campbell, Donald John F79922

Donald was born on March 1, 1919, the son of Angus and Tena (Campbell) Campbell, South Gut. He enlisted in 1942 and served in the Canadian Army 4th Division. Private Campbell served in Germany, Belgium and Holland. He was discharged in September, 1945.

He returned to South Haven and was employed on Ross Ferry. Later he moved to Toronto. He died on July 5, 1998, and his ashes were interred in Harbourview Cemetery, South Haven.

Campbell, Edwin A.

Edwin was the son of William and Alice (MacDermid) Campbell, Hunters' Mountain. Private Campbell served with the Princess Patricia Canadian Light Infantry. He married Hughena MacDonald. He was employed with the Sydney Steel Corporation. He died at 62 years of age and is buried in Forest Haven Memorial Gardens, Sydney.

Campbell, Elizabeth W60715

Betty was the adopted daughter of John and Grace (MacKinnon) Campbell, Big Bras d'Or. She served with the Canadian Women's Army Corps from 1944 to 1945. She married Allan Urquhart and lives in Glace Bay, Cape Breton.

Campbell, Francis Joseph

Francis Joseph was the son of John H. and Margaret (MacNeil) Campbell, Jamesville. He served overseas in the Canadian Army. He married Catherine Matlock. He was a coal miner and operated Campbell's Store in Scotchtown. He died on February 1, 1996, and is buried in St. Michael's Parish Cemetery, New Waterford.

Campbell, John Daniel F89889

Danny was born on July 9, 1909, the son of Henry and Christy (MacDonald) Campbell, Quarry, St. Ann's. He enlisted in 1941. Private Campbell served in the Canadian Army in Canada. He married Hannah MacLennan, Glace Bay. They resided in Baddeck. He died on November 30, 1966, and is buried in Harbourview Cemetery, South Haven.

Campbell, John Russell

Russell was born on January 3, 1915, the son of John A. and Grace (MacKinnon) Campbell, Big Bras d'Or. Leading Seaman Campbell enlisted in the Royal Canadian Navy. He took ill aboard ship and passed away in the military hospital at Prince Rupert, British Columbia, on April 2, 1945.

Stoker Campbell was buried with full military honours and his body was laid to rest in St. James Cemetery, Big Bras d'Or.

Campbell, John Samuel F 87815

John Sam was born on May 19, 1920, the son of Murdoch and Janie (MacRitchie) Campbell, Englishtown. He enlisted on October 9, 1941, in New Glasgow. He served with the Royal Canadian Army Service Corps. Sergeant Campbell served in Canada, United Kingdom and Europe. He was discharged on March 7, 1946, in Sydney. He married Helen Hobson. They resided in Toronto. He died in 1986 and is buried in Bayview Cemetery, Englishtown.

Campbell, Neil Donald R 104292

'Sonny' Campbell was born on June 12, 1919, in Cape North, the son of Allan and Flora (MacKinnon) Campbell, Baddeck Bridge. During his childhood, his family moved to the Big Farm Road. He was a graduate of the Baddeck Academy. He displayed outstanding musical talent as he could play most instruments. After high school, he delivered the mail from Orangedale to Baddeck. This was a time when the mail was sorted on the train and then transported to Whycocomagh, Bucklaw, Nyanza and Baddeck. It was conveyed by car during snowless months, but in winter, a horse and sleigh was the means of transportation.

He enlisted with the Royal Canadian Air Force in 1940 and completed basic training at Guelph, Ontario, where he received his wings as a wireless air gunner. Pilot Officer Campbell served overseas with No. 500 County of Kent Squadron. During coastal patrol, he flew many sorties over enemy territory. On March 7, 1944, his plane Venturio Aircraft # F3546, crashed into the sea and exploded twenty miles north of Capede Laiquelle, Algeria. All crew members were lost. His name is inscribed on the Malta War Memorial, Malta.

Campbell, Neil John MacIver F31666

John was born in 1918, the son of Phillip A. and Mary (MacIver) Campbell, Hunters' Mountain.

Trooper Campbell served in the Duke of Connaught Rifles British Columbia Regiment - 28th Canadian Armed Tank Regiment. He served in Canada, England and France. Trooper Neil John Campbell was killed in action August 9, 1944, in France. His name is inscribed on panel 19, column 3, Bayeux Memorial, France. The following poem was written by his father in his memory.

Two years have passed since you have gone,
We found it sad and pressing,
To think of only a few years passed,
You were to our home a blessing.

The Germans thought they were smart,
To obey their Nazi masters,
They plundered and killed, and killed dear John,
And now they are reaping disaster.

Your brother at the time in the Italy fray,
As you wrote you said you worried,
That Stanley so young and not so strong,
Twas' of him, you said you worried.

We are not alone who felt the foe,
But many thousand others,
We hope and pray we'll see the day,
No one need die for others.

The last cruel battle you were in,
We know your thoughts were true,
Oh, how we wish we were near enough,
To say farewell to you.

High noon and tide will come and go,
But high memory of you will stay,
And those who think of you today,
Are the ones who love you best.

We do not know where your body lies,
Except away off yonder,
Some day not long, we'll meet beyond,
Once more to be home together.

Then sleep dear John, sleep on and take your rest,
Your name indeed is written with the best,
You gave your life without a thought of fear,
Forgive us "John" if we but shed one tear,
For you, whose memory now will linger on,
In fondest dreams - so sweet to look upon.

Campbell, Roy Alexander R 124733

Roy was born on June 9, 1914, the son of Angus and Tena (Campbell) Campbell, South Gut. He enlisted on August 30, 1941, and served with the Royal Canadian Air Force in Canada, United Kingdom and Continental Europe. He flew in Sterling and Lancaster planes. During his thirty-two flying missions over Germany, he was hit twice, but made it back to base. He was discharged on March 2, 1945.

He married Christine MacLennan, Boularderie. They resided in Toronto. He died on April 8, 1995, and interment was at Harbourview Cemetery, South Haven.

Campbell, Roy MacKinnon A 4615

Roy was born on January 1, 1910, the son of John and Grace (MacKinnon) Campbell, Big Bras d'Or. He enlisted on May 14, 1941, with the Royal Canadian Naval Reserve. He served in the North and South Atlantic.

He married Sadie Morrison, Englishtown. They resided in Big Bras d'Or and then moved to Ontario. He died on September 15, 1992, and is buried in St. James Cemetery, Big Bras d'Or.

(brothers Roy Campbell - left, and Donald Campbell - right)

Campbell, Stanley William F54726

Stanley was born in 1921, the son of Phillip and Mary (MacIver) Campbell, Hunters' Mountain. Private Campbell served with the Cape Breton Highlanders. He enlisted on September 3, 1939, and served in Canada, England, Italy and North West Europe. He was discharged on demobilization on September 3, 1945.

He was predeceased by his first wife Mary MacKenzie, Washabuck. He later married Margaret MacLeod, Tarbot. They resided in Hunters' Mountain. He presently resides in Sydney Mines.

Campbell, Stewart Cunard V73823

Stewart was the son of Johnny Sam and Carrie (Giles) Campbell, Ingonish/ Baddeck. He enlisted on January 17, 1944, as an ordinary seaman and served in the Royal Canadian Naval Volunteer Reserve. His theatres of service were in Canada and the North Atlantic. Able Seaman Campbell was discharged on January 16, 1946.

He married and made a career in banking. His father was Governor and lighthouse keeper at St. Paul's Island and also served as M.L.A. for Victoria County.

Campbell, Thomas Donald F32460

Tommy was born on September 20, 1917, the son of Murdoch and Janie (MacRitchie) Campbell, Englishtown. Private Campbell served in the Royal Canadian Army. He enlisted on October 13, 1942, and was discharged on April 11, 1946.

He married Isobel Montgomery, Jersey Cove. He worked for twenty-seven years with the Englishtown Ferry. He became Ferry Captain. He died on April 10, 1992 and is buried in Bayview Cemetery, Englishtown.

Campbell, William F89359

Bill was born on March 10, 1911, the son of William and Barbara (Stephenson) Campbell. He was raised by relatives, Jack and Florence Squires and Malcolm J. and Mrs. MacAulay, Big Bras d'Or. He enlisted on July 21, 1941. He served in Canada and overseas in Holland as a gunner in the infantry. He was discharged on January 11, 1946.

He married Mildred Robertson, Big Bras d'Or. He worked aboard the Big Bras d'Or Ferry. Later they moved to Natick, Massachusetts. He died on October 14, 1980, and is buried in St. James Cemetery, Big Bras d'Or.

Cann, James Walter

Jimmy was born in 1916, the son of William and Maisie (Doyle) Cann, Ingonish Centre. Gunner Cann served in the Light Artillery in Canada (defence at Aldershot). Unmarried, he died in 1985 and is buried in St. Peter's Parish Cemetery.

Cantwell, Henry, O.B.E. F54602

Henry was born in 1908, the son of Daniel and Mary Jane (MacAulay) Cantwell, Baddeck. Warrant Officer Cantwell served overseas with the Cape Breton Highlanders - R.Q.M.S. He was awarded the Member of the **ORDER OF THE BRITISH EMPIRE**.

The following is taken from *The Breed of Manly Men*:

"Regimental Quartermaster-Sergeant Cantwell, who has had twenty-four years of service in the army, was appointed Regimental Quartermaster-Sergeant of The Cape Breton Highlanders on the commencement of hostilities in 1939, and has served continuously in that appointment to the present time.

During the week commencing 25 September 1944, the battalion was occupying positions on the RUBICON, FIUMICINO, Italy. Due to lack of roads, supplies had to be hauled a distance of twenty miles and continuous rains and very heavy and accurate enemy shell-fire made the available roads almost impassable. Despite these obstacles this Warrant Officer, who worked continuously with very little sleep for the entire week, supervised the drawing of rations, ammunition and petrol and personally delivered two hot meals each day up to the most forward troops. His cheerfulness and determination was largely responsible for maintaining the morale of all ranks at a high level during the most difficult period. Throughout all operations in which the battalion has been engaged in Italy and North-West Europe, Regimental Quartermaster-Sergeant Cantwell has served his battalion with great distinction. Despite almost unsurmountable difficulties in supply the battalion has never lacked food, ammunition or equipment. His practice of taking food and supplies to the most forward troops under any and all circumstances has enabled him to give personal direction to his subordinates and has set a high example of devotion to duty to all ranks.

The untiring energy and ability with which this Warrant Officer has performed the duties of his appointment over a long period have greatly contributed to the efficiency and success of the battalion."

He married Mary Ann MacDonald, Tarbot. He served as express agent and harbour master in Baddeck. He died on January 12, 1993, and is buried in Knox Auld Kirk Cemetery, Bay Road, Baddeck.

Capstick, Charles

Charlie was born on February 11, 1922, the son of John W. and Annie (Brown) Capstick, Capstick. He enlisted on November 1941 and served in Canada with the Royal Canadian Air Force, Marine Squadron. He was discharged in December, 1945. He married Evelyn Coll, Sydney Mines. He worked at the gypsum plants in Dingwall and Milford. He was residing in Halifax at the time of his death.

Capstick, Duncan Bernard F33046

'Buddy' was born on December 12, 1923, the son of Duncan and Margaret (MacDonald) Capstick, Capstick. Private Capstick served in the Canadian Army from 1943 to 1946. He was a fisherman and resides in Capstick.

Capstick, Francis Leo R65224

Francis was born on June 28, 1920, the son of John D. and Sarah (Brown) Capstick, Capstick. Flight Sergeant Capstick served in the Royal Canadian Air Force, 149 Squadron. His plane was shot down over the English Channel en route to target at Antwerp, Belgium on October 20, 1941. It had been his fourth and final mission. His name is inscribed on Panel 61, Runnymede Memorial Cemetery, Surrey, England.

Capstick, James R183228

Jim was born on February 2, 1912, the son of John W. and Annie (Brown) Capstick, Capstick.

He served in Canada in the Royal Canadian Air Force, Marine Squadron from 1941 to 1946.

He married Marie Kanary, Capstick. He was a fisherman and an employee of the gypsum plant in Dingwall. They reside in Dingwall.

Capstick, Maurice Clarence 176997

Maurice was born on April 7, 1916, the son of John W. and Annie (Brown) Capstick, Capstick. Sergeant Capstick served in Canada with the Royal Canadian Air Force, Marine Squadron.

He married Winnifred M. MacLean, Red River. He worked at the gypsum plant in Dingwall. He died on February 19, 1986, and is buried in Dingwall Cemetery.

Carmichael, Angus Daniel

'Captain Gussie' was the son of Captain Dan and Hattie (Matheson) Carmichael, Goose Cove, St. Ann's. He served as a Captain with the Merchant Navy. He married Catherine MacDonald, Murray. They resided in Goose Cove. He died in 1980 and is buried in Goose Cove Cemetery.

Carmichael, Angus Hector

Hector was born on March 22, 1914, the son of Captain Angus and Mary (MacDonald) Carmichael, Goose Cove, St. Ann's. Captain Carmichael served in the Merchant Marine and the Canadian Navy. He enlisted on March 25, 1940, and was discharged on June 22, 1945. He married Isabelle MacDonald, Middle River. They lived in Thorald, Ontario. He died on November 6, 1980 and interment was in Thorold, Ontario.

Carmichael, Angus John 10963

'A.J. Hector' was born on November 24, 1917, the son of Hector and Mabel (MacAskill) Carmichael, Goose Cove, St. Ann's. He enlisted in Halifax on July 27, 1942. He served with the Atlantic Command. Later he served with the Cape Breton Highlanders. His theatres of service were in Canada, United Kingdom and Continental Europe. He was discharged on April 4, 1946.

He married Murdena Kerr, North River. They reside in Goose Cove, St. Ann's.

Carmichael, Campbell George

Campbell was born on May 23, 1917, the son of Captain Dan and Hattie (Matheson) Carmichael, Goose Cove, St. Ann's. He served overseas and was one of the first "boys" to enlist from the district. He served with the Canadian Army Signal Corp.

After the war he worked as a lineman with the Eastern Light and Power Company. Unmarried, he died tragically on February 13, 1947, when he was electrocuted while working on power lines in Florence, Cape Breton. He is buried in Goose Cove Cemetery.

Carmichael, Dolena, R.N.

Dolly was born on March 10, 1919, the daughter of Daniel and Mary Belle (MacLeod) Carmichael, New Harris. She was a graduate of the Glace Bay General Hospital School of Nursing. Dolly enlisted in Halifax. Nursing Sister Lieutenant Carmichael served in England and Bruge, Belgium.

She married Carl Phillips. After the war, she worked at Sunnybrook Veteran's Hospital and Westminister Veteran's Hospital, London, Ontario. She and her husband presently live in London, Ontario.

Carmichael, Donald Malcolm F56554

Donnie was born on October 10, 1920, the son of Captain Angus and Mary (MacDonald) Carmichael, Goose Cove. He enlisted on March 15, 1943, in the army with the Royal Canadian Ordinance Corps. He was discharged on November 9, 1944.

He married Ethel Robinson, Montreal. He was an accountant. He lived in Phoenix, Arizona. He died on August 1, 1985.

Carmichael, Harry Daniel F97821

Harry was born on June 1, 1923, the son of Ernest and Margaret (MacDonald) Carmichael, South Side Baddeck. He enlisted in Sydney on May 14, 1942, in the Royal Canadian Ordinance Corps. He served in Canada, England, France, Belgium, Holland and Germany. Corporal Carmichael was discharged on January 10, 1947.

He married Muriel Long. They resided in Baddeck. He was a manager of the Victoria Farmers' Co-Op. He died on July 12, 1994, and is buried in South Side Baddeck Cemetery.

Carmichael, Hector Archibald F32184

'Hector Hattie' was born on December 8, 1911, the son of Captain Dan and Hattie (Matheson) Carmichael, Goose Cove. He enlisted on August 28, 1942, and served with the Royal Canadian Engineers in Canada, United Kingdom and Italy. He was seriously wounded during operations in Italy. He was discharged on August 22, 1945.

He married Euphemia Buchanan, Munroe's Point. He worked with the Department of Highways. He died on March 25, 1976, and is buried in Goose Cove Cemetery.

Carmichael, Nelson

Nelson was born on June 21, 1921, the son of Daniel and Mary Belle (MacLeod) Carmichael, New Harris. He enlisted in the army and moved from Sydney to Ottawa. Overseas he was promoted to Corporal. He served in the military police. After the war, he continued with a military career at Camp Gagetown, New Brunswick.

Nelson married Charlotte Glasier. He served as fire marshal. He and his wife retired in Lincoln, New Brunswick. He died in 1995.

Carmichael, Norman John

Normie was born on May 26, 1919, the son of Hector and Katie (MacAskill) Carmichael, Goose Cove. He served overseas in the Corvette Navy. He served on the Murmansk Run (a port in Northern Russia). He worked as a commissionaire in Halifax. Presently, he is retired and he and his wife reside in Halifax.

Carmichael, Roy Albert F36019

Roy was born on September 9, 1924, the son of Albert and Mary (Morrison) Carmichael, Big Harbour.

He enlisted on September 4, 1943, in the Royal Canadian Artillery where he served as a mechanic. Private Carmichael served in Canada and the United Kingdom and was discharged on April 27, 1946. After the War he joined the Royal Canadian Air Force. He married Nielene Nicholson, Baddeck. He died on January 4, 1978, and is buried in Harbourview Cemetery, South Haven.

Carmichael, William Wilfred F58391

Billy was born on September 14, 1925, the son of Ernest and Margaret (MacDonald) Carmichael, South Side Baddeck. He enlisted on May 11, 1944, with the Royal Canadian Army Medical Corps. He served in the United Kingdom and Continental Europe. He married Thelma Forward-MacLeod. He resides in Baddeck.

Chaisson, Howard R137910

Howard was born on January 15, 1922, the son of George and Catherine (MacDougall) Chaisson, Aspy Bay. He enlisted on January 6, 1942, and served in the 127 Air Field Royal Canadian Air Force. He served in England, France, Germany and Holland. He was discharged on May 9, 1946. He married Christina Burton, Bay St. Lawrence. He was a fisherman. He and his wife reside in Aspy Bay.

Chaisson, John

John was the son of David and Catherine (Capstick) Chaisson, Sugar Loaf. He served during the war. He remained in the Canadian Armed Forces after the war. He married and they reside in the Halifax area.

Chaisson, Zepheron F32610

Zeffie was the son of David and Catherine (Capstick) Chaisson, Sugar Loaf. He enlisted on October 20, 1942, and served with the Canadian Postal Corps. Private Chaisson served in England, France, Belgium and Holland. Corporal Zepheron Chaisson, SF800570, re-enlisted in 1950 and served in the Korean War. He was discharged in June 1954.

He married Theresa Petrie, South Harbour. They operated a bakery at Big Bras d'Or and they now reside in Port Hawkesbury.

Cheverie, Theophile Joseph F1113

Theo was born on June 1, 1925, the son of Dan and Catherine (Aucoin) Cheverie, Baddeck. Private Cheverie served with the Canadian Army Service Corps overseas in Continental Europe. He married Marguerite MacDonald, Baddeck. He worked as a clerk at the White Store. This establishment burned on December 18, 1973. He died on June 20, 1997, and is buried in Harbourview Cemetery, South Haven.

Christie, Hugh Patterson F89357

Hugh was born in 1921, the son of David and Christine (MacDonald) Christie, Black Head. He enlisted in Sydney and served with the North Nova Highlanders. Private Christie was killed in action on March 25, 1945, in Germany. He is buried in Groesbeek Canadian War Cemetery.

Christie, John Laurie F89775

John was born on May 21, 1922, the son of David and Christine (MacDonald) Christie, Black Head. He enlisted in Sydney in 1941 with the First Canadian Army Division, Nova Scotia Regiment. He was discharged in Halifax in 1946. He married Jessie MacAskill, Englishtown. He died on April 25, 1965, and is buried in Bayview Cemetery, Englishtown.

Clarke, Alfred John J36345

'A.J.' was born on October 1, 1921, the son of Dan Alex and Cassie (MacRae) Clarke, Cape Dauphin.

He served with the 435 Squadron, Royal Canadian Air Force. Flying Officer Clarke was killed in a flying accident when the transport plane he co-piloted crashed in Surrey Hills south of London on February 13, 1946. He is buried in Brookwood Military Cemetery, Surrey, England.

The following letter was received by the Clarke family from H.L. Campbell, Air Vice Marshal, R.C.A.F., Ottawa.

Mr. D.A. Clark,
Cape Dauphin
Victoria Co., N.S.

Dear Mr. Clark:

It is with deep regret that I must confirm our recent telegram informing you that your son, Flying Officer Alfred John Clark, was killed on Service Overseas.

Advice received from the Royal Canadian Air Force Overseas Headquarters states that your son lost his life in a flying accident on February 13th, 1946, when his aircraft crashed two miles southwest of Warlingham, Surrey, England. The aircraft, of which your son was a member of the crew, hit a cloud covered hilltop due to bad visibility. His funeral will take place at 11:00 A.M. on February 18th at the RAF Regional Cemetery, Brookwood, Woking, Surrey, England.

You may be assured that any further information received will be communicated to you immediately.

I realize that this news has been a great shock to you, and I offer you my deepest sympathy. May the same spirit which prompted your son to offer his life give you renewed courage.

Yours sincerely,

(H.L. Campbell)
Air Vice-Marshal, Air Member for Personnel

Clarke, Leslie

Leslie was born on June 4, 1925, and raised by Alexander and Cassie (MacRae) Clarke, Cape Dauphin. Private Clarke served with the Canadian Artillery in Canada. He died on March 13, 1972.

Collins, Robert Gordon

Gordon was born in 1912 and raised by Robert and Katie Ann (MacKenzie) Collins, Baddeck. He served during the war. He married Angie Aucoin. They resided in Baddeck. He died in 1976 and is buried in St. Michael's Cemetery, Baddeck.

Cooke, John Leo R137762

John Leo was born on January 26, 1919, the son of John and Elizabeth (Gillis) Cooke, Ingonish. Leading Air Craftsman Cooke served overseas in the Royal Canadian Air Force. He and his wife, Dorothy, lived in New Brunswick. He died on January 4, 1988, and is buried in St. Joseph's Cemetery, Saint John, NB.

Cooke, William Valentine F32566

'Val' was born on June 25, 1923, the son of John and Elizabeth (Gillis) Cooke, Ingonish. Gunner Cooke served in Canada, Italy, Belgium, France and Germany (1941 to 1945).

He and his war bride, Ulgisse Maurice from Belgium, came to Ingonish and then took up residence in Sydney. He died on July 10, 1984, and is buried in St. Peter's Parish Cemetery, Ingonish.

(Wedding photo - Val and Ulgisse Cooke)

Courtney, Donald

Donald was born in 1925, the son of Archibald and Effie (MacAskill) Courtney, Cape North. Private Courtney served overseas during the war. He was badly wounded and lost a leg. He died on July 23, 1978, and is buried in MacPherson Cemetery, Dingwall.

Courtney, Norman F7415

Norman was born on May 5, 1919, the son of Archibald and Effie (MacAskill) Courtney, Cape North. He enlisted on May 15, 1942, and served in Canada as a sapper with the Engineers. Private Courtney was discharged on March 23, 1946. He married Effie MacDonald, Big Intervale. They reside in Cape North.

Cremo, Tom

Tom hailed from Wagmatcook. Private Cremo served during the war.

Cross, Matthew 2004A

Matthew was born on July 13, 1909, the son of George and Grace Buffett, Neil's Harbour. He served with the Royal Canadian Air Force in Canada, Newfoundland and Alaska. He married Treva May

Armstrong, Havelock, New Brunswick. After the war, he joined the Merchant Navy. They reside in Hampton, New Brunswick.

Currie, James Albert A3811

'Bussie' was born in 1921, the son of Dr. Bert and Sadie (MacLeod) (World War I) Currie. He enlisted on July 16, 1942, and served in the Canadian Army and Royal Canadian Naval Reserve. Able Seaman Currie served in Canada and Newfoundland. He married Irene Jones. He was an accountant for Dominion Bridge for many years. He was a superintendent for the Department of Highways in Halifax County. He died on January 12, 1996, and is buried in Greenwood Cemetery, Baddeck.

Bussie Currie (background - County Courthouse, Baddeck)

(Bussie Currie and friend, Shirley Dunlop, in front of general store, Baddeck)

Curtis, Joseph Alexander F76087

Joe was born in 1922, the son of James and Helen (Dunphy) Curtis, St. Margaret's Village. Lance Bombardier Curtis served from November 1942 to March 1946 in the United Kingdom, Continental Europe and Central Mediterranean. Fellow veteran George Hardy, Ingonish, states, "Joseph Curtis found me on a burning tank and saved my life." He served as a municipal councillor for the electoral district of Bay St. Lawrence for two terms. He was a farmer and fisherman. He married Margaret MacDonald, Bay St. Lawrence, and they reside at the picturesque point in Bay St. Lawrence.

Curtis, Rupert Leo

Leo was born on June 10, 1919, the son of Rupert and Elizabeth Jane (MacIntosh) Curtis, Ingonish Centre. Private Curtis enlisted in 1939 and served overseas with the North Novas. Twenty-three year old Curtis was wounded while serving in Belgium. He married Kathleen Brown, Avonport, Nova Scotia. They resided in Sydney where he worked at the Steel Plant. He died on September 5, 1994, and is buried in St. Peter's Parish Cemetery, Ingonish.

Daisley, Charles

Charles was born on June 24, 1906, the son of Edward and Mary (Dee) Daisley, Dingwall. Private Daisley served in Canada during the war. He was a fisherman. He is buried in St. Joseph's Cemetery, Dingwall.

Daisley, James Leo

Leo was born on October 10, 1919, the son of William and Elizabeth Ann (Dixon) Daisley, South Harbour. Private Daisley served in Canada during the war. Tragically he was killed in an industrial accident at the National Gypsum Plant in Dingwall on November 22, 1949. He is buried in St. Joseph's Cemetery, Dingwall.

Dauphney, Angus John A4765

A.J. was born on October 5, 1920, the son of George and Katie (Shaw) Dauphney, Indian Brook. He enlisted on May 15, 1941. He served in the navy with convoy duty across the Atlantic. He was discharged on August 8, 1945. He worked for the U.S. Steel Corporation and later he worked for the Nova Scotia Power Corporation. He married Laura MacAskill, North Shore. He died on June 24, 1978, as a result of a motor vehicle accident. He is buried in Indian Brook Cemetery.

Dauphney, David John

Dave was born on September 29, 1921, the son of John and Adeline (LeBeau) Dauphney, Little River. He enlisted on November 9, 1942, at Sydney and served in the army with the military police in Canada. Private Dauphney was discharged on June 7, 1945, in New Brunswick.

He married Theresa Corbett, New Waterford. He worked at various trades and he was also a fisherman. He died on April 16, 1989, and is buried in Ingonish.

Dauphinee, Ronald Joseph F66445

Ronald was born on September 7, 1913, the son of Henry Peter and Clare (Donovan) Dauphinee, Ingonish. Private Dauphinee served as an artillery gunner with the Second Division # 6 District Company. He served in Newfoundland, England, France, Belgium, Holland and Germany (1942 to 1946).

He and his brothers supplied power to the community of Ingonish in the early years. Later he worked for the Nova Scotia Power Commission. He married Agatha Hawley and they resided in Ingonish Beach.

Deveaux, Russell

Russell was the son of William and Florence (MacMaster) Deveaux, Grass Cove. He served during the war. He married a Miss MacNeil, Sydney. They resided in Sydney.

Deveaux, Wilfred Aloysius F75617

Wilfred was the son of William and Florence (MacMaster) Deveaux, Grass Cove. Signalman Deveau served in the Royal Canadian Corps of Signals in the United Kingdom and Continental Europe (1942 - 1946). He worked for the Department of Highways on the Grand Narrows Ferry.

Dixon, Lawrence

Lawrence was the son of William and Kerrie (Daisley) Dixon, South Harbour. Private Dixon served in Canada during the war. He was killed in a motor vehicle accident in 1946. He is buried in St. Joseph's Cemetery, Dingwall.

Doherty, Andrew Wilson V47795

Andrew was born on March 13, 1921, the son of Malcolm and Sarah Belle (Morrison) Doherty, Long Hill, Red Head. He enlisted on September 9, 1942, in the Royal Canadian Naval Volunteer Reserve. He was discharged on March 12, 1945. He married Beulah Gates, New Ross. They resided in Baddeck. He died on May 17, 1975, and is buried in Highland Cemetery, Baddeck Bay.

Doherty, Charles MacIntosh F32115

Charlie was born on March 30, 1912, the son of Malcolm and Sarah Belle (Morrison) Doherty, Long Hill, Red Head. He served overseas with the Royal Canadian Mechanical Engineers. He enlisted in 1942 and was discharged in 1946. He married Mary Ann MacLean, Washabuck. He served as park warden at the Cape Breton Highlands National Park, Northern Victoria County for thirty years. He died on March 4, 1993, and is buried in Highland Cemetery, Baddeck.

Donahue, Francis

Francis was the son of Jack and Mary (Capstick) Donahue, Bay St. Lawrence. He served in the Royal Canadian Navy. He married Catherine Ann MacDonald, Capstick. He was a merchant at Point Tupper. Later they moved to California where he was involved in the fishing industry.

Donovan, Daniel

Joseph Dan was the son of Joseph and Mary (Barron) Donovan, Ingonish Harbour. He served overseas in the Canadian Army. He resided in Ingonish and worked at the Cape Breton Highlands National Park. Unmarried, he died on August 5, 1971, and is buried in St. Peter's Parish Cemetery.

Donovan, Donald

Don was born on July 2, 1916, the son of Leo and Mary Rachel (MacDermid) Donovan, Ingonish Centre. He served with the Royal Canadian Air Force in Canada from 1942 to 1945. He and his wife, Olga, lived in Pittsburgh. He is buried in the United States.

Donovan, Garrett Isadore F32714

Isadore was born on April 13, 1916, the son of Tom James and Flora Beatrice (Doyle) Donovan, Ingonish Beach. Craftsman Donovan served in Canada, United Kingdom, Continental Europe and Central Mediterranean areas (1942 to 1946). He was predeceased by his first wife, Winnifred Hines. His second wife was Ann Cook. He worked at the Cape Breton Highlands National Park. He died on August 31, 1985, and is buried in St. Peter's Parish Cemetery.

Donovan, Gordon F86245

Gordon was born on September 7, 1914, the son of Leo and Mary Rachel (MacDermid) Donovan, Ingonish Centre.

Corporal Donovan served in Canada, United Kingdom and Germany from 1941 to 1945. He was predeceased by his wife, Ann Roberts. They ran the Ingonish Centre post office. He resides in Glace Bay.

Donovan, Hugh

Hughie was the son of John William (Jack Bill) and Jenny (Ross) Donovan, Ingonish Beach. He served in the Canadian Army in Canada. He was a fisherman. Unmarried, he resided in Ingonish. He is buried in St. Peter's Parish Cemetery.

Donovan, James

'Prisoner Jim' was born in 1923, the son of Michael Leo and Mary Rachael (Donovan) Donovan, Ingonish Harbour. He was captured and taken prisoner of war at Normandy. He escaped, but was recaptured and forced to march for days. The prisoners were made to boil grass and potato peelings and then forced to drink this concoction.

He married Vivian MacIntyre, Ingonish. He worked at the Cape Breton Highlands National Park. He died in 1985 and is buried in St. Peter's Parish Cemetery.

Donovan, John Harvey

Harvey was born on February 1, 1914, the son of Jack Bill and Jenny (Ross) Donovan, Ingonish Harbour. Corporal Donovan served with the Royal Air Force in Canada and Continental Europe.

He married Frances (Honey) Doucette (World War II). He was the local magistrate. He died on July 5, 1983, and is buried in St. Peter's Parish Cemetery, Ingonish.

Donovan, Leo Joseph F57597

Leo was born on September 16, 1924, the son of Thomas James and Flora B. (Doyle) Donovan, Ingonish Beach. Private Donovan served with the Nova Scotia Highlanders in England, France, Belgium, Holland and Germany from 1943 to 1945. He married Sarah Ann MacLellan, Margaree. He worked as a lineman for the Nova Scotia Power Commission. They resided in Ingonish. One of their sons, Ken Donovan, is the historian at Fortress Louisbourg.

Donovan, Sanford Paul

Sanford was born on November 10, 1918, the son of James J. and Jane Sarah (Curtis) Donovan, Ingonish. He enlisted in 1939 in the Canadian Army and served in Italy and Europe. He married Blanche Ponee, Westmount. They operated Donovan's Bakery in Bedford. He died in 1990.

Donovan, Traynor

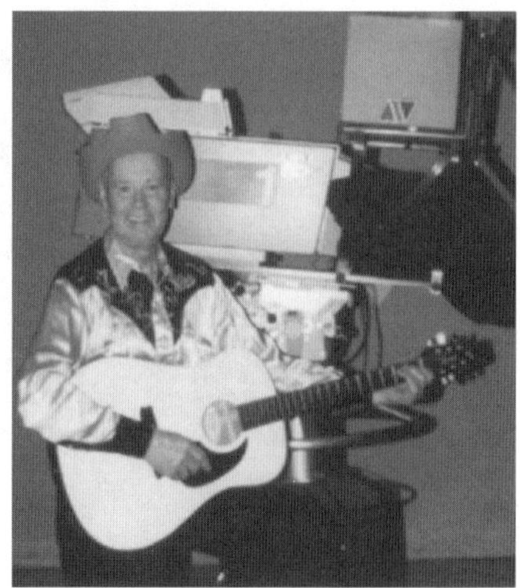

Traynor was born in 1927, the son of Thomas and Flora B. (Doyle) Donovan, Ingonish Centre. Private Donovan served in the Canadian Army in Canada. He married Ann Keilor and they reside in Glace Bay. He worked for C.J.C.B. T.V. for twenty-five years. In 1998, he received the prestigious Stomping Tom Connors Award for his western band - Traynor Donovan and his Radio Ranch Boys.

Donovan, Wilson Leo F32227

Wilson was born on May 28, 1906, the son of Leo and Mary Rachel (MacDermid) Donovan, Ingonish. He served in Canada and Italy.

His wife, Barbara (World War II), hailed from Saskatchewan. They managed the Ingonish Centre post office. He was warden for the Cape Breton Highlands National Park. Tragically, he drowned in Ingonish on April 5, 1953.

Doucette, Frances Margaret

'Honey' was born on June 2, 1926, the daughter of Thomas (World War I) (telegraph office) and Lucy (Devenish) Doucette, Ingonish. She served in the Canadian Army. She married Harvey Donovan (World War II), Ingonish. She died on January 16, 1985, and is buried in St. Peter's Parish Cemetery.

Doucette, James Gordon

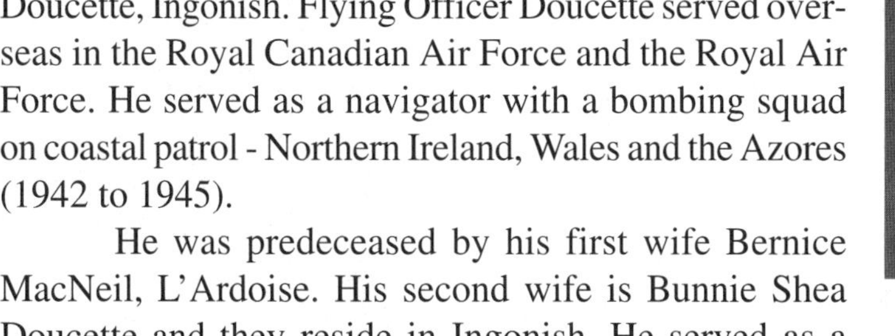

Gordon was born on July 12, 1922, the son of Jack (World War I) and school teacher Mary Helen (Lord) Doucette, Ingonish. Flying Officer Doucette served overseas in the Royal Canadian Air Force and the Royal Air Force. He served as a navigator with a bombing squad on coastal patrol - Northern Ireland, Wales and the Azores (1942 to 1945).

He was predeceased by his first wife Bernice MacNeil, L'Ardoise. His second wife is Bunnie Shea Doucette and they reside in Ingonish. He served as a municipal councillor for a term for the district of South Ingonish prior to serving as a federal fisheries officer for the region.

Doucette, John R.

'Buddy' was born on February 2, 1920, the son of Thomas (World War I) and Lucy (Devenish) Doucette, Ingonish. He served in Canada, Holland and Germany from 1939 to 1945. He and his wife Eva resided in Ontario. In 1995, he attended the 50th Anniversary of World War II in Holland. He died on November 18, 1997.

Doucette, Joseph Francis F59360

Joe was born on May 13, 1926, the son of Leo and Ivy Doucette, Ingonish. Private Doucette served in Canada. He married Dorothy (Dot) Hawley. He worked at the Cape Breton Highlands National Park. He died on July 26, 1992, and is buried in St. Peter's Parish Cemetery.

Doucette, Joseph K.   F75308

Joe was born in July 1920, the son of James J. and Margaret (Donovan) Doucette, Ingonish Beach. Gunner Doucette enlisted in 1941 and served with the Royal Canadian Artillery - 19th Battery - 3rd Field Regiment. Twenty-four year old Doucette was killed in action on September 4, 1944. He is buried in Ancona War Cemetery, Italy.

(left - Val Cooke, right - Joe Doucette)

Doucette, Leo Keats

Keats was born on December 25, 1923, the son of Jack (World War I) and school teacher Mary Helen (Lord) Doucette, Ingonish. Private Doucette served overseas in the Canadian Army in England and Northwest Europe. He was predeceased by his wife, Coralee Shea. He worked at the Cape Breton Highlands National Park. He resides in Dartmouth.

Doucette, Thomas Vincent   F55399

Tom was born on July 17, 1922, the son of Thomas (World War I) and Lucy (Devenish) Doucette, Ingonish. He enlisted on May 28, 1940 and served overseas with the Cape Breton Highlanders from 1941 to 1943. He was posted to the first army in North Africa. In 1943, he was posted to the First Canadian Division in Italy where he served as a scout. He was a sniper with the Royal Canadian Regiment in Italy and Northwest Europe until May, 1945. He was wounded in June, 1944, but continued on duty. At the time of his discharge he had attained the rank of Lieutenant.

While visiting his relatives in England, he met and married Margaret Stevens, Pensensy, England. Like his father, he returned with a war bride. Lieutenant Doucette continued to serve in the Canadian Armed Forces until 1955. He has compiled a remarkable unpublished manuscript about his experiences during the Second World War. The Doucettes reside in Whitby, Ontario.

Dowling, Donald F66442

Don was born on October 11, 1915, the son of Francis and Caroline (Meade) Dowling, Neil's Harbour. He enlisted in the Canadian Army on August 7, 1942. He served overseas as an artillery mechanic. He married Alice Ingraham, Neil's Harbour. He worked as a mechanic for the Cape Breton Highlands National Park. He is now retired and living in Ingonish.

Dowling, Edward F32191

Edward was born on April 1, 1909, the son of Arthur and Eve (Crewe) Dowling, Neil's Harbour. Sapper Dowling served in the Canadian Army. He is buried in St. Andrew's Cemetery, Neil's Harbour.

Dowling, John Gordon F4003

Johnny was born on February 6, 1919, the son of Arthur and Eve (Crewe) Dowling, Neil's Harbour. Private Dowling served overseas with the West Nova Scotia Regiment # 3 from 1942 to 1945. He was wounded in Holland on April 15, 1945, and underwent surgery on May 13, 1945. He married Gertrude Lillington, Neil's Harbour. He worked as a carpenter with the Cape Breton Highlands National Park. He is buried in St. Andrew's Cemetery, Neil's Harbour.

Dowling, Reuben F89956

Reuben was born in 1923, the son of Arthur and Eve (Crewe) Dowling. He enlisted in the Canadian Army in 1941 and served overseas as a gunner He married Greta MacQuinn and they resided in Ontario. He worked as a foreman with a furniture company. He is buried in Ontario.

Dowling, Roger F66504

Roger was born on June 19, 1921, the son of Edward and Fanny (Rogers) Dowling, Neil's Harbour. He enlisted in the Canadian Army on August 13, 1942, and served overseas. He married Renne Fraser and they lived in Dawson Creek, British Columbia, where he worked for a propane company. He died on May 29, 1967, and is buried at Dawson Creek, British Columbia.

Doyle, Francis William F32843

Francis was born on October 14, 1920, the son of William and Euphemia (Robinson) Doyle, Ingonish Centre. Lance Corporal Doyle served in Canada from 1943 to 1946. He married Emma Donovan, Ingonish. He was a fisherman and carpenter. He died on August 4, 1997, and is buried in St. Peter's Parish Cemetery.

Doyle, George James

'Jim' was born in 1922, the son of Joseph and Mary Margaret (Brewer) Doyle, Clyburn, Ingonish. He served in the army in Canada. Coming home from North Sydney on March 25, 1946, he fell overboard and drowned (off Bird Island).

Drake, John Douglas F54656

Jack hailed from Yorkshire, England and was raised by a family in the Hunters' Mountain or Middle River area. He served with the West Nova Scotia Regiment, Royal Canadian Infantry Corps. Thirty year old Corporal Drake was killed in action on March 28, 1944. He is buried in the Moro River Canadian War Cemetery, Italy.

Dunlap, Archibald Roderick FPS/531

Archibald was born on April 26, 1921, the son of Archibald and Amelia (Thompson) Dunlap, Big Bras d'Or. He served overseas in the Merchant Marine from 1940 to 1945. He married Theresa Taylor. He returned and remained in Big Bras d'Or.

Dunlap, John

John was a son of Archie and Amelia (Thompson) Dunlap, Big Bras d'Or. He served in the army. He married Viola MacInnis, George's River. After the war, they settled in Ontario. John Dunlap died there.

Dunlop, Charles David F75902

'Buddy' was born on June 1, 1920, the son of Gerald and Bessie (MacAskill) Dunlop, Baddeck. He first enlisted in the Royal Canadian Air Force in Guelph, Ontario and re-enlisted in the army. He served in the Canadian Postal Corps. He was discharged on January 25, 1946. He married Mary Heuser, River Denys. They are the proprietors of the Telegraph House, Baddeck.

Dunphy, Charles Elmer

Chester was the son of County Councillor William and Christine (Hines) Dunphy, Ingonish Beach. He served overseas in the army. He was predeceased by his wife Sadie Donovan. He remarried Frances Gouthro. He operated a fish business in Ingonish. He is buried in St. Peter's Parish Cemetery.

Dunphy, Freeman

Freeman was born in 1918, the son of Captain Sylvester and Mary (LeBlanc) (St. Pierre) Dunphy, Ingonish Beach. He served in the merchant navy. He married Lila Lee, North Sydney. He was manager of the Ingonish liquor store. He died in 1980 and is buried in St. Peter's Parish Cemetery.

Dunphy, Joseph

Joe was born on June 10, 1924, the son of Caleb and Harriet (Fitzgerald) Dunphy, South Harbour. Private Dunphy served in Canada with the Canadian Army. He married Josephine Mansour. He died in Halifax on January 15, 1993, and is buried in Gate of Heaven Cemetery, Lower Sackville.

Dunphy, Percy

Percy is the son of William and Dorothy (Hines) Dunphy, Ingonish Harbour. He served in the Royal Canadian Navy. He is a master craftsman and builder of model ships. He was predeceased by his wife, Amelia Robinson, North Sydney. He resides in North Sydney.

(Brothers left - Percy Dunphy, right - Sylvester Dunphy)

Dunphy, Russell F97304

Russell was born on January 13, 1918, the son of Patrick and Annie (MacDonald) Dunphy, White Point. Private Dunphy served with the West Nova Scotia Regiment in England and Continental Europe. He married Edna Dixon, White Point. He died on February 23, 1962, and is buried in St. Joseph Cemetery, Dingwall.

Dunphy, Sylvester

Sylvester was the son of County Councillor William and Christine (Hines) Dunphy, Ingonish Beach. He served overseas in the Canadian Army. He married Addie Barron. He worked at the Cape Breton Highlands National Park. He lives at the Beach Crossing, Ingonish.

Eastman, Wesley Earl

Wesley was born on October 29, 1916, the son of William T. and Eliza Ellen (Peach) Eastman, Baddeck.

The following is a portion of an article which appeared in the *Cape Breton Post* on November 9, 1985.

"NORTH SYDNEY - Navy veteran Wesley Eastman, remembering his war years, says he and his comrades aboard the armed cruiser *Prince Henry* saved more lives on patrol in the Caribbean Sea than they sank enemy ships.

The *Prince Henry* rescued the entire 41-man crew of a torpedoed U.S. ship, plucking them from their "carly floats" and landing them in Jamaica during the winter of 1942 in the Caribbean.

Eastman recalls that the Caribbean was a nicer spot than the North Atlantic to be afloat in the life rafts but there were sharks to consider.

"There were lots of sharks", he says.

Receiving a second distress call from another ship about a week later, the *Prince Henry* arrived after the crew had been rescued but put its own crew aboard to try to rescue its cargo of airplane parts. The ship sank anyway as a U.S. Coast Guard vessel was trying to tow it ashore.

Eastman recalled war years when "... we were in close to a lot of action but never seemed to get into the thick of it."

The *Prince Henry*, a cruise ship outfitted with four six-inch guns and several smaller ones, had a "close call" in the port of St. Lucia, Eastman recalled.

The hospital ship *Lady Nelson* sank at that dock after it tied up at a berth left empty by the departure a short time earlier of the *Prince Henry*.

"I wondered if the torpedo was meant for us because it was a close call," he said.

Eastman's Remembrance Day memories include his duty aboard the *Prince Henry* doing convoy duty from Kodiak, Alaska, to Dutch Harbor, when the ship arrived at Kiska Harbor one day after Japanese airplanes had attacked the port.

"I remember seeing a number of ships sunk there with their spars sticking up out of the water," he said.

Eastman's navy career began in August, 1941, on a less serious note, he recalled.

Eastman was ordered to guard a French fishing ship tied up in Sydney Harbor, although the French crew were free to work on farms in Cape Breton.

"We often said we were guarding dead fish," he said.

Starting out as an able seaman and finishing as a petty officer, Eastman's navy years also included service aboard subchasers at the mouth of the St. Lawrence River and the east coast of Cape Breton, Newfoundland, and Labrador before he joined the corvette, *Stellarton*, on the "Newfie-Deerie" run between St. John's, Newfoundland, and Londonderry, Ireland.

Eastman said the corvette was headed for Londonderry when VE-Day occurred and the crew spliced the main brace, getting an extra tot of rum.

He married Phoebe Bernard, Newfoundland. He resides with his daughter in Gabarus.

Eastman, William Anthony V83241

William was born on April 14, 1915, the son of Thomas and Eliza Ellen (Peach) Eastman, Baddeck. He enlisted on August 20, 1942, with the Royal Canadian Navy and served with the engineering section. Seaman Eastman served in the North Atlantic. He married Bertha Anderson. He died in February, 1995.

Edwards, Dr. Nelson George

Nelson was the son of Frank and Anna C. (Johnston) Edwards. He was raised by William and Katie (MacAskill) Matheson, Glen Tosh. He served overseas in the Canadian Army. He was a graduate of veterinary medicine from the Ontario Veterinary College, Guelph, Ontario. He and his wife, Eva, resided in Maine. His ashes were spread over the farm in Glen Tosh.

Englehutt, Georgina W312139

Georgina was born on February 5, 1925, the daughter of Angus and Tena (MacDonald) Englehutt, Wreck Cove. Air Force Woman Englehutt enlisted in June, 1943, and served in the air force. She served as a clerk in Western and Central Canada. She was discharged in June, 1946. She married Sam Penny, Sydney, and they resided in Westmount.

Etheridge, Frank Owen

Frank was born on April 21, 1918, the son of Howard and Charlotte (Carmichael) Etheridge, Big Baddeck. He served overseas. On February 15, 1949, he married Anna MacDonald, North River. They resided in Edwardsville, Cape Breton. He died on July 27, 1980, the result of a drowning accident.

Ferguson, Donald John F3423

Donald was born on June 24, 1914, the son of Roderick and Caroline (Merritt) Ferguson, Rear Big Hill, South Gut. He enlisted on September 12, 1942, with the 85th Bridge Company - Royal Canadian Army Signal Corps. He served in Canada, England, France, Belgium and Germany. He was wounded and hospitalized and in 1945 returned to Halifax on *The Lady Nelson* hospital ship. He returned home to South Haven. He was employed at Englishtown and Ross Ferry's. Unmarried, he died on January 27, 1989, and is buried in Harbourview Cemetery, South Haven.

Fitzgerald, Alexander Buchanan

Sandy was born in 1925, the son of Phillip and Margaret (Buchanan) Fitzgerald, Aspy Bay. Private Fitzgerald served overseas with the Canadian Army. He married Eileen MacLeod, Sunrise. He worked at the gypsum plant in Dingwall and later at the gypsum plant in Milford. They reside in Gay's River.

Fitzgerald, Alphonse F79852

Alphonse was born on April 17, 1916, the son of James and Annie (Marsh) Fitzgerald, South Harbour. Private Fitzgerald served with the West Nova Scotia Regiment in Italy, France, Germany and Holland. He married Lucy Eileen Daisley, South Harbour. He was a mail courier from Ingonish to Bay St. Lawrence for several years. He died on January 2, 1990, and is buried in St. Joseph's Cemetery, Dingwall.

Fitzgerald, Charles Norman F6456

Charlie was born on June 19, 1921, the son of Phillip and Margaret (Buchanan) Fitzgerald, Aspy Bay. He enlisted in February, 1945, and served in the Royal Canadian Army Service Corps. Private Fitzgerald served in Newfoundland and the United Kingdom. He was discharged on April 11, 1946, in Ottawa. He married Florence MacRae, Middle River. He and his wife resided in Dartmouth. He died on February 20, 1995, and is buried in Middle River Cemetery.

Fitzgerald, James Francis

James was born on December 23, 1904, the son of George and Mary E. (Paquet) Fitzgerald, White Point. He enlisted in the United States Army and served overseas with the 3rd Division under the command of General George Patton. He was wounded in St. Lo., France, and was hospitalized for six months. He returned to his division and served until the end of the war. He was awarded the **PURPLE HEART**. He married Ida MacIntosh, White Point. He married again and resided in the United States. He died on November 16, 1967, in Tennessee.

Fitzgerald, John Robert F89363

Jack was born on December 21, 1919, the son of Phillip and Margaret (Buchanan) Fitzgerald, Aspy Bay. He enlisted on July 21, 1941 and served as a gunner with the 2nd Survey Regiment R.C.A. He served in England, France, Holland and Germany. He married Mary Whitley, Sugar Loaf. He worked at the gypsum plant in Dingwall and later at the gypsum plant in Milford. They are presently residing in Cape North.

Fitzgerald, Michael

Michael was the son of Caleb and Sarah (Duggan) Fitzgerald, Dingwall. Private Fitzgerald served in Canada during the war. He worked at the gypsum plant in Dingwall and in construction. He married Jessie MacEachern, Dingwall, and they reside at Dingwall.

Fitzgerald, Winston G. 'Scotty'

Winston 'Scotty' was born on February 16, 1914, the son of harbourmaster George and Mary (Paquet) Fitzgerald, White Point. He served in Canada with the Royal Canadian Army Service Corps from 1942 to 1946. Winston Scotty Fitzgerald was Cape Breton's master fiddle player. He led a celebrated life in the field of musical entertainment. He joined the road show, 'The Merry Makers,' in 1933-34 and then travelled for two and one-half years with Hank Snow. His own radio production was called "Winston Fitzgerald and his Radio Entertainers." He had numerous 78's and LP's to his credit. He travelled the Boston, Toronto and Detroit circuit in the 1950's. He is featured in the *Cape Breton Magazine* # 46 and Allister MacGillivray's book *The Cape Breton Fiddler.* He was predeceased by his first wife, Evelyn Gibson. His second wife was Ann Roland. He died on September 2, 1987, and is buried in St. Joseph's Cemetery, Bras d'Or.

Fortune, Chandler Haliburton V53151

Chandler was born in 1909, the son of Patrick and Maria (Haliburton) Fortune, Upper Middle River - West Side. Chief Petty Officer Fortune served in the Royal Canadian Navy. He married Nellie Jane Munroe (World War II), Inlet Baddeck. They resided in Inlet Baddeck. Chandler Fortune served on the Municipality of Victoria County Council for nine years. He died on September 6, 1992, and is buried in Greenwood Cemetery.

Fortune, Wilfred Walter

Wilfred was born on March 17, 1906, the son of Patrick and Maria (Haliburton)Fortune, Upper Middle River - West Side. Private Fortune served in Canada during the war. He died on December 23, 1980, and is buried in Middle River Cemetery.

(Right -Wilfred Fortune)

Mary Fownes, Dr. C.L. MacMillan, M.D. and Dr. Albert Fownes, M.D.

Fownes, Albert, M.D.

Albert was born in November 1915, the son of Charles and Margaret (Campbell) Fownes, Baddeck. He served with the Royal Canadian Air Force. He married Mary MacPherson (World War II), Baddeck. Dr. Albert Fownes, M.D., graduated from McGill University. He was an internist and cardiologist. He received his fellowship from Canada and England. He practiced his profession in Moncton, New Brunswick. He is retired and living in New Brunswick.

Fownes, Leo Elton, D.F.C. J22528

Leo was born on July 9, 1920, the son of Frank and Mabel (Wilson) Fownes, Big Baddeck. He was a 1939 graduate of Baddeck Academy. On July 17, 1941, he enlisted in Halifax with the Royal Canadian Air Force. He served in Canada, England, France and Belgium with the 409 Squadron. Flight Lieutenant Fownes, navigator, teamed up with F/O R.A. Brittain, Arichat, pilot, to destroy a Nazi plane and to send another down in flames. During two night sorties F/L Fownes participated in destroying three enemy aircraft and damaging a fourth one. F/L Fownes was awarded the **DISTINGUISHED FLYING CROSS**. The award was sent by registered mail on December 21, 1950.

He was a 1948 graduate of Acadia University and a 1955 graduate of Nova Scotia Technical College. He married Vivian Harvey (World War II), Baddeck. He died in Ottawa in 1974. Interment was in St. Andrews Cemetery, Baddeck Forks.

Francis, Dollard MacLean

Dollard was born in 1920, the son of James Kenneth and Mary Grace (Budden) Francis, Newfoundland/Little Narrows. He served in Canada and overseas as a gunner. He and his wife, Mona, resided in Toronto. He died in 1995 in Toronto and is buried there.

Fraser, James Philip

'James P.' was born circa 1904, the son of Rev. John and Johanna Fraser, North Shore/Boularderie. During the prohibition years prior to 1939, he served as a Royal Canadian Mounted Police Cutter Captain. During the World War II Lieutenant Commander Fraser served as the commanding officer aboard the frigate *Waskesiu* in pursuit of enemy U-boats. He married and resided in Halifax. After the war he was a captain aboard the Nova Scotia - Prince Edward Island ferry. Tragically, Captain Fraser was killed in a motor vehicle accident.

Fraser, Kenneth Archibald M.D.

(left - Dr. Ken Fraser)

Kenneth was born on January 18, 1918, the son of Rev. James and Mary (Campbell) Fraser, Boularderie. He received his medical degree from Dalhousie University in 1943. Dr. Fraser served from 1944 to 1946 as a medial officer in the Royal Canadian Army Medical Corps. Captain Fraser served in Canada, England and Germany. Dr. Fraser married Lieutenant Nursing Sister M. Isabel Morrison, Troy. Dr. Fraser practiced as a surgeon in Sydney Mines for thirty-nine years. He died on July 3, 1989, and is buried in Middle River Cemetery.

Fraser, Pringle F58634

Pringle was born on June 9, 1925, the son of Reverend James and May (Campbell) Fraser, Big Bras d'Or. Private Fraser served in Germany with the Canadian Army. He enlisted on July 21, 1944, and was discharged on June 27, 1946. He married Mabel MacLeod, Groves Point. He became an ordained minister in the United Church of Canada. Rev. Fraser died on January 10, 1997, and is buried in Middle River Cemetery.

Fricker, Andrew F89926

Andrew was born on July 19, 1919, the son of Theodore and Jane (Stattler) Fricker, Neil's Harbour. Gunner Fricker enlisted on September 19, 1941 and served overseas with the Canadian Army. He married Susan Petrie, South Harbour. He worked at the Cape Breton Highlands National Park. He died on December 29, 1972, and is buried in St. Andrew's Cemetery, Neil's Harbour.

Fricker, Frederick

Fred was born in 1905, the son of Andrew and Elizabeth (Hatcher) Fricker, Neil's Harbour. He served in the Merchant Navy out of Halifax. He retired to Glace Bay. He is buried in St. Andrew's Cemetery, Neil's Harbour.

Fricker, James F76480

James was born in 1905, the son of John and Elizabeth (Janes) Fricker, Neil's Harbour. He enlisted in the Canadian Army in December, 1942 and served in Canada. He married and spent some years sailing on the Great Lakes. Later he returned to Neil's Harbour where he operated a restaurant. He is buried in St. Andrew's Cemetery, Neil's Harbour.

Fricker, Robert F66451

Bobby was born on July 21, 1922, the son of Hubert and Charlotte (Ingraham) Fricker, Neil's Harbour. He enlisted in the Canadian Army on August 7, 1942. He served overseas as a qualified waterman. He married Rose Hestelten, England. He and his war bride returned to Neil's Harbour. He was a fisherman. He is buried in St. Andrew's Cemetery, Neil's Harbour.

Gardiner, Angus B. F55276

Angus was born in 1912 and was the adopted son of Rory C. and Elizabeth (MacNeil) MacDonald, Washabuck. Corporal Gardiner served with the Cape Breton Highlanders.

He was killed in 1961 in a motor vehicle accident and is buried in Holy Rosary Cemetery, Washabuck.

Garland, John William

'J.W.' was born on April 7, 1922, the son of David and Catherine (Buchanan) Garland, Baddeck Forks.

He served for four years with the Royal Canadian Engineers overseas.

He married Barbara Crocker, New Glasgow. He was a graduate of the Nova Scotia Agricultural College, Truro and Macdonald College, Montreal. He was a professor of Agriculture for five years in Guelph, Ontario. He spent three years in South Africa as a consulting engineer with Larsens Consulting Engineers of Alberta. For twelve years he was a manager of feed mills with the Co-Op in Moncton, New Brunswick. He died on April 10, 1978, and is buried in Baddeck Forks.

Gillis, Donald Wilfred F89978

'Donald W.' was the son of Hugh and Mary Lucy (MacNeil) Gillis, MacKinnon's Harbour. Sergeant Gillis served with the Royal Canadian Army Postal Corps, Royal Canadian Electrical and Mechanical Engineers in Canada and Newfoundland from 1941 to 1947.

Unmarried, he died on November 28, 1969, and is buried in Sacred Heart Cemetery, McKinnons Harbour.

Gillis, Hector

Hector was the son of Rod F. and Catherine (MacNeil) Gillis, Jamesville. He served with the Cape Breton Highlanders in Canada. He was accidentally killed when struck by a train near McKinnons Harbour and is buried in St. Columba Cemetery.

Gillis, James Joseph F2803

Jimmie was the son of Rod F. and Catherine (MacNeil) Gillis, Jamesville. Lance Corporal Gillis served with the Sherbrook Fusillers, 27th Armoured Regiment. He was wounded in Holland on April 12, 1945, and died of first and second degree burns on April 19, 1945. He is buried in Groesbeek Canadian War Cemetery, Holland. His name is also inscribed on the family marker in St. Columba Cemetery, Iona.

Gillis, Lloyd George F97305

Lloyd was born on July 7, 1917, the son of Duncan and Grace (Buchanan) Gillis, Big Baddeck. He served overseas in the army. His discharge date was January 24, 1946.

He married Margaret Phillips. They resided in Baddeck. He died at seventy-five years of age and is buried in St. Andrews Cemetery, Baddeck Forks.

Gillis, Margaret Mary W6005

Margaret was the daughter of Michael A.J. and Annie (MacInnis) Gillis, MacKinnon's Harbour. Corporal Gillis served in the Canadian Women's Army Corps in Canada and Britain from 1941 to 1946. She was a member of the first draft of the Canadian Women's Army Corps to proceed overseas. She served with the staff of the Royal Canadian Army Pay Corps in London, England. She resides in New Glasgow.

(November 9, 1942 - center, Corporal Margaret Gillis, on arrival in England)

Gillis, Neil John F546891

Neil John was born on January 26, 1916, the son of Roderick F. and Catherine (MacNeil) Gillis, Jamesville West.

Company Sergeant Major Gillis served with the Cape Breton Highlanders in Canada, the United Kingdom and Italy (1939 to 1945). Company Sergeant Major Gillis had been serving in Italy and came to London, England to attend to military matters at the Canadian Military Headquarters. His cousin, Corporal Margaret Gillis, was stationed there and when they met, she expressed her condolences to him. She remarked, "Too bad about Jimmie." This was the first that he knew about his brother's death (Killed in Action).

He married Carmel M. Sharkey, New Brunswick. He and his wife are retired and reside in Jamesville.

Gillis, Rodriquez W300459

'Regis' was the daughter of Michael A.J. and Annie (MacInnis) Gillis, MacKinnon's Harbour. Leading Aircraft Woman Gillis served in the Royal Canadian Air Force in Canada from 1942 to 1945. She was the only female air mechanic to serve in Canada. She resides in New York.

Gillis, Walter

Walter was born on July 1, 1924, the son of Angus and Anabel (Donovan) Gillis, Ingonish. He served in the Canadian Army during the war. Affectionately known as 'Boom-Boom', he was the Canadian Army featherweight boxing champion. He died on March 6, 1989, and is buried in St. Peter's Parish Cemetery.

Grant, John William F33059

John William was born on October 31, 1904, the son of Dan and Jennie (MacKenzie) Grant, Garry, Middle River.

Private Grant served with the Cape Breton Highlanders in Canada and overseas. He died on January 16, 1979, and is buried in Middle River Cemetery.

Grant, Rhindress Ian, M.C.

Rhindress was the son of Dr. Hector (M.D.) and Annie Isabel (MacIntosh) Grant, Big Bras d'Or.

He joined the Canadian Army 19th Field Regiment of the Royal Canadian Artillery in March 1940. He was an Artillery Captain and recipient of the **MILITARY CROSS**. He served in France, Belgium, Germany and Holland. He was discharged in 1945. In civilian life he worked at Windsor Gypsum and was manager at the gypsum plant in Little Narrows. He married Brenda Fader of Chester. They retired to Chester and he died there in 1987.

Gwynn, John F56929

John was born on July 30, 1923, the son of Allan and Helen (MacAskill) Gwynn, Aspy Bay. Private Gwynn served in the United Kingdom and Continental Europe from 1943 to 1946. He married Eleanor MacLeod, Cape North. He was light keeper in various locations throughout the province and his last posting was at Black Rock Station, Big Bras d'Or. He and his wife reside in Cape Breton County.

Gwynn, John

'Josie' was the son of Joseph and Effie (Morrison) Gwynn, North Ridge, Cape North. He served in the American Army. He resided in the United States.

Gwynn, Sheridan F79085

Sheridan was born on August 18, 1897, the son of William and Lexie (MacLeod) Gwynn, Cape North. Private Gwynn enlisted in 1941 and served in the Royal Canadian Engineers in Canada and England. He served as a municipal councillor for the Cape North electoral district for two terms. He died on May 16, 1980 and is buried in Aspy Bay Cemetery.

Hanam, Harold Roy F24446

Harold was born on October 30, 1911, the son of John (World War I) and Elizabeth (Williams) Hanam, Baddeck/Neil's Harbour. Lance Corporal Hanam served overseas with the First Hussars Tank Corps from1940 to 1945. He served as a tank driver with the first line reinforcement during the invasion of France. He married Ida Strickland, Neil's Harbour, and they resided in Baddeck. He was employed with the Department of Transportation. He died on June 2, 1994, and is buried in Greenwood Cemetery, Baddeck.

Hanam, Walter Hayward

Walter was born on December 3, 1922, in Baddeck, the son of John (World War I) and Alexandrina R. (Anderson) Hanam, Big Baddeck. He served in the army overseas, including Italy and North Africa. He married twice. His first wife was Margaret Fownes and his second wife was Dorothy MacKay. By trade he was a carpenter. He resided in Boston and Truro, Nova Scotia. He died on June 13, 1976, in Truro and is buried in St. Andrews Cemetery, Baddeck Forks.

Hardy, Clarence Claude

Clarence Claude was born on June 26, 1920, the son of Levi (World War II) and Mary (Canning) Hardy, North Bay, Ingonish. He was a member of the Canadian Merchant Navy. He served as a fireman and trimmer. He was lost at sea on June 26, 1941, when his ship, *S.S. Grayburn*, went down off the coast of Scotland.

His name is inscribed on the Halifax Memorial erected in Point Pleasant Park, Halifax. Listed on the Halifax Memorial are over three thousand names of Canadian men and women who are buried at sea. The dedicatory inscription reads - "Their Graves Are Unknown But Their Memory Shall Endure."

Hardy, George Thomas F32876

George was born on April 12, 1923, the son of John A. and Lily (Wilson) Hardy, Ingonish.

The following is an excerpt from a history paper (213) written by his daughter, Anita Hardy, based on a personal interview with her father, George Hardy, on March 22, 1991.

George Hardy signed up in 1942 at the age of eighteen. All of his friends were in the army and at the time it was "the thing to do."

In the spring of 1943 the fighting began for George when he was assigned to the fourth anti-tank, fifth division and stationed in Italy. There were five men on a tank and George took up the position of radio operator. There were daily rations of food without much variety - usually either cornbeef or beans. There were no hot meals. Sleeping quarters consisted of a big hole dug

under the tank. The five men slept there and were protected by the tank. After being at the lines for two to three weeks a relief crew was sent in. This was their only chance to get rested, cleaned up, and away from the stench of death. George saw many die, enemies and friends, but could not help. This was the toughest of all.

He remembers the Hitler Line and Hill 120. He was on a reconnaissance tank that went ahead of the others to see if it was safe. One morning, after the conditions had been checked out, the officer got out of the tank. Suddenly a shell came. He was not hit but was "killed by concussion." George, who had felt the shock and the gravel flying through the tank, had to report his officer's, his friend's, death. There were those who could not handle it.

There was one day, in the Poe Valley, Italy that George will never forget. They were in the midst of heavy fighting. The troops thought they were driving the Germans back but the Germans circled around. In the turmoil the man who was loading the gun on George's tank went crazy. It was all too much for him. He just ran. There was no time to waste and they were now a man short. The sergeant asked George to leave the radio and quickly load the gun. He was following these orders when another sergeant (whose tank had just blown up) came to help. He put George back on the radio inside the tank and was finishing the gun loading when they received a direct hit from the Germans. The man who had taken George's place was killed instantly, along with two others. George and the driver were alive ... barely.

Feelings at this time are hard to remember. He knows that he crawled over the three dead men in panic and through the flames but he was badly burned and could not see. He distinctly remembers desperately grabbing hold of a man's hand. It was the officer of the unit. He told George they were pulling out and as quickly as he spoke he was gone. The officer left George to die.

George knew they would be heading to the abandoned farm house a long way back but he also knew that he could never make it. He could not even see, or feel anything but the fire until a little while later when he was taken by the hand - this time by someone who would help. It was a friend of his who was taking refuge at the old farm house when the officer and others arrived. He asked where George was and went for him immediately. He found him in bad shape but they ran together, through machine gun fire, feeling the bullets on their boots and made it to shelter.

George woke up four days later in a hospital but he does not remember where. He was blind. His eyes had been burnt shut. He was labelled "dangerously ill" and his family was notified. When he began to improve he was sent to Rome. He was put on a train by himself, still blind, with no one to look after him and no one he knew. Somehow he made it to the hospital and was treated there for two months before he could see. He was not allowed to look in a mirror and the doctors had no idea what he looked like until they received a picture but his burns healed amazingly well. It was not until a month or more in Rome that he learned he had also had malaria.

George went to a convalescence hospital in Rome when he was almost better but he was not treated well there. He only stayed a week and was ready to join his unit that was now in Belgium. No transportation was provided. He had to hitchhike through foreign countries at war and travel on stagnant box cars. When he finally got to Belgium it was the same thing all over again but he was more nervous now. He fought in Holland and was there when the war ended. He was "**MENTIONED IN DISPATCHES**" for bravery.

The officer who did not help George could have been charged with negligence but George did not see him again and had no desire to rethink, retell, or relive the experience. It was January of 1946 before George made it home.

He married Margaret Jackson and they reside in Ingonish.

Hardy, Gordon Walter F56944

Gordon was born on December 18, 1923, the son of Levi (World War II) and Mary (Canning) Hardy, North Bay, Ingonish.

He enlisted in October, 1941 and served as a trimmer, stoker and steward in the Merchant Navy.

Seventeen year old seaman Gordon Hardy was aboard the *Rose Castle* (a merchant vessel headed for Newfoundland to load iron ore) as she sat at anchor awaiting the arrival of a convoy in the cold, U-boat infested North Atlantic the night of November 2, 1942. Before midnight, the *Rose Castle* was torpedoed by the German submarine U518 and sank within one minute. Hardy recalls, "We were a sitting duck." There were eleven survivors out of the crew of forty-six.

Moments before a second torpedo scored a direct hit to the ship's engine room, Gordon jumped sixteen metres into the frigid waters of Conception Bay. The undertow dragged him under and he was barely afloat two hours later when a hand reached out of the blackness and pulled him into a life raft. Unbelievably, his rescuer was his first cousin, George Hardy, from Port Aux Basques whom he had not met before this dramatic moment.

The result of his harrowing experience left him plagued with recurring bouts of pneumonia. Eventually, he was deemed medically unfit to serve overseas and was discharged from the army while undergoing treatment in Camp Hill Hospital, Halifax.

The only living survivor, Gordon Hardy, fifty-two years later fittingly accompanied the Newfoundland Lt. Governor Fred Russell to unveil a monument honouring the sixty-nine victims at Lance Cove, Bell Island, Newfoundland. He married Stella Roper and they reside in Ingonish.

Hardy, Harold Samuel F58095

Harold was born on April 3, 1925, the son of Levi (World War II) and Mary (Canning) Hardy, Ingonish. Private Hardy served in the infantry from 1943 to 1947. He married Florence Hardy. He was an outstanding ball pitcher. He worked at the Steel Plant, Sydney. He resides in Coxheath.

Hardy, Herman

Herman was the son of Thomas Neil (World War II) and Dorcas (MacDonald) Hardy, Ingonish. He served in the Merchant Marine. He was torpedoed while serving aboard the *Lord Strathcona*.

He married Isobel Kennedy, Louisbourg. He was a foreman with a fish plant in Louisbourg. He is buried in Louisbourg.

Hardy, James Richard

Jim was the son of Simon and Mary (Crewe) Hardy, Ingonish. He served overseas in the Canadian Army. He worked in construction. Unmarried, he died in 1990 and is buried in Halifax. James Richard Hardy and his brother, Stanley Crewe Hardy, both wounded while serving in Italy, sent the following poem to their mother:

There's a little path a twisting
to a cottage on the hill,
Where our thoughts are ever creeping
to the one we think of still.
Loving memories of our mother
for years we've been away,
Wondering if she's still the same,
or worries made her gray.

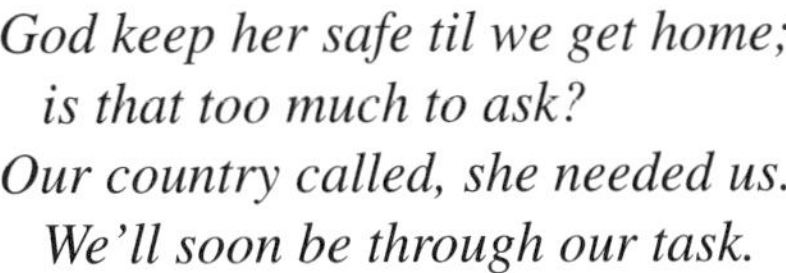

God keep her safe til we get home;
is that too much to ask?
Our country called, she needed us.
We'll soon be through our task.

Then along that path we'll hurry
to a cottage on a hill,
where our thoughts are always creeping,
to the mother we think of still.

Hardy, John Richard

Jack was the son of Thomas Hugh (World War II) and Dorcas (MacDonald) Hardy, Ingonish. He served in the Merchant Marine. He was unmarried and died in Ingonish and is buried in St. John's Cemetery, Ingonish.

Hardy, Levi James F606981

Levi was born on February 23, 1918, the son of Thomas and Dorcas (MacDonald) Hardy, Ingonish.

He served with the artillery in France and Germany from 1942 to 1946.

He married Christine MacDougall (World War II), Ingonish Beach, and they resided in Ingonish Beach. Later they moved to Halifax and he died there.

Hardy, Stanley Crewe F32734

Stan was born on November 11, 1918, the son of Simon and Mary (Crewe) Hardy, Ingonish. Private Hardy served in the army infantry in Italy, France and Germany (1942 to 1945).

He married Mary Neil, Ingonish. He worked at the Cape Breton Highlands National Park. He died in 1997 and is buried in St. John's Cemetery, Ingonish.

Hardy, Thomas Neil

'Thomas N.' was the son of William and Julia (Neil) Hardy, Ingonish. He served in the Merchant Marine. He and one of his sons were both aboard the *Lord Strathcona* when she was torpedoed. He married Dorcas MacDonald and they resided in Ingonish. He is buried in St. John's Cemetery, Ingonish.

Hardy, Wilfred Cecil F75930

Wilfred was born on April 22, 1922, the son of Levi (World War II) and Mary (Canning) Hardy, Ingonish. Corporal Hardy served with the 3rd Light Artillery in Canada and England. While suffering with diphtheria, he returned to Canada aboard the Canadian hospital ship *Lady Nelson*.

He married Jean Ingraham, Newfoundland. He served as the driver of the Victoria County Library Bookmobile. He is the proprietor of a carpet business in Ingonish. He and his wife reside in Ingonish.

Hardy, William Harris F32735

Will was born on July 21, 1917, the son of Levi (World War II) and Mary (Canning) Hardy, Ingonish.

He served as an oiler, trimmer and lineman aboard the *Lord Strathcona* (1940 to 1941). After he underwent sinus surgery, he enlisted with the West Nova Infantry and served overseas. Corporal Hardy was killed in action on December 13, 1944 and is buried in Ravanna British Empire Cemetery, Italy.

Hardy, William Levi

Father & Five Sons In Services

Levi was born on February 13, 1890, the son of William and Julia (Neil) Hardy, Ingonish. He enlisted on January 11, 1941 and served in the Merchant Navy. He served in the North Atlantic on the iron ore ships - *Lord Strathcona* and the *Rose*

Castle (both were torpedoed).

He married Mary Canning, Newfoundland. He was decorated for bravery for rescuing a man who was swamped in a fishing dory when the dory was off their fishing schooner. The incident happened on January 6, 1936, during a severe snowstorm approximately six miles southeast of Ingonish Island. Levi Hardy and his five sons served their country in various branches of the service. He died on February 3, 1974, and is buried in St. John's Cemetery, Ingonish.

Harrington, Mary Belle R.N.

Mary was the daughter of Joseph and Marion (Carmichael) Harrington, New York/ Baddeck.

She served with the Royal Canadian Air Force. Later she graduated from Sydney City Hospital School of Nursing.

She married Robert Anderson, Inlet Baddeck. She practiced her profession for more than thirty years. They resided in Baddeck. Mary Anderson died at age fifty-six and is buried in Middle River Cemetery.

Harris, John Roderick

'Bunny' was born in 1920, the foster son of Thomas A. and Danena (MacRae) MacDonald, Middle River. He enlisted in November, 1939 and Private Harris served with the Canadian Army. In 1948 he died from injuries sustained in a train accident in Ontario. He is buried in Middle River Cemetery.

Hart, Hugh William F76448

Hughie was born July 26, 1916, the son of John Murdoch and Agnes (Nicholson) Hart, Middle River. He enlisted on December 18, 1942, and served as a gunner with the Royal Canadian Army. Private Hart served in Canada, England, France and Germany. He was discharged on March 26, 1946. He died on March 17, 1976m and is buried in Middle River Cemetery.

Hart, Samuel Freeman F54658

Freeman was born in 1923, the son of John Murdoch and Agnes (Nicholson) Hart, Middle River.

He enlisted on September 5, 1939, and served with the Cape Breton Highlanders until January 22, 1946. Private Hart served in Canada, United Kingdom, Continental Europe and the Central Mediterranean area.

He married Janet MacFarlane, Baddeck, and his second wife was Gertrude Geddes. He died on October 26, 1983, and is buried in Middle River Cemetery.

Harvey, Albert F75929

Albert was born on June 6, 1922, the son of Ephraim and Susan (Frampton) Harvey, North Bay Ingonish.

Gunner Harvey served with the Canadian Army Artillery Regiment in France, Germany, Belgium and Holland (1942 to 1946).

He married Susan Hodder, Newfoundland. For thirty-six years he worked at the Cape Breton Highlands National Park. He lives in Ingonish.

Harvey, Leonard Morton

Leonard was born on September 15, 1920, the son of Gordon Stanley (World War I) and Janie (Morrison) Harvey, Murray/Baddeck.

Lieutenant Harvey enlisted on February 10, 1941, in Halifax with the Royal Canadian Artillery. He served as an aerial observation pilot. There were only three squadrons in the Canadian Army with twelve pilots to a squadron. He served in Canada, England, France and Germany. He was wounded twice during the 1858 days he served, 1575 of which were overseas. Captain Harvey was discharged on March 13, 1946, in Halifax.

He was a graduate of Dalhousie University (1948) and Nova Scotia Technical University (1951) with a degree in Civil Engineering. He married Catherine (Chat) Harvey, West Side Middle River. They resided in Baddeck. He died on September 29, 1988, and is buried in Harbourview Cemetery, South Haven.

Harvey, Vivian Marie W310547

Vivian was born on April 2, 1922, the daughter of Gordon S. and Janie (Morrison) Harvey, Murray/ Baddeck. She served in the Royal Canadian Air Force - Women's Division from March, 1943 to November, 1945. She was a graduate of Dalhousie University and Halifax Business College. She married Flying Officer Leo Elton Fownes (World War II). She died on March 23, 1993, and is buried in St. Andrews Cemetery, Baddeck Forks.

Hatcher, James William F27002

Jimmy was born on December 12, 1912, the son of Johnny and Miriam (Smith) Hatcher, New Haven. He enlisted in the Canadian Army and served overseas with the West Nova Scotia Regiment. He married Marge Lamey. He was a fisherman. He is buried in St. Andrew's Cemetery, Neil's Harbour.

Hawley, Alexander

Alex was the son of George and Eliza Hawley, Ingonish. He served in Canada with the Canadian Army. He married Cassie Keddy, Kentville. He worked in the Cape Breton Highlands National Park, Ingonish. He is buried in St. Peter's Parish Cemetery.

Hawley, Charles Joseph F55784

Charlie was born on November 8, 1918, the son of James T. and Annie May (Doyle) Hawley, Ingonish. Private Hawley served in Canada, United Kingdom and Continental Europe (1943 to 1946). He married Eileen Whitty. He was a fisherman and worked at the Cape Breton Highlands National Park. They reside in Ingonish Beach.

Hawley, Henry

Henry was the son of John Daniel and Eliza (Hawley) Hawley, Ingonish. He served the army in Canada. Unmarried, he was a fisherman and resided in Ingonish. He is buried in St. Peter's Parish Cemetery, Ingonish.

Hawley, Oswald

Ossie was the son of Parnell and Blanche (Cann) Hawley, Ingonish Ferry. He served in Canada in the navy. He was a fisherman. He is buried in St. Peter's Parish Cemetery.

Hawley, Russell

Russell was the son of Parnell and Blanche (Cann) Hawley, Ingonish Ferry. He served in the Canadian Army. He was the lightweight boxing champion at Camp Borden. He married and resided in Ontario.

Hawley, Simon Leo

Simon Leo was the son of Reuban and Cassie (MacQuarrie) (schoolteacher) Hawley, Ingonish Ferry. He served overseas in the Royal Canadian Air Force. He married Joyce Erwin, Toronto. They resided in Toronto where he was a policeman with the Ontario Provincial Police.

Hines, Melvin

Melvin was the son of Hugh and Etta Hawley, Ingonish Ferry. He served overseas in the Canadian Army. He was predeceased by his first wife. His second wife was Emma MacLellan, Meat Cove. He worked at the fire tower in the Cape Breton Highlands National Park and later as a fisherman at Black Point. He is buried in St. Margaret's Cemetery, Bay St. Lawrence.

Hunter, Willard Dan F54724

Willard was born on September 9, 1912, the son of William A. and Margaret (MacIver) Hunter, Hunter's Mountain. He enlisted on April 3, 1943, and served in the army, Royal Canadian Highlanders until July 18, 1946, on demobilization. Private Hunter served in Canada, the United Kingdom and Europe (21st Army).

He married Alice Nicholson, Bucklaw. They resided in Sydney. He was a painter by trade. He died on January 26, 1974, and is buried in Little Narrows Cemetery.

Hussey, Benjamin F77547

Ben was born on August 19, 1919, the son of Christopher and Flora Belle (Roberts) Hussey, Ingonish/New Haven.

He enlisted on March 3, 1941, in the Canadian Army and served overseas. Lance Corporal Hussey was wounded twice while in combat in Germany.

He married Rachel Nash, New Haven. He worked at the Cape Breton Highlands National Park. He is buried in St. Andrew's Cemetery, Neil's Harbour.

Hussey, William Thomas A5015

Willie was born on February 21, 1917, the son of George and Sara (Fillier) Hussey, Ingonish.

Able Seaman Hussey served with the Royal Canadian Naval Reserve from 1941 to 1945.

He married Violet Sawler from the South Shore of Nova Scotia. He was a game warden for the Cape Breton Highlands National Park. He died on March 18, 1994, and is buried in St. John's Cemetery, Ingonish.

Hutchison, John F69711

John was born in 1926, the son of Dan and Margaret (MacLean) Hutchison, Inlet Baddeck.

He joined the second battalion of the Cape Breton Highlanders in 1944. He enlisted May 5, 1945, and volunteered for the Europe and Pacific Theatres of War, but the war ended before departure. Private Hutchison was discharged October 6, 1945, on demobilization. He re-enlisted in December, 1947, and served until November, 1949 as a trooper with Lord Strathcona Horse Artillery.

He was predeceased by his wife, Ethel MacRae, Middle River. He presently resides in Middle River.

Ingraham, Arthur Hayman F2054

Arthur was born on September 23, 1922, the son of John James (Jack) and Ethel (Fricker) Ingraham, Neil's Harbour.

He enlisted on July 12, 1943, and served overseas with the North Nova Scotia Highlanders, Royal Canadian Infantry Corps. He was killed in action on July 6, 1944. Private Ingraham is buried in Beny-Sur-Mer Canadian War Cemetery, France.

Jackson, Alfred Fraser F31914

Alf was born on January 2, 1924, the son of James W. and Emiline (Noseworthy) Jackson, North Ingonish.

Signalman Jackson served with the Royal Canadian Signal Corps in Canada, United Kingdom and Continental Europe (1942 to 1946). Besides the fighting, he recalled hardships of enduring no socks, no water, unbearable mosquitoes and washing dishes with salt as there was no soap. Christmas, 1944, was memorable when the sergeants and officers waited on the enlisted men. They enjoyed excellent food, followed by beer and cigars. Signalman Jackson had the honour of being presented to the present day Queen Mother.

He was predeceased by his first wife, Helen M. MacLeod. He later married Anna Vanderwyst who grew up in Holland during the liberation. He resided in Sydney where he was a carpenter. He died on June 5, 1997, and is buried in Ingonish United Church Cemetery.

Jackson, Charles Freeman F59047

Charlie was born on March 11, 1926, the son of James Ward and Emiline (Noseworthy) Jackson, North Ingonish.

Gunner Jackson served overseas with the 2nd Battalion - Heavy Artillery.

He was one of four Jackson brothers who served his country. His first wife was Anne Murphy and his second wife was Helen Joyce Warren. They resided in Sydney where he was a postal letter carrier.

Jackson, George Franklin F32556

George was born on October 13, 1921, the son of James Ward and Emiline (Noseworthy) Jackson, North Ingonish. He served overseas. He married Noreen Humby and lived in Ingonish. He was a clerk at the Cape Breton Highlands National Park. He retired to Sydney.

Jackson, Harry Alexander

Harry was the son of James Ward and Emiline (Noseworthy) Jackson, North Ingonish.

He served overseas and was wounded in France. He convalesced in a Halifax military hospital. He suffered a permanent disability to his arm.

He married Catherine MacKinnon. They resided in Donkin and he worked at the Steel Plant in Sydney.

Jobe, James

Jimmy was born on February 23, 1924, the son of James and Mary Ann (MacIntyre) Jobe, Sugar Loaf. Private Jobe served with the Cape Breton Highlanders in the United Kingdom and the Central Mediterranean from 1942 to 1946. He married Jean Dixon, White Point. He was light keeper at Black Rock, Boularderie. He died on April 4, 1996, and is buried in St. Joseph's Cemetery, New Victoria.

Jobe, Robert Joseph F97051

Bobby was born on June 23, 1921, the son of James and Mary Ann (MacIntyre) Jobe, Sugar Loaf. Private Jobe served overseas with the North Nova Scotia Highlanders. He married Annie MacEvoy, Cape North. He was a construction worker. He is an accomplished violinist. He resides in Westville, Pictou County, Nova Scotia.

Kanary, Alexander James

Alex James was the son of Thomas and Ellen (Donahue) Kanary, Capstick. He served in the Royal Canadian Air Force. He resided in Ontario.

Kanary, Eliza Ann

Eliza was the daughter of Thomas and Ellen (Donahue) Kanary, Capstick. Private Kanary served in the American Army.

Kanary, George

George was the son of Thomas and Ellen (Donahue) Kanary, Capstick. Private Kanary served during the war. He married Lillian Nolan.

Kanary, James Patrick F4000

James was the son of James and Elizabeth (Kavanaugh) Kanary, Capstick. Private Kanary served in the Royal Canadian Signal Corps in France, Belgium, Germany and Holland (1942 to 1945).

He was a fisherman and worked with the Department of Highways. He died on January 30, 1998, and is buried in St. Margaret's Cemetery.

Kane, Dora Catherine

'Doris' was the daughter of James and Elizabeth (Brewer) Kane, Ingonish Centre. She served in Canada with the Canadian Womens Army Corps.

She married Clarence Stevens (WWII), Halifax. They resided in Halifax. Later she moved to British Columbia where she resides at Fraser Lake. She remains very active in the affairs of the local branch of the Royal Canadian Legion.

Kendall, Reuben William F10297

Reuben was born on December 29, 1905, of Newfoundland/Neil's Harbour parentage. He joined the Canadian Army on June 26, 1940, and served overseas as a gunner. He married Gertrude Fricker, Neil's Harbour. He fished out of Louisbourg. He is buried in Louisbourg.

Kerr, Dan John F79745

'D.J.' was born on November 4, 1916, the son of Dan and Mary Ann (MacDonald) Kerr, Quarry, St Ann's.

He enlisted in 1941 and in October, 1942, he was sent overseas with his unit. Private Kerr served with the West Nova Scotia Regiment in England, North Africa and the Italian Front. He had served in Italy since the campaign opened and was killed in action on December 13, 1943. The following was the telegram received by his parents:

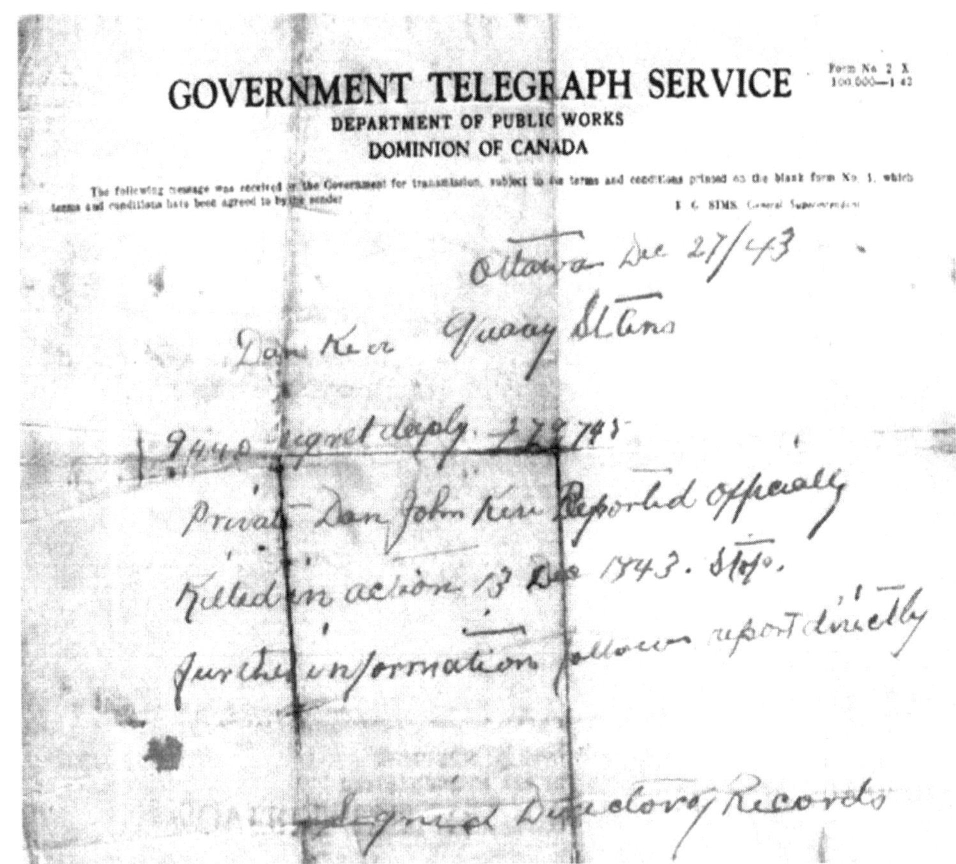

GOVERNMENT TELEGRAPH SERVICE

Form No. 2 X
100,000—1 42

DEPARTMENT OF PUBLIC WORKS

DOMINION OF CANADA

The following message was received by the Government for transmission, subject to the terms and conditions printed on the blank form No. 1, which terms and conditions have been agreed to by the sender

J. G. SIMS, General Superintendent

Ottawa Dec 27/43

Dan Kerr Quarry St Anns

9440 regret deeply F79745

Private Dan John Kerr Reported officially

Killed in action 13 Dec 1943. Stop.

Further information follows report directly

Signed Director of Records

He is buried in Moro River Cemetery, Italy.

Kerr, Hugh Alexander F21406

Hughie Alex was born on October 19, 1915, the son of Dan and Mary Ann (MacDonald) Kerr, Quarry, St. Ann's.

He enlisted on July 22, 1942, and served in the army with the Pictou Highlanders Infantry. He served in Canada, Newfoundland and Bermuda. Private Kerr was discharged January 28, 1946.

He married Norma MacLeod, Smokey. He died on November 26, 1982, and is buried in Greenwood Cemetery, Baddeck.

Kerr, Joseph Angus R280951

Joe was the son of Peter and Mary (MacDonald) Kerr, Cape North. Flight Sergeant Kerr served overseas with the Royal Canadian Air Force. He presently resides in New Brunswick.

Kerr, Peter Abraham R183274

Peter was born on May 30, 1923, the son of Dan Angus and Sarah (Briggett) Kerr, North River. He enlisted in November, 1940, and served with the Royal Canadian Air Force. He was discharged in December, 1945.

He married Shirley Dunlop, Baddeck. They resided in Truro where Mr. Kerr worked for the Municipality of Colchester. They retired to Baddeck.

Lahey, Michael

Michael was the son of John W. and Anna (MacLellan) Lahey, Barra Glen. He served with the Royal Canadian Air Force and the Royal Canadian Corps of Signals.

He married Cecilia MacIsaac, Frenchvale. He worked at the Steel Plant in Sydney. He and his wife are retired and residing in Sydney.

(left - Michael Lahey, right - Frank Nicholson)

LaRusic, Anthony F32013

Tony was born on February 3, 1914, the son of Patrick and Lena (Capstick) LaRusic, St. Margaret's Village. Private LaRusic served with the Royal Canadian Engineers in England, France, Germany, Holland and Belgium. He married Francis Plumridge. He and his war bride returned to St. Margaret's Village. They now reside in Sydney.

LaRusic, Emery Patrick F33066

Emery was born on March 17, 1923, the son of Patrick and Lena (Capstick) LaRusic, St. Margaret's Village. He enlisted on February 12, 1943, and served with the 8th New Brunswick Hussars. Private LaRusic served in France, Germany, Italy and North Africa. He was discharged on October 8, 1945. He married Alice Sanford, Windsor, Nova Scotia. He worked for the Nova Scotia Power Corporation. He is buried in Dartmouth.

LaRusic, Martin Francis V46974

(left - Martin LaRusic)

Martin was born on October 30, 1909, the son of John and Mayo (Dee) LaRusic, Dingwall. Shipwright 3rd Class LaRusic served in the Canadian Navy. On demobilization he was serving on the HMCS *Protector* (1942 to 1945).

He was a carpenter by trade. He was predeceased by his first wife Catherine MacDonald. He remarried and was residing in Sydney at the time of his death and is buried in Holy Rosary Cemetery, Westmount.

Lawrence, John

Jack was the son of William and Mary (Wills) Lawrence, Neil's Harbour. He enlisted in the Canadian Army and served in Canada. He married Elsie Best. He was a fisherman. He died on January 23, 1948, and is buried in St. Andrew's Cemetery, Neil's Harbour.

Leaver, George Clarence

George was born on February 19, 1920, the son of Jack and Eliza (MacDonald) Leaver, Baddeck. He served overseas with the Regina Rifles and the North Novies. He married Anne Warner, Sydney. They resided in Sydney. He was a painter by trade. He was predeceased by his wife, and presently resides in Taigh Mara Veterans Home in Glace Bay.

Lillington, Edgar F97575

Edgar was the son of Joshua and Sarah (Harvey) Lillington, Neil's Harbour. He enlisted in the Canadian Army on April 13, 1942, and served in Canada.

He married Susan Best, Neil's Harbour. He was a fisherman. He is buried in St. Andrew's Cemetery, Neil's Harbour.

Lillington, Wendell F97067

Wendell was born on December 12, 1922, the son of Joshua and Sarah (Harvey) Lillington, Neil's Harbour. He enlisted in the Canadian Army in November, 1941, and served overseas. After the war, he worked in the Merchant Navy. He retired to Neil's Harbour.

(Left, Wendell Lillington)

Long, Alexander Daniel F2820

Alex was born on August 6, 1919, the son of Thomas and Edith (Cantwell) Long, Baddeck. Lance Corporal Long went overseas in November of 1942. He served in Canada, England and Continental Europe. He served with the Princess Louise Fusiliers in Italy.

He married Sadie MacRae, Baddeck. He was a plumber by trade. They reside in Halifax.

Long, Kilmer Leon F75933

Kilmer was born on April 3, 1922, the son of Thomas and Edith (Cantwell) Long, Baddeck. Private Long went overseas in May 1943. He served in Continental Europe and with the Princess Louise Fusiliers in Italy. He married Anne Beers, Dartmouth. They resided in Dartmouth. He died on October 3, 1998, and is buried in Knox Auld Kirk Cemetery, Bay Road, Baddeck. Another brother, Clarence William Long (SF 90676) served as a gunner with the Royal Canadian Heavy Artillery in Korea.

MacAskill, Charles Duncan B64172

Charlie was born on March 8, 1916, the son of Norman and Mary (MacDonald) MacAskill, St. Margaret's Village. He served in the Queen's Own Rifles of Canada Infantry (1940 to 1945). He served in the United Kingdom, France and Germany and he was wounded in Normandy, France. His wife hailed from British Columbia. He was killed in a motor vehicle accident near Ingonish and is buried in Aspy Bay Cemetery.

MacAskill, Donald M. 31158741

Donald was born on November 24, 1904, the son of Norman and Mary (MacDonald) MacAskill, St. Margaret's Village.

He enlisted on August 18, 1942, in the United States Army, 1620 Service Unit and was discharged on February 9, 1945.

MacAskill, James G. F55227

Jim was born on June 23, 1916, the son of Norman and Mary (MacDonald) MacAskill, St. Margaret's Village. Private MacAskill served in the North Nova Scotia Highlanders. He was wounded and captured as a prisoner of war in Germany.

He married Mary Postlethwaite, New Victoria. He is buried in Aspy Bay Cemetery.

MacAskill, Kenneth John

Kennie John was born the son of Kenneth and Jessie (MacLeod) MacAskill, North Shore.

Private MacAskill served overseas with the Army Service Corps.

He married Margaret Wilson, New Waterford. He sailed on the Great Lakes and was lost in a storm on Lake Erie on November 12, 1956. His body was never recovered. His name is inscribed on a monument in the MacAskill Family Cemetery, North Shore.

MacAskill, Norman Daniel

Norman was born in 1904, the son of Norman and Mary (Campbell) MacAskill, Mill Cove, St. Ann's.

He served overseas with the Royal Canadian Air Force. Two older brothers served in World War I. One of them, Campbell was killed in action.

Norman served for twenty-eight years as a detective with the Sydney Police Department. He retired in 1973 as deputy police chief. He married Violet House, Sydney. He died on April 9, 1987, and is buried in St. James Cemetery, Big Bras d'Or.

MacAskill, Norman Phillip

Norman was born on July 3, 1920, the son of Malcolm and Rachael (MacDonald) MacAskill, Meadow, North River.

He enlisted in April, 1942, with the Royal Canadian Army Service Corps. He served in Europe - Italy, France and Germany. He was discharged with the rank of Sergeant. He served with the United Nations in Cyprus.

He married Alexandra MacKenzie Briggett, Boularderie. They retired to Munroe's Point. He died on October 13, 1997, and is buried in Goose Cove Cemetery.

MacAulay, Alexander Malcolm F33136

Alex was born on May 24, 1920, the son of Murdoch and Annie (MacDonald) MacAulay, Baddeck Bay. Lance Corporal MacAulay served overseas in the Canadian Army from February, 1943 to demobilization on March 27, 1946.

He married Doris MacKay, Big Baddeck. He was a founding partner of MacAulay's Garage, Baddeck. He was killed in a motor vehicle accident on January 18, 1958, and is buried in Highland Cemetery, Baddeck Bay.

MacAulay, Charles Evans Peter

Charlie was born in 1910, the son of John D. and Catherine (MacInnis) MacAulay, Baddeck.

He served overseas with the Royal Canadian Engineers. He was **MENTIONED IN DISPATCHES** for distinguished service against the enemy. He married Susan Danella MacFarlane, Pictou Island. They resided at Roger's Hill Crossroads, Scotsburn, Pictou County. He died on August 7, 1980.

MacAulay, Daniel Duncan V25980

Danny was born on May 25, 1915, the son of Murdoch and Annie (MacDonald) MacAulay, Baddeck Bay. He served from May, 1940, to August, 1945, with the Royal Canadian Naval Volunteer Reserve in Canada and England. He married Isabel MacDonald, Estmere. The Inverary Inn Resort in Baddeck is owned by the MacAulay family.

MacAulay, Donald Norman

Donald was born on April 20, 1907, the son of Norman and Norrie (Morrison) MacAulay, North Gut.

He served in the Canadian Army at Brantford, Canada.

He married Agnes Matheson, St. Patricks Channel. They resided in Baddeck. He died on February 27, 1977, and is buried in Harbourview Cemetery, South Haven.

MacAulay, Ian

Ian was the son of John D. and Catherine (MacInnis) MacAulay, Baddeck. He served during the war. Ian MacAulay resided in La Crosse, Wisconsin.

MacAulay, John Edwin F69706

John Edwin was the son of Malcolm John and Rachel (MacLeod) MacAulay, Hazeldale. He served in the army during the war.

He and his wife, June, resided in Toronto where he was an auto body mechanic. He died in 1996 and is buried in Little Narrows Cemetery.

MacAulay, Lionel Frederick F4956

Lionel was born on January 4, 1917, the son of George and Mae (MacKay) MacAulay, Baddeck Bay.

He served from May 1942 to March 21, 1946 with the Royal Canadian Army - Royal Canadian Army Medical Corps. He served in Canada and overseas in Continental Europe.

He married Marjorie Gillis, Skye Glen. They resided in the old home in Baddeck Bay. He died on March 26, 1971, and is buried in Highland Cemetery, Baddeck Bay.

MacCluskey, George J. F54685

George was the son of Frederick and Catherine (MacNeil) MacCluskey, Ottawa Brook.

Corporal MacCluskey served with the Cape Breton Highlanders and the West Nova Scotia Regiment. Twenty-five year old MacCluskey was wounded January 5 and subsequently died on January 13, 1944.

He was a graduate of Iona High School and had attended Nova Scotia Agricultural College, Truro. He was closely associated with the co-operative movement and the credit union. Besides his parents, he was survived by a young widow, Dorothy MacCluskey.

MacCuspic, Malcolm John F33457

Malcolm was born on June 7, 1924, the son of Dan and Annie (MacLean) MacCuspic, Hunter's Mountain.

He enlisted in 1943 and served with the 1st Canadian Parachute Battalion in Continental Europe. Paratrooper MacCuspic was wounded in France on the 14th of August, 1944. He was involved in the Battle of the Bulge and served in Belgium and Holland for about two months. His battalion dropped over the Rhine not far from Wesel, Germany on March 24 and remained in Wismar, Germany until the end of the war. He was discharged on September 11, 1945.

He married Kathryn Joyce Pride, Sydney. They resided in Port Hawkesbury. He died on November 10, 1998, and is buried in Forest Haven Memorial Gardens, Sydney.

MacDonald, Abraham

Abraham was born on June 27, 1905, the son of John J. (Ban) and Bella (Morrison) MacDonald, Baddeck. He was raised at the home of Dougal MacDonald at Red Head. He served in the Canadian Army. He married Nita Anderson, Pictou. He died in 1942.

MacDonald, Adam Joseph F89291

Adam was born in 1921 the son of Hector and Mary (Dixon) MacDonald, Gillis Point. Corporal MacDonald served in the Argyll and Sutherland Highlanders. He was killed in action on October 29, 1944, and is buried in Bergen-op-Zoom Cemetery, Netherlands. He was survived by a young widow (née Monica Connors) of St. John's, Newfoundland.

MacDonald, Ainslie Ford R65383

Ainslie was born on July 14, 1920, the son of Forbes and Katie (Ford) MacDonald, Middle River. He enlisted in September, 1940 and served as a Flight Sergeant with the Royal Canadian Air Force, 2nd Tactical Air Force. He served in Canada, Newfoundland, United Kingdom, Belgium, Holland and Germany. His first wife was Frances Rickey, Kingston, Ontario. His second marriage was to Catherine MacKenzie, Marion Bridge. He died on February 11, 1986, and is buried in Middle River Cemetery.

MacDonald, Alexander A1623

'Sander' was born on February 11, 1911, the son of Captain Dan (World War I) and Bessie (MacLeod) MacDonald, Baddeck. He enlisted on May 10, 1940, and served in the Royal Canadian Navy until October, 1945.

He married Margaret Ann MacDonald, French River. He died on May 11, 1984, and is buried in Greenwood Cemetery, Baddeck.

MacDonald, Alexander F33485

Alex was born on October 27, 1912, the son of Alexander and Elizabeth (Budge) MacDonald, Sunrise. He enlisted on June 4, 1943 in the Canadian Army and served overseas as a gunner in the artillery. He married Edna Rogers, New Haven. He worked at the Cape Breton Highlands National Park. He is retired and living in New Haven.

MacDonald, Alexander, M.D.

Sandy was the son of Dr. Daniel, M.D., and Margaret (MacNeil) MacDonald, Bay Pond, Baddeck. Dr. MacDonald served with the Canadian Medical Corps. Major MacDonald was 1st Clinical Surgeon in a 200 bed military hospital at Aldershot. He married Astra (Toot) Buckley, Sydney. 'Dr. Sandy' practised medicine in Sydney until his retirement.

MacDonald, Alexander John F33313

'Alex Big Johnny' was born in 1906, the son of John and Margaret (MacCharles) MacDonald, Upper Middle River.

He enlisted on April 6, 1943, and served in the Army - 20th General, Royal Canadian Army Medical Corps. Private MacDonald served in France, Belgium and England. His discharge was on March 23, 1946. He died in 1970 and is buried in Middle River Cemetery.

MacDonald, Alexander John

'Alex Big Angus' was born on June 7, 1902, the son of Angus and Bella (MacPherson) MacDonald, Middle River. Private MacDonald served in the United States Army.

His two older brothers served in the first Great War. He died on August 13, 1972, and is buried in Roselawn Park Cemetery, Detroit, Michigan.

MacDonald, Alexander Kitchener

'Alex John A.' was born on March 3, 1915 the son of John A. and Margaret (MacRae) MacDonald, Middle River. Sgt. MacDonald served overseas in the Royal Canadian Air Force. He operated a trucking business and was involved with the construction of the AlCan Highway. Later he worked with the British Columbia Telephone Company. His brother, Kenneth, was the founder of the Middle River firm, Midway Motors Limited. Unmarried, Alex MacDonald died in 1997 in Vancouver and is buried there.

MacDonald, Alexander Young F32481

'Sandy A.Y.' was the son of Lauchlin (World War I) and Sarah (Brown) MacDonald, Baddeck. He served overseas with the Canadian Army, Royal Canadian Signals, 3rd Division. He married Daisy MacKillop, Baddeck Bay. In civilian life, he was a banking executive with the Royal Bank. They reside in British Columbia.

MacDonald, Charles Campbell R252286

Campbell was born on January 9, 1924, the son of Neil and Dolena (Matheson) MacDonald, Estmere.

Flight Sergeant MacDonald served with the # 24 Operational Training Unit. He served as a wireless air gunner in the Royal Canadian Air Force. His Wellington aircraft was lost on a night cross-country exercise when they went down in the North Sea on April 5, 1945. His name is inscribed on Panel 282, Runnymede War Memorial, Surrey, England.

MacDonald, Charles John F55228

Charlie John was born in 1909, the son of Duncan H. and Flora (MacDonald) MacDonald, Bay Road Valley. Private MacDonald served overseas with the North Nova Scotia Highlanders, Infantry Corps. Weekly, Duncan H. MacDonald wrote to his sons. When he learned that Charlie had been killed in action and Gordon taken prisoner of war, he wrote:

August 1944
Dear Charlie and Gordon,

Again on this fine Sunday afternoon we write you these lines as oft we done in answer to your welcome cheerful and never failing letters which sorry to relate we receive no more and Dear Charlie you have made the Supreme Sacrifice and your body rests far away from your native shores and kindred but we trust and pray that your soul is at rest with God in his Eternal home and Gordon we still have hopes that you are still living and will return to us and if fates prove otherwise we hope your soul is in that happy haven.

Tomorrow would be your thirty fifth birthday Charlie and in my mind's eye I can plainly see you as a little lad with your little pail carrying cold water from the old spring, later plodding to Post Office for our mail and telling us tall stories of the Germans you had met on way and destroyed later on but when seven years old travelling miles to school alone, then later in years leaving the parental roof and going to North River lumber woods later on to wheat fields of Alberta then home again on the Rawleigh route with your faithful horse Jumbo. Thence to Gypsum Plant at Dingwall and when I heard our country was at war I well knew by your ideals you would be one of the first loyal boys that would enlist for country and freedom and it takes lots of courage to leave home, loved ones and friends and embark on the great adventure you and all your brothers we well knew would be in ranks only ye did not wish we be left alone and we are proud to be the parents of such a family but we miss the empty chairs. But ye got your Patriotism honestly from your forebears. Well do I remember being thrilled by father with the tales of the exploits of Nelson at Trafalgar, Wellington at Waterloo, Wolfe at the Plains of Abraham and in our countries early days singing the praises of MacDonald, Tupper and Cartier and you Charlie visiting travelling a long way to see the home of your ancestors all goes to prove that your heart was true and you gave your precious manly life fighting to the last for us and the freedom you believed in greater love hath no man than that he gives his life for his friends. You will always live in our memories as one of nature's gentlemen, a friend of all and a son any parents and brothers and relatives may well be proud to own kinship to and its sad to see so many of the cream of our country go under but such is cruel war.

So farewell Dear Son for the Present but we trust and pray we will all meet again over yonder where there will be no more parting and cruel war which parted us from a loving faithful Son and Brother we'll see no more.

From Father, Mother and Brothers

Private MacDonald was killed in action the day after D-Day, June 7, 1944. He was buried in Beny-Sur-Mer Cemetery, France.

MacDonald, Dan Allister Murray

Murray was born on May 25, 1919, the twin son of John A. and Kate (MacDonald) MacDonald, Tarbot. Murray served in the Canadian Merchant Navy. He was aboard the *Watuka* when she left in convoy from Louisbourg. Murray was lost at sea thirty-five miles out of Halifax on March 22, 1944, at six o'clock in the morning. The *Watuka* was sunk by enemy action.

MacDonald, Daniel F54605

Danny was born on May 22, 1906, the son of Archie and Sarah (MacDonald - widow MacIvor) MacDonald, Baddeck. He enlisted on August 28, 1939, and served with the Cape Breton Highlanders in Canada and Britain. Company Quartermaster Sergeant MacDonald was discharged at Halifax on January 23, 1946.

He was a long distance runner and a participant in the 1929 Boston Marathon which was won by Nova Scotia's Marathon King Johnny Miles. Dan MacDonald placed 32nd out of a field of 198. He married Gertrude May, Newfoundland. They resided in Baddeck. He died on June 22, 1986, and is buried in Harbourview Cemetery, South Haven.

MacDonald, Daniel Francis F56375

Dan F. was born on November 15, 1923, the son of Angus Ranald and Sarah E. (MacNeil) MacDonald, Washabuck. He served overseas with the Royal Canadian Artillery (ACK-ACK) and Canadian Forestry Corps. He served in Canada and the United Kingdom. He married Kathleen Murphy, Washabuck, where they resided.

He died on December 17, 1997, and is buried in Holy Rosary Cemetery, Washabuck.

MacDonald, Daniel John R264961

'D.J.' was born on August 11, 1926, the son of Dan and Katie Ann (Peterson) MacDonald, Quarry, St. Ann's. He enlisted on August 24, 1943, and served as a postal clerk in the Royal Canadian Air Force. LAC MacDonald was discharged on April 26, 1946.

He married Phyllis MacKenzie, Baddeck. He operated a barber shop in Baddeck. D.J. died on July 13, 1972, and is buried in Greenwood Cemetery, Baddeck.

MacDonald, Daniel Murdoch F97828

Donnie was born on October 20, 1917, the son of Big Jack and Elizabeth (Morrison) MacDonald, Port Bevis.

He enlisted on May 14, 1942, and served as a craftsman in the Royal Canadian Electrical and Mechanical Engineers. He served in England, France, Holland and Germany. Private MacDonald was discharged on March 30, 1946.

Unmarried, he died tragically in a house fire on December 2, 1973, and is buried in Harbourview Cemetery, South Haven.

MacDonald, Daniel Ranald F14413

'Dan R.' MacDonald hailed from Capstick. He was born on May 15, 1921. Gunner MacDonald served in the Royal Canadian Army in Italy, France and Germany (1940 to 1945).

He married Mary Rita Curtis, St. Margaret's Village. He was a warden in the Cape Breton Highlands National Park. He died on March 15, 1966, and is buried in St. Margaret's Village Cemetery.

MacDonald, Donald James F92118

Donald James was the son of Angus and Veronica (MacNeil) MacDonald, Ottawa Brook. Flying Officer MacDonald served with the Royal Canadian Air Force - 46783 Squadron Air Crew.

He married Mary MacNeil, Little Bras d'Or. His unpublished manuscript about World War II Cape Breton veterans who were killed in action is at the Royal Canadian Legion, Branch # 12, Sydney. He is buried in Resurrection Cemetery, Sydney.

MacDonald, Donald John F32182

'D.J. Bheag' (Beag) is Gaelic for 'little' - Gaelic pronunciation is VEK was born on August 27, 1909, a twin child of Murdoch and Alexis (Montgomery) MacDonald, West Tarbot. He enlisted on August 28,

1942, as a mechanic in the Royal Canadian Electrical and Mechanical Engineers. He served in the United Kingdom. He was discharged on March 20, 1946.

He married Anna Mae Dauphney, Indian Brook. They resided at Indian Brook. He died on November 16, 1988, and is buried in Riverside Cemetery, North River.

MacDonald, Donald John F 56960

Donald John was born on March 11, 1923, the son of Angus and Philena (Smith) MacDonald, Rocky Side, St. Ann's. He enlisted on June 1, 1943, and served with the Cape Breton Highlanders - The Stormont, Dundas and Glengarry Highlanders in England, France, Belgium, Holland and Germany. He was wounded in action and was discharged on March 12, 1946.

He married Martha MacLean, Big Baddeck. They resided in Big Baddeck and later in Baddeck. Donald John died on June 28, 1996, and is buried in Harbourview Cemetery, South Haven.

MacDonald, Donald Seward

'Donald Willie Danny' was born on August 7, 1917, the son of William and Annie (MacEachern) MacDonald, West Side Middle River. Private MacDonald served in the Royal Canadian Signal Corps.

He married Rita Ford, Newfoundland. They resided in Ontario. He died on April 23, 1988, and is buried in Pinehill Cemetery, Scarborough, Ontario.

MacDonald, Duncan B.

Duncan was the son of John (caretaker at Corson's Estate) and Lena (Roberts) MacDonald, Ingonish. He served overseas in the Royal Canadian Air Force. He married a school teacher, Jean MacEwen. They resided in Sydney.

MacDonald, Duncan John F3980

'D.J.' was born on April 17, 1921, the son of Murdoch Angus and Mary (Smith) MacDonald, Rocky Side.

He enlisted on July 27, 1942, and served as a gunner with the Heavy Antiaircraft Regiment in Canada, Newfoundland and England. While serving in England he was transferred as reinforcement to the Black Watch Regiment, 2nd Battalion. Private MacDonald was wounded during combat in France in September, 1944, and was hospitalized for two and one-half months. Following his recuperation he served as an instructor in an Officer Training School in England. He married a school teacher, Ann Matheson (Glen Tosh). They resided at Rocky Side, South Haven. He served as a federal fisheries officer until his retirement.

MacDonald, Ewen F2862

Ewen was born on March 28, 1918, the son of John B. and Sarah (MacDonald) MacDonald, Quarry, St. Ann's. He served overseas with the North Nova Scotia Highlanders. While a member of the invasion force, Private MacDonald was killed in action on June 7, 1944, in France. He is buried in Beny-Sur-Mer Canadian War Cemetery, France.

MacDonald, Francis Joachim A117741

Francis Dan A. was the son of Dan A. and Isabel (MacNeil) MacDonald, St. Columba/Iona. Rifleman MacDonald served with the Royal Winnipeg Rifles in Canada, England, France and Northwest Europe (1943 to 1946). Unmarried, he died on March 22, 1980, and is buried in St. Columba Cemetery, Iona.

MacDonald, Franklin Donald F51779

Frank was born on July 16, 1922, the son of Angus J. and Frances (MacRae) MacDonald, Middle River. He enlisted on January 1, 1943, and served with the Black Watch Highland Light Infantry. Private MacDonald served in Canada, England, France, Belgium and Holland. He was wounded in Holland on October 8, 1944, and was hospitalized in Antwerp and England. He was discharged on July 24, 1945. He married Margaret L. MacKay, Big Baddeck. They resided in Middle River. He died on December 26, 1982, and is buried in Middle River Cemetery.

MacDonald, George Brown F10997

George was born on May 12, 1921, the son of Dan P. and Katie (Peterson) MacDonald, Quarry, St. Ann's. He enlisted in 1942 and served in Canada. He was discharged in 1946. He married Hettie Dunford. They reside in Sydney.

MacDonald, Gordon Duncan F55329

Gordon was born on January 27, 1917, the son of Duncan and Flora (MacDonald) MacDonald, Bay Valley Road. He enlisted on June 14, 1940, with the North Nova Scotia Highlanders. He disembarked for overseas on July 15, 1941. Private MacDonald was taken prisoner of war in France on June 6, 1944. He married Joan MacLean, Cape North. He worked for the National Gypsum Company in Dingwall. He died on March 25, 1977, and is buried in Aspy Bay Cemetery.

MacDonald, Gordon Neil F32116

Gordon was born on April 19, 1914, the the son of Frederick and Catherine (Ferguson) MacDonald, Baddeck.

Lance Corporal MacDonald served from August, 1942, to March 26, 1946, with the Royal Canadian Signal Corps. He served in the United Kingdom and Continental Europe.

He married Wilhelmina Creelman, R.N. (Matron of Victoria County Memorial Hospital). He died on April 15, 1991, and is buried in St. Andrew's Cemetery, Baddeck Forks.

MacDonald, Gordon William

Billy was raised by Angus and Catherine (MacDonald) Urquhart, Little River. He enlisted on November 4, 1943, in Montreal, Quebec, in the Royal Canadian Air Force. He was discharged on May 21, 1946, at Lachine, Quebec. Following the war he continued his career in the military. He and his wife, Theresa, resided in Ontario. He died on June 21, 1984, and is buried in Riverview Cemetery, North River Bridge.

MacDonald, Reverend Hugh A.

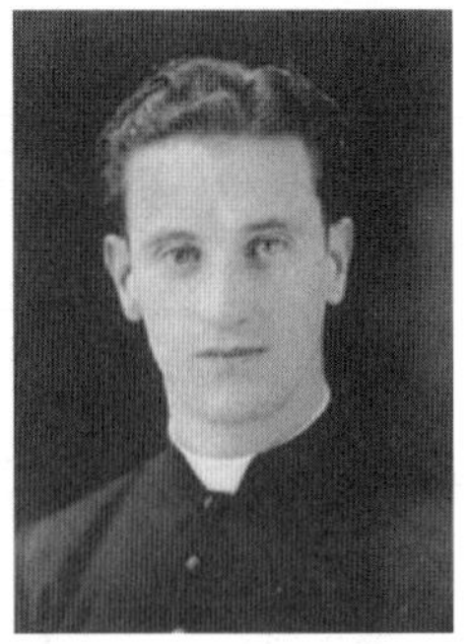

'Hugh A.' (World War I) was the son of Michael A.J. (World War I) and Mary (MacDonald) MacDonald, Iona.

Reverend MacDonald was ordained in 1936. Captain MacDonald served with the Canadian Chaplain Services in the Royal Canadian Navy. Father MacDonald died in 1979 in Detroit, Michigan, and is buried there.

MacDonald, Hugh W.

'Hugh W.' was the son of James Jonathan and Elizabeth Effie (MacKinnon) MacDonald, Ottawa Brook. Lieutenant MacDonald served with the Cape Breton Highlanders in Canada, the United Kingdom and Italy. He married Irene Belliveau, Musquodoboit Harbour. He died on February 10, 1980, and is buried in Sacred Heart Cemetery, McKinnons Harbour.

MacDonald, James Fraser F58582

James was born on April 11, 1917, the son of Alexander and Annie (MacLennan) MacDonald, Boularderie. He served in the army in England, France and Germany.

He married Tena Dauphney, Indian Brook. He sailed for many years on the Great Lakes. They resided in North River. He died on July 14, 1983, and is buried in Riverside Cemetery, North River.

MacDonald, James Robert F32662

'Carpenter Jim' was born on March 20, 1923, the son of Robert and Clare (Young) MacDonald, Ingonish Beach. Corporal MacDonald served in Canada from 1943 to 1944. He married Mary Frances Doucette and they resided in Ingonish. He was a carpenter. He died on February 9, 1996, and is buried in St. Peter's Parish Cemetery, Ingonish.

MacDonald, John Angus MacIver

Johnny was born on December 2, 1922, the son of Murdoch and Mary J. (MacDonald) MacDonald, Little River.

'Johnny Skir Dhu' enlisted in 1939 in Sydney. He served in the Royal Canadian Air Force. He served in Canada off the Atlantic Coast in crash boats. He was discharged in 1945. He was the last baby delivered on the North Shore by the legendary midwife Granny Urquhart. He was a carpenter and salesperson. He married Dolly Beck and they reside in Catalone.

MacDonald, John Bernard

Johnny was born on June 1, 1926, the son of Angus Ranald and Sarah Liza (MacNeil) MacDonald, Washabuck. He served with the North Nova Scotia Highlanders and the Carlton York. Private MacDonald served in Canada, United Kingdom, Northwest Europe and Italy. Unmarried, he died on October 17, 1978, and is buried in Holy Rosary Cemetery, Washabuck.

MacDonald, John Charles 3393

John Charles was the son of Archibald and Flora (Patterson) MacDonald, Boularderie East. He served in the Canadian Army. He was unmarried. He was a surveyor and worked with the provincial Department of Highways. He died suddenly at fifty-four years of age and is buried in St. James Cemetery, Big Bras d'Or.

MacDonald, John Cyril K51259

Cyril was the son of James and Margaret (MacNeil) MacDonald, Ottawa Brook. Private MacDonald served with the North Shore Regiment in Canada, United Kingdom and Northwest Europe. He was wounded in action in Normandy in 1944. He married Dolena MacNeil, Christmas Island. They resided in Westmount. He was an electrician by trade. He is buried in Holy Rosary Cemetery.

MacDonald, John David F88479

'John D.' was born on May 1, 1919, the son of Duncan and Flora (MacDonald) MacDonald, Bay Valley Road. He enlisted on June 30, 1941, and served with the Cape Breton Highlanders in the United Kingdom and Central Mediterranean region. He was wounded in Italy on May 26, 1944.

He married Theresa Curtis, St. Margaret's Village. He was a warden in the Cape Breton Highlands National Park. He died on January 9, 1994, and is buried in Aspy Bay Cemetery.

MacDonald, John Duncan

'John D.' was born on October 24, 1918, the son of Angus and Cassie (MacKenzie) MacDonald, Meadow, North River. He served in the Canadian Army with the Lincoln and Welland Regiment. He served in active duty in Continental Europe. He married Irene Mouland, Sydney. They moved to Ontario in 1947 and reside in Brantford, Ontario.

MacDonald, John Hugh F58471

John Hugh was born on September 19, 1925, the son of Angus and Theresa (MacLellan) MacDonald, Capstick. Private MacDonald enlisted in 1941 with the Cape Breton Highlanders and served in the United Kingdom. He married Alexina Fraser. He died on March 23, 1988.

MacDonald, John James F8812

John was born on June 5, 1919, the son of Hugh and Helen (Goodfellow) MacDonald, Baddeck. Private MacDonald served with the Pictou Highlanders in Canada and Newfoundland (1940 - 1945). He married Marguerite Cain, Millville, and resided in Baddeck. He died on April 27, 1979, and is buried in Greenwood Cemetery, Baddeck.

MacDonald, John Jeremiah F58028

Johnny was born on May 20, 1918, the son of Jack and Margaret (Calahan) MacDonald. He was born in Montana and came to Estmere when he was a preschooler. He was the step-son of Malcolm Campbell.

He enlisted in 1943 with the Merchant Marine. In 1944 he enlisted with the Canadian Army, Royal Canadian Engineers, 86th Bridge Company and served in Canada and overseas until June 1, 1946. He married Charlotte MacNeil, Gabarus. They resided in Sydney where he worked with the Canadian National Railway. He died on February 4, 1975, and is buried in Forest Haven Cemetery, Sydney.

MacDonald, John Neil

John Neil MacDonald hailed from Sugar Loaf. He served in the navy. He married during the war and his wife died overseas. Subsequently he and his young family returned home. Following the war he remained a seaman. He presently resides in Cheticamp.

MacDonald, John Peter F78511

Johnnie was born on September 9, 1919, the son of Dan P. and Katie (Peterson) MacDonald, Quarry, St. Ann's. He enlisted on April 17, 1941, with the Cape Breton Highlanders at New Glasgow. He served in Italy, Belgium, Holland, France, England and Canada. Private MacDonald was discharged on December 7, 1945, at Halifax. He married Annie MacDonald, Baddeck. He was employed as an auto body repairman. He resides in Baddeck.

MacDonald, Joseph

Joe was the son of Robert and Clare (Young) MacDonald, Ingonish Beach. Sergeant MacDonald served overseas in the Canadian Army. He married Edna Donovan. He served in the Canadian Armed Forces following the war until his retirement. They reside in Fredericton, New Brunswick.

MacDonald, Kenneth

Kennie was born on May 9, 1918, the son of Big Jack and Elizabeth (Morrison) MacDonald, Port Bevis. He served overseas with the Cape Breton Highlanders.

He married Annie Andrews, R.N., North River/ Sydney Mines. He was a carpenter. He died on August 18, 1988, and is buried in Harbourview Cemetery, South Haven.

MacDonald, Kenzie F 24466

Kenzie was born in 1917, the son of Red Murdoch D. and Christena (Carson) MacDonald, Ross Ferry. He enlisted on July 18, 1940, with the Royal Canadian Artillery. He served as a gunner. He served in Canada, England and North West Europe. He married Ethel Marian MacPhail, River Denys. He died on June 22, 1979, and is buried in MacDonald Cemetery, Boularderie.

MacDonald, Leo

Leo was the son of M.L.C. John A. (World War I) and Mary Agnes (MacKinnon) MacDonald, Iona. Lieutenant MacDonald served with the Cape Breton Highlanders in 1939 and with the West Nova Scotia Regiment in Northwest Europe. Major MacDonald pursued a career in the military following the war.

MacDonald, Malcolm

Malcolm Louie was a son of Malcolm and Christy (MacPhee) MacDonald, Meadow, North River. He served as a flight officer with the Royal Canadian Air Force. He was a Gaelic language instructor at the Gaelic College from 1941 to 1943. He taught Gaelic at the North River school. He married and he worked in the administration office for the Nova Scotia Liquor Commission. It is believed that he is buried at Musquodobit.

MacDonald, Margaret

Margaret was born on May 31, 1922, the daughter of Angus Ranald and Sarah Liza (MacNeil) MacDonald, Washabuck.

Private MacDonald served in the Canadian Women's Army Corps in Canada. Unmarried, she died on June 25, 1990, and is buried in Holy Rosary Cemetery, Washabuck.

MacDonald, Margaret Ellen

Margaret was born on November 23, 1909, the daughter of George H. and Mary Ann (Buchanan) MacDonald, Sugar Loaf.

She was a graduate of the Provincial Normal College, Truro, and the United Church Training College, Toronto. Lance Corporal MacDonald served with the Royal Canadian Air Force (Women's Division) from January 16, 1942, to August 15, 1945, in Canada.

She served with the United Church of Canada in Angola, Africa. She was employed by the Department of Health and Welfare and the University of Toronto for a number of years. She died on June 30, 1997, and is buried in Aspy Bay Cemetery.

MacDonald, Dr. Martin S., M.D.

Martin was the son of M.L.C. John A. (World War I) and Mary Agnes (MacKinnon) MacDonald, Iona.

He enlisted in the Cape Breton Highlanders and later Captain MacDonald served with the Royal Canadian Army Medical Corps in Canada and overseas.

He was a 1939 Arts graduate of St. Mary's University. He received his M.D.C.M. from Dalhousie University Medical School in 1945. He married Olive Petrie, New Waterford. Dr. MacDonald practiced medicine in Glace Bay before opening his own general practice in Dartmouth in 1955. He died at sixty-three years of age and is buried in Gate of Heaven Cemetery, Lower Sackville.

MacDonald, Michael Bernard, D.C.M. F54680

Mike was born on August 27, 1920, the son of Dan Ambrose and Isabel (MacNeil) MacDonald, St. Columba.

The following was taken from the *Cape Breton Post*, November 10, 1986.

'On the night of April 30, 1945, MacDonald was a Platoon Sgt in "D" Company of the Cape Breton Highlanders, which was attacking the key strong-point in the defences of the port of Delfzijl.

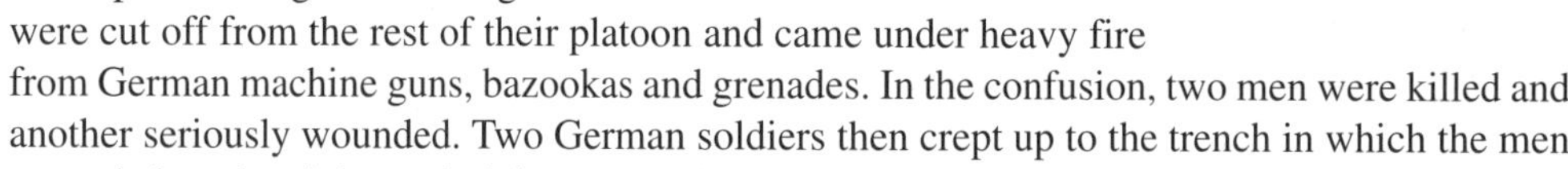

According to the citation that led his being awarded the medal, at one point during the battle Sgt. MacDonald and five of his comrades were cut off from the rest of their platoon and came under heavy fire from German machine guns, bazookas and grenades. In the confusion, two men were killed and another seriously wounded. Two German soldiers then crept up to the trench in which the men were sheltered and demanded they surrender.

Sgt. MacDonald would have none of this. When the enemy soldier closest to him allowed the barrel of his gun to stray out of line for an instant, he grabbed it, knocked the man down and headed back towards the trench.

He was seriously wounded in both legs as the enemy opened fire from a pill-box, but was able to crawl to the safety of the trench. He remained there for seven hours with the two remaining comrades until help arrived.

From the trench, he was taken to a tent behind the lines, then was moved by ambulance to Germany and by air to Brussels. From Brussels, he was sent to England.

In all, he was in hospital from May 2, 1945 until late 1946.

"We were in the process of surrendering, all lined up" recalls the soft-spoken 68-year-old when asked about that fateful night. "When the rifle got off line, I grabbed it. Then the whole batch of us took off running. We weren't that far from the trench; I took a dive and got hit."

"It's all very well to stay alive, but you've got to have your dignity; that's all there is".

MacDonald doesn't hold much hope for mankind learning a lesson from the horrors of the last world war, despite there not having been another one since.

"No, we never learned anything from war," he says, "just that, with the atomic bomb, we can never have another one ..."

In fact, it's likely that few among his friends and neighbours know that the Iona native was awarded a **DISTINGUISHED CONDUCT MEDAL** for bravery on the battlefield during the closing days of World War II.

Like many who fought for their country in either of the two world wars, Mike MacDonald is reluctant to talk about his experiences.'

He married the Cape Breton author and playwright, Beatrice MacNeil. They reside in North Side East Bay.

MacDonald, Murdoch MacKenzie F77515

Murdoch was a son of Daniel and Annie (Buchanan) MacDonald, South Harbour. He enlisted on February 27, 1941, and served in France, Holland, Belgium and Germany. Bombardier MacDonald was discharged on December 1, 1945. He married Martha Budge, New Haven. His territory as a mail carrier was from Ingonish to Bay St. Lawrence. They reside in South Harbour.

MacDonald, Neil Roderick

Neil Roddie was born on May 25, 1919, twin son of John A. and Kate (MacDonald) MacDonald, Tarbot.

He enlisted for overseas service. He served in Canada. His twin brother, D. Murray (World War II), was lost at sea. He married Mae Bezanson. He was a rural mail carrier for many years. He died on February 18, 1991, and is buried in Pine Hill Cemetery, River Bennett.

MacDonald, Norman A. V6559

Norman was the son of Reverend Malcolm N. and Bessie (MacDonald) MacDonald, Big Bras d'Or. He enlisted in Ottawa on July 12, 1940 and served as a writer with the Naval Volunteer Reserve. He served overseas from July 1942 to July 1943 on the HMCS *Nioke* and HMCS *Snowflake*. On February 14, 1945, he was promoted to Paymaster Lieutenant, Royal Canadian Naval Volunteer Reserve.

He married Sheila Robinson, Scotland. He and his war bride returned to Big Bras d'Or. He worked for the civil service in Ottawa and with the Unemployment Insurance Office in Sydney Mines. He is buried in St. James Cemetery, Big Bras d'Or.

MacDonald, Norman Daniel F55022

Norman was born on April 6, 1915, the son of Duncan H. and Flora (MacDonald) MacDonald, Bay Road Valley. He enlisted on March 27, 1940, and served with the Cape Breton Highlanders in Italy and Africa. Private MacDonald was wounded in Italy on September 6, 1944. He married Harriett Maloney, Dingwall. He worked at the National Gypsum Plant in Dingwall. He died on May 9, 1970, and is buried in Aspy Bay Cemetery.

The following are excerpts from his father's diary - Aspy Bay - 1944.

May 2 - Set nets: May 5 - two plaster boats: May 26 - John D. wounded in Italy: May 27 - Put in potatoes: June 3 - Strong NE wind with rain and snow: June 6 - Allies start invasion of France: June 7 - Charlie and Gordon reported missing in action: July 5 - Christy left for Sydney: July 8 - Thomas MacDonald killed in action: July 18 - began haying: August 8 - received word that Charlie was killed in action June 7: September 2 - Johnnie Wilkie, Joe Alex and I to Sydney Mines: September 6 - N.D. wounded in Italy: October 6 - Charlie MacAskill wounded in France, finished digging potatoes - 32 bushels, John A. MacNeil killed in action in France.

MacDonald, Peter Frederick F33198

Freddie was born on July 24, 1923, the son of James and Margaret (MacNeil) MacDonald, Ottawa Brook. Corporal MacDonald served in Canada and overseas - United Kingdom, Italy and Northwest Europe in the Royal Canadian Artillery and West Nova Scotia Regiment.

He married Mary Ratchford, New Victoria, and they resided in London, Ontario. He died on March 20, 1996, and he is buried in St. Peter's Cemetery, London, Ontario.

MacDonald, Phillip Joseph

Phillip Joseph was the son of Angus and Veronica (MacNeil) MacDonald, Ottawa Brook. He served with the Royal Canadian Artillery. He was predeceased by two wives and is married to Jeannie MacDonald. They reside in Sydney.

MacDonald, Ranald F54988

Ranald was born on January 25, 1914, the son of Angus Ranald and Sarah Liza (MacNeil) MacDonald, Washabuck. Private MacDonald served with the Cape Breton Highlanders in Canada and the United Kingdom. He married Joan MacKenzie, Washabuck. He died on August 5, 1983, and is buried in Holy Rosary Cemetery, Washabuck.

MacDonald, Robert Capstick F32648

'Bob Reddy' was born on April 29, 1921, the son of County Councillor Angus D. and Alice (Capstick) MacDonald, St. Margaret's Village. Private MacDonald served in the Royal Canadian Signal Corps in Italy, France, Germany and Holland (1942 to 1946). He married Mary Alice Capstick from Capstick. He is buried in St. Margaret's Village Cemetery.

MacDonald, Roderick Columbus

Roddie was born on May 19, 1918, the son of Angus Ranald and Sarah Liza (MacNeil) MacDonald, Washabuck. He served with the West Nova Scotia Regiment, Cape Breton Highlanders and North Nova Scotia Highlanders. Private MacDonald served in Canada, Italy, United Kingdom and Northwest Europe. He was predeceased by his first wife, Olive Hunter. His second wife was Helen Chester. In civilian life he worked as a pipe fitter. He died on May 23, 1996, in Vancouver, British Columbia.

MacDonald, Ronald

Ronnie was the son of John F. and Elizabeth MacDonald, Big Bras d'Or. He served in the Merchant Marine and he was lost en route overseas. He was unmarried.

MacDonald, Stephen F56524

Stephen was the son of Dan A. and Isabel (MacNeil) MacDonald, St. Columba. Private MacDonald served with the Calgary Highlanders in Canada, United Kingdom and Northwest Europe. He married Margaret MacDonald, Antigonish. They resided in Iona. He died on June 10, 1983, and is buried in St. Columba Cemetery.

MacDonald, Stewart Rindress F37383

Stewart was born on March 29, 1924, in Massachusetts, the son of D.J. and Catherine (Stewart) MacDonald, North River. He enlisted in Nova Scotia and served in the army with the North Nova Scotia Highlanders. He was killed in action on March 25, 1945. He is buried in Groesbeek Cemetery, Holland. Private MacDonald was survived by a young widow, Margaret Clarke MacDonald, sister of A.J. Clarke (World War II killed in action).

MacDonald, Thomas Joseph F55320

Tom was born in 1904, the son of Michael and Sarah Jane (Kanary) MacDonald, St. Margaret's Village. He served overseas with the North Nova Scotia Highlanders, Infantry Corps. Lance Corporal MacDonald was killed in action on July 8, 1944, in France. He is buried in Beny-Sur-Mer Cemetery, France.

MacDonald, William Alexander

'Willie Murdoch' was born on September 3, 1900, the son of Murdoch and Mary (Carmichael) MacDonald, Yankee Line. Private MacDonald served with the army in Canada. He married Violet Lelacheur, Cap la Ronde, Richmond County. He died in Camp Hill Hospital, Halifax.

MacDougall, Christine Katherine

Christine was born on November 28, 1924, the daughter of Daniel R. and Mary Ann (Whitty) MacDougall, Ingonish. Wren MacDougall served with the Royal Canadian Navy in Canada. She married Levi James Hardy (World War II), Ingonish. She died on November 14, 1997, and is buried in St. Peter's Parish Cemetery, Ingonish.

MacDougall, Dougal

Dougal was the son of Dan and Flora (MacCormick) MacDougall, Upper Washabuck. He served with the Cape Breton Highlanders in Canada and the United Kingdom. Later he served in the Canadian Merchant Navy. He married and resided in Montreal. He retired to Toronto and is buried there.

MacDougall, James Lawrence

James was born in 1918, the son of Daniel and Flora (MacCormick) MacDougall, Upper Washabuck. Lance Corporal MacDougall served with the North Nova Scotia Highlanders and the Canadian Provost Corps. He served in Canada and was left permanently disabled while serving with the Canadian Provost Corps. He died on July 28, 1953, and is buried in Holy Rosary Cemetery, Washabuck.

MacDougall, Joseph H. F3916

Joe was born in 1918, the son of Jim Alex and Sarah (Murphy) MacDougall, Upper Washabuck. Private MacDougall served with the Cape Breton Highlanders in Canada, United Kingdom and Italy. He was wounded in action and, as a result, used an artificial eye. Unmarried, he died in 1993 and is buried in Holy Rosary Cemetery, Washabuck.

MacDougall, Phillip Joseph

Phillip was born in 1911, the son of Daniel and Flora (MacCormick) MacDougall, Upper Washabuck. He served with the Cape Breton Highlanders and the Royal Canadian Engineers. Unmarried, he died on November 18, 1986, and is buried in Holy Rosary Cemetery, Washabuck.

MacEachern, Murdoch A.

Murdoch was a son of Murdoch and Mary (MacDonald) MacEachern, Quarry, St. Ann's. He served in the Royal Canadian Navy. His older brother. Murdoch MacEachern served in World War I.

He married Mary MacLennan, Quarry, St. Ann's. He worked with Sydney Steel Corporation. He died on October 7, 1987, and is buried in Goose Cove Cemetery, St. Ann's.

MacFarlane, Gordon John F32312

Gordon was born on June 1, 1914, the son of John and Lillian (Wareham) MacFarlane, Baddeck. He enlisted in September, 1942, with the Royal Canadian Ordinance Corps and served in Canada. Staff Sergeant MacFarlane was discharged on January 28, 1946.He married Isabel Matheson, Whycocomagh. They resided in Baddeck. He was a partner in the firm of MacFarlane Motors, Baddeck. He was also Prothonotary for Victoria County. He died on April 19, 1976, and is buried in Greenwood Cemetery, Baddeck.

(Left - Livingston MacFarlane; Right - Norman Ross)

MacFarlane, Livingstone Strachan F32185

'Lig' was born on September 10, 1911, the son of Malcolm and Jennie (Strachan) MacFarlane, Baddeck. Signalman MacFarlane served from August, 1942, in the Royal Canadian Corps of Signals until December, 1945, in Canada and the United Kingdom. He married Dolly Morrison, Goose Cove. He was an engineer with the Department of Highways, Ferry Division. He died on October 20, 1982, and is buried in Harbourview Cemetery, South Haven.

MacFarlane, Ralph Peter F97301

Ralph was born on September 20, 1913, the son of John and Lillian (Wareham) MacFarlane, Baddeck. He enlisted on February 4, 1942, and served with the Royal Canadian Electrical and Mechanical Engineers.Sergeant MacFarlane was discharged on January 29, 1946. He married Pauline Long, St. John's. He was a partner in the firm of MacFarlane Motors, Baddeck. He died in 1986 and is buried in Greenwood Cemetery, Baddeck.

MacFarlane, Russell Fraser F3562

Russell was born on July 27, 1919, the son of William A. and Margaret (MacKenzie) MacFarlane, Kempt Head. He enlisted with the Pictou Highlanders. He went overseas with the West Nova Scotia Regiment, Canadian Army. He served in Canada, the North Atlantic, United Kingdom, Central Mediterranean and Continental Europe.

He married Ruth MacKenzie, Ross Ferry. They resided in Kempt Head. He died on April 19, 1991, and is buried in MacDonald Cemetery, Boularderie.

MacFarlane, Stewart F606702

Stewart was born on April 18, 1921, the son of Neil A. (World War I) and Christy Belle (Stewart) MacFarlane, South Side Baddeck. He enlisted on June 23, 1942 with the Royal Canadian Engineers, 23 Field Company. Private MacFarlane served in Canada and was discharged in 1945. He married Amy Taylor, Baddeck. He was a carpenter by trade. He died on September 8, 1993, and is buried in Highland Cemetery, Baddeck Bay.

MacGovern, Malcolm

Malcolm was the son of William and Catherine (MacInnis) MacGovern, Iona. He served with the Royal Canadian Artillery, the 6th Canadian Anti Tank Regiment. He served in Canada, United Kingdom and Northwest Europe. He married and he and his wife resided in New Brunswick.

MacGregor, Alexander James F89890

Alexander was born in 1921, the son of Murdoch and Grace (MacInnis) MacGregor, Nyanza. He enlisted on September 3, 1941, and served as a gunner in the 4th Field Regiment, Royal Canadian Army. He served in Canada and Continental Europe until demobilization January 11, 1946.

He married Catherine Hart, Baddeck. He died from injuries sustained in a motor vehicle accident in 1951.

MacInnis, Anna

Anna was born on March 17, 1916, the daughter of Murdoch and Christine (MacLeod) MacInnis, North Shore.

She was working in Cleveland when she left her job to enlist in Toronto in December, 1942. She served overseas in London with the Canadian Army. She was discharged in April, 1946. She resides in Austin, Texas.

(centre - Anna MacInnis)

MacInnis, Cecil Stubbs F36065

Cecil was born on July 16, 1924, the son of John and Hattie (Stubbs) MacInnis, Little Narrows. He enlisted on September 11, 1943, in Halifax. Private MacInnis served overseas in France and Germany. He was discharged on May 8, 1946. He married Janie Munroe, Little Narrows. He was killed on February 5, 1953, as the result of an accident while engaged in highway construction. He is buried in Little Narrows Cemetery.

MacInnis, Clarence Wilfred   193774

'Scotty' was born on April 16, 1916, the son of Malcolm A. (World War I - K.I.A.) and Christena (MacInnis) MacInnis, Indian Brook. He enlisted on February 28, 1938, in Cleveland, Ohio, and was discharged on March 20, 1946, in New York City. He served as an able seaman with the United States Merchant Marine. He married Mary Urquhart, Skir Dhu. He died on November 15, 1977 and is buried in Riverside Cemetery, Skir Dhu.

MacInnis, Donald Fraser

Donald Fraser was born on November 30, 1918, the son of Murdoch John and Annie (MacDermid) MacInnis, Breton Cove.

He enlisted in 1940 in New Glasgow. He was a corporal with the anti-aircraft artillery. He served in Labrador, England and Holland.

He married Louella MacNaughton, New Brunswick. He worked as a carpenter in Massachusetts. He died on October 30, 1994, in Watertown, Massachusetts.

MacInnis, John Angus F31912

John was born on April 2, 1915, the son of Murdoch and Christy (MacLeod) MacInnis, Indian Brook. He grew up in Skir Dhu. He enlisted on July 16, 1942, with the Canadian Army Signal Corps. He trained in England and served in France, Belgium, Holland and Germany. During the final days of the war his unit crossed the Rhine in Germany. He recalls two terrifying incidents. A comrade thought an overhead plane was one of their own. It was a Nazi plane and the pilot dove and strafed the area. They escaped by diving into the cellar of an abandoned house. Another time an American aircraft mistakenly bombed a unit attached to the Canadians. It was John's worst war experience.

He fondly remembers the camaraderie among the men in his unit. They often shared their "goodie parcels" from home with English children.

Since he was the tallest of the North Shore John MacInnis', he acquired the name 'Long John.' He is a fisherman. He married Jessie Carmichael, Tarbot, and they reside in French River.

MacInnis, John Daniel

Danny was born on October 23, 1911, the son of Neil J. and Jessie (Montgomery) MacInnis, Jersey Cove. He served as a campaign sergeant with the 197th Regiment in the United States Army. His theatres of service were in Southeast Asia, New Guinea and Australia. Unmarried, he resides in Pasadena, California.

MacInnis, John Donald

John Donald was born on April 1, 1900, the son of Neil and Jessie (Montgomery) MacInnis, Jersey Cove. He grew up in Breton Cove. Chief Warrant Officer MacInnis served with the American Air Force - 460 Base Unit on crash boats. Eight or nine crew members manned these high powered rescue boats. After the war, he remained a sea captain in the United States. He married Louise MacLennan, Sydney Mines. They resided in California. He died in 1965 and is buried in MacDonald Memorial Cemetery, Breton Cove.

MacInnis, John Norman

John Norman was born on January 14, 1910, the son of Neil and Jessie (Montgomery) MacInnis, Jersey Cove. He was a sergeant in the Royal Canadian Air Force. He married Marion Webster, R.N., Sergeant of Nurses, New Caledonia Island. They resided in the United States. He worked as a carpenter and was involved as a clan historian. He died in California in 1984 and is buried in MacDonald Memorial Cemetery, Breton Cove.

MacInnis, Kenneth Murray

Kenneth was the son of Peter and Dora (MacInnis) MacInnis, River Bennett. Private MacInnis served overseas in the Canadian Army. Somewhere in Europe, during that time, he unexpectedly met his brother, Norman. It must have been an emotional reunion for these brothers. He married Mae Skillen, Glasgow, Scotland. They resided in Edmonton, Alberta. He died April 15, 1998.

MacInnis, Malcolm Neil 69706

Malcolm Neil was born on August 22, 1926, the son of John and Hattie (Stubbs) MacInnis, Little Narrows. He enlisted on May 5, 1945, in the infantry of the Canadian Army. Private MacInnis served in Canada and was discharged October 16, 1945, in Halifax. He married Rachel Mary Robinson, Alba. They reside in Little Narrows where he was employed with Little Narrows Gypsum Company.

MacInnis, Norman Malcolm F75759

Norman Peter was on October 6, 1909, the son of Peter and Margaret Ann (MacDonald) MacInnis, River Bennett. He enlisted on September 13, 1942. He served overseas with the 3rd Anti-tank Unit Royal Canadian Artillery. He was discharged on December 7, 1945. He was a lobster fisherman and fur trapper and worked aboard the Englishtown Ferry for sixteen years. He married Annie (Mickey) Carmichael, Tarbot. He died on September 9, 1998, and is buried in Pine Hill Cemetery, River Bennett.

MacIntosh, Donald Robert F2980

Donald was born on September 19, 1918, the son of John H. and Ellen (MacDonald) MacIntosh, Bay St. Lawrence. Private MacIntosh served with the 4th Anti Tank Artillery in Canada, England, Continental Europe and Italy (1941 to 1946). He married Eleanor Farquhar, Sydney. They were the proprietors of Hotel Baddeck, Baddeck. He died on December 27, 1988, and is buried in St. James Cemetery, Big Bras d'Or.

MacIntosh, James Bryon F57401

James was born on January 4, 1924, the son of Edward Roderick and Sarah (MacDonald) MacIntosh. When his mother died, he was raised at the home of Dannie (Painter) MacLean, Little Narrows. He enlisted with the Royal Canadian Army Signal Corps on August 20, 1943, in Halifax # 6 District Depot. Private MacIntosh served in Canada and the United Kingdom. He was discharged on November 4, 1946. He married Margaret Ruby Meddlemiss, England and later married Ann MacIntosh, Orangedale. They reside in River Denys. He was an electrician by trade.

MacIntosh, Kendrick F86173

Kendrick was born on October 2, 1921, the son of Thomas and Sarah (Daisley) MacIntosh, South Harbour. Sergeant MacIntosh served with the North Nova Scotia Highlanders in the United Kingdom (1941 to 1945).

He married Beatrice Davidson, England. He and his war bride returned to Canada. He worked on the St. Lawrence Seaway. They reside at South Harbour.

MacIntyre, Frederick Burnaby F87851

Fred was born in 1917, the son of Sea Captain Byron (Bino) and Hazel (Ross) MacIntyre, Ingonish Ferry. Private MacIntyre served overseas with the 3rd Field Regiment (1940 - 1945). He was a carpenter and died in 1985 and is buried in St. Peter's Parish Cemetery.

MacIntyre, Georgina

Georgina was the daughter of Sea Captain Byron (Bino) and Hazel (Ross) MacIntyre, Ingonish. She served as a wireless operator. She married and resided in Western Canada.

MacIsaac, Donald

Donald was the son of Roderick and Mary (MacDonald) MacIsaac, Washabuck. He served with the Royal Canadian Engineers in Canada, United Kingdom and France. He was serving at Dieppe on August 19, 1942. He married and resided in Sydney.

MacIver, Arthur

Arthur was born in 1920, the son of Jack and Mary Margaret (MacLeod) MacIver, Port Bevis. Private MacIver served with the Service Corps in Canada and North West Europe. He married and lived in Cape Breton and Ontario. He was killed in 1964 in a car/pedestrian accident in London, Ontario. He is buried in Harbourview Cemetery, South Haven.

MacIver, Daniel

Danny was born the son of James and Margaret (Buchanan) MacIver, Baddeck. He served in the Canadian Army with the Cape Breton Highlanders. He married Helen Bond, Sydney. They resided in Sydney where he was a postmaster. He died in 1976 and is buried in Sydney.

MacIver, Daniel

Buster was the son of John Charlie and Christy (Ferguson) MacIver, Upper Washabuck. He served during the war. He married Lillian MacLean, Washabuck. They resided in Sydney. Their son, Daniel MacIver, is a playwright and producer in Toronto. He has written a play based on his father's life entitled 'Present Times.' Buster MacIver is buried in Holy Rosary Cemetery, Washabuck.

MacIver, Donald Fraser F36067

Donald Fraser was born in 1924, the son of Dan and Hannah (MacDonald) MacIver, South Cove. He enlisted in the Canadian Army. Private MacIver served in Canada. He married Roseanna MacKay, Whycocomagh Portage. They resided in South Cove. He died in 1976 and is buried in the Little Narrows Cemetery. His uncle, Dr. John Angus MacIver, M.D., practiced medicine in Baddeck.

MacIver, Edward Watson

Eddie was the adopted son of Murdoch and Mary (Smith) MacIver, Boularderie Centre. He served overseas. He returned with his war bride and they resided for a while in Boularderie.

MacIver, Harold R264977

Harold was born in 1926, the son of Mrs. Lexina Morrison, Red Head. Leading Aircraftman MacIver enlisted on August 21, 1943, and served overseas with the Royal Canadian Air Force. He was discharged on demobilization on November 13, 1945. He married Mary Harrison, Trenton, Ontario and they resided in British Columbia. He died in 1981 and is buried in Vancouver.

MacIver, Henry Norman F54677

Henry was born in 1915, the son of James and Margaret (Buchanan) MacIver, Baddeck. He enlisted on September 4, 1939, with the Cape Breton Highlanders. Private MacIver served in Canada. He married Eileen Earle, North Sydney. They resided in North Sydney where he was employed with Thompson and Sutherland Ltd. He died on January 8, 1996, and is buried in North Sydney. His father, 'Little Jimmie MacIver,' was the faithful legendary teamster for Dr. C.L. MacMillan, M.D., Baddeck.

MacIver, Malcolm John F54676

Malcolm was born on June 4, 1916, the son of Neil and Eunice MacIver, Hunters' Mountain. He enlisted on September 4, 1936 and served until demobilization on October 13, 1945, with the Cape Breton Highlanders. Corporal MacIver served in England, Italy, Belgium and Holland.

"Perhaps the closest call I had was on Graveyard Hill when we were under continuous fire about a week. One day there was a lull in the shelling so I had just decided to stand up in my slit trench and clean my rifle when a mortar shell dropped right in front of my trench knocking me down in my trench and blowing my rifle out of my hands about 20 feet from the trench. When I picked up the rifle later, the wood on it was all riddled from shrapnel and the bolt I couldn't find until the next day. I cannot till this day figure out how I wasn't killed or badly wounded, but I guess the Good Lord didn't want me." Source - *The Breed of Manly Men.*

He married Evelyn MacNaughton, St. Patrick's Channel. They retired to Baddeck. He died on November 29, 1996, and is buried in Middle River Cemetery.

MacIver, Margaret Christine W303375

Peggy was born on October 14, 1918, the daughter of Neil and Eunice (MacDermid) MacIver, Hunter's Mountain. Leading Air Woman Margaret MacIver served in the Royal Canadian Air Force - Women's Division. She enlisted in May, 1942, and took her basic training at Rockcliff, Ontario. She was posted to Moncton and Wayburn, Saskatchewan. Then she was posted overseas to England. She was discharged on demobilization in October, 1945.

She married John K. MacKay (World War II), Big Baddeck. They resided in the United States and retired to Tarbot and she presently resides there.

MacIver, Norman Dan F30054

Norman Dan was born in 1912, the son of John E. and Mary (Gillis) MacIver, South Cove. Corporal MacIver served in the Royal Canadian Engineers in Canada, United Kingdom and North Western Europe. He married Jessie (Danny Painter) MacLean, Little Narrows. They resided in Little Narrows. He died on September 2, 1991, and is buried in the Little Narrows Cemetery.

MacIver, William Malcolm F54848

Billy was born in 1911, the son of James and Margaret (Buchanan) MacIver, Baddeck. He enlisted on September 4, 1939, with the Cape Breton Highlanders. Private MacIver served in Canada and England.

His first wife was Jean Scott, a sister to Charlie Scott (World War II). His second wife was Jessie MacDonald, Baddeck. He was killed in a motor vehicle accident in 1958 and is buried in Greenwood Cemetery, Baddeck.

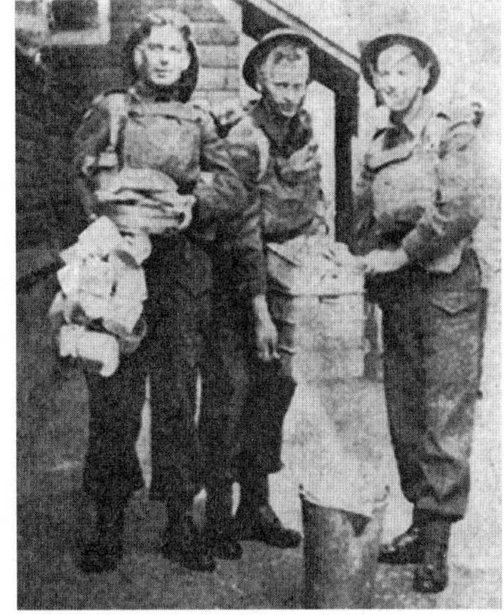

Taking Dinner to the Guardhouse. Right - William MacIver, Baddeck

MacKay, Angus Dan R124878

'A.D.' was born on May 30, 1919, the son of John Archie and Annie (MacLean) MacKay. He was raised by Angus and Nina (Morrison) MacLeod, Nyanza. Leading Aircraftman MacKay enlisted on August 21, 1941 and served in the Royal Canadian Air Force until demobilization on January 21, 1946. He married Vivian Hart, Baddeck. They resided in Little Narrows and later in Blues Mills. He died on May 21, 1991, and is buried in Little Narrows Cemetery.

MacKay, Catherine May

Kaye was born on June 28, 1919, the daughter of John Dan and Jennie (Latham) MacKay, Upper Baddeck River. Corporal MacKay served in the Royal Canadian Air Force. She married J. Norman Austin, Skye Glen. They resided in the United States where her husband was a manager of several businesses. They retired to Salmon River, Nova Scotia. She died on January 7, 1990, and is buried in Valley, Colchester County.

MacKay, Donald Frank F32596

Frank was born on April 25, 1922, the son of John and Jessie (MacLennan) MacKay, Boularderie. He enlisted on November 5, 1942 with # 6 District Depot Canadian Army. Trooper MacKay served in the United Kingdom and Continental Europe. He returned to civilian life on January 31, 1946. He had served with the West Nova Scotia Highlanders prior to active service. He joined the militia on March 5, 1957, and Master Warrant Officer MacKay served until April 25, 1973.

Frank held the office of Grand Master of the Masonic Lodge in Nova Scotia for the 1993-1994 term. He married Margie Bona, Richmond County. They reside in Glace Bay.

MacKay, Duncan Roderick

Duncan was born on February 27, 1923, the son of John Dan and Jennie (Latham) MacKay, Upper Baddeck River. Duncan served overseas including service in Continental Europe.

He married Frances Quinn, Millville. They resided in Massachusetts where he was employed with a manufacturing company. They retired to Millville, Cape Breton. Presently, they are residing in North Sydney.

MacKay, John Kenneth

John was born on July 26, 1920, the son of John Dan and Jennie (Latham) MacKay, Upper Baddeck River. He enlisted on February 8, 1942 and served as a gunner with the 16 Coast Regiment, Royal Canadian Army. His wife, also a World War II veteran, was Margaret MacIver, Hunter's Mountain. They resided in Massachusetts during their working lives. Upon retirement, they returned home to live in Tarbot. He died on May 24, 1992 and is buried in St. Andrews Cemetery, Baddeck Forks.

MacKenzie, Alden Jack

Alden Jack was born in 1917, the son of Jack and Jessie (MacLeod) MacKenzie, Rear Little River. He enlisted in the Navy in 1940. He served on the Atlantic Coast and in Greenland. He married and moved to Ontario. He died circa 1980.

(Right - Alden MacKenzie (in suit))

MacKenzie, Archibald Joseph F77518

Archie was the son of Dan Joseph and Cassie (Walker) MacKenzie, Ottawa Brook. Sergeant MacKenzie served with the Royal Canadian Artillery in Canada, England and Europe. He married Catherine Ann MacNeil, Jamesville. He was a noted fiddler. He is buried in Sydney.

MacKenzie, Catherine

Catherine was the daughter of Dan Joseph and Cassie (Walker) MacKenzie, Ottawa Brook. She served with the Royal Canadian Air Force. She married John Angus MacLean, Ottawa Brook. They reside in Sydney.

MacKenzie, Charles John Duncan F37354

'Buddy' was born on January 4, 1927, the son of Jack and Georgie (MacRae) MacKenzie, Yankee Line. He served in the Canadian Army in Canada. He married Charal Rowe, Sydney. For sixteen years he operated C.J.D. Fuels Ltd. in Baddeck. He died on June 26, 1989, and is buried in Middle River Cemetery.

MacKenzie, Fraser Phillip F3900

Fraser was the son of George and Agnes (Carmichael) MacKenzie, New Harris. Fraser enlisted on September 17, 1942, in the 104th Coast Battery, Royal Canadian Army and served with the Cape Breton Highlanders. He served in Canada, the United Kingdom and Continental Europe. He was shot during in the battle of Dieppe, France. He lost his leg and spent nine months in an English hospital. He married Florence Morrison, Sydney. He worked as a hotel clerk in Sydney.

MacKenzie, Fraser Drummond 33433

(Right - Fraser D. MacKenzie)

Fraser was born on June 30, 1918, the son of Fraser and Margaret (Matheson) MacKenzie, Ross Ferry.

He enlisted on May 14, 1943, with the West Nova Scotia Regiment. Private MacKenzie served in Canada, Continental Europe, United Kingdom and the Central Mediterranean area. He received a shrapnel wound to his hip. He was discharged on November 10, 1945.

He married Murdella MacFarlane, Kempt Head. They resided for some years in the United States. They returned to Boularderie and North Sydney.

MacKenzie, Gordon Christie F524612

Gordon was born on July 15, 1919, the son of Adam and Agnes (MacLeod) MacKenzie, Boularderie Centre. He enlisted on November 22, 1940, with the 2nd Battalion Pictou Highlanders. He served in Canada. He married Katherine MacDonald, Black Rock. They reside in Boularderie Centre on the family farm.

MacKenzie, Hector Matheson

Hector was born on April 8, 1912, the son of Fraser and Margaret (Matheson) MacKenzie, Ross Ferry. He enlisted on August 13, 1942, and served overseas with the Canadian Electrical Mechanical Engineers. Craftsman MacKenzie served with # 2 Canadian Advanced Space Workshop. He married Arabel MacFarlane, Kempt Head. They resided in Ross Ferry. Hector worked with the Department of Transportation. He and his wife are retired and living in Boularderie.

MacKenzie, James Donald F97268

'J.D.' was the son of Dan Joseph and Cassie (Walker) MacKenzie, Ottawa Brook. Gunner MacKenzie served in the Royal Canadian Artillery in Canada, England, France and Germany (1942 to 1945). He resided in Detroit, U.S.A. Unmarried, he died in May, 1991, and is buried in Sacred Heart Cemetery, McKinnons Harbour.

MacKenzie, John Dan F10813

John Dan was the son of George and Mary (Carmichael) MacKenzie, Cain's Mountain. He enlisted in 1942 in Sydney and served in the Army Service Corps. He served overseas until his discharge in 1946. He married Theresa MacDonald of Ottawa Brook where they resided. He died on February 15, 1984, and is buried in McKinnons Harbour Cemetery.

MacKenzie, John Hector F 33070

Johnny was born on July 13, 1904, the son of John A. and Mary (MacKenzie) MacKenzie, Kempt Head. He enlisted on February 12, 1943, in Sydney. Corporal MacKenzie served with the Royal Canadian Engineers. He was discharged on February 28, 1946. He married Phyllis Grant, Point Edward. He died on June 25, 1985, and is buried in Forest Haven Memorial Gardens, Grand Lake Road.

MacKenzie, Murray Murdoch A 86111

Murray was born on April 16, 1914, the son of Adam Allan and Agnes (MacLeod) MacKenzie, Boularderie Centre. He enlisted in July, 1942, and served with the Canadian Ordinance Mechanical Engineers Reserve Unit. He served in Canada and England. He received a shrapnel wound to his leg. He married Margaret Riggs, Glace Bay. Murray worked for the Ford Motor Company, Windsor, Ontario. They resided in Windsor. He died on December 31, 1995, and is buried in Windsor, Ontario.

MacKenzie, Nelson

Nelson was the son of George and Agnes (Carmichael) MacKenzie, New Harris. He enlisted with 104th Coast Battery, Royal Canadian Army, Cape Breton Highlanders. He served in Canada, United Kingdom and Continental Europe. He suffered wounds to his hand and shoulder. He married Fairlie Carmichael. He lived in Ontario.

MacKenzie, Roy Alexander F57540

Roy was born on February 16, 1923, the son of John Phillip (World War I) and Catherine (MacQueen) MacKenzie, Plaister Mines. He enlisted on September 9, 1943, in Halifax in the Canadian Army, No. 6 District Depot. He served as a gunner in France, Belgium and Holland. He was discharged on demobilization on January 12, 1946. In civilian life, he worked with the Customs Department in Yarmouth. He resides in Yarmouth.

MacKenzie, Sadie

Sadie was born on January 15, 1920, the daughter of Kenneth Angus and Margaret (Gunn) MacKenzie, New Harris. Sadie enlisted in the Royal Canadian Air Force and served in Canada as an office worker. She married Alfred Hoover. She presently lives in Ottawa.

(left - Sadie MacKenzie, right - Dolly Carmichael)

MacKenzie, Dr. Walter Campbell, O.C., BSc., M.D., C.M., M.S., F.A.C.S.,F.R.C.S.(C), Hon F.R.C.S., Hon F.R.C.S. (Edin), Hon F.R.C.S. (Ire), Hon F.R.C.S. (Glas), L.L.D. (McGill), L.L.D. (Dalhousie), L.L.D. (Manitoba)

Walter was born in 1909, the son of J.K. and Annie (MacAulay) MacKenzie, Baddeck.

Dr. MacKenzie was a 1933 graduate of Dalhousie Medical School. He joined the Royal Canadian Navy in 1940 as Surgeon-Lieutenant. He was posted in Halifax, Sydney and St. John's while serving as Surgeon-in-Chief to Royal Canadian Navy hospitals.

He was Dean of Medicine at the University of Alberta from 1959 to 1974. In 1971 he was awarded the **ORDER OF CANADA**. He was awarded the **F.N.G. STARR** by the Canadian Medical Association. This is often referred to as the Victoria Cross of Canadian medicine. The Walter C. MacKenzie Health Sciences Centre at Edmonton, Alberta is named to commemorate " ... his inspirational leadership in medical education and surgery, not only at the university where he was based but throughout the world." He truly earned the epithet "Citizen of World Surgery."

He married Dorothy Rossier, Newport, Nova Scotia. He died on December 19, 1978, in Edmonton, Alberta.

MacKenzie, Wilfred

Wilfred was the son of Kenneth Angus and Margaret (Gunn) MacKenzie, New Harris. He served with the Royal Canadian Air Force in Canada. He was an engineer with the Canadian National Railroad. He was unmarried. He died in Sydney in 1951 and is buried in New Harris Cemetery, New Harris.

MacKillop, Allan MacLeod F65137

Allan was born on September 24, 1916, the son of Malcolm and Minnie (MacAulay) MacKillop, Baddeck Bay. He enlisted on February 20, 1942, in Halifax with the Royal Canadian Signal Corps. Signalman MacKillop served in England, Sicily, Italy, France and Holland. He was discharged on demobilization on February 7, 1946.

A letter written to his mother dated May 31, 1942, reads:

"Dear Mom, Sunday again. I guess I'll have to write again. We were Duty Platoon so I have been all day in the kitchen. I've washed more damn pots and pans than enough. I thought they would never end. They are not the small ones like you use but from five gallon size to fifteen gallon and believe me it takes plenty of scrubbing to get them clean. However, I've got my hands clean anyway. I see Big Kennie MacDonald every day. He is doing O.K. There is sure one awful whack of Cape Bretoners here. The Gaelic sure flies around when they start talking what with McNeils and McKenzies from Iona and McDonalds and McLeods from North River and McIsaacs from Inverness it sure sounds

like Cape Breton. If I keep on the first thing I know I'll be able to speak it. Now I guess I've said enough for this time so I'll have to say so long. As ever, Allan."

Allan married Patricia Watts, Alberta. He was a prospector in the Canadian North and Queen Charlotte Islands. He and his wife reside in Vancouver, British Columbia.

MacKillop, Angus Duncan

'Gussie' was born on March 17, 1915, the son of Malcolm and Minnie (MacAulay) MacKillop, Baddeck Bay. He served during the war in the Royal Canadian Navy. He married Giselle Monpetit, Hull, Quebec. He served as superintendent at York Structural Steel for over twenty-five years. He died on March 31, 1989, in Fredericton. He is buried in Harbourview Cemetery, South Haven.

MacKillop, Christena Helen R.N.

Tena was born on March 12, 1922, the daughter of Malcolm and Minnie (MacAulay) MacKillop, Baddeck Bay. She was a registered nurse and a graduate of the Ottawa Civic Hospital School of Nursing. Nursing Sister MacKillop served in Canada.

She married Flight Lieutenant Leonard Jones (World War II), London, Ontario. They operated a store and tourist business in St. Ann's. Later her husband served as Executive Director of the Gaelic College, St. Ann's. She died on April 14, 1978, and is buried in Harbourview Cemetery, South Haven.

MacKinnon, Alexander

Alex was the son of Archie and Marcella (MacLellan) MacKinnon, Ingonish. He served overseas during the war. He was predeceased by his first wife. He later married a school teacher, Lucy Millet, Cheticamp. He worked at the Cape Breton Highlands National Park in Cheticamp. He is buried in Cheticamp.

MacKinnon, Angus Harold

'Bus' was born on June 27, 1926, the son of Big Donald (World War I) and Mary (MacDonald) MacKinnon, Ingonish Ferry. He served as a gunner in the Royal Air Force and made many sorties over Germany.

He married Kaye MacLeod, New Haven. He worked and resided in Toronto. He was killed on November 22, 1962, in a motor vehicle accident in Toronto and is buried in the United Church Cemetery, Ingonish Ferry.

MacKinnon, Columbus

Columbus was the son of Dan and Catherine (MacKenzie) MacKinnon, Washabuck/Cain's Mountain. He served with the Cape Breton Highlanders in Canada and the United Kingdom.

This family (father and sons) were accomplished musicians. He married and resided in the Yukon. He died tragically as a result of a drowning accident. Six members of the MacKinnon family served during the World Wars.

MacKinnon, Daniel

Dan was the son of Archie and Marcella (MacLellan) MacKinnon, Ingonish. He served in Canada during the war. He married and worked in the coal mines in New Waterford.

MacKinnon, Daniel Joseph

Dan Joe was the son of Dan and Catherine (MacKenzie) MacKinnon, Washabuck and Cain's Mountain. He served with the Cape Breton Highlanders and the West Nova Scotia Regiment in Canada, United Kingdom, Italy and Northwest Europe.

His wife hailed from New Zealand. They resided in New Zealand for a while and then moved to British Columbia and then to the Yukon. Tragically, he was killed in an industrial accident while working in the Yukon.

MacKinnon, Donald C.

Donald was the son of Rory S. and Margaret Monica (MacNeil) MacKinnon, McKinnons Harbour.

Lieutenant MacKinnon served with the North Nova Scotia Highlanders. He was attached to the Third Canadian Division in its invasion of France on D-Day. He was killed in action on July 8, 1944, and he is buried in Beny-Sur-Mer Canadian War Cemetery, France.

MacKinnon, Hector F605627

Hector was born on September 19, 1919, the son of Archie and Martha (MacDonald) MacKinnon, White Point. Private MacKinnon served in the Canadian Army. He married Effie Mae Rambeau, White Point. He died on May 27, 1953, and is buried in St. Joseph's Cemetery, Dingwall.

MacKinnon, John Neil

Johnnie was the son of Dan and Catherine (MacKenzie) MacKinnon, Washabuck/Cain's Mountain. He served during the war. He was predeceased by two wives and resides in Hamilton, Ontario.

MacKinnon, Malcolm J.

'Malcolm J.' was the son of John N. and Mary Catherine (MacNeil) MacKinnon, MacKinnon Settlement. He served in Canada, the United Kingdom and Italy. He was seriously wounded in Italy. He married and resided in Ottawa. He died in 1993 and is buried in Ottawa.

MacKinnon, Phillip F77677

Phillip was the son of Dan and Catherine (MacKenzie) MacKinnon, Washabuck/Cain's Mountain. He served with the Royal Canadian Engineers in Canada, United Kingdom and Northwest Europe. He was wounded in action. He married Kay MacDonald, Glace Bay, and he and his wife resided in Ontario.

MacKinnon, Robert

Bob was the son of Malcolm and Annabel (MacLeod) MacKinnon, Ingonish Ferry. He served in the Royal Canadian Air Force. He married and resides in Hagarville, Ontario.

MacKinnon, Roderick

Roddie was the son of Norman MacKinnon. He was raised by Archibald and Catherine (MacKinnon) Campbell, Rear Baddeck Forks Road. Roddie served overseas. He married Edith Fadgen, Amherst, Nova Scotia. They resided in Ontario. He died on July 8, 1995.

MacKinnon, Roderick James

Roddie was born December 3, 1922, son of Angus (World War I) and Catherine Jane (Gillis) MacKinnon, Washabuck. He served in the Royal Canadian Artillery in Canada, United Kingdom and Europe. He married Ellen Louise O'Mara, Ontario. He died on July 22, 1991, and is buried in St. Catharines, Ontario.

MacKinnon, Roderick John F19294

Roderick was the son of John N. and Mary Catherine (MacNeil) MacKinnon, MacKinnon Settlement. Private MacKinnon served in the Royal Canadian Artillery and Royal Canadian Engineers in Canada (1943 to 1946). He was struck by a train and died on August 10, 1968. He is buried in St. Columba Cemetery.

MacLean, A. Hector 4459

Hector was born in 1912, the son of Hector and Catherine (MacDonald) Mac Lean, Gillis Point. Seaman MacLean served as a radio operator in the Merchant Marine. Radio Officer MacLean tried to no avail to send an S.O.S. from the *Vineland* (a paper carrier which belonged to the Mersey Paper Company) at 2:30 p.m. on April 20, 1942, when she was torpedoed by a German U-boat. They were situated forty miles north of Mayaguana Island in the South Atlantic sea. When the German U-boat surfaced, all the crew were in lifeboats. The German commander gave the crew packets of cigarettes and ensured that the lifeboat had provisions and left them to make their own way to land.

Hector MacLean was a sales employee of the Mersey Paper Company, Liverpool. He wrote an interesting article entitled "The Last Day of the *Vineyard*" for the Mersey Quarterly - Liverpool, Nova Scotia (1960s). He married Johanna MacDougall. He died on March 26, 1984 and is buried in St. Columba Cemetery.

MacLean, Alexander Columba F24404

(Left - Michael J MacLean; Right Alexander C MacLean, twin brothers)

Alexander was a twin son of John J. and Cassie (MacDonald) Mac Lean, Ottawa Brook. Sergeant MacLean served with the 7th Anti Tank Regiment, Royal Canadian Artillery, 3rd Division in Canada, the United Kingdom and Northwest Europe (1940 to 1946).

He married a school teacher, Sarah E. (Ada) MacKenzie, Ottawa Brook. He was employed with Little Narrows Gypsum until his retirement. He served on the executive of the Nova Scotia Highland Village Society. He died on May 4, 1998, and is buried in Sacred Heart Cemetery, McKinnons Harbour.

MacLean, Alexander Donald

'Alex Aulay' was born on September 7, 1902, the twin son of Aulay and Hannah (MacLeod) MacLean, Middle River.

Private MacLean enlisted in 1943 and served in the service corps of the United States Army.

He was a twin brother to Johnny Aulay MacLean, Middle River. He resided in Waltham, Massachusetts and he retired to Middle River and presently resides in Baddeck.

MacLean, Angus George F32737

'A.G.' was born in 1923, the son of Daniel A. and Annie (Stockley) MacLean, North Ingonish. Private MacLean served with the North Shore (New Brunswick) Regiment, Royal Canadian Infantry Corps. He was killed in action by a land mine on July 6, 1944. He is buried in Beny-Sur-Mer Cemetery, Calvados, France.

MacLean, Archibald Daniel R88377

Archie was the son of Roderick Campbell and Annie (MacRae) MacLean, Cape Dauphin. He served in the Royal Canadian Air Force. He married Isobel MacDonald, North Sydney. He worked for St. Francis Xavier University, Antigonish. He resides in Antigonish.

MacLean, Benedict

Bennie was born in 1919, the son of Neil P.S. and Christina (MacLean) MacLean, Washabuck. He served with the Cape Breton Highlanders and later he served with the Royal Canadian Air Force. He served in Canada and the United Kingdom. He married Ann MacKenzie, Washabuck Bridge. He was a school teacher in Baddeck and Little Bras d'Or. He died on May 16, 1980, and is buried in Holy Rosary Cemetery, Washabuck.

MacLean, Dan Edward

Dan Edward was born in 1918, the son of Ferry Captain Allan and Sadie (Campbell) MacLean, Englishtown. He enlisted on December 7, 1942, in Halifax. Leading Air Craftsman MacLean served with the Royal Canadian Air Force in the Canadian North and Germany. Unmarried, he died in 1978 in Toronto. He is buried in Bayview Cemetery, Englishtown.

MacLean, Daniel Angus

Dan Angus was the son of John Archie and Sarah (Gillis) MacLean, Ottawa Brook. He served during the war. He and his wife Beatrice resided in Montreal. He is buried in Sacred Heart Cemetery, McKinnons Harbour.

MacLean, Donald

Donald was the son of Roderick and Annie (MacRae) MacLean, Cape Dauphin. He served in the Royal Canadian Air Force. He married Ruth Putnam, United States. He worked as a building contractor in Massachusetts. He is deceased.

MacLean, Donald John F 2900

'D.J.' was born on December 7, 1921, the son of Phillip and Hughena (MacKay) MacLean, Upper Baddeck River. He enlisted at the Canadian Army Base New Glasgow. He first joined the Ordinance Corps and then transferred to the Cape Breton Highlanders. He served in Canada, Continental Europe, United Kingdom and in the central Mediterranean. He was discharged in Halifax, # 6 Depot, on January 22, 1946.

He married Elizabeth Moser, New Glasgow. He was employed in the construction business. They live in Caledonia, Guysborough County, Nova Scotia.

(Left - Donald MacLean)

MacLean, Donald Torquil

Donald was the son of Kenneth and Mary Belle (Sutherland) MacLean, Englishtown. He served with the United States Navy. He is married and resides in Toledo, Ohio.

MacLean, Ernest Gordon F60781

Ernie was the son of Daniel and Ann (Stockley) MacLean, Ingonish. He served in the Merchant Marine from September 1939, to February, 1942. He enlisted on September 11, 1942, in the Canadian Army. Rifleman MacLean served in Canada. He was discharged on April 15, 1944. He married Violet Hardy, Ingonish. They resided in Detroit where he was a barber. Eventually they returned to Ingonish. He died on September 4, 1978, and is buried in St. John's Cemetery, Ingonish.

MacLean, George Robert L108056

George was born on January 28, 1925, the son of Kenneth and Sadie (MacLeod) MacLean, Skir Dhu.

He enlisted in Regina on January 1, 1944, and served with the Lake Superior Regiment, 4th Canadian Armoured Brigade. He served in Canada, the United Kingdom and Continental Europe. After the cessation of hostilities in Europe he volunteered for the Pacific Theatre and was discharged on April 5, 1946. He was later recalled to serve as a Lieutenant with the Cape Breton Highlanders (Reserve Force) and while stationed at Camp Borden, Ontario, trained recruits to serve in the Korean War.

He married Jean Dechman, R.N., Bridgetown. He and his wife are retired and residing in Englishtown.

MacLean, James A.

Jimmy was born in 1902, the son of Neil P.S. and Elizabeth (MacNeil) MacLean, Washabuck. He served as Company Quartermaster with the Cape Breton Highlanders. C.Q.M. Sgt. MacLean served in Canada and the United Kingdom.

He married Irene Deon, Pomquet. He died on September 1, 1981, and is buried in Holy Rosary Cemetery, Washabuck.

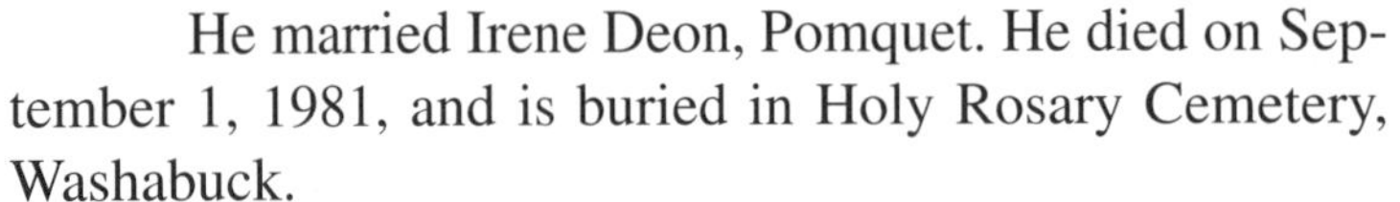

MacLean, John A.

'John A.' was born on November 16, 1895, the son of Dan Rory and Flora (MacLean) MacLean, Hunter's Mountain. Private MacLean served during the war. He resided and died in 1975 in Vancouver, British Columbia. His older brother, Sgt. Roderick MacLean, served during World War I.

MacLean, John Campbell D122628

'Buddy' was born in 1921, the son of Ferry Captain Allan and Sadie (Campbell) MacLean, Englishtown.

He enlisted in New Brunswick with the Royal Canadian Ordinance Corps 44 LAD # 3 Infantry. During his training in England, while driving a R.C.O.C. motor vehicle, Private MacLean was accidentally killed on May 8, 1944. He is buried in Brookwood Military Cemetery, Surrey, England.

MacLean, John Charles 721188

'Johnny Washabuck' was born in 1925, the son of Red Rory and Ellen Ann (MacLean) MacLean, Lower Washabuck. Private MacLean served in the Canadian Army from 1945 to 1946. He married Jean Currie, MacAdam's Lake. He was a noted fiddler and step dancer. They resided in Ontario and retired to Northside East Bay. He died in 1984 and is buried in Holy Rosary Cemetery, Washabuck.

MacLean, John Daniel F32716

Johnnie was born on February 28, 1918, the son of William and Dolena (MacKay) MacLean, Boularderie Centre. He enlisted on December 4, 1942, in Sydney. He served with the Canadian Army. Private MacLean was discharged on August 18, 1943 in Halifax. He resided in Boularderie. He was a mechanic and truck driver. Unmarried, he died on November 15, 1992, and is buried in Man O' War Cemetery.

MacLean, John Joseph F32760

Joe was born in 1916, the son of Paul and Mary (MacNeil) MacLean, Shore Road, Baddeck. He enlisted in 1942 and served with the Royal Canadian Electrical and Mechanical Engineers. He was discharged in 1946. 'Big Joe' MacLean was a mechanic by trade. He died in 1957 and is buried in St. Michael's Cemetery, Baddeck.

MacLean, Joseph Ignatius

'Joe Lighthouse' was the son of Hector and Catherine (MacDonald) MacLean, Gillis Point. Major MacLean served with the Cape Breton Highlanders in England and Canada (1939 to 1946).

He married Isabel MacLean, Grand Narrows. He was a teacher and school principal prior to his retirement. He died at seventy-three years of age and is buried in St. Barra's Parish Cemetery, Christmas Island.

MacLean, Kenneth Edward

Kenneth was a son of Kenneth and Mary Belle (Sutherland) MacLean, Englishtown. He enlisted on April 7, 1943, with the United States Merchant Marine. He served in the Atlantic, Middle East and Pacific war zones. He was discharged on November 26, 1946. He resides in Ashland, Ohio, with his wife, Eileen, and son, Eddie.

MacLean, Michael Daniel A1368

'Michael Dan Red Rory' was born on August 18, 1910, the son of Red Rory and Ellen Ann (MacLean) MacLean, Lower Washabuck. He served in the Royal Canadian Naval Reserve in Newfoundland and Canada. He served as a commissionaire at the Alexander Graham Bell Museum in Baddeck until his retirement. He married Mary Ann MacNeil, Gillis Point. He died on August 8, 1992, and is buried in St. Michael's Cemetery, Baddeck.

MacLean, Michael John

Michael John was the twin son of John J. and Cassie (MacDonald) MacLean, Ottawa Brook. He served with the 5th Light ACK-ACK Regiment, Royal Canadian Artillery, 5th Division in Canada, United Kingdom, Italy and Northwest Europe.

He married Isabel Bonaparte, McKinnons Harbour. His twin brother, Alexander, also served during World War II. He worked at the Sydney Steel Plant. He is buried in Resurrection Cemetery, Sydney.

(Left - Michael J MacLean; Right Alexander C MacLean, twin brothers)

MacLean, Murdock William F97054

Murdock was born on November 24, 1906, the son of Donald and Ann (Ingraham) MacLean, Neil's Harbour. He enlisted on November 17, 1941, in the Canadian Army and served overseas. He married Flora Strickland, Neil's Harbour. He worked as a fisherman and coal miner in Glace Bay. He died on September 3, 1969, and is buried in St. Mary's Cemetery, Glace Bay.

Murdock and Ann MacLean

MacLean, Peter Neil

Neil was born on September 11, 1906, the son of Captain James and Alice (Capstick) MacLean, St. Margaret's Village. He enlisted in the United States Navy in May, 1942, and served in the Naval Air Section of the fleet. He was discharged in July, 1946. He died while residing in the United States.

MacLean, Phillip F59272

Phillip was born on May 24, 1924, the son of Phillip and Hughena (MacKay) MacLean, Upper Baddeck River. He enlisted in February, 1944, at Halifax and served in Canada. He was discharged in 1946.

For many years he was employed in the trucking business in New Glasgow. He married Barbara Fownes MacKay, Big Baddeck, and they are presently living in South Side Baddeck.

MacLean, Roland Stewart

Roland was born on October 27, 1923, the son of Peter and Ella (MacDonald) MacLean, Ingonish. He served with the Royal Canadian Air Force in Armprior, Ontario (1944 to 1945). He married Ann MacRae, Sugar Loaf. They resided in Waverley, Nova Scotia. He died on February 20, 1996, and is buried in St. John's Cemetery, Ingonish.

MacLean, Russell Grant

Russell was born on September 29, 1922, the son of John A. and Carrie (Russell) MacLean, Estmere. He served in Canada in the army. He died on December 10, 1995, in North York, Ontario. He is buried there.

MacLean, Seward Edward F33586

Seward was born on October 24, 1908, the son of Mrs. Jessie Ann (Nicholson) MacDonald, Middle River.

He enlisted on August 31, 1943, in Sydney with the Cape Breton Highlanders. He served with the North Shore New Brunswick Highlanders in the United Kingdom and Continental Europe until demobilization April 29, 1946. He married Isobel Katherine Morrison, Point Clear. They resided in Boularderie. He worked for many years on the Ross Ferry. He died on February 21, 1986, and is buried in MacDonald Memorial Cemetery, Boularderie.

MacLean, William

Billy was born on May 2, 1922, the son of Roderick and Annie (MacRae) MacLean, Cape Dauphin. He served in the Merchant Marine and later in the Royal Canadian Air Force. Billy married Pat Hillier, Glace Bay. He was a tobacco company salesman. They lived in Sydney. He is deceased.

MacLellan, Charles

Charlie was the son of Angus and Cassie (MacLean) MacLellan, Ottawa Brook. He served with the North Shore Regiment in Canada, United Kingdom and Northwest Europe.

He married Lillian Ackland, Sudbury. He worked at the Sudbury Nickle Mine and is buried in Sudbury, Ontario.

MacLellan, Hector Daniel F78585

Hector was born on November 26, 1920, the son of Paul and Effie (MacDonald) MacLellan, Black Point. He enlisted in 1940 and served with the Cape Breton Highlanders, Royal Canadian Infantry Corps. Sergeant MacLellan was killed in action on May 1, 1945, and is buried in Holten Cemetery, Netherlands.

MacLellan, Hugh Daniel F97308

Hughie Dan was the son of John J. and Marcella (MacEachern) MacLellan, Black Point. Private MacLellan served in the Canadian Army in the United Kingdom and Continental Europe from 1942 to 1945.

He married Maisie Madison, Scotland. He and his war bride returned to Nova Scotia. He worked with National Gypsum in Dingwall. They reside in Dartmouth.

MacLellan, James Angus
F89245

Jim Angus was the son of Angus and Catherine (MacLean) MacLellan, Ottawa Brook. Private MacLellan served with the Cape Breton Highlanders in Canada and England (1941 to 1943). He resided in Reserve Mines. Unmarried, he died on April 18, 1993, and is buried in Reserve Mines.

(Right - Jim Angus MacLellan)

MacLellan, John A.

John A. was the son of Allan D. and Jessie (MacEachern) MacLellan, Black Point. Private MacLellan served in the Merchant Marine. He married Florence MacLean, Pleasant Bay. They were proprietors of the Bonnie Doon Restaurant, Pleasant Bay. He died in New Waterford.

MacLellan, John Neil B37389

John Neil was born on October 6, 1913, the son of Angus and Cassie (MacLean) MacLellan, Ottawa Brook. Corporal MacLellan served in the Royal Hamilton Light Infantry, Royal Canadian Infantry Corps. He was killed at Dieppe on August 19, 1942, and is buried in Calais Canadian War Cemetery, France.

MacLellan, Peter Allan F54691

Allan was born on July 21, 1918, the son of Angus and Catherine (MacLean) MacLellan, Ottawa Brook.

Private MacLellan served with the Cape Breton Highlanders and the West Nova Scotia Regiment in Canada, England and Italy (1939 to 1945). He was wounded twice. He married Rhodena MacNeil, Ottawa Brook. He died on October 5, 1974, and is buried in Sacred Heart Cemetery, McKinnons Harbour.

World War II soldiers. The following was written on the reverse of the photo: left to right standing - Peter Allan MacLellan. Billy ?, Archie, Pat, Willie, Hughie (Dan X.) MacNeil. Seated - Angus, Billy, George, Neil, John Joseph (Dodo) MacNeil. Seated on ground - unidentified

MacLennan, Alexander Murdock F57628

Sandy was the son of John A. and Mary (Lane) MacLennan, Nyanza. Private MacLennan enlisted on October 19, 1943, and served in Canada with the Canadian Infantry.

He married Doris Crossman. He was employed at the Moncton Airport. He died on November 30, 1991, and is buried in Sackville, New Brunswick.

MacLennan, Calder

Calder was the son of Peter M. (World War I) and Florence (Robinson) MacLennan, Money Point/Baddeck. He served overseas with the Canadian Army.

He married Ann MacAskill, Cape North. After the war he worked with Trans Canada Airlines in Toronto. They lived in Scarborough, Ontario. He died there and his ashes were interred in the family plot in Greenwood Cemetery, Baddeck.

(Brothers left - Fred MacLennan, centre -Buddy MacLennan, right - Calder MacLennan, seated - their mother Mrs. Peter MacLennan)

MacLennan, Colin Robinson F55109

'Buddy' was the son of Peter M. (World War I) and Florence (Robinson) MacLennan, Money Point/ Baddeck. Private MacLennan served overseas in the Argyll and Sutherland Highlanders of Canada (Princess Louise's), Royal Canadian Infantry Corps. He was killed in action on April 23, 1945, and is buried in Holten Canadian War Cemetery, Netherlands.

MacLennan, Dan Alexander

Dan was the son of John and Mary (Lane) MacLennan, Nyanza. Sergeant MacLennan served during the war. He married Margaret Jewisson, England. He was a jeweller and they reside in Halifax.

MacLennan, Donald Archibald

Donald was born on June 25, 1925, the son of Donald and Annie (Campbell) MacLennan, West Middle River. He served in the Royal Canadian Air Force in Canada and overseas. Flight Sergeant MacLennan returned to overseas duty for four years after the war.

He married Jean Matheau, Prince Edward Island. They resided in Manitoba. He died on December 13, 1973, and is buried in Portage La Prairie, Manitoba.

MacLennan, Frederick

Fred was the son of Peter (World War I) and Florence (Robinson) MacLennan, Money Point/ Baddeck. He served in the Canadian Army with the Cape Breton Highlanders. Fred was killed as a result of a motorcycle accident during training exercises in Newfoundland on October 8, 1943. Thirty-five year old Fred MacLennan was survived by his widow, Nina Reid MacLennan, and two young sons.

MacLennan, Josie Alene

(Right-Alene MacLennan)

Alene was born on March 5, 1919, the daughter of Alexander and Jessie Belle (MacKenzie) MacLennan, North River Centre. Sergeant MacLennan served in the Canadian Army as a comptomist in Halifax. She married Walter Lovegrove, England. She presently resides in Georgetown, Ontario.

MacLennan, Kenneth Hadley

Kenneth was born in 1922, the son of Alexander and Lena (Hadley) MacLennan, Little Narrows. He served in the Royal Canadian Air Force in Labrador. He married Ann Florence Allen, North Sydney. He died in a motor vehicle accident in 1982. He is buried in the Little Narrows Cemetery.

MacLennan, Murdock Fraser B144919

Murdock was born on June 9, 1913, the son of John and Mary (MacDermid) MacLennan, Middle River. Private MacLennan served with the 48th Highlanders of Canada. He enlisted March 26, 1943 and served in Canada, United Kingdom and the Central Mediterranean area. He was severely wounded in action. He was discharged on June 28, 1945, due to the effects of his injuries. He married Mary Grant, Garry. He carried on farming and lumbering at Middle River. He died on February 14, 1985, and is buried in Middle River Cemetery.

MacLennan, Murdoch James R183185

(right - M.J. MacLennan)

'M.J.' was born on September 12, 1914, the son of Alexander and Jessie Belle (MacKenzie) MacLennan, North River Centre. He enlisted in September, 1942, and served as a sergeant in the medical corps in the Royal Canadian Air Force. He served in Canada, Goose Bay, England and Northern Europe. He was discharged in May, 1946.

M.J. was a Registered Nurse and a graduate of the Nova Scotia Hospital and Victoria General Schools of Nursing, Halifax. For twenty-eight years he worked for Fisher Scientific Company, Toronto. He married Mamie Paley, Elmsdale. They are retired and residing in North River.

MacLeod, Alexander Fraser F77416

Alexander was born on February 2, 1919, the son of Norman R. and Ida (Urquhart) MacLeod, Fifes Hill, Big Bras d'Or. Spr. MacLeod served overseas with the Royal Canadian Engineers - 3rd Division. Alexander's brothers, Roderick C. and Murray U., also served their country during World War II.

Alexander married Ada Taylor, Florence. He was a watchmaker and jeweller and operated a business in New Waterford. Eventually, they moved to the United States. He died in New Hampshire on May 11, 1994, and is buried there.

MacLeod, Allan Archibald F79807

Allan was born on July 12, 1916, the son of Norman C. and Agnes M. (MacMillan) MacLeod, Big Baddeck. He enlisted on June 22, 1942, with the Canadian Army Signal Corps. He served in Canada, England and North West Europe. He was discharged on February 7, 1946.

He married Elsie MacLeod (World War II), Glen Tosh, St. Ann's. They resided in Baddeck. Allan died on August 19, 1967. He is buried in St. Andrews Cemetery, Baddeck Forks.

MacLeod, Angus F58225

Angus was born on November 7, 1921, the son of Neil J. and Mary (Morrison) MacLeod, Ross Ferry. He enlisted on March 8, 1944, in the Canadian Army. He served in Canada. He was discharged in October, 1945. He married Christine Caldwell, Sydney Mines. They reside in Ross Ferry.

MacLeod, Angus Donald V2607

'A.D.' was born on November 2, 1912, the son of Angus and Nina (Morrison) MacLeod, Nyanza. He served for five years with the Royal Canadian Naval Volunteer Reserve on the high seas. Chief Petty Officer MacLeod was chief motor mechanic 3rd class.

He married Dolores Sullivan. They resided in Baddeck. He died in 1963 and is buried in Greenwood Cemetery, Baddeck.

MacLeod, Angus Roderick

'Red Angus' was born on February 15, 1910, the son of Roderick and Catherine (MacLeod) MacLeod, Big Glen. His parents died during his childhood and he was raised by his uncles Malcolm and Norman MacLeod, Backlands, Baddeck Forks.

Angus served overseas in the army. Afterwards, he worked as a hard rock miner in the Canadian West. He married Georgie Shaw, Margaree. They retired to Edwardsville. Angus died in August, 1969, and is buried in St. Andrews Cemetery, Baddeck Forks.

MacLeod, Bertram Yorke F97929

(Background - North River and Smith's Mountain)

Bert was born on September 1, 1922, the son of Dan K. and Nellie (MacMillan) MacLeod, North River Bridge. He enlisted on June 4, 1942, in Sydney. In May, 1943 he graduated from Brockville, Ontario's Officers' Training School as 2nd Lieutenant. He then completed infantry training at Aldershot and qualified as Lieutenant. He served as a training officer in various locations in Canada. In 1944 he went overseas and served as field platoon commander with the Algonquin Regiment, 4th Armoured Division in North West Europe. He was wounded in Germany. He then served in England. He was discharged in Halifax on April 18,

1946. He served in the militia with the Cape Breton Highlanders for several years. He was a foreman at the Sydney Steel Plant. He and his second wife, Joyce, are retired and residing in Sydney.

MacLeod, Clarence Kenneth F54684

Clarence was raised at the home of his MacLennan grandparents in Middle River. He enlisted on September 5, 1939, in the Royal Canadian Engineers. As a sapper, he served with the Cape Breton Highlanders and the West Nova Scotia Regiment. He served in Canada, the United Kingdom and Continental Europe. He was discharged on demobilization on April 23, 1946.

He married Dolena MacPhee, Big Baddeck, and they resided in Middle River. He died on November 27, 1995, and is buried in Middle River Cemetery.

MacLeod, Dan Chester V47411

Dan Chester was born in 1911, the son of John Edward and Bella (MacRae) MacLeod, Middle River. He enlisted on September 2, 1942 in the Royal Canadian Navy. He served as a shipwright 3rd class in the North Atlantic. Chief Petty Officer MacLeod was discharged on demobilization on August 6, 1945. He married Agnes Morrison, Hunters' Mountain. He resided in Middle River. He died in 1972 and is buried in Middle River Cemetery.

MacLeod, Dan Nichol

Dan Nichol was born 1925, the son of Angus and Dinah (MacLeod) MacLeod, Tarbot. He served with the United States Army and now resides in California.

MacLeod, Dan Wilson

Dan Wilson Bain MacLeod was born on August 11, 1919, and raised by his grandmother Esther MacLeod and her second husband, Norman MacLeod, Tarbotvale. He served overseas in the Canadian Army. After the war, Dan married and resided in Michigan, USA. Presently they reside in North Ridge, California.

MacLeod, Donald James F33199

'Jimmie King' was the son of James and Kate (MacDonald) MacLeod, South Gut. He enlisted on November 5, 1943, and served with the Merchant Marine and the Royal Canadian Army Medical Corps. Private MacLeod was discharged on September 13, 1944. For fifteen years he drove the school bus between Baddeck and North Shore. He later worked as a commissionaire in Halifax. Unmarried, he died in Halifax on August 28, 1993. He is buried in Harbourview Cemetery, South Haven.

MacLeod, Donald Murdoch

'Donald D.B.' was born on December 25, 1911, the son of D.B. and Christine (MacDonald) MacLeod, Breton Cove. He enlisted on July 1, 1940, as a 2nd Lieutenant. He was discharged on November 16, 1945, as a Lieutenant. He served with Unit BE & M Company Royal Canadian Engineers in Canada, Newfoundland and overseas. He received his Bachelor of Science from Acadia University and also earned an engineering certificate. He served as Highway Engineer for Victoria County. He married Doris Goobie, Newfoundland, and they resided in Baddeck. He died in December, 1975, and is buried in Harbourview Cemetery, South Haven.

MacLeod, Elsie May W60697

Elsie was born on April 1, 1926, the daughter of Alexander Miles (World War I and II) and Catherine (Stowe) MacLeod, Glen Tosh. She enlisted in October, 1944, and served in Canada. Private MacLeod was discharged in November, 1945. She married Allan A. MacLeod (World War II), Big Baddeck. They resided in Baddeck. She was the recipient of the Rose Medallion for Community Service. She died on June 13, 1994, and is buried in St. Andrews Cemetery, Baddeck Forks.

MacLeod, Fraser K. F56453

Fraser was a son of Kenneth and Katherine (MacLennan) MacLeod, New Campbellton. He enlisted in March, 1943 and served with the North Nova Scotia Highlanders, Infantry Corps. He was sent overseas in April, 1944, and went to France on D-Day. Lance Corporal MacLeod was killed in action in France on August 14, 1944, and is buried in Bretteville-Sur-Laize Canadian War Cemetery.

MacLeod, Gordon Alexander R76393

Gordon was born in 1918, the adopted son of Big Kenneth (World War I) and Annie (Ross) MacLeod, Little Narrows. He enlisted on December 23, 1940, and served as a leading aircraftsman in the Royal Canadian Air Force. Leading aircraftsman MacLeod served in Canada and was discharged on November 21, 1945. He married Ruth MacKenzie, West Bay. They reside in Sydney where he worked with the Canadian National Railway. Now retired, he is actively involved with the work of the Salvation Army. His father, a blacksmith at Little Narrows, played the role of Rev. Norman MacLeod in one of the re-enactments of the departure of the Highlanders from St. Ann's for New Zealand (Gaelic College - 1951).

MacLeod, Gordon Fraser Campbell F97604

'Gordon Mike' was born on February 7, 1913, the son of Phillip and Christy (MacAulay) MacLeod, Baddeck. He served in the Royal Canadian Artillery as a gunner. He served from 1942 to 1944.

He married Sadie Russell, Estmere. They resided in Baddeck. He died in 1960 and is buried in Greenwood Cemetery, Baddeck.

(Gordon F. MacLeod, his wife Sadie, Jonena and Douglas MacLeod)

MacLeod, Hannah

Hannah was the daughter of John Alexander and Christie Belle (MacIver) MacLeod, Indian Brook. She served in the Women's Royal Canadian Naval Service in Ottawa. She married Mr. Koneig and resides in Ontario.

MacLeod, Herbert Kitchener

Herbert was born on July 4, 1916, the son of Johnny J.P. and Catherine (MacLeod) MacLeod, Baddeck. He served in the Royal Canadian Air Force. He married Edith MacKenzie, Baddeck. He was a school teacher, teaching at Trois Rivieres, Quebec, where he died on January 30, 1969. He is buried in Greenwood Cemetery. Baddeck.

(Herbert K. MacLeod and wife Edith. 'Ready to board' - Baddeck wharf.)

MacLeod, J. Harold R88268

Harold was born on June 17, 1920, the son of John Joseph and Helen (Stephens) MacLeod, New Haven. Sergeant MacLeod served in the Royal Canadian Air Force. He was stationed in India and served as a communications repair technician (R.D.S. mechanic) from 1941 to 1945.

He was a 1938 graduate of Mount Allison University, Sackville, New Brunswick. He married Nelda MacKillop, R.N., Grand River (Matron of Buchanan Memorial Hospital, Neil's Harbour). He was a merchant (MacLeod and Sons firm) at New Haven. He died on August 7, 1986, and is buried in St. Peter's Cemetery, Neil's Harbour.

MacLeod, James F1136

Jimmy was born on May 8, 1917, the son of Angus C. and Mary (MacMillan) MacLeod, Upper Baddeck River. Lance Corporal MacLeod enlisted in 1943 with the Royal Canadian Army and served until 1946. He served in Canada. He married Blanche Richards, Englishtown. He was a carpenter by trade. He is presently retired and living in Baddeck.

(Brothers James MacLeod - left and Roddie MacLeod - right)

MacLeod, John Angus F57436

John A. was born on June 2, 1924, the son of Roderick and Mary Grace (Royal) MacLeod, Cape North. Private MacLeod served with the Cape Breton Highlanders in Canada, United Kingdom, Italy and Northwest Europe (1943 to 1945). He was injured by a bomb and "this twenty year old soldier was lucky to be alive." Spr. MacLeod, SF 57436, served in the Korean War with the 23 FD Squadron Royal Canadian Engineers in Canada and Korea (1951 to 1953).

He was predeceased by his first wife Eva Hatcher, New Haven. He and his wife, Margaret Grant, reside in Ontario. After his years of war service he continued to serve in the Canadian Armed Forces. In 1995, seventy year old John MacLeod revisited Holland. Looking back he expressed his thoughts about what it was really like fifty years before:

" ... After a few days, and a few trips to battle sites, the memories kept flooding back. The horror, destruction, the starving populous, terror filled children, and for three weeks the Dutch people opened their homes, their arms and poured out their love for the surviving Canadian vets who risked all for them.

The Dutch people gave up vacations to be with us vets.

One of my most memorable experiences was when our host family took us to the town of Delfzijl, the last town the Cape Breton Highlanders liberated. Fifty years later the town has grown into a fair size city.

The center of town is as I remember. When I found the town square and water fountain I recognized the buildings and streets. I found the building I was billeted in and unbelievable as it seems, it was the same as fifty years ago, even to my bedroom. The only notable change was a new window in the bedroom.

It was a strong flood of emotions, after fifty years, sadness and happiness. How does it feel to be royalty? I will never know, but they made me feel like a king, and all I can say to them is: you were worth it."

MacLeod, John William

Jack was born on May 4, 1911, the son of William Henry and Mary Susan (Cann) MacLeod, Ingonish. He served in the Merchant Navy - S.S. *Strathcona*. He married Emily MacLean. He died on January 11, 1988, and is buried in St. John's Cemetery - Presbyterian Side, Ingonish.

MacLeod, Kenyon

Kenyon was the son of Rev. Kenneth MacLeod and his first wife. He was born in the United States, but came to live with his uncle, Charles MacLeod, in St. Patrick's Channel. He served in the Royal Canadian Air Force. He married and lived in Toronto where he later died.

MacLeod, Malcolm Roderick

'Malcolm John Alex' was the son of John Alexander and Christy Belle (MacIver) MacLeod, Indian Brook. Private MacLeod served in Canada, England and Continental Europe. He was wounded during active service in France. He married Murdena MacKenzie, Boularderie, and they resided in Sydney. He was a bricklayer. He died on March 16, 1982, and is buried in Forest Haven Memorial Gardens, Sydney. His family donated the land for the war monument in Indian Brook. The dedication service was held on November 9, 1997.

MacLeod, Mary Margaret W305427

Mary Margaret was born on June 15, 1921, the daughter of Neil and Christy (Matheson) MacLeod, North River Bridge. She served with the Royal Canadian Air Force. Leading Air Force Woman MacLeod enlisted on August 8, 1942, and served in Canada. She was discharged on December 13, 1944. She married Charles Backus (World War II), Quebec. They resided in Stanbridge East, Quebec. She died on June 22, 1998 and is buried in Quebec.

MacLeod, Melvin William SF58972

Melvin was born on December 19, 1925, the son of Roderick and Mary Grace (Royal) MacLeod, Cape North. Gunner MacLeod served with the 3rd and 4th Royal Canadian Heavy Artillery in Canada and Germany from 1944 to 1946. After the war he continued to serve in the Canadian Armed Forces. He died on May 4, 1996 and is buried in MacPherson's Cemetery, Cape North.

MacLeod, Murdoch

Murdoch was born on August 14, 1918, the son of Dan R. and Florence (Reid) MacLeod, Big Bras d'Or. He served during World War II. He died in Ontario in 1987.

MacLeod, Murdock F35781

'Buster' was born on January 21, 1915, the son of William and Annabel (Ferguson) MacLeod, Baddeck. Private MacLeod enlisted in Halifax with the Canadian Section - 2nd Echelon. He served in Continental Europe.

He married Joyce Porter, Wolfville. He was an accountant and served as a mayor of the town of Wolfville. He and his wife reside in Wolfville.

MacLeod, Murdoch Angus F56789

Murdoch Angus was born on November 22, 1906, the son of Alexander (Mason) and Christy Ann (MacLeod) MacLeod, Goose Cove/St. Ann's. Private MacLeod served overseas with the Signal Corps in the Canadian Army from 1942 - 1946. He worked with Ferguson's Transfer Company in Sydney. Unmarried, he died on January 16, 1971, and is buried in Riverside Cemetery, North River.

MacLeod, Murdoch Murray

Murray was born in 1924, the son of Angus N. and Christy (Smith) MacLeod, Big Hill. Murray was raised at the home of Dan Neil MacMillan, Big Baddeck. He served overseas and was wounded in Italy. After undergoing hospital treatment for many years, he died in 1966 at the Queen Mary Veteran's Hospital, Montreal. He is buried in Greenwood Cemetery, Baddeck.

MacLeod, Norman A. F58426

Norman was born on August 25, 1913, the son of Robert and Annabel (Morrison) MacLeod, Cape North. Private MacDonald served in Canada.

He married Lillian Burton, Cape North. He worked in construction as a heavy equipment operator. He presently resides in North Sydney.

MacLeod, Norman Phillip

Norman was born in 1917, the son of Phillip and Maggie (James) MacLeod, Smokey. First Class Seaman MacLeod served as a gunner in the navy. He became deaf as a result of the noise concussion. He resided in Smokey. He is unmarried and presently resides in the Breton Bay Veteran's Home, Sydney.

MacLeod, Norman Roderick

'Red Norman' was born on October 11, 1908, the son of Roderick and Catherine (MacLeod) MacLeod. His parents died during his childhood, and he was raised by Murdoch "Webber" and Mary MacLeod, Baddeck Bay. He served overseas in the army artillery. He married Evelyn MacPhee, Baddeck Bay. He was a gifted singer and a commentator on the Gaelic program heard over radio station CBI. He died on July 9, 1971, and is buried in St. Andrews Cemetery, Baddeck Forks.

MacLeod, Robert Strachan R252272

'Robert S.' was born on November 8, 1924, the son of Murdoch "Robert" (World War I) and Catherine (MacFarlane) MacLeod, South Gut. He enlisted on May 13, 1943, in the Royal Canadian Air Force. He served as a rear gunner. He began flying with the 158 Squadron in Bridlington, England and then with 199 Squadron in North Creek, Norfolk, England. He flew 33 missions in a four engine Halifax III. Although never shot down, He and his crew members had very narrow escapes and unpleasant flights. They experienced being lost in fog, shot at over Berlin and coming in over the English Channel very low in fuel. He signed up for a further tour of duty in the Pacific War Zone. He came home on leave in July, 1945, but; fortunately, he did not return to war service as the Pacific War ended in August, 1945. He married Eveline Dunbar, Lorne, Pictou County. He served as fishery officer for many years. They reside in South Haven.

MacLeod, Roderick Alexander

Roddie was a twin son born on July 12, 1924, to Angus C. and Mary (MacMillan) MacLeod, Upper Baddeck River. Roddie enlisted in Halifax on July 7, 1942. His basic training was at Lachine, Quebec. He completed a wireless air gunner course at Guelph # 4 Wireless School and completed his gunnery course in Ontario. He graduated as a pilot officer. Flying Officer Roddie MacLeod served with the Royal Canadian Air Force in Canada.

Following the war he worked at the Canadian Pacific Railroad until his retirement. He married Evelyn Fitzpatrick, Ontario and they reside in Woodstock, Ontario.

MacLeod, Roderick Donald F1512

Roderick was born on November 20, 1918, the son of Norman and Mary (Matheson) MacLeod, Breton Cove. He enlisted on January 8, 1942, in the Army Ordinance Corps. He served in Canada, Newfoundland and England. He was discharged on March 21, 1946. Roderick married a school teacher, Grace MacDonald, Goose Cove. He was a carpenter and a lobster fisherman. They reside in Breton Cove.

MacLeod, Walter S. J23358

Walter was born on January 8, 1922, the son of John Joseph and Helen (Stephens) MacLeod, New Haven. Pilot Officer and Navigator MacLeod served overseas in the Royal Canadian Air Force and Royal Air Force in the United Kingdom (1942 to 1945). He served with the Bomber Squadron 158 in England. He attended Mount Allison University and he married Clara Fricker, Neil's Harbour. He was an accountant and they resided in Fall River, Nova Scotia. He died in June, 1990, and is buried in St. Peter's Cemetery, Neil's Harbour.

MacLeod, Wilfred

Wilfred was born on December 17, 1917, the son of William D. and Annabel (Ferguson) MacLeod, Baddeck. Private MacLeod served from 1941 to 1945 in the infantry. He served in the Carleton Tank and York Regiment in Africa and Italy. He married Millicent Walton, R.N., England. They resided in Baddeck. He died on March 4, 1978, and is buried in Greenwood Cemetery.

MacLeod, Wilfred F58744

Wilfred was born on March 19, 1925, the son of John and Christine MacLeod, Ingonish, Smokey. Private MacLeod served with the Stormont, Dundas and Glengarry Highlanders in England, France, Belgium, Holland and Germany (1943 to 1945). He married Thelma Rideout, Ingonish and they reside in the ancestral home in Ingonish.

MacLeod, William FH1602

(Scotty and Evelyn MacLeod)

'Scotty' was born on July 17, 1911, the son of Donald and Lexina (Finlayson) MacLeod, Middle River. Regimental Sergeant Major MacLeod served with the 21st Mortar (N.B. Regiment) in France, Gibraltar, Italy and Africa. He married Evelyn Wambolt, Annapolis Royal, and they resided in Berwick. He was a service station operator. He died in Berwick and is buried there.

MacLeod, William F 33318

William was the son of Daniel R. and Florence (Reid) MacLeod, Big Bras d'Or. He served in Normandy, France with the North Nova Highlanders in the Tank Corps. Unmarried, he was killed in action. Private MacLeod was reported missing in action on July 25, 1944, and is buried in Bretteville-Sur-Laize Canadian War Cemetery.

MacMillan, Allison F2573

Allison was born on August 18, 1916, and raised by Malcolm and Jane (MacKenzie) MacMillan, Big Harbour. He enlisted on May 11, 1943, and served in the Lanark and Renfrew Scottish Regiment Canadian Army. He served in Canada, the Central Mediterranean and the United Kingdom. For approximately a year after peace was declared, Private MacMillan remained in the army.

He married Florence MacLeod, Glen Tosh. He worked on Ross Ferry. He was a qualified captain for any size passenger boat in minor waters. He served as a rural school bus driver for eighteen years. They reside in Big Harbour.

MacMillan, Joseph Kenneth Norman R65413

Joseph Junior MacMillan was born to Joseph and Ella (MacDonald) MacMillan, Big Baddeck. His father died at a young age, leaving two sons, who then lived with their grandmother, Mrs. Sarah MacMillan, and their uncle, Dan Neil MacMillan. For his senior high school year, Joseph Junior moved to Westville, Nova Scotia and resided with his uncle, Reverend Malcolm MacMillan, and his family. He was a 1939 graduate of New Glasgow High School. For one year he taught (with a permissive license) at the Upper Baddeck School.

He enlisted in the Royal Canadian Air Force and served as a wireless operator and air gunner with the No. 459 Australian Squadron. His Hudson Aircraft stalled while turning at low altitude and crashed five miles northwest of Landing Ground Z, Egypt. Twenty-one year old Flight Sergeant MacMillan was killed on August 25, 1942, and is buried at Tel-El-Kebir War Memorial Cemetery, Egypt. Unmarried, news of his death came to his uncle, Dan Neil MacMillan, Big Baddeck.

MacMillan, Roderick Murdoch A2468

Roddie was born on October 9, 1898, the son of Malcolm and Jane (MacKenzie) MacMillan, Big Harbour. He enlisted on August 6, 1940, as Chief Petty Officer in the Royal Canadian Navy Reserve. He served as a marine engineer in Canada and on the high seas. He was involved with the Battle of the Atlantic. He was discharged on November 29, 1945.

He married Ethel Ross, Sydney. He served as Chief Engineer on Ross Ferry and then he became the superintendent of the ferry. They resided in Big Harbour. He died on October 22, 1985, and is buried in Harbourview Cemetery, South Haven.

MacNeil, Alexander James

Alex James was born in 1918, the son of Emma Jane MacNeil, St. Margaret's Village. Able Seaman MacNeil served in the Royal Canadian Naval Volunteer Reserve. He resided in Whitney Pier. He died on June 21, 1986, and is buried in St. Margaret's Village Cemetery.

MacNeil, Alexander Joseph

Alex Joseph was born on October 27, 1923, the son of Sarah MacNeil, St. Margaret's Village. He served in the Royal Canadian Air Force from 1943 to 1945. He married Leona Lahey.

MacNeil, Archibald

'Archie D.Y.' was the son of Dan Y. and Eliza (MacLean) MacNeil, Ottawa Brook. Private MacNeil served with the Royal Canadian Army Signal Corps in Canada, United Kingdom and Northwest Europe. He married Margie MacNeil, Sydney. They reside in Sydney.

MacNeil, Benedict

Bennie was raised by Murdock Paul and Kate Paul MacLean, Washabuck. He served with the Cape Breton Highlanders in Canada, United Kingdom, Italy and Northwest Europe. He was wounded in battle. He married and he and his wife lived in Montreal.

MacNeil, Benjamin Joseph Columba

Bennie was the twin son of Charles S. and Mary Sarah (Campbell) MacNeil, Red Point. He served with the Canadian Army in Canada. He married Peggy Crysdale, Toronto, and they resided in British Columbia. His twin brother John Francis 'Mosey' MacNeil (World War II) was raised in Baddeck.

MacNeil, Catherine W6034

'Honey' was born on June 10, 1921, the daughter of Francis X.S. and Christina (MacDougall) MacNeil, Iona. Corporal MacNeil served in the Canadian Women's Army Corps in Canada, United Kingdom and Northwest Europe (1942 to 1946).

She married Lieutenant Francis X. MacNeil (World War II), MacNeil's Vale. She was the switchboard operator at Iona for many years.

MacNeil, Cecil

Cecil was the son of John Murdoch and Tena (Devoe) MacNeil, Gillis Point. Corporal MacNeil served with the North Nova Scotia Highlanders in Canada, United Kingdom and Northwest Europe. He was with the North Nova Scotia Highlanders when they landed on the beaches of Normandy.

During the summer of 1944, his mother received word that her son was killed. In fact, he had been wounded in an engagement with the enemy while on patrol duty. He managed to make his way to the home of a Dutch couple where he received first aid and makeshift shelter. He remained there until the Canadian forces advanced and he was taken to a military hospital.

He married Marie Gillis, Ingonish. They resided in Ingonish where he worked at the Cape Breton Highlands National Park. He died on August 22, 1982. He is buried in St. Peter's Parish Cemetery, Ingonish.

MacNeil, Daniel Aloysius

'Danny Michael D.' was born on June 6, 1915, the son of Michael D. and Catherine (MacNeil) MacNeil, Iona. Lance Corporal MacNeil served with the Cape Breton Highlanders in Canada.

He married Kaye 'Johnny Y.' MacLean, Gillis Cove, Inverness County. He was an engineer on the Iona/Grand Narrows ferry. He died on March 25, 1991, and is buried in St. Columba Cemetery, Iona.

MacNeil, Daniel Thomas, D.F.C. J85961

'Dan T.' was born on October 10, 1915, the son of James E. and Elizabeth (Brown) MacNeil, St. Margaret's Village. He enlisted in July, 1940, in the Royal Canadian Air Force and served overseas until 1945. He was a member of the No. 419 Squadron. He flew forty-seven sorties. Also, he was stationed on the Isle of Man in charge of a heavy navigational unit. He was awarded the **DISTINGUISHED FLYING CROSS** on May 10, 1945. "Flying Officer MacNeil's work in the air was of a very high standard showing precision of timing and track keeping. By his example, through his work in the air and his constructive ideas and suggestions on the ground, he became very valuable to the section and an inspiration to all new navigation." The medal presentation was made in Halifax on July 27, 1949.

Prior to his enlistment, he was a school teacher. He married Dorothy Haggar, England. He and his war bride returned to Cape Breton. He was a district fishery officer stationed in Baddeck. He died on July 29, 1982, and is buried in St. Margaret's Village Cemetery.

MacNeil, Donald J.

'Donald J.' was the son of Rory G. and Margaret (MacNeil) MacNeil, Iona Rear. He served in Canada, United Kingdom and Northwest Europe with the Algonquin Regiment and the Cameron Highlanders of Ottawa. He was wounded twice. He married Eugenie Oliver, Ontario and they resided in Ontario. He died on November 14, 1970, and is buried in St. Columba Cemetery, Iona.

MacNeil, Donald J.

Donald was born on December 26, 1918, the son of Dan and Minnie (MacDonald) MacNeil, Bay Road Valley. Corporal MacNeil served in the Royal Canadian Air Force. He worked for the Canadian National Telecommunications Operation at Money Point Mountain. He mar-, ried Susan Gillis, Big Intervale. He died on April 2, 1982 and is buried in Sydney.

MacNeil, Francis Xavier

'Francis X.' was the son of Dan S. and Katie Anne (MacDonald) MacNeil, MacNeil's Vale. Lieutenant MacNeil served with the Cape Breton Highlanders in Canada, the United Kingdom, Italy and Northwest Europe. He was taken prisoner of war for about two years. He married Catherine (Honey) MacNeil, Iona. He died on August 16, 1994, and is buried in St. Columba Cemetery, Iona.

MacNeil, George MacIntosh

George was the son of Roderick and Mary (MacNeil) MacNeil, Iona. Gunner MacNeil served with the Royal Canadian Artillery in Canada and the United Kingdom. He married Theresa Massairo, New Brunswick. They resided in New Brunswick and he is buried there.

MacNeil, Gerald Leo

Gerald Leo was the son of Hugh and Elizabeth (MacLean) MacNeil, Gillis Point. He served with the Cape Breton Highlanders, Hastings and Prince Edward Regiment, 8th Hussars and the Royal Canadian Artillery in Canada, United Kingdom, Italy and Northwest Europe.

MacNeil, Gordon Leo French, M.C.

Gordon was the son of Major Gordon M. (World War I) and Annie Laurie (MacNeil) MacNeil, Iona. Captain MacNeil served with the Cape Breton Highlanders and West Nova Scotia Regiment in Canada, United Kingdom and Italy. He received the **MILITARY CROSS** at Buckingham Palace from His Majesty King George VI on May 22, 1946, which he had earned while fighting on the Italian front with the West Nova Scotia Regiment. His citation for the **MILITARY CROSS** follows:

' ... Captain MacNeil, while on a reconnaissance in a platoon area during the daylight attack upon Catenanuova July 30, 1943 was informed of a strong enemy patrol which had been apparently dispersed in confusion by our artillery fire and had taken cover in an area of cactus scrub. This officer, commanding "C" Company of a Canadian regiment realizing the value of prompt and vigorous offensive action at the right time, immediately organized the platoon and led them in a bayonet charge over a 100-yard stretch of fire swept ground, routed the Germans and took 25 prisoners.

The example, the initiative, the personal courage and the gallantry of this officer on this occasion merits the highest praise.'

Gordon MacNeil Sr., his father, was awarded the **MILITARY CROSS** during World War I.

He married Mary 'Toni' Wiles, R.N., England. He died in October, 1983, and is buried in St. Columba Cemetery, Iona.

(Major Gordon MacNeil, eldest son Gordon III, and his wife Toni Wiles MacNeil, taken on the day he received the Military Cross from His Majesty George VI at Buckingham Palace)

MacNeil, Harold Alexander F 97918

Harold was born on June 8, 1914, the son of Alexander and Janie (Dennison) MacNeil, Baddeck. He enlisted on September 2, 1940, in the Royal Canadian Signal Corps where he served as a signalman. His theatres of service were in Canada, England, France, Holland and Belgium. Signalman MacNeil was discharged on October 26, 1945.

He married Sadie MacDonald, Baddeck. He died on October 21, 1987, and is buried in Harbourview Cemetery, South Haven.

MacNeil, Hector Joseph F89385

Hector was the son of Francis X.H. and Mary (MacNeil) MacNeil, Iona. He served in Canada, United Kingdom, Italy and Northwest Europe. Five of Hector Joseph MacNeil's brothers served in the First World War. He married Mildred MacNamara. They resided in New Waterford. He died on September 2, 1973.

MacNeil, Hector Matthew F54000

'Hector M.' was the son of Joseph H. and Katie Anne (MacNeil) MacNeil. He served with the Cape Breton Highlanders in Canada. He married Anna MacNeil, Jamesville. He was post master at Iona. He died on August 10, 1979, and is buried in St. Columba Cemetery.

MacNeil, Hugh Benedict

Hugh Benedict was born on March 25, 1921, the son of Joseph H. and Katie Ann (MacNeil) MacNeil, Iona. Private MacNeil served with the Cape Breton Highlanders in Canada, United Kingdom, Italy and Northwest Europe (1940 to 1946).

He married Dolly Ratchford, Barra Glen. He worked with the Department of Highways on the Grand Narrows Ferry. He died on November 24, 1973, and is buried in St. Columba Cemetery, Iona.

MacNeil, Hugh Columba J17016

Hugh Columba was the son of Joseph and Sarah (MacNeil) MacNeil, Red Point. He was teaching school at Ottawa Brook when he enlisted for war service. In 1939 he served with the Cape Breton Highlanders and later he served in the Royal Canadian Air Force. Pilot Officer Navigator MacNeil was killed in action on May 13, 1943. Twenty-four year old MacNeil was serving with the 57 Squadron when his Lancaster aircraft was shot down near Netterden. He is buried in the Roman Catholic Cemetery, Gelederland, Holland.

MacNeil, James

James was born on September 26, 1914, the son of Alexander and Mary (MacNeil) MacNeil, St. Margaret's Village. He served in the Royal Canadian Air Force. He married Helen Dowling. He taught school in St. Margaret's Village. He was a graduate of Nova Scotia Agricultural College, Truro, and an agricultural representative in the Truro area. He died on August 5, 1993, and is buried in St. Margaret's Village Cemetery.

MacNeil, James Roderick Joseph

'James R.J.' was the son of Edward A. and Margaret (Campbell) MacNeil, Iona. He served with the Cape Breton Highlanders and also in the navy in Canada and the United Kingdom. He married C.W.A.C. Catherine G. Carr, England (World War II). They resided in Ottawa. He is deceased and his widow presently resides in Hamilton, Ontario.

MacNeil, John Alexander

John Alex was the son of Alex P. and Catherine (MacNeil) MacNeil, Gillis Point. Able Seaman MacNeil served with the Canadian Merchant Navy. He was serving aboard the S.S. *Indier* (Belgium) when he was lost at sea on April 3, 1941. Thirty-seven year old Able Seaman MacNeil's name is inscribed on Panel 19 on the Halifax Memorial, Point Pleasant Park, Halifax - War Graves Registry.

MacNeil, John Alexander E97412

'Big Jack' was the son of Alexander R. and Mary (MacNeil) MacNeil, St. Margaret's Village. Corporal MacNeil served overseas with the North Shore New Brunswick Regiment. He was killed in action on October 12, 1944, and is buried in Adegem Canadian War Cemetery, Belgium.

MacNeil, John Alexander Joseph

'John A.J.' was the son of Edward A. and Margaret (Campbell) MacNeil, Iona. Lieutenant MacNeil served in the Cape Breton Highlanders in 1939 and later in the Royal Canadian Navy. He was a graduate of St. Francis Xavier University, Antigonish and he worked for the Ontario Provincial Government. Unmarried, he died in Ontario.

MacNeil, John Charles F76143

John Charlie was born on April 29, 1920, the son of Dan Angus and Katie (MacCormick) MacNeil, Highland Hill. Signalman MacNeil served with the Royal Canadian Signal Corps in Canada, United Kingdom and Northwest Europe (1942 to 1946).

He married Catherine MacNeil, Glace Bay. He and his wife resided in Glace Bay.

MacNeil, John Dan

John Dan was the son of Neil H. and Mary Ann (MacKenzie) MacNeil, Barra Glen. He served in Canada. He married Catherine MacNeil, Sydney. He was a noted Gaelic singer and is featured on a tape produced by Rosemary MacCormack. He is buried in Sydney.

MacNeil, John Francis

John Francis was the son of Alexander J. and Sarah (MacNeil) MacNeil, Iona. He served in Canada, United Kingdom and Italy. He was wounded and lost a leg. He married Geraldine MacIsaac. They resided in New Waterford and he is buried there.

(Mother Sarah MacNeil and John Francis MacNeil)

(Baddeck Paratrooper Receives Wings, March 1943. Left - Pte. J.F. MacNeil receiving his Wings from Brigadeer General George P. Powell at Fort Bennington, Georgia)

MacNeil, John Francis

'Mosey' was the twin son of Charles S. and Mary Sarah (Campbell) MacNeil, Red Point. He was raised by Louise MacNeil, Baddeck. In March, 1943, Private J.F. MacNeil received his wings from Brig. General George P. Howell, Commandant of the U.S. Paratroop School, Fort Bennington, Georgia. He was a member of the final graduating class of the First

Canadian Paratroop Battalion which afterwards trained its recruits at a Canadian centre. He served with the Canadian Paratroopers in Canada, United Kingdom and Northwest Europe. He also served in combat in the Korean War. He married Norma Fetterly, Port Arthur, Ontario, and they resided in British Columbia.

MacNeil, John Hugh F55024

'John H.' was the son of Malcolm and Annie (MacNeil) MacNeil, Jamesville. He served with the Cape Breton Highlanders and Veterans' Guard of Canada (1940 - 1945). He married Mary Catherine MacNeil, Jamesville. He died on June 15, 1969, and is buried in St. Columba Cemetery, Iona.

MacNeil, John James F32255

Jimmie was born in 1916, the son of John D. (World War I) and Freda (Casey) MacNeil, Baddeck. He enlisted on September 8, 1942, with the Royal Canadian Army Medical Corps. He served in Canada, England, Italy and Belgium. Corporal MacNeil was discharged on October 30, 1946. He married Claudette Cheverie, Baddeck. They reside in Toronto.

MacNeil, John Joseph F55025

John Joseph 'Do-Do' was born in 1922, the son of Rory John and Catherine (MacNeil) MacNeil, Iona. Private MacNeil served with the Cape Breton Highlanders in Canada, United Kingdom and Italy (1940 to 1944). He was wounded in Ortona. By trade he was an electrician. Unmarried, he died on October 24, 1986, and is buried in St. Columba Cemetery, Iona.

MacNeil, John Joseph F54666

'John J.H.' was born on November 2, 1907, the son of Joseph H. and Katie Anne (MacNeil) MacNeil, Iona. Sergeant MacNeil served with the Cape Breton Highlanders in Canada, the United Kingdom, Italy and Northwest Europe (1939 to 1946). He married Mary Brown, Glace Bay. He died on January 10, 1975, and is buried in St. Columba Cemetery.

MacNeil, John Michael

Jackie was the son of John A.J. and Mary (MacNeil) MacNeil, Barra Glen. He served in the Merchant Navy. He married Faye MacLean, Washabuck. He and his wife reside in Toronto.

MacNeil, John Michael F605699

Johnnie was born on December 16, 1917, a twin son of James E. and Elizabeth (Brown) MacNeil, St. Margaret's Village. He served as a gunner with the Royal Canadian Artillery in Canada. He was tragically killed by a runaway horse on July 20, 1942, in St. Margaret's Village. He is buried in St. Margaret's Village Cemetery

MacNeil, Reverend John Michael

John Michael was born in 1913, the son of Dan D. and Mary (MacNeil) MacNeil, MacNeil's Vale. Captain MacNeil served in the Canadian Chaplain Service in Canada. Father MacNeil served as a Roman Catholic Chaplain in the Army and the Royal Canadian Navy. Father MacNeil died in 1988 and is buried in Ottawa.

MacNeil, John P.

'John P.' was the son of Neil S. and Annie (MacKinnon) MacNeil, Gillis Point. He served with the Cape Breton Highlanders in Canada. He married Jessie Campbell, Sydney. He died on July 17, 1978, and is buried in St. Columba Cemetery, Iona.

MacNeil, John Patrick F56406

John Pat was the son of Red Dan and Margaret Anne (Campbell) MacNeil, Jamesville. Spr. MacNeil served in the Royal Canadian Engineers in Canada, England and Northwest Europe (1943 to 1946). Unmarried, he died in North Sydney.

MacNeil, John Roderick A2447

Roddie was the son of John A.J. and Mary (MacNeil) MacNeil, Barra Glen. Prior to joining the Navy, he had been a member of the Dominion Coal Company. Thirty year old 'Stoker' (1st class) MacNeil served in the Royal Canadian Navy on the SS *Rose Castle*, *Lord Strathcona* and other cargo ships. He had twenty-two crossings to his credit. In the last letter that he had written from overseas, he stated that he was due furlough the next month. He was lost at sea while serving on the *Mayflower* on October 1, 1942. His name is inscribed at Londonderry City Cemetery - R.C. Plot Sec. M, Grave 7, County Londonderry, United Kingdom.

MacNeil, John Stephen F58909

John Stephen was the son of James S. and Mary Ann (MacInnis) MacNeil, Grass Cove. Piper MacNeil served with the North Nova Scotia Highlanders in Canada, England and Continental Europe. He is a past president of the Royal Canadian Legion, Branch # 124, Iona. He is a retired school bus driver and he resides in Iona.

MacNeil, Joseph F97201

'Joe Neil A.' was the son of Neil A. and Annie (MacNeil) MacNeil, Ottawa Brook. Private MacNeil served with the Cape Breton Highlanders and the Carlton and York Regiment in Canada, United Kingdom and Italy (1942 to 1945). He died in Toronto in 1996 and is buried there.

MacNeil, Leonard

Leonard was the son of Hugh and Elizabeth (MacLean) MacNeil, Gillis Point. He enlisted in Montreal with the Canadian Army and served in Canada and possibly overseas.

MacNeil, Malcolm

'Malcolm Dan D.' was the son of Dan D. and Mary Anne MacNeil, Ottawa Brook. He served with the Cape Breton Highlanders in Canada, United Kingdom, Italy and North-west Europe. He married Greta MacLean, Big Baddeck. They resided in Newmarket, Ontario. He is buried there.

MacNeil, Malcolm

Malcolm was born on June 11, 1915, the son of Neil M. and Sarah Emma (Burke) MacNeil, Iona. He served during the war. He married twice. His first wife was Rose MacDonald and his second wife was Patricia Fellowes. They resided in St. Thomas, Ontario. He died on November 24, 1996, and was buried in St. Thomas, Ontario.

MacNeil, Malcolm

Malcolm was the son of Alexander P. and Mary Ann (MacLeod) MacNeil, Grass Cove. He served in the Canadian Army in Canada, United Kingdom and Northwest Europe. He was wounded in action. He married and resided in Oshawa, Ontario.

MacNeil, Malcolm James F9213

'Malcolm Big Rory' was the son of John Rory and Mary Margaret (MacNeil) MacNeil, Iona. Gunner MacNeil served with the Royal Canadian Artillery, 6th Canadian Anti-Tank Regiment, 103 Battery in the United Kingdom and Continental Europe (1942 to 1946). He married Kay MacNeil, Big Beach. They reside in Iona. He was a captain on the Iona/Grand Narrows Ferry.

MacNeil, Michael

'Michael J.A.J.' was the son of John A.J. and Mary (MacNeil) MacNeil, Barra Glen. He served as an engineer in the Merchant Marine during the six war years. He had served on the *Rose Castle* and the *Lord Strathcona*. Both were torpedoed and sunk by the enemy. While serving on the *Lord Strathcona*, two nearby ships were sunk by a German U-boat off Newfoundland. Since there was no protection for the oar laden *Lord Strathcona*, the captain ordered the crew into lifeboats. She was torpedoed and went to the bottom. All hands survived.

During peacetime he served on the *Patrick Morris*. He had gone on vacation just before the *Patrick Morris* made its final ill fated voyage in April

1970. The captain and three engineers were lost. He married Mary MacKenzie, Christmas Island. He is buried at Christmas Island.

MacNeil, Michael

'Michael Neil D.' was the son of Neil D. and Katie (MacLean) MacNeil, Jamesville. He served with the Royal Canadian Artillery in Canada. He married Lillian Gillespie, Manitoba, and they resided in Winnipeg.

MacNeil, Michael Hector

Michael Hector was born in 1909, the son of John M. and Christy (MacDonald) MacNeil, Barra Glen. He served in the Merchant Marine and was injured when his ship was torpedoed. He joined the Canadian Army after this incident. He married Catherine Isabel MacNeil. He died in Toronto in 1968.

MacNeil, Michael John F76267

Michael John was born on February 5, 1917, the son of Joseph H. and Katie Ann (MacNeil) MacNeil, Iona. Private MacNeil served with the 23rd Canadian Field Ambulance, Royal Canadian Army Medical Corps, and served in Canada, United Kingdom and Northwest Europe. He died in October, 1965, while serving in the Armed Forces and is buried in St. Columba Cemetery, Iona.

MacNeil, Michael Roderick

'Michael R.' was the son of Neil R. and Mary Ann (MacNeil) MacNeil, Barra Glen. He served in the Canadian Army in Canada. Unmarried, he died on February 14, 1995, and is buried in St. Columba Cemetery, Iona.

MacNeil, Murdock Dan F58952

Murdock Dan was the son of Frank M. and Margaret (MacNeil) MacNeil, Barra Glen. He served with the North Shore Regiment in Canada, United Kingdom and Northwest Europe. He was an engineer on the Grand Narrows Ferry. Unmarried, he died in December, 1989, and is buried in St. Columba Cemetery, Iona.

MacNeil, Murray Leonard F40100

Murray was a son of Angus and Mae (Oram) MacNeil, New Campbellton. He joined the Royal Canadian Army Signal Corps on January 15, 1940. He was discharged on April 17, 1946. He married and lived in Ontario. He died there.

MacNeil, Neil

Neil was the son of Murdoch and Mary (MacDonald) MacNeil, Bay St. Lawrence. He served in the Navy. He was light keeper at Money Point. He died on May 25, 1977, and is buried in St. Joseph's Cemetery, Bras d'Or.

MacNeil, Neil A. F33216

'Neily Neil D.' was born on October 24, 1924, the son of Neil D. and Katie (MacLean) MacNeil, Jamesville. Private MacNeil served in the Canadian Army, Armoured Carrier Regiment in Canada, United Kingdom and Northwest Europe (1943 to 1945). He married June Bessonette, Ontario.

MacNeil, Neil R.

'Neil R.' was the son of Dan Y. and Eliza (MacLean) MacNeil, Ottawa Brook. He served with the American Army and was wounded in action. He resided in the United States and is buried there.

MacNeil, Norman

'Norman A.P.' was the son of Alex P. and Mary Ann (MacLeod) MacNeil, Grass Cove. He served during the war. He married Rose MacNeil, Point Tupper.

(left to right - Norman A.P. MacNeil, Michael Dan MacNeil, Helen MacNeil and Rose MacNeil)

MacNeil, Norman R271969

'Norman M.D.' was the son of Malcolm Dan (World War I - Benacadie) and Christy (MacDonald) MacNeil, Grass Cove. Seventeen year old Norman MacNeil was awarded the **CARNEGIE MEDAL** for saving three young girls from drowning when they broke through the ice on the lake near Iona on February 9, 1943. The girls that he rescued were Mary MacNeil, Florence Gillis and Wilma Gillis. Tragically, a fourth girl, Claire MacNeil, was a drowning victim.

Leading Aircraftsman MacNeil served in the Royal Canadian Air Force and the Fleet Air Arm in Canada and the United Kingdom.

In civilian life, he was an accountant. He married Betty Taylor and they reside in Bridgewater.

MacNeil, Ralph Gordon R65104

Ralph was born in 1913, the son of Alexander and Janie (Dennison) MacNeil, Baddeck. The following letter was received by his mother, Mrs. Janie (John N. World War II) Nicholson, Baddeck.

R.C.A.F. Iceland
May 1/45

Dear Mrs. Nicholson:

There is no further word about "Mac" or any of the lads in his crew and to be quite frank with you there seems little, if any, hope that they will turn up. Our aircraft, and aircraft from the United Kingdom, are daily patrolling the area but have seen or heard nothing.

Your son will be listed as missing for some period and even now a committee of the boys on this squadron are packing his personal belongings to send back to you. The rules of the R.C.A.F. are that no clothing of R.C.A.F. issue or sale, will be sent out. Any money accruing from the sale of R.C.A.F. uniforms or equipment will be sent. So you will receive only those articles listed as "personal belongings". As to his will and such things, all that is handled from Ottawa and you should hear from them very soon.

Again may I pass on the sincere sympathy of all our lads and of myself especially.

Sincerely,

F.A. Lawrence S/L
S/L F.A. Lawrence
Chaplain
 # 162 Bomber Reconnaissance Squadron

The crew of Canso aircraft # 11066 took off on a twelve hour anti-sub patrol and a wireless report was received from the aircraft thirty minutes after takeoff and that was the last that was ever heard from the crew. Search action was undertaken, but nothing was seen. Due to good weather in the area and an absence of wreckage, enemy action was assumed to be the cause. On April 3, 1945, a crew of eight were on board including Flight Sergeant Ralph Gordon MacNeil. Flight Sergeant, Flight Engineer MacNeil has no known grave, his name is inscribed on the Runnymede War Memorial, Panel 282, Surrey, England.

Besides his mother, Janie, and step-father, Jack N. Nicholson (World War I), Baddeck, he was survived by a young widow, Sarah Florence MacNeil, Bear Lake, Ontario.

MacNeil, Roderick Cyril F36810

'Roddie C.' was the son of John Dan and Annie C. (MacNeil) MacNeil, Barra Glen. Private MacNeil served with the West Nova Scotia Regiment in Canada, the United Kingdom and Northwest Europe from 1944 to 1946.

He married Helen Devon, Sault Ste. Marie, Ontario. They reside in Barra Glen where they maintain the family farm. Veteran Roddie C. was an invaluable member of the research committee that compiled this book. He is a Gaelic scholar and singer, Gaelic College Gaelic Choir member, weaver of the Cape Breton Tweed, Gaelic song composer and board member of the Highland Village in Iona - a worthy upholder of the Highland Scottish culture of this province. In honour of departed comrades he composed the following Gaelic song "Lest We Forget Our Departed Comrades" which appeared in *The Victoria Standard* in November, 1995.

Mas Dio-Chuimnhnich Sinn Ar Cuideachd Nach Maireann

Siest:

A bhith fagail ar baile
'S na coir ann
Abhith fagail a'chala
Ga seoladh na mara
Measg gach cunnairt's cafaig
Air an fhairge throm.

Chorus:

Leaving our community
And the fine kind people there.
Leaving the pier
for the sailing of the ocean,
amidst every danger and rushing
on an angry sea.

Rann:

Mor ghruaimean ar duthcha
Leis an naidheachd a fhuair sinn
Tha a'Ghearmailt 'gar gluasad

Verse:

Much gloom covers our country
with the news we heard.
The Germans are on the move

'S gar n imrich gu blar.

Ged a bha sinn an dochas
Nach tigheadh i ri cogadh
'S beag a tha i nis coltach
Gum bidh solas 's an tir.

Turus againn ri sealadh
Ann am mionach an T-soithich
Leis an eascaraid 'feitheamh
Fo iochdar nan stuaidh.

'S nuair a bha sinn a fagail
Le mor bheannachd ar cairdean
Feuch gan till sinn gu sabhailt
Gu'n duthaich ar gaoil.

Sia bliadhnachan cianail
Dortadh fala neo-chriochnach
Ach le cuideachadh an Tighearna
Thainig solus na sith.

Tha am piobair a'gleusad
Cur a-mach ceol 's sgeula
Leis an duanag as speiseil
Gun do chriochnaich am blar.

Saoil seo: am a bhith ri mireadh
Ach cha slanaich sin na cridhean
No cuir stad air deoir sileadh
Airson fir tha fuar fo'n fhoid.

Daor 's cosgail an T -saorsa
Ann an airgead 's uine
Surach sin 's neo-phriseil
coimeas sgrios air fuil blath.

and marching to battle.

Although we were in hope
that it wouldn't come to war,
little does it now look like
there will be solace in the land.

We have a journey to sail
in the bowels of the ship
with the enemy awaiting
down under the waves.

We were leaving
with many blessings from our loved
ones, for a safe return
to the land of our love.

Six dreary years
of unending bloodshed,
but with the help of the Lord
the light of peace appeared.

The piper is tuning,
delivering music and a message
with the tune most loved
that the battle has ended.

Imagine now, a time for merry-making
but that won't heal the hearts
or stop the flow of tears
for men cold under the sod.

In the air and on the land
on the ocean, among the seaweed
without a coffin and without linen
and without the wake-fold to
mourn.

'S an iarmailt 's air fearann *Air a'mhuir a-measg an fheamann* *Gun chiste 's gun anart* *'S gun luchd-faire re bron.*	*Dear and costly the freedom* *in money and time.* *Trifling and of little value that,* *Compared to the destruction of* *warm blood.*
Og fallainn 's gun chreuchdachd *Bha air falbh 's cha d'fhuair tilleadh* *Airson nach maireann, ar cuideachd* *Guidh gur Parras an diol.*	*Young and healthy and without* *ailments* *were away and did not return* *for the departed, our comrades* *pray, paradise is their reward.*
Cairdean curanta, as uaisle *Fad a bhios sibh 'nar cuimhne* *Ged is meirg an gunna* *'s ged a thiormaich an-T suil.*	*Friends, gallant, the noblest,* *long will you be in our memory* *although the gun has rusted* *and the tears have dried.*

MacNeil, Stephen Albert   F55241

Albert was the son of John P. and Mary Catherine (MacDonald) MacNeil, Iona. Corporal MacNeil served with the Cape Breton Highlanders in Canada, United Kingdom and Italy. He was wounded in active service. He met his nephew, Fred Cederberg, in Carians, Italy (World War II). He married Violet Wilson and remained in Scotland after the war. He died in Scotland.

(left - S. Albert MacNeil and his nephew, Fred Cederberg)

MacNeil, Thomas Featherstone   F57147

Tommy was born in England on May 23, 1907. As a child, he was sent to Canada from the Middlemore Home, Birmingham, England. He was raised by George and Grace (MacLeod) MacNeil, Tarbot. He enlisted on July 13, 1943, in the Canadian Army - North Shore (New Brunswick) Regiment. He served overseas in active duty in France and Germany. Private MacNeil was discharged on October 31, 1945. He married Maude MacLean, Tarbot. They resided in Tarbot.

MacPhee, Norman Dan

Norman was born on May 12, 1912, the son of Dan and Effie (Buchanan) MacPhee, Big Baddeck.

Norman took his basic training at Esquimalt, British Columbia. Private Norman MacPhee saw active duty in theatres of service in Continental Europe. He married Erma Margaret Ross, Lorne, Pictou County. They operated a service station business in Landsdowne, Pictou County. He died on July 17, 1999 and is buried in Lorne Cemetery, Pictou County.

MacPherson, Mary

Mary was the daughter of Donald J. (World War I) and Florence (MacLeod) MacPherson, Baddeck. She served with the Royal Canadian Air Force. She married Dr. Albert Fownes, M.D., (World War II). She was a physical education instructor. She died on November 8, 1998, and her ashes are interred in the family plot, Greenwood Cemetery, Baddeck.

Mary Fownes, Dr. C.L. MacMillan, M.D. and Dr. Albert Fownes, M.D.

MacPherson, Vimy Katherine C49067

Vimy was born on May 29, 1917, the daughter of Malcolm and Dolena (MacDonald) MacPherson, Lower Middle River. She was a Registered Nurse and a graduate of the Royal Victoria Hospital School of Nursing, Montreal. She enlisted in the Royal Canadian Air Force in Montreal and was commissioned as Flying Officer (Nursing Sister) on January 4, 1944. Flying Officer Nursing Sister MacPherson served at the Command Hospital, Lachine, Quebec, and the Rockcliffe Military Hospital, Ottawa. She was discharged on March 4, 1948. She married Squadron Leader O. Stephen Comishen. She presently resides in Ottawa.

MacQuarrie, David Peter V26105

Dave was born on January 10, 1910, the son of Dan and Margaret (MacNeil) MacQuarrie. He spent his early years in Middle River. He served with the Royal Canadian Navy. He married Marguerite MacLennan, Baddeck. They resided in Baddeck. He died on October 10, 1991, and is buried in Greenwood Cemetery, Baddeck.

MacQueen, Daniel Alexander R213093

Dan Alex was born on April 9, 1917, the son of Kenneth C. and Sarah (MacDonald) MacQueen, Little River. Leading Air Craftsman MacQueen served overseas in the Royal Canadian Air Force. He enlisted in 1942 and served until June, 1946. He married Edna Strickley and they resided in Preston, Ontario. He died there.

MacQueen, Thomas F79329

Tommy was born on September 24, 1919, the son of Kenneth C. and Sarah (MacDonald) MacQueen, Little River. He enlisted in Kentville on November 17, 1941, in the Canadian Army Provost Corps. Lance Corporal MacQueen served in Canada and Newfoundland. He was discharged in Kentville on March 30, 1946.

He married Mary Eleanor Maloney, North Sydney. They resided in Little River where he was a fisherman. He is a fluent Gaelic speaker. A widower, he presently resides in Baddeck.

MacRae, Alexander Thomas

'A.T.' was born in 1909, the son of Thomas and Annabel (Nicholson) MacRae, West Middle River. Leading Air Craftsman MacRae served during the war. He married Alena MacIsaac. He died in 1988 and is buried in Middle River Cemetery.

MacRae, Archibald John F55091

Archie was born in 1907, the son of Dan and Margaret (MacKinnon) MacRae, Upper Middle River. Private MacRae served overseas with the Cape Breton Highlanders. He married Hannah MacLeod, Framboise. They resided in Sydney where he was a merchant and later employed in car sales. He died on August 6, 1998 and is buried in Forest Haven Memorial Gardens, Sydney.

MacRae, Donald Duncan F89200

'D.D.' was born on August 25, 1912, the son of Dan and Margaret (MacKinnon) MacRae, Upper Middle River. He enlisted on July 4, 1941, and served in the Army, 18 Field Regiment, Royal Canadian Engineers. Private MacRae served in Canada, England, France, Holland and Germany. He was discharged on demobilization on November 8, 1945.

He married Georgie Fortune, R.N., Middle River. He carried on farming in Middle River. He is presently retired and living in Baddeck.

(D.D. MacRae and wife, Georgie)

MacRae, Donald J.

Donald was the son of Thomas and Annabel (Nicholson) MacRae, West Middle River. Private MacRae served during the war. He married and resided in Montreal where he worked for the Dominion Bridge Company. He died in Montreal.

MacRae, Duncan Earle F 36102

Earle was born on October 29, 1924, the son of John and Jessie (MacLennan) MacRae, Middle River. He enlisted on September 16, 1943, and served as a gunner. Gunner MacRae was discharged on November 13, 1945.

He was a graduate of the Nova Scotia Agricultural College, Macdonald College and McGill University. He was employed with the Nova Scotia Department of Agriculture in the Farm Management Division and later went on to hold positions in various other companies. He married Georgina Boast. They resided in Regina. He died on April 21, 1982, and is buried in Middle River Cemetery.

MacRae, Edna Isabel W40446

(right - Edna MacRae)

Edna was born on May 17, 1921, the daughter of Kenneth P. and Bessie (MacLeod) MacRae, Sugar Loaf. She served with D Company Canadian Women's Army Corps. She married Thomas Lally and they resided in California.

MacRae, Eric D.   F4001

Eric was born on July 19, 1919, the son of Kenneth P. and Bessie (MacLeod) MacRae, Sugar Loaf. Private MacRae served with the West Nova Scotia Highlanders in England and Italy. He was assistant light keeper at Betty's Island, Prospect Bay, Nova Scotia. Unmarried, he died on September 7, 1979, and is buried in Aspy Bay Cemetery.

MacRae, Gordon Donald   F55829

'Gordon Dan D.' was born on January 20, 1921, the son of Daniel and Annie (Livingstone) MacRae, Middle River. He enlisted on January 11, 1943, and served as a trooper with the 17th Duke of York, Royal Canadian Hussars, Canadian Army. Trooper MacRae served in Canada, France, Germany and Holland. He was wounded by shrapnel during combat. He was discharged on demobilization in February, 1946.

He was predeceased by his first wife Edith MacLennan, Middle River. He later married Margaret MacKay MacDonald and they reside in Middle River.

MacRae, Ida May   W40431

Ida was born on July 3, 1915, the daughter of Kenneth P. and Bessie (MacLeod) MacRae, Sugar Loaf. Private MacRae served in the Canadian Women's Army Corps. She married Eddie Avon and they resided in Montreal. She died in 1972 and is buried in Last Post Field Cemetery, Point Claire, Quebec.

MacRae, Kenzie

Kenzie was born in 1922, the son and only child of Murdoch A. (World War I) and Katie Belle (MacKenzie) MacRae, Baddeck. He was a graduate of Baddeck Academy. He served overseas. This young veteran returned from overseas service in March, 1946, and died from poliomyelitis in September, 1946. He is buried in Greenwood Cemetery, Baddeck.

MacRae, Murdock Donald (Dan) F33015

'Murdock Dan' was born on July 1, 1914, the son of Dan and Margaret (MacKinnon) MacRae, Upper Middle River. He enlisted in January, 1943, and served in the Army with the Royal Canadian Artillery. Private MacRae was discharged in November, 1945. He married Annie Florence MacInnis, Skye Glen. They resided in Middle River. He died on December 22, 1977, and is buried in Middle River Cemetery.

MacRae, Phillip Kenneth

Phillip was born on September 21, 1909, the son of Alexander and Jane (MacDougal) MacRae, Upper Middle River. Private MacRae served overseas in the army in Continental Europe. He returned to the family farm. He worked with the Department of Lands and Forests. He presently resides in Baddeck.

MacRae, Roderick

Rory was born on March 19, 1927, the son of Kenneth P. and Bessie (MacLeod) MacRae, Sugar Loaf. He served in the United States Navy. He worked for the firm, Cape Breton Battery in Sydney. He married and they reside in Sydney.

MacRae, Roderick Angus F1544

'Roddie Charlie Angus' was born on July 11, 1925, the son of Charles R. (World War I) and Catherine Mae (Morrison) MacRae, Baddeck. He enlisted on March 10, 1944, with the Royal Canadian Corps of Signals and served as a signalman. He served in Canada, the United Kingdom and North West Europe. He was discharged on August 1, 1946, on demobilization.

He married Doris C. MacDonald, R.N., Middle River. He was a 1950 graduate of St. Francis Xavier University and a graduate of Nova Scotia Technical University in 1952. He served as an engineer with the Department of Highways. He and his wife reside in Baddeck.

MacRae, Roderick Norman F55283

Roderick was born on November 14, 1914, the son of John N. and Dolena (MacKenzie) MacRae, Upper Middle River. He served with the North Nova Scotia Highlanders, Royal Canadian Infantry Corps. Private MacRae was taken prisoner of war during D-Day Battle on June 7, 1944, and ordered killed shortly after he was taken by the enemy. He is buried in Beny-Sur-Mer Cemetery, France. His name is engraved on the family monument in Middle River Cemetery.

MacRae, William David R104026

William was born on November 5, 1919, the son of David Archie (Brook) and Flora M. (MacRae) MacRae, West Middle River. He enlisted in 1941 at Halifax in the Royal Canadian Air Force. Flight Sergeant MacRae's aircraft crashed on January 9, 1943, during submarine patrol near Yarmouth, Nova Scotia, while returning to base. He was killed in the crash. Flight Sergeant William David MacRae is buried in Middle River Cemetery.

MacRitchie, Arthur

Arthur was a foster son of Dan and Mary (MacLeod) MacRitchie, Tarbot. He served overseas. He died in 1995 in Vancouver.

MacRitchie, Donald Archibald

Don was born on November 2, 1914, the son of Angus J. and Mary J. (Carmichael) MacRitchie, Baddeck Bay. He enlisted in August, 1944 in Halifax. He served as a gunner - Artillery (A.O.P.) Division - 12th Artillery. He served in England, France, Belgium, Holland and Germany. He was discharged on June 21, 1946, in Halifax. He married Laura Steeves, Sydney. He resides in Massachusetts.

MacRitchie, Duncan J.

'D.J.' was born on September 11, 1898, the son of Norman and Annie (Matheson) MacRitchie, Englishtown. D.J. served in the Merchant Navy in Canada and overseas. He was killed at the Steel Plant in Sydney on June 19, 1943. He is buried in Bayview Cemetery, Englishtown.

MacRitchie, Mary R.N. N753141

May was born on July 20, 1920, the daughter of Angus and Carrie (Matheson) MacRitchie, Bucklaw. She was a 1943 graduate of the Bath Memorial Hospital School of Nursing, Maine, U.S.A. Nursing Sister MacRitchie enlisted in the United States Army in August, 1944, as 2nd Lieutenant N 753141. She served in Europe as a nurse anaesthetist. 1st Lieutenant MacRitchie was discharged in March, 1946. She joined the United States Army Reserve in 1948 and was promoted to full Colonel in 1974. She was an operating room supervisor at New England Deaconess Hospital, Boston. She died in New Port Richie, Florida, on October 18, 1993. She is buried in the St. Patrick's Channel Cemetery.

MacRitchie, Norman John

Norman was born on January 1, 1911, the son of Angus J. and Mary (Carmichael) MacRitchie, Baddeck Bay. He enlisted on August 28, 1942 with the South Alberta Regiment. He served in Canada, England, France, Germany, Belgium and Holland. Private MacRitchie was discharged on December 3, 1946, in Halifax. He married Madeline Alice Tarrant, Isle of Jersey, England. They had resided in Massachusetts since 1948. He died on November 6, 1991, and is buried in Brookdale Cemetery, Dedham.

MacVicar, Emiline Jean

Jean was born April 1, 1919, the daughter of John and Norrie (MacDermid) MacVicar, Englishtown. She enlisted in the army on August 4, 1942, in Sydney. Private MacVicar served with the Canadian Women's Army Corps in England and Holland. She was discharged on January 26, 1946. She married Alex Dupe, Ingonish. She lived in Englishtown and Sydney and retired to Ingonish. She died on April 2, 1981, and is buried in the Anglican Church Cemetery, Ingonish.

Maloney, David

Dave was born in 1919, the son of Sheppard (World War I) and Jennie (Harvey) Maloney, Dingwall. Private Maloney served with the Canadian Infantry Corps in Canada. He married Jessie Burton, South Harbour. He died in 1953, after which his widow and family moved to Big Harbour. He is buried in Aspy Bay Cemetery.

Matheson, Alexander Laughlin

'Alexander L.' was born on August 19, 1920, the son of John Edward and Alena (MacLean) Matheson, Little Narrows. He served overseas for four years in the Royal Canadian Air Force. Corporal Matheson was **MENTIONED IN DISPATCHES** from His Majesty King George VI.

He married Elsie Mingarelli, Sydney. They resided in Sydney and he worked for thirty-nine years with the Canadian National Railway. He died on December 24, 1988, and is buried in Little Narrows Cemetery.

Matheson, Alfred J.

Alfred Matheson was born in September, 1924, the son of Alexander and Mabel (Parsons) Matheson, Big Harbour. Private Matheson served with the Canadian Army in Italy. Presently, he resides in Northern Ontario.

Matheson, Alexander Roderick

Alexander was born in September, 1919, the son of Alexander and Mabel (Parsons) Matheson, Big Harbour. He served in Canada. He married Mary Kennedy, Louisbourg and worked as a pipe fitter. He is now retired and resides in Sydney.

Matheson, Angus Dan F9246

Angus Dan was born in Jubilee, the son of Charlie and Mary Jane (Smith) Matheson, Jubilee. He served in the Canadian Army - West Nova Scotia Regiment. He served in Britain, France, Germany and Italy. He married Theresa MacNeil, Ottawa Brook. They resided in Ontario.

Matheson, Angus James

'Angus Klondike' was the son of Norman and Katie Belle (MacLeod) Matheson, Estmere. He served in the Canadian Army in Canada. He is buried in the Estmere Cemetery.

Matheson, Angus Samuel

Angus was born on March 23, 1922, the son of Malcolm and Catherine (Beaton) Matheson, Baddeck. He served in the Royal Canadian Air Force. He and his wife, Janet, live in Chester Basin. He was a member of the marine division of the Royal Canadian Mounted Police.

Matheson, Dan Alexander V46710

Dan Alex was born on October 20, 1912, the son of William and Katie (MacAskill) Matheson, Glen Tosh. He enlisted on August 20, 1942, in Halifax. He served as ship's cook from December 31, 1942, to January 4, 1946, on the HMCS *Pictou* (corvette) on convoy duty in the North Atlantic. He was discharged in Halifax in January, 1946.

He married Donna Buchanan, River Bennett. They resided in Sydney where Dan Alex was a barber. He is retired and still resides in Sydney.

Matheson, Duncan James

'D.J.' was the son of Phillip and Christy (MacLeod) Matheson, Crescent Grove. Leading Air Craftsman D.J. Matheson served during the war. He married Hazel Law, R.N., Saint John, New Brunswick. He died on January 26, 1992, and is buried in Highland Cemetery, Baddeck Bay.

Matheson, George Murray

Murray 'Big Alex' was born in June, 1917, the son of Alexander and Mabel (Parsons) Matheson, Big Harbour. He served in the Merchant Navy. He was shipwrecked twice. One ship was torpedoed off Wabana, Newfoundland. Unmarried, he died in January, 1980, and is buried in Harbourview Cemetery, South Haven.

Matheson, John R65036

Jack was born in 1904, the son of Phillip and Christy (MacLeod) Matheson, Crescent Grove. Flight Sergeant Matheson served with the Royal Canadian Air Force in Canada and Newfoundland (1940 - 1945). He married Bertha MacKay. He died on August 5, 1993, and is buried in Highland Cemetery, Baddeck Bay.

Matheson, Murdoch

Murdoch 'Big Alex' was born on November 23, 1912, the son of Alexander and Mabel (Parsons) Matheson, Big Harbour. He served overseas with the Cape Breton Highlanders. One of his theatres of service was in Italy. Unmarried, he died in June, 1997, and is buried in Harbourview Cemetery, South Haven.

Matheson, Murdoch F58379

Murdoch was born on September 2, 1925, the son of Phillip and Christy (MacLeod) Matheson, Crescent Grove. He enlisted on May 9, 1944, in the Royal Canadian Army. He was a gunner and served in Canada, England, Belgium, Holland and Germany. He was discharged in June, 1946.

A very community spirited citizen, Murdoch Matheson supported many worthy organizations. He was active in politics and served as district municipal councillor. He and his wife, Edna MacRae, resided in Baddeck. He died on December 27, 1992, and is buried in St. Andrew's Cemetery, Baddeck Forks.

Matheson, Murdoch Montgomery D141215

'Bucky' was born on May 8, 1915, the son of John J. and Lena B. (MacKenzie) Matheson, Goose Cove. He enlisted on June 25, 1943, in Montreal # 4 District Depot. He served in the 2nd Survey Regiment, Canadian Army as a gunner. He served in the United Kingdom and Canada. Private Matheson was discharged in Halifax on demobilization. Dr. Matheson is a retired chiropractor. He and his wife, Barbara, resided in Sarnia, Ontario.

Matheson, Murdock William

Murdock was born in 1904, the son of Little Donald and Bella (MacLeod) Matheson, Little Narrows Crossing. Sergeant Matheson served in the American Army. He married Martha Gile. He died in 1957 in Florida. He is buried in the Little Narrows Cemetery.

Matheson, Sandy Alvin F10038

Sandy was born on November 24, 1924, and was raised by J.P. and Bessie (Matheson) Matheson, Goose Cove. He enlisted on November 19, 1943, in Halifax in the Canadian Army. Private Matheson served in Canada, Britain and North West Europe. He was discharged on April 13, 1946. After the war, he worked with the Department of Lands and Forests. He and his wife, Georgina (MacLeod) Matheson, reside in North River.

Meade, Charles F2353

Charles was born on March 16, 1903, the son of George and Mary Ann Meade, Neil's Harbour. Leading Stoker Meade served in the Royal Canadian Navy. He married Selena Kettle and they resided in North Sydney. After the war, he was a merchant mariner. At the time of his death, he was residing with his son in Port Aux Basques, Newfoundland. He is buried in North Sydney.

Montgomery, Angus Malcolm R176894

Angus was born on November 5, 1913, the son of Dan and Martha (MacRitchie) Montgomery, Jersey Cove. Angus enlisted on August 20, 1942, with the Marine Squadron Royal Canadian Air Force. Corporal Montgomery served overseas with supply and salvage on the high seas. He was discharged on December 6, 1945. He married Christine MacDonald, Rocky Side, and they resided in Jersey Cove. He was a fisherman and captain on the Englishtown Ferry. He died on May 26, 1989, and is buried in Pine Hill Cemetery, River Bennett.

Montgomery, Norman Dan A4603

Norman was born on December 27, 1904, the son of John and Annie (Buchanan) Montgomery, Meadow, North River. He served in the Corvette Navy from May 10, 1941, as an able seaman and was discharged on August 9, 1945. He was a recipient of the **AFRICAN STAR MEDAL**. He married Katherine MacDonald, Meadow. They resided there where he was a farmer. He died on April 25, 1992, and is buried in Riverside Cemetery, North River.

Morley, Alexander

Alex was the son of Malcolm and Philena (Campbell) Morley, Black Rock. He enlisted in July, 1940, and served with the Motor Transport Division, Sydney. He married Mae MacKenzie MacPherson. Following the war, they moved to the United States. He died in Massachusetts.

Morris, Donald Frederick

Don was born on September 19, 1918, the son of Charles Freeman and Edna (Jackson) Morris, Ingonish. Private Morris served overseas with the Medical Corps. He and Signalman Alfred Jackson returned to Canada aboard the HMT *Mauretania*. In January, 1946, the two khaki clad veterans were stranded in North Sydney, so they walked a distance of eighty-five miles to their homes in Ingonish. They departed at six o'clock Monday morning and reached their destination at noontime Tuesday. He was predeceased by his first wife, Sarah MacDonald, Wreck Cove. His second wife was Beatrice Lawrence. He worked at Camp Hill Hospital, Halifax. He died in 1968 and is buried in St. John's Cemetery, Ingonish.

Morrison, Catherine Hannah W310549

Kay was born on December 18, 1918, the daughter of Harry and Flora A. (Morrison) Morrison, Hunter's Mountain. Kay enlisted on February 13, 1943, in the Royal Canadian Air Force. Leading Air Force Woman. Morrison served in Canada and was discharged on December 18, 1945, on demobilization. She married Melvin MacLean, Big Baddeck. She was a Certified Nursing Assistant and she worked at the Victoria County Memorial Hospital for many years. She died on December 30, 1996, and is buried in Middle River Cemetery.

Morrison, Catherine Lorraine

Lorraine was born on October 30, 1913, the daughter of Malcolm (Buck) and Catherine (MacLeod) Morrison, Bucklaw. She enlisted in the Royal Canadian Air Force in 1942. She took her basic training in Toronto and served as a clerk in the Western Provinces. She is retired and residing in Orangedale. Castle Moffett is located on her family homestead.

Morrison, Christopher Daniel F31812

'C.D.' was born on November 4, 1923, the son of John James and Mary Belle (Morrison) Morrison, Point Clear, Boularderie. Lance Corporal Morrison served in the Provost Corps Canadian Army. He married twice. His first wife was Jessie MacNeil. His second wife is Margaret MacGillivray. He resides in Massachusetts.

Morrison, Dan 9559

Dan was born on August 13, 1917, the son of Malcolm and Mary (MacLean) Morrison, Englishtown. He enlisted in 1942 in Halifax. He served with the Canadian Army, Royal Winnipeg Rifles. Private Morrison served in Continental Europe. He was captured in October, 1944, and taken prisoner of war in France for over a year. He married twice. He resided in Toronto and died there in March, 1988.

Morrison, Daniel Roderick

Dan Rory was the son of D.W. and Margaret (Morrison) Morrison, Gillis Point. He served with the Cape Breton Highlanders in Canada, United Kingdom and Italy. He was wounded in combat. He married Mary Bates. He resides in Sydney.

Morrison, Donald

Donald was the son of Kenneth and Hannah (MacDermid) Morrison, Big Bras d'Or. He served in the postal department of the army. After 1945, he continued as a career soldier. Unmarried, he died in 1978. He is buried in St. James Cemetery, Big Bras d'Or.

Morrison, Donald R176959

Donnie was born on June 3, 1914, the son of John and Annabel (MacDonald) Morrison, Cape North. He enlisted in September, 1942, in the Royal Canadian Air Force. Corporal Morrison served in Canada. He married Martha Fitzgerald, Aspy Bay. He worked at the National Gypsum plant in Dingwall and at the gypsum plant in Dartmouth. He died on September 1, 1986, and is buried in Cape North Cemetery.

Morrison, Donald Norman F1527

Donnie was born on March 1, 1913, the son of John L. and Peggy Ann (Morrison) Morrison, Wreck Cove. He enlisted on August 13, 1942, with the Ordinance Corps North Nova Scotia Highlanders. Private Morrison served in England, France, Belgium, Holland and Germany. He was discharged on July 20, 1946. He married Mary Ann Buchanan, Indian Brook. They resided in Wreck Cove. He was a Gaelic speaker and member of the St. Ann's Gaelic Choir. He was a fisherman and he also worked with the Nova Scotia Power Corporation. He died on May 9, 1995, and is buried in Ocean View Cemetery, Birch Plain.

Morrison, Donald Roderick

(Donald R. Morrison and his wife, Lieut. Sally Miller Morrison)

Donald was born on December 10, 1910, the son of Daniel and Annie (MacDonald) Morrison, Big Baddeck. Sergeant Donald Morrison, on New Year's Day, 1945, wed Lieutenant (Nursing Sister) Sally J. Miller, daughter of Mr. and Mrs. Donald Miller, Garden of Eden, Pictou County at St. Nicholas Episcopal Church, Taplow, England. He served as an engineer with the occupation army in Germany. Upon their return to Canada, they resided in New Glasgow. Donald died in New Glasgow on February 14, 1991.

Morrison, Donald Simon F78907

Donnie was born on February 27, 1920, the son of Murdoch and Jessie Ann (MacKenzie) Morrison, Goose Cove. He enlisted on August 12, 1941, in the army - Royal Canadian Ordinance Corps. He served in England, Italy, France and Germany. He was discharged on February 8, 1946. He married Muriel Smith, Murray. He died on February 22, 1994, and is buried in Harbourview Cemetery, South Haven.

Morrison, Edward 176814

Edward was born on May 14, 1914, the son of Malcolm and Mary (MacLean) Morrison, Englishtown. He enlisted in 1942 with the Royal Canadian Air Force. Leading Air Craftsman Morrison served in Canada.

He married Anna MacAskill, Englishtown. They resided in Westmount. He was employed with the Canadian National Railway. He died on November 16, 1992, and is buried in Forest Haven Memorial Gardens, Sydney.

Morrison, George F30558

George was born on September 16, 1915, the son of George and Elizabeth Louise (Grezel) Morrison, Dingwall. Sergeant Morrison served with the Halifax Rifles in the United Kingdom (1941 to 1946). He married Margaret Fitzgerald, Dingwall. He died on September 2, 1974, and is buried in St. Joseph's Cemetery, Dingwall.

Morrison, Gordon F79806

Gordon was born on May 28, 1916, the son of Malcolm and Mary (MacLean) Morrison, Englishtown. He enlisted in June, 1943, in Halifax. He served in the Canadian Army with the Princess Louise Fusiliers. He served in Italy, Holland, Belgium, France, Germany and England. He was discharged in April, 1946. He married Margaret MacDonald, Murray and they resided in Sydney. He was an employee at the Steel Plant, Sydney. He died on July 17, 1996, and is buried in Forest Haven Memorial Gardens, Sydney.

Morrison, Henrietta

'Etta' Morrison was born on December 18, 1907, the daughter of Angus and Mary Jane (Campbell) Morrison, Englishtown. She served in the United States Navy. She worked with I.B.M. in New York as private secretary to the president of the company. Unmarried, she died on November 23, 1984. She is buried in Bayview Cemetery, Englishtown.

Morrison, Hubert F55234

Hubert was born on June 10, 1922, the son of John James and Catherine (MacKillop) Morrison, Munroe's Point. He served overseas in the army as a Lance Corporal with the Cape Breton Highlanders. He married Rose Anne Steele, Westmount. They resided in Sydney and St. Ann's. He died in July, 1981.

Morrison, Hugh Reid F66523

Reid was born on August 10, 1915, the son of John and Annabel (MacDonald) Morrison, Cape North. Private Morrison served overseas in the Royal Canadian Army Signal Corps, 71st General Transport Corps (1942 to 1946). He married Edith MacDonald, U.S.A. He worked at the National Gypsum plant in Milford. He died on September 20, 1983, and is buried in Cape North Cemetery.

Morrison, Jessie Grace R.N.

Jessie Grace was born on September 15, 1904, the daughter of Neil and Mary (MacKinnon) Morrison, Cape North.

She was a 1926 graduate of Winnipeg General Hospital School of Nursing. Nursing Sister Morrison was initiated into the service at Halifax Military Hospital. She served in Canada and England with the Royal Canadian Army Medical Corps. She retired in 1969 after twenty-two years service with the Department of Veterans Affairs. She died on August 5, 1997, in Edmonton, Alberta.

She was featured in the *Cape Breton Magazine* Issue # 66. In that article she says, "So the journey through life had its beginnings in Cape North, Cape Breton. When the curtain drops, I, like my parents, will be far from the old sod. But where we rest that shall be forever Cape Breton. With the Psalmist, I can say 'Lord my heart is not haughty, nor mine eyes lofty: neither do I exercise myself in great matters, or in things too high, for me. Life has been very good and I am very grateful'." - excerpt from an interview with Jessie Morrison by Ronalda Sutherland Reichwein, Edmonton.

Morrison, John Phillip F33172

John Phillip was born on March 10, 1903, the son of Daniel and Annie (MacDonald) Morrison, Big Baddeck. He enlisted on March 5, 1943, and served in Canada, England and with the occupational army in Germany. He was discharged on April 3, 1946.

By trade he was a mechanic and was employed for many years at Bethune's Garage, Baddeck. He married Christine MacLeod, Big Baddeck. They resided in Baddeck. He died on October 13, 1978, and is buried in St. Andrews Cemetery, Baddeck Forks.

Morrison, Kelvin Joseph R252275/24910

Kelvin was born on May 31, 1924, the son of Murdoch and Jessie Ann (MacKenzie) Morrison, Goose Cove. He enlisted in May, 1942, in Sydney and served in the Royal Canadian Air Force. Corporal Morrison served for the entirety of the war. He married Lillian Embury. They reside in Roslin, Ontario.

Morrison, Kinnon John

Kinnon was born on February 21, 1920, the son of Dan and Catherine (MacRae) Morrison, Long Hill, Red Head. He served during the war in Canada. He married

Ethel Isobel MacRae, Boularderie. He worked as a stevedore with Canadian National Marine. They resided in Sydney Mines. He died on January 25, 1998, and is buried in St. James Cemetery, Big Bras d'Or.

Morrison, Malcolm F32193

Malcolm was born on May 1, 1912, the son of Murdoch J. and Bella (MacKay) Morrison, Tarbotvale. He enlisted in Sydney on August 31, 1942 and served overseas as a sapper in the Canadian Army (No. 6 Depot). He was discharged on December 4, 1945, in Halifax.

He married Katie Dauphney, Indian Brook. He was a carpenter and they lived in Tarbot and Whitney Pier. Malcolm presently resides in Whitney Pier.

Morrison, Malcolm Roderick F87794

Roy was born on December 12, 1918, the son of William and Katie Ann (Morrison) Morrison, Sunrise. Sergeant Morrison served with the North Nova Scotia Highlanders in Canada and the United Kingdom from 1941 to 1946. He married a school teacher, Frances MacKillop, St. Ann's. He was Customs Officer in Baddeck. They presently reside in Baddeck.

Morrison, Margaret, R.N.

Margaret was born on August 1, 1897, the daughter of John and Catherine (MacDonald) Morrison, Baddeck Bay. She was a graduate of Faulkner Hospital, Jamaica Plains, Massachusetts. She joined the United States Army Nursing Corps in 1942 and was one of the first nurses ashore at Normandy. Captain Morrison was awarded the **BRONZE MEDAL** for her meritorious service overseas.

She was employed as an industrial nurse by Abbot Industries of Winton, New Hampshire, for seventeen years. She retired to her home in Baddeck Bay. She died in 1968 and is buried in Highland Cemetery, Baddeck Bay.

Morrison, Murdena May, R.N. NF2893

Murdena was born in 1916, the daughter of Angus and Catherine (MacKenzie) Morrison, North Gut, St. Ann's.

She was a 1939 honours graduate of the Victoria General Hospital School of Nursing, Halifax. Nursing Sister Morrison began active duty on February 28, 1944, and served overseas from January 27, 1945, to May 28, 1946. She was posted to the Embarkation Transit Unit from September 20, 1946, to January 27, 1947. She then served at the Montreal Military Hospital and the Toronto Military Hospital. Lieutenant Nursing Sister Morrison was discharged from service on September 20, 1950. She married Jack Eldridge (World War II). They resided in Dartmouth, Nova Scotia. She presently resides in Halifax.

Morrison, Murdock A2788

Murdock was born on September 24, 1912, the son of Alexander J. and Molly (MacLeod) Morrison, Wreck Cove. He enlisted on October 2, 1940, as an able seaman in the navy. He served as a carpenter in the shipwright department. He was discharged on June 18, 1945.

He was predeceased by his first wife and war bride, Mary Menzies Smith, and his second wife, Rita MacLeod, North River. He operated Morrison's General Store in Wreck Cove for twenty-two years. He died on December 10, 1998, and is buried in Hillcrest Cemetery, Wreck Cove.

Morrison, Rev. Murdock Dan

Murdock D. was born on April 12, 1905, the son of Dan and Catherine (MacRae) Morrison, Long Hill, Red Head. He was ordained in 1931 and served as the minister of a Baptist church in Modesto, Oakland, California. He served as a United States Air Force Chaplain and spent twenty-six months serving in the Aleutian Islands. He married Margaret MacLeod. They resided in the United States. He died on August 11, 1983, in Alhambra, California.

Morrison, Neil Allan

Neil was born on October 31, 1906, the son of Malcolm and Mary (MacLean) Morrison, Englishtown. He served in the United States Merchant Navy. He served on the SS *Knute Rochne* which sailed to England. He married

Dolly MacAskill. He sailed on the Great Lakes for sixteen years starting in 1927. He and his wife resided in Michigan. He died there in 1994.

Morrison, Nelson

The name Nelson Morrison appears on the Roll of Honor in St. James Church, Big Bras d'Or. He has not been identified.

Morrison, Roy John

Roy was born on March 22, 1920, the son of Murdoch and Mabel (MacAskill) Morrison, Goose Cove, St. Ann's. He served in the American Navy. He married Betty MacInnis, Big Pond. They resided in Minnesota. He died in July, 1975, and is buried in the United States.

Morrison, Sadie Margaret

Sadie was the daughter of Kenneth A. and Annie (MacLean) Morrison, Rear Little River. She served in the Army Corps. She was predeceased by her first husband, Patrick MacNeil, and her second husband, Francis Delaney. She died on December 1, 1998, and is buried in Resurrection Cemetery, Sydney Forks.

Morrison, William Charles

'Buster' was born on February 7, 1924, the son of William and Clara (Benny) Morrison, Kempt Head. He enlisted in Blue Waters, California with the United States Army. Private Morrison was a gunner and brakeman with the American Transportation Corps. He served in France, Belgium and Holland. Unmarried, he was killed in Idaho while working on the railroad on November 17, 1946. He is buried in Drummond Cemetery, Boularderie.

Mudge, Thomas F2932

Thomas was born on July 13, 1920, the son of Thomas and Lucy (Graves) Mudge, Englishtown. He enlisted on June 1, 1942, in New Glasgow. He served in the Canadian Army with the Royal Canadian Electrical Mechanical Engineers. He was discharged in Halifax on February 11, 1946. He married Jessie MacAskill, Englishtown. He was an employee with the Englishtown Ferry. They reside in Englishtown.

Munro, Allan

Allan was born in 1909, the son of Norman and Margaret (MacDonald) Munro, Jersey Cove. Six of the Munro sons served their country. Two made the supreme sacrifice. Allan served as a fireman in the Merchant Marine. He was lost at sea aboard the SS *Swiftpool* on August 5, 1941. Unmarried, his parents received the following message from His Majesty King George VI, Buckingham Palace:

"The Queen and I offer you our heartfelt sympathy in your great sorrow. We pray that the Empire's gratitude for a life so nobly given in its service may bring you some measure of consolation. George R.I."

His name is inscribed on his parents' marker in Pine Hill Cemetery, River Bennett.

Munro, Carnot

Carnot was born in 1916, the son of Norman and Margaret (MacDonald) Munro, Jersey Cove. He served as a Merchant Seaman. He was lost at sea when his ship the *Lisieux* was sunk by enemy action on December 4, 1939. His two brothers were in the same convoy, but on different ships. His name is inscribed on his parents' marker in Pine Hill Cemetery, River Bennett.

Munro, Claude

Claude was born in 1913, the son of Norman and Margaret (MacDonald) Munro, Jersey Cove. He served as a seaman with the Merchant Navy. He married Donna MacAulay, Englishtown. He worked on the Big Bras d'Or Ferry. He died in 1978 and is buried in Pine Hill Cemetery, River Bennett.

Munro, Ernest C.

Ernest was born in 1922, the son of Norman and Margaret (MacDonald) Munro, Jersey Cove. He enlisted in the Royal Canadian Air Force - Marine Division before the end of the war and served in Canada.

He was an accomplished artist and a graduate of the Nova Scotia College of Art. He studied under the English landscape artist Elizabeth M. Nutt. The late Rev. A.W.R. MacKenzie, Director of the Gaelic College, commissioned him to do several historical paintings. They remain on permanent display at the Gaelic College, St. Ann's. Unmarried, he died in Montreal in 1979. His name is inscribed on a marker in the Pine Hill Cemetery, River Bennett.

Munro, John Roy

Roy was born in 1905, the son of Norman and Margaret (MacDonald) Munro, Jersey Cove. At seventeen years of age, he left home on his first sea voyage aboard the *Canadian Pioneer* which went to Australia.

He served in the Merchant Marine. The *A.D. Huff* was torpedoed on February 22, 1941, by the 26,000 ton German battle cruiser *Genesiau*. It was posted as missing for several months and all hands were presumed lost. Later information revealed that the ship's crew were taken prisoner by the Nazis after the vessel was destroyed. They were sent to a prisoner of war camp in one of the German occupied countries.

He was a prisoner of war for almost the entire period of the war. He spent four and one-half years in enemy camps. He and his fellow prisoners witnessed the advance of the Allies which brought their freedom. They watched and waited as thousands of planes flew across the skies. The light created by fires, searchlights and flares made it possible to read a newspaper at night twenty-six miles from the action.

Roy was an internationally recognized seafarer and was affectionately known as 'Seaboots.' Unmarried, he died in 1965 and is buried in Pine Hill Cemetery, River Bennett.

Munro, Murray Edward PY15380

Murray was born in 1917, the son of Norman and Margaret (MacDonald) Munro, Jersey Cove. He enlisted as a seventeen year old private in the Canadian Army. He served with the Royal Canadian Regiment in the first contingent to go overseas. He served in England, North Africa, Sicily and Italy. He was wounded twice while in active service. Sergeant Munro returned to Canada and became an instructor at Debert, Nova Scotia. He was discharged on July 1, 1947.

After the war Murray worked on the Great Lakes and in the Canadian North. He retired to Jersey Cove. Unmarried, he died in 1982 and is buried in Pine Hill Cemetery, River Bennett.

Munroe, David George

Davie was the son of John and Annie (MacLeod) Munroe, Inlet Baddeck. He served in the army in France, Germany, Belgium and Holland. He married Eva Margeson, Kentville. They resided in London, Ontario.

Munroe, John D.
106551716

John D. was born in 1924, the son of George A. (World War I) and Annie (MacDonald) Munroe, Baddeck. He enlisted in 1941 and served in the Royal Canadian Air Force. He continued his career in the military after the war. Captain Munroe retired in 1969. He married Gladys Smith, Birch Grove, and they reside in Glace Bay.

Munroe, Nellie Jane

Nellie was born in 1916, the daughter of John Munroe and Annie (MacLeod) Munroe, Inlet Baddeck. She served with the Canadian Women's Army Corps. She married Chandler Fortune (World War II), Middle River. They resided in Inlet Baddeck. She died in 1971 and is buried in Greenwood Cemetery, Baddeck.

Munroe, Robert H.

Robert was born in 1910, the son of Alphonse and Margaret (Nicholson) Munroe. He spent his early years in West Middle River and Gairloch Mountain. Sergeant Munroe served in the United States Air Force - 57th Fighter Group. He served in Suez, North Africa, Sicily, Malta, Corsica and Italy (1942 to 1945). He married Denzella Heal. They reside in Camden, Maine.

Munroe, Samuel E.

Samuel was the son of Alphonso and Margaret (Nicholson) Munroe. Sergeant Munroe served in the United States Army. He married Laura Green. They resided in Massachusetts.

Murphy, Charles F455388

Charlie was born in 1919, the son of Daniel and Mary Ann (MacKenzie) Murphy, Washabuck. He served with the Pictou Highlanders in Canada. Unmarried, he died on May 9, 1982, and is buried in Holy Rosary Cemetery, Washabuck.

Murphy, Donald John B. F88424

Donald John B. was the son of Joseph F. and Mary (MacNeil) Murphy, McKinnons Harbour. Corporal Murphy served with the Cape Breton Highlanders and the Canadian Provost Corps in the United Kingdom, Central Mediterranean and Northwest Europe (1941 to 1946). He served with the peace keeping forces in Egypt in 1964. He died on January 18, 1996, and is buried in Sacred Heart Cemetery, McKinnons Harbour.

Murphy, Hugh James F54668

Hugh J. was the son of Joseph F. and Mary (MacNeil) Murphy, McKinnons Harbour. Sergeant Murphy served with the Cape Breton Highlanders and the Canadian Provost Corps in Canada, England, Italy and Northwest Europe from 1939 to 1945. He served as President of Grandona Legion and as a Zone Commander. He was a machine operator with the Department of Transportation and later with the Little Narrows Gypsum Company. He died on April 26, 1971, and is buried in Sacred Heart Cemetery, McKinnons Harbour.

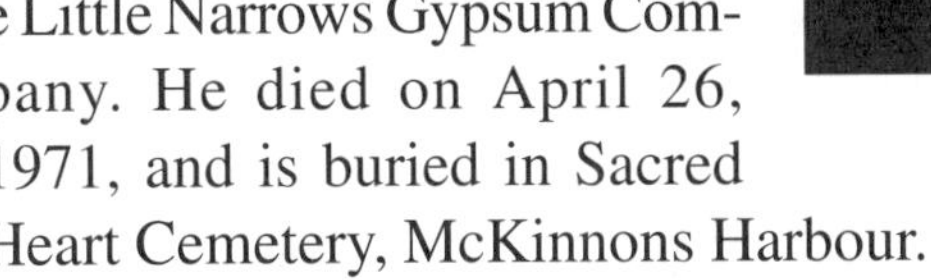

Murphy, Michael Peter F88430

Peter was the son of Joseph F. and Mary (MacNeil) Murphy, McKinnons Harbour. He served with the Cape Breton Highlanders in Continental Europe, United Kingdom and Central Mediterranean areas. He married Margaret Theresa MacNeil, Iona. They resided in Iona where he was an engineer on the Grand Narrows/Iona Ferry.

Murphy, Roderick Joseph

Roddie was the son of Joseph F. and Mary (MacNeil) Murphy, McKinnons Harbour. Sergeant Murphy served with the Cape Breton Highlanders in Canada, United Kingdom, Italy and Northwest Europe. He served overseas in Egypt as a peace keeper for two years (1959 to 1960 and 1965 to 1966). He married Mary MacNeil, Jamesville. He worked on the Iona/Grand Narrows Ferry. He died on December 31, 1993, and is buried in Sacred Heart Cemetery, McKinnons Harbour.

Murray, Austin V26157

Austin was the son of Austin George and Marie C. Murray. His family lived in Murray, North River. He enlisted on May 17, 1941, and was discharged on August 1945. He served as a signal man in the navy. He married Jennie Clarke, New Campbellton. A widower, he presently resides in New Campbellton.

Nicholson, Allison

Allison was born on April 7, 1920, the son of John T. and Rhoda (MacKay) Nicholson, Crescent Grove. He enlisted in the Army and served overseas. He married a school teacher, Mildred Murphy, Port Hood. They reside in Bedford.

Nicholson, Catherine A. W312114

Catherine was born on August 29, 1915, the daughter of Alexander and Effie (Buchanan) Nicholson, Jersey Cove. She served as a leading airwoman. Catherine married James Forbes, Prince Edward Island. She died on September 26, 1973, and is buried in Prince Edward Island.

Nicholson, Charles MacKay F97299

Charlie was born on November 3, 1922, the son of John T. and Rhoda (MacKay) Nicholson, Crescent Grove. He enlisted on February 6, 1942, and served in the Royal Canadian Artillery. He served in Canada, Newfoundland and the United Kingdom. Corporal Nicholson was discharged on April 6, 1946.

He married Christabel Jolly (W144360) World War II), England, who was serving in the Medical Corps with the British Forces. Corporal Nicholson and his war bride returned to Baddeck where they still reside.

Nicholson, Donald John R183281

'Dukie' was born on August 16, 1923, the son of Frank and Christina (MacLennan) Nicholson, Upper Middle River. He enlisted on November 18, 1942, in the Royal Canadian Air Force. He graduated from training in Quebec in January, 1944. Warrant Officer Nicholson was sent overseas in March, 1944, to the South of England and then over the skies of Germany.

He married Alice Fudge. They resided in Sydney where he was employed at the Steel Plant. Dukie Nicholson is an accomplished musician, hence the name. They reside in Sydney.

Nicholson, Donald Malcolm F87814

Donnie was born on February 29, 1920, the son of Alexander and Effie (Buchanan) Nicholson, Jersey Cove. L/Bdr Nicholson served overseas with the Royal Canadian Artillery, 95th Battery 15 F # Regiment.

The following letter was written by him to Mrs. Cassie MacAskill, President of the Englishtown Red Cross:

"Dear Mrs. MacAskill: -

I wish to thank you and all others of the Red Cross Organization for the cigarettes which I received some time ago. I would have written and acknowledged them much sooner but for the fact that I went on ten days leave to England the very day that I received them.

We are having a very quiet and restful time over here now - too much so for most of us. After the past year in particular, it seems strange not to have a war on one's hands, though of course everyone is thankful that at last it is all over.

For several weeks after the "Cease Fire" we were stationed in Germany, in the vicinity of Oldenberg. We had an ideal camp there, a former Hitler Youth centre. After working for over a week getting the place cleaned up, just when we got it well organized, the powers that be decided that we had to move out of Germany, so we are now in a little village in Holland. We are supposed to stay here until it is time to go home, but of course one never knows - we may move a dozen times before we finally leave the country.

My boss has just handed me some typing to do for him, so I must close. Thanks again for the cigarettes, and the best of luck to the Red Cross.

Sincerely, Donnie Nicholson"

He married Margaret Buchanan, Englishtown. He was employed at the Englishtown Ferry. He served as municipal councillor for his electoral district. He died on September 3, 1993, and is buried in Bayview Cemetery, Englishtown.

Nicholson, Frank Daniel F38093

Frank was born on August 20, 1926, the son of William W. (World War I) and Melissa (Watson) (World War I) Nicholson, South Side Baddeck.

He enlisted in November, 1944 and served in the army. Private Nicholson was scheduled for duty in the Pacific when the war ended. He was a graduate of Nova Scotia Agricultural College and Macdonald College, Montreal. His career as a broadcaster and CBC executive spanned thirty-one years. He married Anna MacLeod, R.N., Baddeck. They retired to Big Baddeck. Frank died on March 21, 1992. Interment was in St. Andrews Cemetery, Baddeck Forks.

Nicholson, Harvey MacRae F58990

Harvey was born on March 18, 1926, the son of Colin and Ruby (MacRae) Nicholson, Big Baddeck. Harvey served as a signal man in the Royal Canadian Signal Corps (Army). Unmarried, he died in Vancouver on August 14, 1987.

...son, Helen Watson W6640

Helen was born on March 1, 1922, the daughter of William W. (World War I) and Melissa (Watson) (World War I) Nicholson, South Side Baddeck. She enlisted on August 3, 1943, with the Canadian Women's Army Corps. She served as a typist. Lance Corporal Helen Nicholson was discharged on April 8, 1946. She was a graduate of Acadia University. She married Reverend Donald Martin, Springhill. Presently, they reside on Vancouver Island.

(Sisters Helen Watson Nicholson - left and Jean C. Nicholson - right)

Nicholson, Ian Dan F79510

Ian was born on October 8, 1921, the son of Donald and Jennie (Finlayson-Davidson) Nicholson, Bucklaw. He enlisted on April 17, 1941, in the Canadian Army. He served in the "C" Company, Royal Canadian Infantry Corps, Cape Breton Highlanders. Private Nicholson proceeded overseas in March, 1942. He was wounded in April, 1944, and returned to combat in May and was killed in action on May 26, 1944. He is buried in Cassino War Cemetery, Cassino, Italy.

Nicholson, Jean Catherine

Jean was born on January 6, 1925, the daughter of William W. (World War I) and Melissa (Watson) (World War I) Nicholson, South Side Baddeck. She enlisted in August, 1943, in the Canadian Women's Army Corps. She was a graduate of Acadia University. Jean married Dr. Dave Chabassol, PhD, Westville. Presently, they reside in Victoria, British Columbia.

Nicholson, John Bane F11013

'Red John' was born on November 18, 1923, the son of John A. and Mary (MacDonald) Nicholson, West Middle River. He enlisted on January 7, 1944, in the Canadian Army with the Brockville Rifles. Private Nicholson served in Canada and the South Atlantic. He was discharged on demobilization on May 11, 1946.

He married Irene MacRae, Middle River. He was employed with the Department of Highways. He and his wife resided on their farm in Middle River. He died on August 22, 1998, and is buried in Middle River Cemetery.

Nicholson, John Charles

Charles was born on January 20, 1921, the son of Frank and Christina (MacLennan) Nicholson, Upper Middle River. He enlisted in November, 1939, along with his chum, Bunny Harris (World War II). Private Nicholson served overseas. He married Goldie

Timmons. They resided in Sydney. Charles was a Police Sergeant with the City of Sydney. He died in August, 1982, and is buried in Middle River Cemetery.

Nicholson, Malcolm MacLeod F66285

Malcolm was born in August, 1917, the son of John T. and Rhoda (MacKay) Nicholson, Crescent Grove. He enlisted on July 29, 1942, with the 86 Bridge Company, Royal Canadian Army Signal Corps. Corporal Nicholson served overseas. He was discharged on March 28, 1946. He married Grace MacKinnon, Cape North. They reside in Toronto, Ontario.

Nicholson, Mora May W6652

Mora was born on October 7, 1924, the daughter of Donald and Jennie (Finlayson-Davidson) Nicholson, Bucklaw. Private Nicholson served in the Canadian Army in Halifax. She married Allister Beaton, Skye Glen. She later married Duncan Johnston, Whycocomagh. They reside in North Bay, Ontario.

Nicholson, Murdoch Donald A5666

Murdoch was born on December 26, 1911, the son of Alexander and Effie (Buchanan) Nicholson, Jersey Cove. He enlisted on September 11, 1942, and served with the Merchant Marine and the Royal Canadian Navy. He served with the corvettes in the North Atlantic. He was discharged on November 5, 1945. He was employed with the Department of Transportation at the Englishtown Ferry. He died on February 21, 1995, and is buried in Pine Hill Cemetery, River Bennett.

Nicholson, Neil Duncan

Neil D. was born on March 13, 1908, the son of Roderick and Flora (Campbell) Nicholson, Gairloch Mountain, West Middle River. Seaman Nicholson served in the United States Navy. He married and resided in the United States. His ashes were interred in Middle River Cemetery.

Nicks, Bert Ernest F30962

Bert was the son of Bert E. and Dolena (Ford) Nicks, Ingonish. Trooper Nicks served with the 27th Armoured Regiment (The Sherbrooke Fusiliers Regiment), Royal Canadian Armoured Corps. Twenty-one year old Nicks was killed in action on July 8, 1944, and is buried in Beny-Sur-Mer Canadian War Cemetery, France.

Nicks, Harry

Harry was the son of Bert E. and Dolena (Ford) Nicks, Ingonish. He served overseas in the Canadian Army. He married Tillie Gillis, Ingonish. He worked at Point Edward Naval Base and later at Camp Gagetown, New Brunswick. He and his wife reside in Fredericton, New Brunswick.

Nolan, John Abraham Thomas A5871

Johnny was the son of Duncan and Violet (Hardy) Nolan, Ingonish. In 1939, Ordinary Seaman Nolan served in the Merchant Navy on the St. Lawrence Seaway. He enlisted on February 25, 1942, in the Royal Canadian Naval Volunteer Reserve and transferred on March 4, 1943, to the Royal Canadian Naval Reserve. Leading Patrolman Nolan served on shore patrol between Halifax and Sydney until the end of the war.

He married Edith MacVicar, Whitney Pier/ Englishtown. They were proprietors of Nolan's Store, Ingonish. They reside in Ingonish.

Northen, Cosmos Jerome F31870

Cosmos was born on July 19, 1915, the son of Charles and Margaret (MacLean) Northen, Ottawa Brook. Charlie Northen (father of World War II veterans Cosmos and Peter) lived in Ottawa Brook and was a veteran of both World Wars. Private Northen served in the West Nova Scotia Regiment in Canada from 1942 to 1946.

He was predeceased by his first wife, Rhodena MacLean. His second wife was Daphne Bonaparte. He was an excellent accordion and fiddle player. He worked at Little Narrows Gypsum Company. He is retired and he and his wife reside in Ottawa Brook.

Northen, Peter Joseph F66275

Peter was the son of Charlie and Margaret (MacLean) Northen, Ottawa Brook. Corporal Northen served in the West Nova Scotia Regiment in the United Kingdom, Continental Europe and Central Mediterranean (1942 to 1945). He was wounded twice.

He married Madeleine MacLean, Washabuck. He operated the Little Narrows Ferry for many years. Later he worked at the Little Narrows Gypsum Company. He died in April, 1984, and is buried in Sacred Heart Cemetery, MacKinnon's Harbour.

O'Donnell, Raymond

Raymond was born on November 20, 1921, the son of Phillip and Mamie (MacDonald) O'Donnell, Jamesville West. He served in Canada with the Cape Breton Highlanders. He resided in Jamesville West and Sydney. He is retired and resides in Baddeck.

Ongo, Andrew

Andy was born in 1919, the son of Emmanuel and Emily (Hickey) Ongo, Baddeck. He served overseas with the Canadian Army. He married Jennie Stysh. They resided in South Bar. He was employed for forty-five years at the Sydney

Steel Plant in the railway department. He died on June 25, 1997, and is buried in Low Point, Cape Breton County.

Palmer, Leonard

(Canadian Hospital Ship Lady Nelson*, 1945. Second row left to right - #1 Cpt. R.O. Bethune, Baddeck. Fifth row left to right - # 12 Pte. Leonard Palmer, Big Baddeck, and # 24 Pte. Leslie Buffett, Neil's Harbour)*

Leonard was born in England and raised by James H. and Rosalie A. (Crowdis) MacIver, West Side Baddeck, Big Baddeck. He served on the Canadian Hospital Ship *Lady Nelson*. He married Hilda Ashe, Big Baddeck. They lived in Hunter's Mountain, Boularderie and North Sydney and eventually moved to Massachusetts.

Patterson, Angus F333144

Angus was the son of Charles John and Lena Belle (Murray) Patterson, Boularderie East. He enlisted in the army in 1943. He served with the 5th Medium Artillery invasion of Italy. He was discharged in 1945. He married Mary MacLeod. The Patterson farm was located on the Cape Breton/Victoria County boundary. They resided in Ontario. He died on July 19, 1999 and is buried in Mount Hope Cemetery, Brantford, Ontario.

Patterson, Neil Fraser 104234

Neil Fraser was born on May 19, 1917, the son of John and Lena Belle (Murray) Patterson, Boularderie East. He joined the forces on July 15, 1941, and was discharged in December, 1945. Twice married, his first wife was Lena MacAulay and his second wife is Adrienne MacLennan Fraser, Sydney Mines. He farmed in Millville and worked for the Department of Transportation. He is a resident in the Veterans Unit, Harbour View Hospital, Sydney Mines.

Payne, John Henry

John Henry was born in 1915, the son of William and Lissie (MacLellan) Payne, Neil's Harbour. He enlisted in the Canadian Army and served in Canada. He died on May 1, 1994 and is buried in St. Andrew's Cemetery, Neil's Harbour.

(Brothers John H. Payne - left, and Thomas Payne - right)

Payne, Thomas

Tom was the son of William and Lissie (MacLellan) Payne, Neil's Harbour. He enlisted in the Canadian Army and served in Canada. He married a Miss Sweet, Neil's Harbour. He worked in the coal mines in Glace Bay. He returned to Neil's Harbour. He is buried in St. Andrew's Cemetery, Neil's Harbour.

Peck, James

James hailed from Wagmatcook. Private Peck served during the war.

Peters, Milton Leo

Milton was born on June 15, 1916, the adopted son of Michael Leo and Bridget (Curtis) Peters, Ingonish. He served overseas in the Canadian Army. He married Helene Dolores Barron, Ingonish. He worked at the Sydney airport. He died on August 18, 1984, and is buried in St. Peter's Parish Cemetery, Ingonish.

Phillips, Susie

Susie was the daughter of Aaron and Margaret (MacLeod) Phillips, Big Baddeck. She served in the Royal Canadian Air Force, Women's Division, as a dietitian. She enlisted in June, 1942, and was discharged in November, 1945. She married J.C. (Jack) Taylor. Presently, they live in Penticton, British Columbia.

Probert, Alexander David F76430

Alexander was born in 1922, the son of William and Rachel (MacQuarrie) Probert, Middle River. He enlisted on December 18, 1942, in the Canadian Army. He served as a bombardier. His theatres of service were in Canada, United Kingdom and Continental Europe. He re-enlisted in the army and served in the Royal Canadian Army from 1953 to 1968. He retired with the rank of Sergeant. He married Violet Kelley, Ontario. He resided in Toronto.

Probert, Donald F 56255

Donald was born on January 12, 1923, the son of William and Rachel (MacQuarrie) Probert, Middle River. He enlisted on February 17, 1943, in the Army, 3rd Division, Fort Garry Horse. He served as a trooper in Canada, United Kingdom and Continental Europe. Trooper Probert was discharged on February 17, 1946. He married Lillian Gilbert, Ontario and they resided in Ontario. He is presently living in Middle River.

Rambeau, Pius

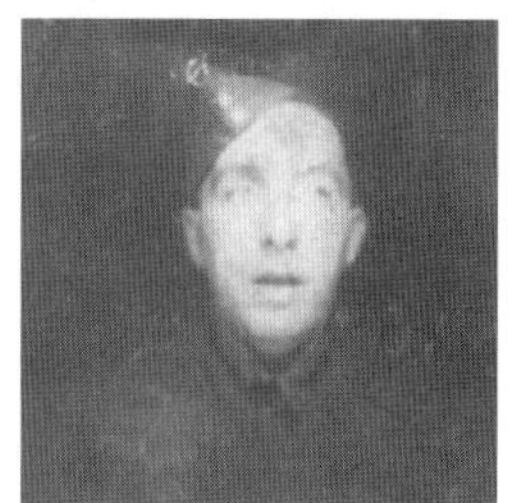

Pius was the son of Stephen and Fanny (Fitzgerald) Rambeau, South Harbour. Private Rambeau served overseas during the war. He worked for the National Gypsum Company and as a carpenter. He married Hannah Theriault, Smelt Brook. They resided in Halifax and he is buried there.

Ramsey, George William F107050

George was born on September 23, 1904, the son of James and Edith (Janes) Ramsey, Neil's Harbour. He enlisted on June 15, 1943 and served in Canada with the Royal Canadian Artillery.

He married Eliza Heaney from Prince Edward Island. He worked at the fish plant in Neil's Harbour. He died on March 15, 1999 at Neil's Harbour. He is buried in St. Peter's Presbyterian Cemetery, Neil's Harbour.

Ratchford, Patrick

Paddy was the son of James and Mary Ratchford, Barra Glen. He served with the Royal Canadian Army Signal Corps in Canada, United Kingdom and Northwest Europe. He married Margaret MacMillan. He died in 1973 and is buried in New Waterford.

Richards, Fred F607257

Fred was born on May 13, 1911, the son of James and Martha (Meade) Richards, Englishtown. He enlisted on November 12, 1942, in Halifax, No. 6 Depot. He served as a gunner with the 104th Royal Canadian Artillery. He served on the North Atlantic and in Newfoundland. He was discharged on April 10, 1946. He married Gwen Hooper. He was employed with the Canadian National Railway. He and his wife reside in Westmount.

Rideout, Robert William Edwin

Bob was born on August 31, 1913, the son of John and Ida (Murphy) Rideout, North Ingonish. He served in the Canadian Army in Canada. He married Emma Hardy and they resided in Ingonish where he was a fisherman.

Rideout, Sanford

Sanford was born on June 15, 1912, the son of Fred and Sarah (Murphy) Rideout, North Ingonish. He served in Petawawa in 1943. He was a fisherman. Unmarried, he resided with his aged father in the family home in Ingonish. He is buried in St. John's Cemetery, Ingonish.

Roberts, John Norman F24349

John Norman was born on October 3, 1918, the son of John W. and Christie (MacLeod) Roberts, Bucklaw. He enlisted in the Royal Canadian Artillery on June 22, 1940. Gunner Roberts was discharged on December 18, 1945. He married Emma Jane (Mayme) Boutilier, Sydney Mines. He was a partner in Brown & Roberts Electric, Sydney Mines. He died on September 3, 1970. His daughter, Mary MacNeil, Christmas Island, wrote the song, "Little Buck The Reindeer," recorded by Duncan Wells.

Roberts, Morris John F32860

Morris was born on July 4, 1920, the son of Tom and Annie (MacInnis) Roberts, Baddeck. He enlisted on January 12, 1943, and served until March 21, 1946. He served as a sapper with the Royal Canadian Engineers in France, Germany, Belgium and Holland. He married Anne McIlmoyle, Ontario. He was a Building Contractor in Niagara Falls. They are retired and living in St. Catharines, Ontario.

Roberts, Simon Carl F52061

Simon was born on December 3, 1920, the son of Clement Hayden and Sadie (Hardy) Roberts, North Ingonish. Private Roberts enlisted in 1939 and served with the Cape Breton Highlanders, C Company - Canadian Army Occupational Force, in England and Continental Europe.

He married Carrie Hardy, Ingonish, and they resided in Oshawa. He died on December 30, 1991.

Roberts, Thomas Felix

Tom was the son of William and Elsie Roberts, Ingonish. He served in Canada with the Canadian Army. He married Bertha Roberts, Halifax. He was a fisherman and truck driver. Tragically, he was drowned when he fell off his fishing boat in North Bay Wharf, Ingonish. He is buried in St. John's Cemetery, Ingonish.

Robinson, Fabian

Fabian was the son of Thomas and Julia (Whitty) Robinson, Ingonish Ferry. He served overseas during the war. He married Regis Frances Marsh, Mill Creek. He was a painting contractor in North Sydney. He is buried in Holy Cross Cemetery, North Sydney.

Robinson, Fredell A.

Fred was the son of Thomas and Julia (Whitty) Robinson, Ingonish Ferry. He served in the Canadian Army during the war. He married Ethel Hatcher, North Sydney. He was a painter by trade. He died on December 19, 1983, and is buried in Holy Cross Cemetery, North Sydney.

Rogers, Henry

Henry was born in 1909, the son of John R. and Elizabeth (Neal) Rogers, New Haven. He served in the Canadian Army during the war. He married Margaret Burt. He was an employee with J.W. Stephen's Ltd., Sydney. He died on July 1, 1998, and is buried in Lakeside Cemetery, North Sydney.

Roper, Benjamin Harvey F33462

Ben was born on December 5, 1924, the son of Harvey (World War I) and Mary (MacGean) Roper, North Ingonish. He enlisted on May 21, 1942 and served with the 5th Division Princess Louise Fusiliers in England, Central Mediterranean, Italy, France and Germany. He was a victim of a motorcycle crash and spent one and one-half years in bed in a military hospital in England. He returned home in a body cast to the hospital in Debert.

He married Blanche Roper, Ingonish. He served as the Chief Warden in the National Park at Louisbourg. At the time of his death, he and his wife were residing in Westmount, Cape Breton.

Roper, Harry Cecil CDN-652

Harry was the son of Charles Purcell and Annie Mae (Towns) Roper, Ingonish. Lieutenant Roper was a Canadian officer loaned to the British Army. He served with the Royal Canadian Infantry Corps, Attd. 5th Btn., The Wiltshire Regiment. He was killed at The Battle of Arnhem on October 1, 1944, and is buried in Arnhem Oosterbeek Cemetery, Netherlands. He was unmarried.

Roper, Henry George Wesley F78512

Henry was born on September 18, 1919, the son of Percy and Georgina (Jackson) Roper, Ingonish. He enlisted on July 8, 1941, and served with the 6th Field Regiment, 2nd Division, 91 Battery Artillery in England and Continental Europe. He was on parade for the King's Inspection. He and "all the boys from home" - George and Alfred Jackson, Ben Hussey, Albert Harvey and Henry Brewer - were all in attendance for an impressive meeting at Canada House. He married Ida Hardy, Ingonish. He worked in Point Edward and Halifax. He now resides in Sydney.

Roper, Leslie Bowden

'Bowdy' was the son of William and Charlotte (Murphy) Roper, Ingonish. He served overseas in the Forestry Corps building bridges from 1940 to 1945. He married Eva MacLean, Ingonish. He operated a sawmill and trucking business. They resided in North Ingonish. He is buried in the United Church Cemetery, Ingonish.

Ross, Donald Fraser

Donald was born on March 17, 1916, the son of Tom and Catherine (MacAskill) Ross, Little Narrows. He served during the war from 1940 to 1943 in Canada. He married Jamie Matheson, R.N., Aberdeen. He was a merchant and post master and worked for thirty-five years at the gypsum plant in Little Narrows. He died on April 12, 1978, and is buried in the Little Narrows Cemetery.

Ross, Duncan Alexander MacAskill

'Dick' was born on July 20, 1909, the son of Tom and Catherine (MacAskill) Ross, Little Narrows. He enlisted on August 19, 1943 in the United States Army. He served in England, Germany and France and from France to Okinawa. Sergeant Ross was discharged on December 12, 1945.

He married Margaret Bailey, Prince Edward Island. They lived in the United States and retired home to Little Narrows. He died on March 20, 1998, and is buried in Little Narrows Cemetery.

(Family photo - Duncan Ross in uniform)

Ross, George Arthur F45682

George was born in April, 1924, the son of John R. and Nellie (MacDonald) Ross, Baddeck. He enlisted in 1941 with the Pictou Highlanders - North Nova Scotia Highlanders. He served overseas in communications with the Signal Corps. He was injured during conflict in Germany. He followed a military career after the war. He married Alice Reason, Ontario. Major Ross and Mrs. Ross are retired and living in Barrie, Ontario.

Ross, Hubert MacIntosh F45725

Hubert was born in 1922, the son of John R. and Nellie (MacDonald) Ross, Baddeck. He enlisted on March 28, 1941, and served with the Pictou Highlanders and the Cape Breton Highlanders. He served in Canada, the United

Kingdom, Carribean and Central Mediterranean areas. He was critically injured in Italy in 1944. He was discharged on May 25, 1945. He married Betty MacDonald, Baddeck. He worked in construction at the Steel Plant in Sydney. They reside in Sydney.

Ross, John F91682

Jack was born on September 13, 1905, the son of William (World War I) and Christine (MacLeod) Ross, North Gut. He enlisted on March 12, 1940 and served as a sapper with the Royal Canadian Engineers. He was with the Canadian Army during the invasion of Sicily. He served in Italy and was in the Battle of Britain. He was a recipient of the **AFRICAN STAR**.

He and his second wife, Angeline MacDonald, Big Harbour, resided in Baddeck. He passed away on January 5, 1996, and is buried in Harbourview Cemetery, South Haven.

Ross, John Fraser F66566

Fraser was born in 1915, the son of John R. and Nellie (MacDonald) Ross, Baddeck. He enlisted on August 20, 1942 in the Signal Corps. He served overseas as a signalman. He served in the United Kingdom and Continental Europe. He died on December 7, 1980, as a result of a fire accident. He is buried in Greenwood Cemetery, Baddeck.

Ross, Joseph S.

Joe was born on November 29, 1920, the son of William (World War I) and Christine (MacLeod) Ross, North Gut. He served in the United States Army. He was posted in Corsica when his brother Murdoch was killed in action.

He became a rehabilitation counsellor at a Boston clinic. He resides in Massachusetts.

Ross, Murdoch John F97030

Murdoch was born on October 27, 1919, the son of William (World War I) and Christine (MacLeod) Ross, North Gut.

He served in the Royal Canadian Army Medical Corps as a stretcher bearer. He was wounded on July 24, 1944, during the fighting in Normandy, France. He died of wounds the following day. He is buried in Beny-Sur-Mer Cemetery, Calvados, France.

Private Murdoch Ross was named after his uncle, Private Murdoch J. Ross of the 85th Battalion, Canadian Expeditionary Force, who was killed at the Battle of the Somme.

Ross, Neil MacDonald F318778

'Buddy' was born in 1917, the son of John R. and Nellie (MacDonald) Ross, Baddeck. He served in Canada with the Army Signal Corps. He married Pearl Hillman, Sydney. They reside in Sydney.

Ross, Norman F32166

Norman was born on October 20, 1906, the son of William (World War I) and Christine (MacLeod) Ross, North Gut. He enlisted on April 24, 1942, and served as a trooper with the Royal Canadian Armoured Corps. He served in Canada and Newfoundland. Norman married Nora Morrison, South Gut. They lived in South Haven. Norman died on November 30, 1997, and is buried in Harbourview Cemetery, South Haven.

Ross, Walter

Walter was born on November 29, 1915, the son of William (World War I) and Christine (MacLeod) Ross, North Gut. He enlisted in the United States Army and served in the Solomon's Unit. He lived in the United States. In the 1940's, he completed a comprehensive genealogical manuscript of the highland settlers and their descendants in the St. Ann's Bay region. It remains an invaluable source for those tracing such ancestral roots. Unmarried, he died on August 27, 1973. He is buried in Massachusetts.

Ryan, Donald Alphonse A5046

(Right - Donald Ryan)

Donnie was born on November 24, 1922, the son of Dan Martin and Florence (Decoste) Ryan, Baddeck.

In 1941, he enlisted in the navy in Halifax and served on convoy duty on the North Atlantic for three years.

He made eighty crossings. He received the **AFRICA STAR** for his escorts to North Africa. For three months he was without shore leave. He was Acting Petty Officer in charge of watch on board ship. On two different occasions he helped pick local men out of the water when their ships were torpedoed - one was John R. Fraser, Boularderie, and the other was Murray Matheson, Big Harbour. He was discharged in Halifax in 1945.

He married Dolly MacLeod, Quarry, St. Ann's. They reside in Baddeck where he worked as Legion Manager and later was in charge of maintenance at the Victoria County Memorial Hospital.

Ryan, Joseph

Joe was the son of Frank and Eva (DeCoste) Ryan, Plaister Mines. He served on convoy duty in the Navy on the North Atlantic. He married Agnes Campbell, Point Clear. They lived in Kempt Head and then moved to Antigonish. He died in 1996.

Ryan, Patrick Martin A 2801

Patrick was born on November 14, 1918, the son of Dan Martin and Florence (DeCoste) Ryan, Baddeck. He enlisted in Halifax in 1940 and served on convoy duty in the navy on the North Atlantic. Able Seaman Ryan was discharged in 1945.

He married Donna Hamm, Baddeck. He worked as a carpenter in Toronto before they retired to Baddeck. He died on October 21, 1992, and is buried in Harbourview Cemetery, South Haven.

Ryan, Thomas Joseph R1271923

Tommy was born on October 5, 1927, the son of Dan Martin and Florence (DeCoste) Ryan, Baddeck. He enlisted on September 18, 1943, in the Royal Canadian Air Force and served in Canada until September 23, 1946. He married and he and his wife reside in Orangeville, Ontario. In civilian life, he worked as an auto body mechanic.

Samways, Eli Richard

Eli was the son of Oliver and Emma (Hardy) Samways, North Ingonish. He served overseas during the World War II and in the Korean War. He married Charlotte Knowles and they resided in Ingonish after the war. They later moved to Yarmouth.

Samways, Norman C.

Norman was the son of Oliver and Emma (Hardy) Samways, North Ingonish. Gunner Samways served overseas during the war. He and his wife, Rita LeBlanc, lived in New Victoria. He worked as a leverman at the Iron Ore Pier at Sydney Steel.

Scott, Charles Pryde

Charlie was raised by Archie and Christine (Morrison) Matheson, Goose Cove. He served overseas with the Canadian Corps of Engineers. He saw active duty in Continental Europe. He married Charlotte MacAulay, Grand River. They resided in Sydney where he was employed with Dominion Steel and Coal Company. He died on September 20, 1989, and is buried in Goose Cove Cemetery.

Seymour, Ephriam F89955

Ephriam was born in 1915, the son of George and Emily (Fricker) Seymour, Neil's Harbour. He enlisted in 1941 in the Canadian Army. He served with the Royal Canadian Electrical and Mechanical Corps in Canada. He married Ann Boyland. They resided in Halifax. After the war, he served for twenty-five years in the Canadian Armed Forces (Army). He died in 1976 and is buried in St. Andrew's Cemetery, Neil's Harbour.

Seymour, Thomas Freeman F89405

Freeman was born on December 18, 1921, the son of George and Emily (Fricker) Seymour, Neil's Harbour. He enlisted on July 21, 1941, in the Royal Artillery and served in Canada. He married Marion Williams and worked at the Cape Breton Highlands National Park. He died on April 5, 1998, and is buried in St. Andrew's Cemetery, Neil's Harbour.

Shea, Theodore

Ted was the son of Thomas and Mary Agnes (Barron) Shea, Ingonish Beach. He served overseas in the Canadian Army. He married Bridget Dunphy, Ingonish. They resided in Sydney where he was employed at the Steel Plant.

Small, John William

'J.W.' was the son of George and Catherine (MacNeil) Small, Red Point. Sergeant Small served in the Royal Canadian Signal Corps in Canada. He married Peggy MacNeil, Mabou. They resided in Westmount. He was an electrician and the superintendent of maintenance for the Point Edward Industrial Park and the Canadian Coast Guard College in Point Edward. He died on October 1, 1998 and is buried in Holy Rosary Parish Cemetery, Westmount.

Small, Michael

Mickie was the son of George and Catherine (MacNeil) Small, Red Point. He served with the Royal Canadian Signal Corps. He was predeceased by his first wife, Mary MacKenzie, Benacadie. His second wife was Josephine MacNeil, Jamesville. They resided in Sydney.

Smith, Alexander F8852

Alexander was born on September 15, 1915, the son of Dan and Mary A. (MacDonald) Smith, Indian Brook. From August, 1939, to August, 1942, he served in the Merchant Navy as an able seaman. His work involved transport of supplies to convoys going overseas. On August 12, 1942, he enlisted in the Canadian Army. He was discharged on August 12, 1945.

He married Evelyn MacDermid, Wreck Cove, and they settled in Wreck Cove. He worked as a lobster fisherman and carpenter. A very community-minded citizen, he is a tireless advocate for the betterment of others and his community. He served as a municipal councillor for the North Shore electoral district. He was a driving force behind the war monument unveiled in Indian Brook on November 9, 1997. A widower, he presently resides in his own home in Wreck Cove.

Smith, Angus

Angus was born in 1908, the son of Hugh and Effie (MacInnes) Smith, Ingonish Ferry. He served in the Merchant Navy. The ship on which he was posted was torpedoed twice. Fortunately, he survived both attacks. He resided with his parents. Unmarried, he died in February, 1988, and is buried in the United Church Cemetery, Ingonish Ferry.

Smith, Arthur William F33400

Arthur was born on May 28, 1924, the son of Dan Murdoch (World War I) and Mary (MacKenzie) Smith, Big Hill. He enlisted on April 27, 1943, in Sydney in the # 6 District Depot C.A. He served in the North Atlantic area.

Private Smith returned to civilian life on demobilization on April 30, 1946. He married Margaret Campbell, New Waterford. He was a coal miner and carpenter. He died on May 27, 1977, and is buried in Scotchtown Cemetery, New Waterford.

Smith, Daniel F97722

Dan was born in 1911, the son of Hugh and Effie (MacInnes) Smith, Ingonish Ferry. He served with the Royal Canadian Corps of Signals, 97 1st Canadian Division Sigs. Thirty-two year old Signalman Smith was killed on July 5, 1943. He is buried in La Rellnion War Cemetery, Algeria.

Smith, John MacRae

Johnny was born on October 22, 1913, the son of Hugh and Effie (MacInnes) Smith, Ingonish Ferry. He studied navigation in Halifax and St. John's, Newfoundland. He served as a mate on the oil tankers in the Merchant Marine during the war years. Captain Smith was the recipient of a Bravery Award from the Royal Canadian Humane Association for his heroism in assisting in the rescue of a drowning victim from the frigid waters of Sydney Harbour on January 29, 1938.

He married Elizabeth Burton, South Harbour. He served as first mate and captain on the *Aspy* and as harbour pilot for the gypsum boats in Dingwall. Later he was captain on *Ross Ferry* and then captain in charge of all Cape Breton ferries. They resided in Big Harbour. He died on January 5, 1980, and is buried in Harbourview Cemetery, South Haven.

Smith, Peter William F33299

'Peter Will' was born on August 19, 1911, the son of William and Johanna (MacAskill) Smith, Oregon, North River. He enlisted in Sydney on April 2, 1943, and served with the Cape Breton Highlanders in the searching for buried mines.

When his mother died on August 13, 1943, he was granted furlough to come home for her funeral. As he returned to war, he bade farewell to his family and friends and told them he knew that he would never return. While mine sweeping an Italian beach, Private Smith and a comrade were killed as a result of a mine accident on June 19, 1944. He is buried in Minturo Cemetery, Italy.

Smith, Roderick

Roderick was the son of Alexander and Mary (MacDonald) Smith, River Bennett. He served in the Canadian Army. He was stationed in Canada and Newfoundland. He is buried in Pine Hill Cemetery, River Bennett.

Smith, Roger F33383

Roger was born on July 18, 1922, the son of Dan Murdoch (World War I) and Mary (MacKenzie) Smith, Big Hill. He enlisted on April 20, 1943, in Sydney and served in the North Nova Scotia Highlanders. He served as an infantry man in Canada, United Kingdom and North West Europe. He arrived on Scheldt battlefield on October 13, 1944. He served in front line action from

October, 1944 to March, 1945. In battle near the Rhine, he was struck by German shell-fire and suffered a concussion and wounds which sent him to a succession of convalescent hospitals. He was discharged on March 25, 1946, in Halifax.

As a young drifter, he hitchhiked to a London, Ontario mission and arrived there on September 4, 1951. His life's work lay ahead of him and for the next thirty-five years, he would administer to the needs of the homeless and destitute. He became Executive Director of Mission Services of London, Ontario. In 1988, the city of London honoured him as their "Citizen of the Year." He married Iris Rogers. They are retired and he enjoys painting and recently published a book entitled *Big Hill, A Memoir.* It is a compelling account of his formative years in the community of Big Hill, his wartime experiences and his career with the mission services of London, Ontario.

Snow, Dr. Timothy, M.D.

Timothy was raised by Jack Corbett and Abigail Snow, Dingwall. He served in the navy during the war. Dr. Snow was a graduate of Dalhousie Medical School, Class of 1957. Dr. Snow is a beloved country doctor who carried on a family practice at Kennetcook, Nova Scotia. He also served as warden for the County of Hants for eighteen years. In 1998 he is serving his thirty-fourth year as a Hants County Councillor.

Southwell, Phillip

Phillip was born in England. He was raised by Margaret and Catherine MacLennan, Little Narrows. He served overseas in the Royal Canadian Air Force. He returned to Little Narrows after the war to visit and then went back to England to marry. He and his wife came to Winnipeg where he was employed as a chef. Eventually they returned to Salisbury, Wiltshire, England. He died there circa 1991.

Squires, Edward R88042

'Teddy' was the son of Jack and Florence (Stephenson) Squires, Big Bras d'Or. He enlisted on February 4, 1941. He transferred to the Royal Canadian Air Force Reserve on September 27, 1945. He was a leading aircraftsman. He married Irene Hefford in England and he and his war bride came to live in Big Bras d'Or where they still reside. He worked on the Big Bras d'Or Ferry.

Squires, John Robert R104363

John Squires was born on July 23, 1915, the son of Jack and Florence (Stephenson) Squires, Big Bras d'Or. He enlisted on July 22, 1941, and served with the Royal Canadian Air Force. Corporal Squires was discharged on July 23, 1945. He married Hilda Boyce, Sydney Mines. They reside in Big Bras d'Or. He worked in the mines and farmed in South Side Boularderie.

Squires, William 78564

(Brothers Ted Squires - left, and William Squires - right)

Willie was the son of Jack and Florence (Stephenson) Squires, Big Bras d'Or. Private Squires served in the army. He married twice. His first wife was Janette Campbell. His second wife was Catherine Emery, Florence. He was a carpenter and he and his wife resided in the family home in Big Bras d'Or. He died on April 17, 1984, and is buried in St. James Cemetery, Big Bras d'Or.

Stephenson, John William

John was born on December 4, 1921, the son of Gavin and Mary Alice (MacLennan) Stephenson, Big Bras d'Or. He enlisted in the army in 1941. He was discharged in 1944. At the time of his marriage to Christine Jane MacLeod, West Tarbot, Private Stephenson was an instructor in Motor Transport, Aldershot, Nova Scotia. They resided at Fife's Hill, Big Bras d'Or.

Stevens, Andrew

Andrew hailed from Wagmatcook. Private Stevens served during the war.

Stevens, Thomas F56262

Tom hailed from Wagmatcook. Private Stevens served in the army in Canada (1943). He was a caretaker of the old school at Wagmatcook. He died on January 18, 1993, and is buried in Membertou Memorial Gardens.

Stockley, Arthur M.

Arthur was the son of John and Ann Maria (Roberts) Stockley, Ingonish Centre. Sergeant Stockley served during the war. He married and lived in Halifax. He died in 1995.

Stockley, Charles R. F45700

Charlie was born on January 15, 1918, the adopted son of Albert and Gertrude (Roper) Stockley, Ingonish Centre. Private Stockley served with the Pictou Highlanders in Canada and Bermuda. He was the middleweight champion of the Canadian Armed Forces and won the Golden Glove twice in Bermuda. He married Loretta Brewer, Ingonish. He died on July 28, 1992, and is buried in St. John's Cemetery, Ingonish.

Stockley, Clifford M. F32739

Clifford was born on December 26, 1923, the son of Purves and Letetia (Brewer) Stockley, Ingonish. Quartermaster Stockley served overseas with the Canadian Army. He and his brother, Wesley, were in their dory tending to their lobster traps when they were both tragically drowned on July 5, 1946.

Stockley, Frances

Frances was born on December 9, 1922, the daughter of Alfred and Louise (Dupe) Stockley, Ingonish Centre. She enlisted in 1943 and served in the Medical Corps. She married Allan Porter, U.S.A., and they resided in New York. She died on February 28, 1997, in Stoney Creek, Ontario.

Stockley, George Hayden F78568

George was born on December 18, 1919, the son of John and Annie Maria (Roberts) Stockley, North Bay, Ingonish. Gunner Stockley served with the Royal Canadian Artillery, 13th Field Regiment, in Canada and overseas from 1941 to 1945. He married Mary Ann Hardy, Ingonish. He died on July 26, 1948, in Camp Hill Hospital and is buried in St. John's Cemetery, Ingonish.

Stockley, Henry Herbert F79363

Henry was born on October 23, 1918, the son of Francis and Mary Elizabeth (Payne) Stockley, Ingonish Centre. Gunner Stockley served with the North Nova Scotia Highlanders Artillery (1941 to 1944). He married Carrie Mackley, R.N., administrator of the Buchanan Memorial Hospital. He worked at the Cape Breton Highlands National Park. They reside in North Bay, Ingonish.

Strickland, Nathan F97058

Nathan was born on May 6, 1920, the son of Wilson and Mabel (Sweet) Strickland, Neil's Harbour. He enlisted in November, 1940 and served with the North Nova Scotia Highlanders, Royal Canadian Infantry Corps. Private Strickland was killed in action on July 8, 1944 and is buried in Beny-Sur-Mer Cemetery, France.

Strickland, Richard F97068

Richard was born on November 11, 1922, the son of Wilson and Mabel (Sweet) Strickland, Neil's Harbour. He enlisted in November, 1940, in the Canadian Army and served overseas. He married Eva Ingraham, Neil's Harbour, and resided in Toronto. He was a stationary engineer. He is presently retired and living in Neil's Harbour.

Strickland, William George F78639

Billy was born on January 3, 1916, the son of Wilson and Mabel (Sweet) Strickland, Neil's Harbour. He enlisted on May 27, 1940, in the Canadian Army and served during the war. He also served in the Korean War. He resided in Toronto and later returned to Neil's Harbour. He is buried in St. Andrew's Cemetery, Neil's Harbour.

Sweet, Ernest

Ernest was born in Neil's Harbour, the son of Richard and Jane (Dowling) Sweet, Neil's Harbour. He enlisted in September, 1940, and served in Canada and overseas as an oiler in the Merchant Navy. He was discharged in November, 1945. He married Leonora Nicholson, Baddeck. He worked in construction and then as an engineer with the Englishtown Ferry. He died on December 31, 1975, and is buried in Bayview Cemetery, Englishtown.

Sweet, James

James was born in 1901, the son of Richard and Jane (Dowling) Sweet, Neil's Harbour. He served as a steward in the Merchant Marine. He served on coal boats during and after the war.

He was a church organist. He resided in Englishtown. Unmarried, he died in 1971. He is buried in the United Church Cemetery, Englishtown.

Sweet, Victor D91106

Victor was born on January 14, 1916, the son of Richard and Jane (Dowling) Sweet, Neil's Harbour. Private Sweet served with the Royal Canadian Army Service Corps. Unmarried, he was killed in England on July 12, 1943, and is buried in Brookwood Military Cemetery, Surrey, England.

Sweet, W. Martin F89810

Martin was born on July 18, 1917, the son of James and Hattie (Clark) Sweet, Neil's Harbour. Corporal Sweet served in the Royal Canadian Army from 1940 to 1945. He married Augustus (Scotty) Amirault. They lived in Toronto and later moved to Halifax. He died on July 29, 1982, and is buried in Fairview Cemetery, Halifax.

Toomey, Allister Cameron F33027

Allister was born on December 9, 1922, the son of Arthur and Christine (MacInnis) Toomey, Indian Brook. Private Toomey enlisted on February 3, 1943, in Sydney and served overseas with the Irish Regiment of Canada. He was wounded (shelled) on August 31, 1944, and died on September 2, 1944. He is buried in Italy.

Toomey, Archibald Theodore

Ted was born on October 19, 1920, the son of Arthur and Christine (MacInnis) Toomey, Indian Brook. Private Toomey served overseas with the Sherbrooke Tank Regiment. He was a sapper with the Royal Canadian Engineers. He served in Italy and France.

He married Anna Hart. They resided in Ontario. He died on November 19, 1991, and is buried in Riverside Cemetery, French River.

Tracy, Daniel

Dan was the son of Jerry and Sadie (MacNeil) Tracy, Grass Cove. He served with the Royal Canadian Navy. He married Genevieve Lynch. They resided in New Brunswick.

Turner, George F97055

George was born on May 26, 1920, the son of Albert and Minnie (Burrage) Turner, New Haven. He enlisted in the Canadian Army and served overseas. He married Theresa LaRusic, Bay St. Lawrence. He was the light keeper at Money Point. He is now retired and living in New Haven.

Turner, Margaret Eliza W30072

'Peggy' was born on September 30, 1903, the daughter of Charles and Christine (Burton) Turner, Dingwall. Corporal Turner served with the Royal Canadian Air Force from 1941 to 1945. She married Raymond Skinner, Newfoundland. She is buried in Aspy Bay Cemetery.

Turner, Thomas F76477

(Left - Tom Turner)

Tommy was born on January 16, 1914, the son of Alfred and Minnie (Burrage) Turner, New Haven. He enlisted in October, 1942, in the Canadian Army Corps and served overseas. On October 6, 1945, Private Turner went to the rescue of a boy who was in imminent danger of drowning in a water tank at Archwick Green, Manchester. He gallantly saved the boy and for his deed of bravery was presented with a parchment citation from the Royal Humane Society dated December 11, 1945.

He married a school teacher, Elizabeth Taylor, New Haven. He was a fisherman. They reside in New Haven.

Turner, Walter F32698

Walter was born on July 21, 1923, the son of Alfred and Minnie (Burrage) Turner, New Haven. He enlisted on November 27, 1942, in the Canadian Army and served overseas in the Continental Armoured Corps. He re-enlisted in 1946 and served until January 19, 1953. He married and resided in Dartmouth. He was a welder and is now retired and still lives in Dartmouth.

Urquhart, John Alexander

John Alec was born on December 4, 1916, the son of Dan and Sarah (MacInnis) Urquhart, Skir Dhu. He served overseas in the Navy. He married Anna MacKay, Whitney Pier. They resided in Sydney where he worked for a car dealership. He died on August 27, 1997, and is buried in Forest Haven Cemetery, Sydney.

Urquhart, Malcolm Alexander F607256

Malcolm was born on October 11, 1911, the son of Malcolm and Katie Ann (MacDonald) Urquhart, Skir Dhu. He enlisted in 1940 with the Canadian Army. He served in Canada and Newfoundland. Unmarried, he died on May 1, 1988, and is buried in Riverside Cemetery, French River.

Urquhart, Roderick J.

Roderick was the son of Neil and Annie (MacLeod) Urquhart, Skir Dhu. He served in the Navy. He moved to the United States after the war. He and his wife resided in Haverill, Massachusetts.

Walker, Leonard

Leonard was the son of Dan and Catherine (MacDonald) Walker, Ottawa Brook. He served in the Royal Canadian Army Signal Corps in Canada, the United Kingdom and Northwest Europe. He married Effie Morrison, East Bay. He worked at the Steel Plant in Sydney. He is buried in Sydney.

Walton, William

William was born in England and raised by Sandy and Christie (MacLean) Ross, Little Narrows. He served overseas in the Air Force during the war. He married and lived in Hamilton, Ontario, where he is buried.

Warner, Thorold Edward

Thorold was the son of Althea Warner and stepson of Duncan MacAskill, Hazeldale. He served during the war.

Warren, Fred F89406

Fred was born on November 4, 1917, the son of Matthew and Clara Mae (MacKinnon) Warren, Neil's Harbour. He enlisted in the Canadian Army and served as a gunner in Continental Europe. He married Inez Lawrence. They resided in Neil's Harbour where he was a fisherman. He is buried in St. Andrew's Cemetery, Neil's Harbour.

Whitfield, Christene Anna

Christene was born on March 7, 1924, the daughter of George and Annabel (MacAskill) Whitfield, Englishtown. She enlisted on January 21, 1943, in North Sydney. Leading Airwoman Whitfield served in Canada as a secretary with the Royal Canadian Air Force. She was discharged on June 12, 1946. She married George Carruthers of Sydney Mines. She died on February 2, 1991, and is buried in Field of Honour Forest Hills Cemetery, Fredericton.

Whitfield, George J.

George F. Whitfield, Sr., WWI

George was the son of George F. and Annabel (MacAskill) Whitfield, Englishtown. He served in the Merchant Navy. He served in the Canadian Armed Forces after the war and managed the armed forces bakery in Whitehorse, Yukon. He resides in New Brunswick.

His father, George Frederick Whitfield, was born in Shewsbury, England on March 3, 1884. He served with the 185th Overseas Battalion in World War I and he also served during World War II. The Whitfield family resided for a number of years in Englishtown. George F. Whitfield, Sr., died on January 28, 1953, in Toronto.

Whitfield, James Edward R104121

Ted was the son of George F. (World War I and II) and Annabel (MacAskill) Whitfield, Englishtown. He enlisted in June, 1941, in North Sydney and served with the Royal Canadian Air Force. He was discharged in 1946. He worked as a millwright in an Ontario paper factory. He resides in Niagara on the Lake, Ontario.

Wilkie, Donald F58469

Donald was born on July 15, 1918, the son of George T. and Flora (MacDonald) Wilkie, Sugar Loaf. Private Wilkie served overseas with the D Company - Canadian Infantry. He worked for the National Gypsum Company. He died on July 17, 1962, and is buried in Aspy Bay Cemetery.

Wilkie, Gifford Dan F1078

Gifford was born on December 12, 1921, the son of Alexander K. and Christine (MacDonald) Wilkie, Sugar Loaf. Private Wilkie served in the Canadian Army Signal Corps in the United Kingdom from 1943 to 1946.

He married Gertrude Moore. He and his second wife, Allie Fricker, reside in Eastern Passage. He is retired from the National Gypsum Company.

Williams, Wilbert F76239

Wilbert was born in 1922, the son of Herbert and Alice (Strickland) Williams, Neil's Harbour. He enlisted on November 25, 1942, in the Canadian Army and served overseas. In 1949, he was tragically killed in a hunting accident. He is buried in St. Andrew's Cemetery, Neil's Harbour.

Young, Augustus

Gus was born on September 25, 1906, the son of George and Julia (Wadden) Young, Ingonish Beach. Wing Commander Young served overseas in the Royal Canadian Air Force. He married Jean Mann, Sydney. He worked as a designer for the Chrysler Corporation, U.S.A. He died on April 4, 1991, and is buried in Resurrection Cemetery, Sydney Forks.

Young, Joseph Austin

Joe was born on July 28, 1907, the son of Thomas A. and Louise (Rambeau) Young, Ingonish Beach. Corporal Young served with the Royal Canadian Air Force in the United Kingdom from 1939 to 1945. He married Sarah Bernadette Gillis-Peters, Ingonish. He worked at the Cape Breton Highlands National Park. He died on August 6, 1981, and is buried in St. Peter's Parish Cemetery, Ingonish.

(Wedding photo - Joseph and Bernadette Young)

Zwicker, George Albert F55585

George was the son of Albert and Mary (MacIntosh) Zwicker, Bay St. Lawrence. He enlisted on July 15, 1940, with the Cape Breton Highlanders, 5th Division. He served as an instructor in the military training school, Bren Guns, and then transferred to the New Brunswick Carlton and York Regiment. He remembered landing in Italy in the Second Wave. Their landing was successful as they did not encounter the same resistance experienced by the First Wave. He believed that James MacAskill of Bay St. Lawrence was in the First Wave with the Royal Canadian Regiment and they were badly shot up. Corporal Zwicker was wounded while serving in Italy. He was discharged on October 19, 1945.

He married Stella Maude May, Halifax. They reside in Halifax.

Bibliography

Allison, Les and Hayward, Harry
They Shall Not Grow Old *A Book of Remembrance*
This book has been produced as a memorial to all those Canadians who took part in the Air War 1939-1945. It contains a short biography of over 18,000 Canadians, airmen, airwomen, and other nationals wearing the uniform of the RCAF, who lost their lives between September 3, 1939 and August 12, 1945.
Published by the Commonwealth Air Training Plan Museum.
Brandon, Manitoba, 1992.

Berton, Pierre
Vimy
An easy readable account of the famous battle of Vimy Ridge carried out by Canadian troops.
McClelland and Stewart; 1986.

Cape Breton's Magazine
Devoted to the history, natural history and future of Cape Breton Island.
Wreck Cove, Nova Scotia

Catholics of the Diocese of Antigonish, N.S.: The War 1914 - 1919
Nominal Enlistment Rolls by Parishes
Included in the Diocese of Antigonish was the parishes of Victoria County. The book provided names, rank and units served in as well as photos of members of the armed forces that were killed in action.

Farmiloe, Dorothy
The Legend of Jack Munroe
A Portrait of a Canadian Hero
Published by Black Moss Press
Windsor, Ontario, 1994

Hayes, Lt. Col. J.
The Eighty-Fifth in France and Flanders
A History of the 85th Canadian Infantry Battalion
(North Nova Scotia Highlanders)
Served with the 4th Canadian Division on the Western Front
Nominal Roll and Services
Halifax, N.S. 1920

Hunt, M. Stuart
Nova Scotia Part in the Great War
Halifax, N.S. 1920

MacDonald, Rev. D.
Cape North and Vicinity
Pioneer Families, History and Chronicles, 1933

MacDonald, F.B. and Gardiner, John G.
The 25th Battalion: Canadian Expeditionary Force
Sydney, N.S. 1983

MacLean, Alexander D.
History of Victoria County
Unpublished manuscript at the Beaton Institute, University College of Cape Breton

MacNeil, Roddie C. etal
The Story of St. Columba Parish: Iona, Cape Breton
Sydney, 1994

Morrison, Alex and Slaney, Ted
The Breed of Manly Men
The History of the Cape Breton Highlanders
Published by The Canadian Institute of Strategic, Studies and The Cape Breton Highlanders Association
Sydney, 1994

Nicholson, G.W.L.
Canada's Nursing Sisters
Canadian War Museum, Historical Publication # 13
Toronto, 1975

Nicholson, G.W.L.
Canadian Expeditionary Force 1914 - 1919
Official History of the Canadian Army in the First World War
Ottawa, 1962

Nicholson, John etal
Middle River
Past and Present

History of a Cape Breton Community 1806 - 1985
Middle River Area Historical Society
Sydney, 1985

Nova Scotia Highland Brigade, C.E.F.
85th Nova Scotia Highlanders
185th Cape Breton Highlanders
193rd Nova Scotia Highlanders
219th Overseas Highland Battalion
Each unit is covered with a short history and a photographic record of the personnel. This photographic record was done before the brigade embarked to England on the *Olympic* on the 13th of October, 1916.

Parker, Mike
Running the Gauntlet
An Oral History of the Canadian Merchant Seamen in World War II
Halifax, 1994

Schull, Joseph
The Far Distant Ships
An Official Account of Canadian Naval Operations
Department of National Defence
Ottawa, 1952

Stacey, C.P. and Nicholson, G.W.L.
Six Years of War: The Army in Canada, Britain and the Pacific - Vol. I
The Canadians in Italy - 1943-45, Vol. II
The Victory Campaign: The Operations in North-west Europe 1944-45, Vol. III
The three volume set published by the Minister of National Defence in 1966 provides an excellent account of all Canadian units that served with the land forces.

Tucker, Gilbert Norman
The Naval Services of Canada: Its Official History
Ottawa, 1952

Wigney, Edward H.
The Canadian Expeditionary Force Roll of Honour
Members and former members of the C.E.F. who died as a result of service in the Great War 1914 - 1919.

Other Sources:

Oral Interviews with Veterans, and relatives and friends of Veterans
Beaton Institute of The University College of Cape Breton
Cape North Museum
Cape Breton Highlanders Museum, Victoria Park, Sydney
National Library of Canada
National Archives of Canada
Department of National Defence
Nova Scotia Public Archives
Commonwealth War Graves Commission
Veterans Affairs Canada
Victoria County Archives, Baddeck
Census for Canada - 1901

Addresses for additional information on the veterans:

Secretary-General
Canadian Agency
Commonwealth War Graves Commission
66 Slater St.
Ottawa, Ontario
K1A 0P4
Merchant Marine
Canadian Coast Guard
Transport Canada
344 Slater St.
Ottawa, Ontario
K1A 0N7

Personnel Records Unit
National Archives of Canada
395 Wellington St.
Ottawa, Ontario
K1A 0N3

"I have fought a good fight,

I have finished my course,

I have kept the faith."

Second Timothy 4:7